ECONOMICS
A Complete Course

Dan Moynihan • Brian Titley

Third Edition

OXFORD
UNIVERSITY PRESS

OXFORD
UNIVERSITY PRESS

Great Clarendon Street, Oxford OX2 6DP

Oxford University Press is a department of the University of Oxford.
It furthers the University's objective of excellence in research, scholarship,
and education by publishing worldwide in

Oxford New York

Athens Auckland Bangkok Bogotá Buenos Aires Calcutta
Cape Town Chennai Dar es Salaam Delhi Florence Hong Kong
Istanbul Karachi Kuala Lumpur Madrid Melbourne Mexico City
Mumbai Nairobi Paris São Paulo Shanghai Singapore Taipei
Tokyo Toronto Warsaw
with associated companies in Berlin Ibadan

Oxford is a registered trade mark of Oxford University Press
in the UK and in certain other countries

© Dan Moynihan and Brian Titley 1989, 1993, 2000

Database right Oxford University Press (maker)

First published 1989
Second edition 1993
Third edition 2000

British Library Cataloguing in Publication Data

Data available

ISBN 0 19 913413 8

Typeset by Advance Typesetting Limited, Oxon.
Printed in Hong Kong

Contents

Acknowledgements

We are grateful to the following for permission to include the following copyright material in this textbook.

Barclays Bank plc for 'World Population 1950–2025' from *Barclays Bank Review*, February 1984.

Centre for World Economic Development for the cartoon 'Depending on just ourselves'.

Daily Mail: for 'Inflation on target to hit 35 year low of 1pc', 16 June 1999.

The Economist: for 'Gola', 16 May 1999; 'Official Aid', 13 March 1999.

Evening Standard: for 'Air traffic sell off will make passport fiasco look line peanuts', 20 July 1999.

Financial Times: for 'Rampant Inflation hits Israeli Economy', 20 March 1984; 'Prices collapse on oil markets' 11 December 1985.

The Guardian: for 'Bradford and Bingley vote could be last straw for mutual societies', 27 April 1999; 'Exports slump sparks record deficit in goods', 27 May 1999; 'Pound surges as traders bet on interest rate increase', 31 July 1999.

Les Gibbard: 'IOU' cartoon from *The Guardian*, 12 October 1984.

The Mirror: for 'Wine sinks beer', 30 January 1999.

Organisation for Economic Co-operation and Development: for 'The Russian Federation 1995' from OECD Economic Surveys.

Times Newspapers Limited: for 'Unemployed drown their sorrows', *The Times*, 11 January 1985; 'BSE sparks mad rush for other meat', *The Sunday Times*, 31 March 1999; 11 January 1985; 'Coca-Cola raided by EU officials', *The Times*, 10 July 1999; 'Volvo admits rigging prices', *The Times*, 20 July 1999.

The Sunday Mirror: for 'Gap Happy', 5 April 1999.

Virgin Atlantic Airways Ltd: for 'It won't be a monopoly', July 1996.

The publishers would like to thank the following for permission to reproduce photographs:

A & M Records: p 21 (bottom); Abbey National: p 51 (bottom); Bryan and Cherry Alexander: p 9 (left); Apple Computer UK Ltd: p 213; Ark Communications: p 3 (top right); ASDA: p 133 (top); Associated British Ports, Southampton: p 136 (bottom); Bank of England: pp 403 (left), 416; Birmingham City Engineers Department: p 38 (bottom right); Bolton Business Ventures: p 113; Brighton Borough Council Technical Services: p 20 (top); British Airways: p 206; British Coal: p 3 (top left); British Nuclear Fuels: p 133 (bottom); BP: p 205 (middle); British Rail: p 191; British Steel: p 133 (top middle); Citizens Advice Bureaux: p 223; Corbis UK Ltd/ AFP: 292 (right); Corbis UK Ltd/Owen Franken: pp 292 (left), 389; Corbis UK Ltd/Christian Liewig/Temp Sport: p 22 (bottom); Fiona Corbridge: pp 195 (bottom), 199; Cull Photographic: pp 16 (bottom), 19 (bottom centre), 84 (right), 196, 299 (bottom right); Cussons/Grant Spreckley Williams: p 212 (left); Daily Telegraph: p 97; Esso: p 205 (right); Evening Standard: pp 108, 130; Giorgio Ferrari Retail: p 57 (top right); Financial Times: pp 7 (centre), 196 (top); Ford Motor Company: pp 19 (top), 52 (top), 56, 136 (top); Format Photographers/Sheila Gray: pp 141 (middle), 245; Format Photographers/Jenny Matthews: pp 4 (top), 22 (middle), 38 (top left and right, bottom left); Format Photographers/Michael Ann Mullen: pp 33 (right), 141 (right); Format Photographers/Maggie Murray: pp 4 (bottom), 247 (left); Format Photographers/Joanne O'Brien: p 423 (left); Format Photographers/Brenda Prince: pp 423 (right), 430; Freeserve: p 118; Sally and Richard Greenhill: pp 3 (bottom left), 9 (right), 16 (top), 85, 141 (left), 195 (middle left & middle); Harrods: p 22 (top); J K Heinz Company: p 76 (right); Holt Studios: p 31; Chris Honeywell: p 19 (bottom right); Hulton Getty: p 269; Hunters Franau: p 57 (top left); International Stock Exchange Photo Library: pp 12, 84 (left), 95, 122, 313; Kellogg Company Ltd: p 202; Frank Lane Picture Agency: pp 3 (bottom right), 7 (left), 195 (middle right); Tony Lees: pp 99 (right), 343 (bottom), 415; Lever Brothers Ltd: p 212 (right); Lloyds Bank: p 94 (middle); London Features International: p 21 (top); Marks & Spencer: p 94 (left); Mercedes-Benz: pp 133 (bottom middle), 299 (top left); Military Archive and Research Services: p 20 (bottom); The Mirror: p 151; National Westminster Bank: p 213; Omega: p 57 (bottom left); Alan Owens: pp 11, 48, 197, 410; PA Photos: pp 244, 343 (top); Philips: p 297 (left); Phonogram: p 49; Report/John Harris: p 247 (right); Rolls Royce: p 213; Royal Mint: p 405; H Samuel: p 299 (bottom left); Sanyo UK Ltd: p 57 (bottom right); Sealand Aerial Photography: p 10; Shell: pp 205 (left), 291, 301 (left); St Ivel: pp 18, 229 (top), 301 (right); Martin Sookias: p 99 (left); Tate & Lyle: p 213; William Teacher & Sons: 57 (top middle); Toshiba: pp 8, 248, 299 (top right); VAG (UK): p 213; Volvo: p 76 (left); Woolworths/Paragon Communications: p 94 (right); Zefa: pp 7 (right), 33 (left), 50, 112, 190 (right), 297 (right).

Illustrations are by Barking Dog Art, Matt Buckley and Ian Heard.

Preface

This text has been completely revised for its third edition. Tables, charts and other statistical information have been brought up to date with official statistics available in January 2000. There is an entirely new section on European Economic issues, and there are updates on the latest developments in macroeconomics and economic policy.

The book meets the latest requirements for GCSE, Standard Grade, and International GCSE. In addition, the text provides an excellent primer for the first year of A-Level Economics.

Dan Moynihan
Brian Titley
June 2000

Aims

At the end of this chapter you should be able to:

1 Realize that people's wants for **goods and services** are unlimited.

2 Understand that **resources** used to make goods and services are **scarce**.

3 Distinguish between a **need** and a **want**.

4 Understand the use of **advertising** to persuade people to buy goods and services, that is, to create wants.

5 Explain why **scarcity** of resources leads to **choice**.

6 Evaluate the real or **opportunity cost** of choice.

7 Understand that **economics** involves trying to increase people's choice.

8 Recognize that **conflicts of interest** are caused by scarcity on a local, national and international scale.

9 Analyse the economic dimensions of a problem.

1

The Mirror
www.mirror.co.uk

OIL RUNS OUT

Today the world's oil supply has dried up. A crisis meeting of world leaders took place in Washington last night.

Yesterday the top oil producing companies of the world declared that the world's supply of oil was now exhausted. The last barrel of oil has been filled and the oil rigs will drill no more. The world now faces an energy crisis. No more oil will mean no more petrol for transport or machinery. There can be no more plastic for components in many household devices like satellite television, digital tape recorders and telephones.

Energy ministers for around the world are meeting today in Switzerland to discuss the crisis and try and find a solution. Solar, wind and nuclear powered stations are already over-worked to meet the demand for electricity. The world could face a black-out in the next ten years.

Section 1 | What is the economic problem?

Resources   The newspaper article above paints a gloomy picture of what might happen in the future. It is hard to imagine a world without oil but even now there is only a limited amount of oil left in the ground. In other words it is **scarce** and as more and more is used up there will come a time when no oil remains. The world's oil took millions of years to form – we may use it all in little over a century!

However, it is not just oil that is scarce, but all natural materials, such as iron ore, coal, gold. Even the clean air that we breathe and the water we drink are limited in amount and may eventually run out.

If you imagine the world as a round ball then it is possible to see that only a limited amount of materials can be squeezed from it. All of these scarce materials are called **resources**.

Problem | Resources are scarce

Resources include natural resources, machinery, people and land

Resources are important because they are used to make goods, like televisions, cars, houses, fruit and vegetables, and to provide **services**, like banking, insurance, transport, decorating and hairdressing.

Problem | Scarce resources are used to make goods and sevices

Any resources that are not scarce are called **free goods**. The air that we breathe seems without limit and so is considered to be a free good. However, with increasing pollution in the world, fresh, clean air may be scarce!

At first sight it may seem that even though there is only a limited amount of resources in the world, the world is such a big place that these things might not be so scarce. Before you agree with this view look at the following exercise.

Exercise 1   Needs and wants

A

B

Look at the two photos A and B. Photo A represents modern city life; photo B represents a group of people living in a poor African village.

1   What needs have the two families in common?

2   Which family will not be able to satisfy all its needs?

3   What do you think are the wants of the family in picture A?

4   What do you think are the wants of the family in picture B?

5   Why can't the wants of either family be satisfied?

6   What do you think are the main differences between **needs** and **wants**?

Needs and wants   All people have the same basic needs. Whether rich or poor, we all need food, clothing, shelter and air to survive. However, people usually want more than they need. The human race is like an ever hungry beast – its wants are without limit. If we asked all of the people in the world to list what they wanted and then added these lists together we would find that not all of these things could be made. This is because the resources needed to make goods and services are scarce compared with people's wants. This is the central economic problem.

Problem | Human wants are unlimited

Exercise 2   What do we need and what do we want?

Below is a jumbled collection of pictures of goods and services. Draw a table like the one on page 6 and sort them into needs and wants giving reasons for your choice.

NEEDS	WANTS	REASON
EGGS	COMPACT DISCS	EGGS ARE FOOD DISCS BRING PLEASURE— BUT NOT ESSENTIAL FOR SURVIVAL

You should now understand the difference between needs and wants. Write a sentence to explain what these two words mean.

The creation of wants

The goods and services that we *need* are the things necessary for survival, for example, food and clothing. Whereas goods and services that we *want*, for example, televisions and video-recorders, may bring pleasure, but they are not necessary for us to survive. We have discovered that people have unlimited wants: we always want more. But why do we keep wanting more and more? This might be because some wants are created for us by others.

Exercise 3   Why do I want what I want?

Choose five of the wants that you listed in Exercise 2 and write down why you want them.

WANT	REASON
BICYCLE	MY FRIEND HAS ONE

Now compare your reasons with a partner and write down the most popular reasons for wanting goods and services.

Many wants are created by advertising. Advertisements use clever slogans and catch-phrases to try to persuade people to want particular goods and services (see Chapter 10).

Exercise 4   Catch-phrase

1   Try to write down four catch-phrases or slogans used by advertisers.
2   Now try these out on your partner to see if s/he can name the good or service that the advert is trying to create a want for.

Choosing what we want

We have learned that wants are unlimited but the resources used to produce the goods and services to satisfy these wants are limited. That is, there is **scarcity**. Nobody can have sufficient goods and services to satisfy all their needs and wants, so people must choose which wants they will satisfy. Choice is necessary because scarce resources can be used in lots of ways to make many different goods and services. Scarce resources have alternative uses.

Problem | Scarce resources have alternative uses

For example, many soccer clubs have spare land next to their grounds. The problem facing these clubs is to choose what to do with this land. They could build a sports complex or leisure centre to serve the community, or a supermarket, or a block of flats or even an office complex. Whatever they do, they can only choose one of these options because land is a scarce resource.

Exercise 5   Alternatives

Below is a list of resources. See how many alternative uses you can find for them, that is, see how many different goods and services they can help to produce.

1   An area of farm land.

2   A person who is good at maths.

3   A shovel.

4   An egg.

For example, a piece of land can be used as:

motorway   farmland

People, nations and the world must choose how scarce resources are to be used; they must choose which goods and services to make because they cannot make everything that they want.

| Section 2 | Opportunity cost: The cost of choice |

Exercise 6　The next best thing

Choosing between goods and services involves a very special cost. Imagine that you have just bought the list of items below. Now imagine that you were unable to get any of these items. Copy and complete the table.

What I have just bought	What could I have bought instead?
DVD video player Four bedroom house Box of chocolates A ticket to the Cup Final	

In the second column you have listed your second best choices, or your next best alternatives to the objects in column one. For example, if you had bought a DVD video player, you may be going without the benefit of a holiday. The benefit of the holiday given up is the real cost of owning the DVD video player. The real cost of choosing one thing and not another is known as the **opportunity cost**. This measures the benefit you could have had from the next best alternative you have gone without.

Opportunity cost arises not only when we buy things, but also when we choose what goods and services to produce. For example, in deciding to use a piece of land to build a new sports complex, we may be going without the benefit of new houses.

Exercise 7

If there were enough resources to produce everything everybody wanted, would there be any opportunity cost? Explain your answer.

| Section 3 | What is Economics for? |

We have now discovered the central problem in economics: resources are scarce and have alternative uses, but people's wants are unlimited. As raw materials, such as metals and chemicals, are extracted from the ground, less and less is left for the future, whilst people's wants are forever increasing. As the world develops and as its population grows, more and more wants are created, but not all of these wants can be satisfied. As a result scarcity on a worldwide basis is increasing all the time. The choice of alternative goods and services an individual country has depends upon its share of resources in the world.

Exercise 8 Free to choose?

An Innuit boy

A Western boy

1   Look at the photographs above and copy the list below. Copy the table and put a tick in the first column if you think the Innuit boy is free to choose. Tick the second column if the Western boy is free to choose.

Free to choose? ✗ or ✓	Innuit boy	Western boy
Can go to a soccer match. Can eat in a restaurant. Can catch their own food. Can drive a car. Can visit foreign countries. Can own his or her own house. Can obtain medical help when needed. Can receive an Economics education. Can receive a daily paper. Can be independent. Can receive radio and TV.		

2   Which person has more choice and why?

The people in the second picture have a greater choice of goods and services to enjoy than the person in the first picture. This is because the people in the second picture live in a country which has far more resources to produce more of the goods and services people want.

The Innuit boy has far less choice. There are fewer resources in his country that can be used to produce goods and services to satisfy wants.

In some countries, people have virtually no choice at all. For example, in the poorest countries of Africa, one of the few choices available to people is for parents to choose if they should eat and let their children starve or if the children should eat and let their parents die. In these countries not even needs can be satisfied with the available resources. This great difference in choice is caused by the relative lack of resources in the poorer countries. Yet in both rich and poor nations people want more resources than are available.

The purpose of Economics involves advising how best to use scarce resources in order to make goods and services to satisfy as many wants as possible. In other words, Economics attempts to increase people's choice. When people have more goods and services to choose from, they are better off. For example, the Western boys are better off than the Innuit boy simply because they have the ability to choose between more goods and services.

However, the satisfaction of wants by the making of goods and services has also brought with it the problems of pollution and the destruction of the environment. We will return to this in Chapter 9 when we investigate social and private costs and benefits.

| **Section 4** | Choice: A conflict of interests |

The M25 motorway cutting through farm land

The above example illustrates the choices that face people because of scarcity of resources with alternative uses. If resources are used in one way, for example, to build the M25 motorway, they cannot be used in some other way, for example, as farm land. Whilst the M25 motorway may satisfy the wants of motorists, it does not satisfy the wants of farmers, nature lovers and people who live near the motorway who must suffer the noise and pollution that it causes.

Clearly choice involves a conflict of interest. Everybody cannot get what they want so some people will always be disappointed by the choices made by others.

Case study

Exercise 9   Anytown conflict: A case study

Anytown local council is under pressure from its local taxpayers. This is because Anytown council has £10 million remaining of its budget to spend on resources.

The local housing estate is in urgent need of repairs and the residents are angry.

'It is inhuman that we should have to live in such conditions; damp and dirt are everywhere. The council should build some new properties.'

OR

But in the north of the town, the old hospital has been forced to close due to lack of funds for repairs. People who live in the north have to travel to the southern Anytown hospital for treatment.

'It is intolerable that people like me have been forced to travel such a long way to receive health care. The council should modernize and re-open the old hospital.'

The council faces a choice. It can either build a new housing estate or modernize the old hospital. Each scheme would cost an estimated £10 million but whatever choice the council makes, only some of the local people's wants will be satisfied.

Your task
The people living in the north of Anytown and the people living in the estate are locked in disagreement. They both want the council to satisfy their wants, but only one of them can win.

Split up into an even number of groups of three or four students. Half of the groups are to represent the people in the north of Anytown and the other half are to represent the people from the estate.

1   In your group write a speech to be read to the class outlining why your group should be satisfied by the council.

2   Choose one pair of opposing groups. These groups now read their speeches to the whole class and are then given five minutes to argue their case. The rest of the class will be the council which then decides by majority vote how it will spend the £10 million.

Questions

1 Why is there disagreement or conflict in Anytown?

2 To avoid all conflict in Anytown, what is needed?

Exercise 10   International conflict: Acid rain

A power station pumping out waste gases into the atmosphere

Many European factories and power stations which make goods and services use gas and coal for fuel. Waste gases from burning these resources are pumped into the atmosphere and then turn to acid as they mix with the air and water droplets in the clouds.

The cloud then travels across national boundaries, and when it rains the acid falls on other countries with damaging effects: water in lakes and rivers becomes poisoned, animals and plants die. About 5% of the acid found in rain in Germany and Sweden is from the UK. In Norway, between 9 and 12% of the acid in rain is from the UK. Countries which suffer the bad effects of acid rain would prefer the UK to filter the waste gases from its power stations and factories. However, it would be more costly for UK industry to do this.

The choice is therefore between cheap power in the United Kingdom and a clean environment in Europe.

1 What are the scarce resources under threat from acid rain?

2 What is the opportunity cost of the pollution to the world?

3 What conflict is illustrated in this dilemma?

Disagreements or conflicts like those in Anytown occur because of scarcity. On a larger scale different countries can also suffer a conflict of interests as we have seen in Exercise 10. Clearly there are not enough resources to provide all the goods and services to satisfy everybody. With scarcity there will always be winners and losers and because nobody wants to lose there will always be conflict.

Exercise 11 Conflicts

- Should we build buses or hospitals?
- Should we plough up farm land for motorways or continue to farm it?
- Should we build more nuclear weapons or feed the Third World?
- Should we use up all of our natural resources, such as oil and coal, now or should we keep some for the future?

1 Copy out a table like the one started below. In the column headed conflict, write down the questions listed above.

2 Answer these questions on your own in the second column, explaining your answer.

3 Compare your answers with those of your neighbour and make a note in your table of which answers you agree on and which cause disagreement. Why is there disagreement?

4 For the questions upon which you agree with your neighbour, can you prove that your choices are the correct ones? Explain why you may not be able to prove this.

5 For the questions upon which you disagree is it possible for you to prove definitely that you are correct? Explain.

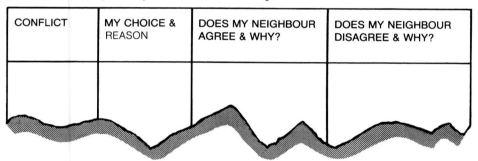

CONFLICT	MY CHOICE & REASON	DOES MY NEIGHBOUR AGREE & WHY?	DOES MY NEIGHBOUR DISAGREE & WHY?

Section 5 **Value judgements**

When attempting to provide an answer to important questions like those in the previous exercise, it is difficult to avoid using your own opinions. The problem is opinions differ because what is right and fair for one person may not be for another. If we decide that we **ought** to build hospitals and feed countries with food shortages then we are making **value judgements**, that is judgements based upon our own opinions.

Economics is not about value judgements or opinions that cannot be proven. Instead the subject is concerned with statements which can be tested or proved against facts. For example, statements suggesting there are over four million unemployed can be tested by counting the number out of work.

On the other hand, suggesting the government should spend more money on reducing unemployment and less on giving aid to poor countries is a value judgement, which cannot be tested by looking at the facts. It is not possible to prove definitely that the government should do one thing or another.

The problem is that because Economics deals with satisfying people's wants and because conflicts arise due to scarcity, we cannot always avoid making value judgements and saying what should be or what ought to be.

Exercise 12   A matter of opinion

Which of the following statements would be of concern to a person who studies Economics. That is, which statements can be tested against facts?

1   Prices are on average rising by 10% per year.

2   Wealth should be more equal.

3   A tax on wealth would reduce the differences in people's wealth.

4   Old age pensions ought to be increased.

5   An increase in pensions would cause an increase in spending in the economy.

6   An increase in taxation on petrol will reduce the quantity of petrol sold.

7   If wages were lower firms would employ more workers.

8   Wages should be lower because firms would employ more workers.

9   Using scarce resources involves an opportunity cost.

10   We should use fewer scarce resources today so that we will have some left for the future.

Key words

In your own words write down what you understand by the following:

Resources	**Wants**
Goods	**Scarcity**
Services	**Opportunity cost**
Free goods	**Value judgements**
Needs	

Now go back to the chapter to check your understanding of the above terms.

| **Chapter 2** | The Language of Economics |

Blah! Blah! Blah! Blah! Blah!

Aims

At the end of this chapter, you should be able to:

1 Use some of the language of the economist.

2 Understand what is meant by an **economy**.

3 Define what is meant by **production, consumption** and **exchange**.

4 Recognize the existence of **markets**.

5 Classify the **factors of production**.

6 Distinguish between **consumer goods** and **capital goods**.

7 Acknowledge the provision of **public goods** and **merit goods**.

8 Define **income** and **wealth**.

| **Section 1** | What is an economy? |

An **economy** is an area in which people make, or produce, goods and services. This area can be of any size, with any number of people involved. For example, we can talk of a local economy, such as a village, town or city. We can also talk of a national economy, such as the UK economy. In turn, the United Kingdom is part of the economy of Europe along with countries like France, Spain and Germany. Indeed, every country in the world can be considered an economy as long as it is involved in the production of goods and services. Similarly, all countries together make up the world economy.

Production, consumption, and exchange

The meaning of production

Production is any activity designed to satisfy people's wants. The things that satisfy people's wants are **goods**, like televisions, cars, furniture and food, and also **services** like teachers, window-cleaners, doctors, and shop assistants. Production, therefore, involves the making and selling of goods and services. However, if people do not want a certain good or service, like a plant that withers, a television without a picture, or a comedian who doesn't make people laugh, then the making and sale of such goods and services would not be classed as production by an economist. The people who make and sell goods and services are known as the **producers**.

The meaning of consumption

The using up of goods and services to satisfy our wants is known as **consumption**. When we eat we are consuming food. When we watch television we are consuming electricity, the television set and the services of a television company. When we go to schools and colleges, we are consuming the services of teachers. We are consuming when we read books, sit on chairs, sleep on beds, put money into a bank account, ask a policeman the time, listen to the radio and use up any other goods and services in order to satisfy our wants.

The people who buy goods and services to satisfy their wants are known as **consumers** and their spending is called **consumption expenditure**.

The meaning of exchange

People can satisfy some of their wants by producing some goods and services themselves. For example, keen gardeners may grow some vegetables to eat to satisfy their want for food. Very few people, however, can make many of the things they want. In order to obtain the goods and services they cannot produce themselves, they must swap or exchange what they can make for the things they cannot make. To be able to do this, most people go to work to earn money. They then swap this money for goods and services produced by other workers.

Section 3 What is a market?

A **market** is a group of people who wish to exchange goods and services with each other. This group of people is made up of all those who wish to make and sell a particular good or service, and all those willing to buy it. Any market therefore is made up of producers and consumers.

We can say that the market for CDs consists of all producers and all consumers of CDs. Similarly, there is a market for food, clothing, televisions, houses, insurance, and all other goods and services.

A market need not be in just one particular place, like Billingsgate fish market in London. For the economist, anyone who wishes to buy or sell a good or service, wherever they are in the world, is part of a market. Markets can be spread over a small area or a very large area. For example, people living in Scotland would not wish to buy a local newspaper from Cornwall in England. Therefore, we say the market for the Cornish newspaper is **local**, whilst the market for daily newspapers like *The Times*, or *Daily Mirror*, is **national**. Japanese video-recorders are sold all over the world. This is a **world** or **international** market.

If an economist talks of a **perfect market**, then it is one where no one producer or consumer alone can influence the price charged for goods and services. On the other hand, an **imperfect market** is one where perhaps a powerful producer or powerful consumer can affect the price charged for goods and services to their own advantage. (See Chapter 10 for a full discussion.)

Section 4 | Resources: The factors of production

The scarce resources available for use in the production of goods and services to satisfy wants are called **factors of production**. These are the **inputs** into a production process from which an **output** of goods and services emerges.

Factors of production can be grouped under three headings.

Land The fertile soil vital to the growth of plants, minerals such as coal and oil, and animals for their meat and skins, are known as **natural resources**, but to simplify the economist calls all of these **land**. Land therefore includes the seas and rivers of the world, forests and deserts, all manner of minerals from the ground, and chemicals and gases from the air and earth's crust.

Labour Nothing can be produced without people. They provide the physical and mental effort to make goods and services. People who work with the hand and with the mind are **human resources**, or what is termed **labour**.

The size and ability of an economy's labour force are very important in determining the quantity and quality of the goods and services that can be produced. The greater the number of workers, and the better educated and skilled they are, the more a country can produce.

Whilst most people have the ability to contribute to the production of goods and services, not everyone could be a successful business person and be able to employ and organize resources in a **firm**. A firm is a business that owns a factory or a number of factories, offices, or perhaps even shops, where goods and services are produced. Business know-how, or the ability to run a production process, is known as **enterprise**. The people who have enterprise and can control and manage firms are called **entrepreneurs**. They are the people who take the risks and decisions necessary to make a firm run successfully.

Capital To make the task of production easier, man has invented many tools: pens to write with, computers to calculate, screwdrivers, spanners, shovels, rulers, and many more. On a grander scale, turbines drive engines, tractors plough the land, ships transport goods, lathes shape and refine metals and wood, and factories and offices have been built to house many man-made tools and machines. These **man-made resources** which help to produce many other goods and services are known as **capital**.

Economists tend to talk of **units** of factors of production. For example, an economist might say that 'a firm has employed thirty more units of capital'. This simply means that it has bought thirty new machines. Similarly, if an economist talks of units of land, it could mean tonnes of coal, barrels of crude oil, or acres of land. Likewise working people become units of labour for the economist.

Exercise 1 Classifying resources

Task A
Below is a list of many of the scarce resources that are used to produce cartons of orange juice. Draw three columns and label them **natural resources, human resources** and **man-made resources**, and then in pairs decide in which column each item should go.

Telephones	Oil	Shops
Advertising people	Lorries	Ship's crew
Cotton for clothing	Printing machines	Factory buildings
Fertile soil	Peeling machines	Drink tasters
Squeezing machines	Orange trees	Insecticide sprays
Orange pickers	Economists	Oranges
Packaging machines	Power stations	Roads
Package designers	Coal	Accountants
Calculators	Warehouse workers	Shop assistants
Water	Lorry drivers	Dock workers
Bank clerks	Wood	

Task B
Now try to produce a list of resources you think help to produce cars. Compare your list with the rest of the class, and again sort them out into natural, human and man-made resources.

Section 5 — What do resources produce?

Consumer goods and services

A **consumer good** is any good that satisfies consumers' wants. Some of these consumer goods are called **consumer durable goods** because they last a long time, for example, cars, washing-machines, televisions, compact disc players, computers. **Non-durable goods** are those which have a short life, for example, food, drink, matches, petrol, washing powder.

Durable and non-durable goods

Sometimes our wants are satisfied by someone doing something for us. These are called **consumer services**. Examples would include the services of a doctor, banker, insurance agent, window-cleaner, teacher, policeman.

Capital goods

Man-made resources which help to produce other goods and services are known as **capital goods**. For example, screwdrivers, drills, tractors, ploughs, lorries, power stations and factory buildings are capital goods because they are not wanted for themselves, but for what they can help to produce. Capital goods are bought by producers. The buying of capital goods is known as **investment**. Therefore, we can talk of a firm investing in new machinery and buildings to allow them to produce other goods and services. Investment in capital goods, like factories and machines, will increase production and help an economy grow.

Public goods

Imagine that someone came to your door and asked you to pay twenty pounds towards the cost of powering the lamp-post out in the street for another year. The collector argues that the street lamp provides you with light to help you see at night when you are driving or walking home. It also benefits your neighbours and the people across the street. You know that, if they all give twenty pounds to the collector, this will keep the street lamp shining at night, whether you pay or not, and you can still enjoy the benefits of street-lighting even though you have not paid towards it. In this case consumption cannot be confined to those who have paid for it.

However, if all your neighbours thought in the same way as you, the collector would be unable to get twenty pounds from anyone and the street light could not be kept running. The only way that street-lighting can be provided is if the government provides it and forces everyone to pay for it by collecting taxes.

Goods and services which are provided by the Government because everyone benefits from them, even if they do not pay for them, are called **public goods**. The Government provides these goods and services as no private firm would wish to produce them, because nobody would pay for their use. Examples of public goods include defence, the police, law and order, cleaning of the environment, lighthouses, the Thames Barrier and, of course, street-lighting.

Street-lighting and defence are examples of public goods

Merit goods Sometimes the Government provides goods and services because they think that people ought to have them, even if they cannot afford to buy them. Such goods and services are called **merit goods**. Examples of these goods are health care and education. We are entitled to these goods and services, even if we do not have the money to pay for them.

| Section 6 | What do resources earn? |

Payments to factors of production Unless resources are freely available firms must pay the owners of land, labour and capital to use them to produce goods and services. For example, labour is paid wages (see Chapter 11). However, in economics we can also think of payments to factors of production as transfer earnings and economic rent.

In everyday use the word rent means the amount of money people pay in order to benefit from the use of a good for a certain period of time. For example, when people talk about the weekly rent of land or of housing, they mean the price of using housing or land for one week, one month or one year.

In economics, rent has a different meaning to the sort of rent that people usually talk about. To avoid confusion, the sort of rent that economists are interested in is called **economic rent**.

Before we can understand economic rent, it is necessary to understand something called **transfer earnings**.

Transfer earnings

Transfer earnings are how much a factor of production could earn in its next best use. For example, in the centre of London two acres of land used as office space might earn £2 million for its owners each year. If the land could not be used as office space its next best use might be as a car-park. As a car-park, the two acres of land might earn £500 000 per year. This £500 000 is what the land could earn in its next best use. The transfer earnings of the land is therefore £500 000. If land could only be used for one purpose and had no alternative use then its transfer earnings would be zero.

Economic rent

Economic rent is the amount of money that a factor earns over and above its transfer earnings. In the example above, the land used as office space could earn £2 million but in its next best use could only earn £500 000. Its economic rent therefore is £1 500 000.

Exercise 2   Economic rent

Consider the factors of production below. What are their transfer earnings and economic rent?

Labour
John Cleese (comedian and writer). Earned £50 000 for one Sony commercial in one week. In his next best use as a lawyer he could earn £2 000 in the same week.

Labour
Sting (pop and film star). Earns about £5 million each year. He used to be a teacher and would earn about £25 000 each year.

Capital

A computer earned about £1 000 in its first year in use, storing data at the Inland Revenue. Billy Smith's sweet-shop has a computer just like it to keep a record of his stock and takings. In its first year in operation it enabled him to raise his profits by £100.

Land

The Harrods department store in London occupies a piece of land for which it pays a rent of £3 million each year. In its next best use as residential land for housing the land could command a rent of £1 million.

Labour

Anne Galaxy is a bus driver. She earns £20 000 a year. Her next best use would be a car-part assembler in a local factory earning £9 000 a year.

Exercise 3   Reaching their goal

Ian Wright (footballer and TV personality) can earn over £20 000 each week. He was a window cleaner before he became a professional footballer and would have earned around £200 a week.

1   What are Ian's transfer earnings?
2   **a**   What is his economic rent?
     b   Why is his economic rent so high?

3   Which of the following would be likely to earn a high economic rent? Explain your answers.

    a   a pop star
    b   a carpenter
    c   a film actress
    d   a road-sweeper
    e   a brilliant economist

Ian Wright is able to command such a high economic rent because he has very special footballing talents which are much in demand. Similarly, actors and pop stars, like John Cleese and Sting, have very special abilities that no one else has, and, because they are so much in demand, this pushes up their earnings way above what they could earn in their next best use. Where a job does not require special talents there will be a large supply of people able to do the job and their earnings will be much lower than those of people, like pop and film stars and footballers, who earn what is called a **rent of ability**.

Section 7	Income and wealth

What is wealth?

Private wealth consists of a stock of goods which has a money value and includes such assets as video-recorders, cars, houses, jewellery, paintings and other possessions. An entrepreneur's stock of wealth may include land, factories and machines. People's savings in banks, building societies and other financial institutions also form part of their wealth.

Social wealth consists of assets owned by the government for the benefit of the general public. These assets include roads, hospitals, parks, schools, colleges, weapons.

The **national wealth** is the total amount of wealth owned by the general public, including entrepreneurs, and the Government, both in this country and abroad.

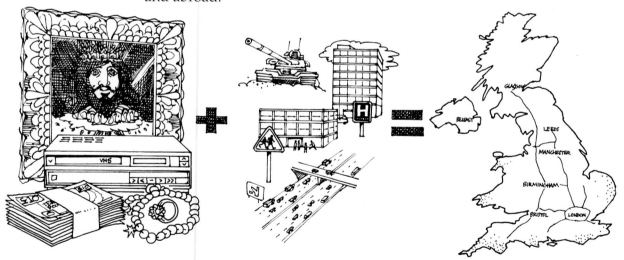

Private wealth + Social wealth = National wealth

What is income?

Income can be divided up into two parts: **earned income** and **unearned income**.

Earned income is money paid to people for the work they do. Some people may be paid a weekly wage or salary, others may be paid each month. Some people might only be paid for each job they complete. For example, a builder is paid an amount of money for each house, or each building, completed. Window-cleaners are paid for each window, or each house of windows they clean.

Unearned income is money gained from owning assets or wealth. It is money for which no work has to be done. It includes savings earning interest in a bank or building society, gifts of money from relatives or friends, or a win on the lottery or bingo.

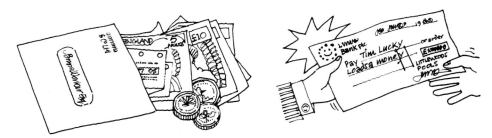

Earned income   Unearned income

The **Gross Domestic Product (GDP)** of an economy measures the total value of output or income of the economy. That is, GDP is a measure of the national income of an economy.

Section 8 The public and private sectors of the economy

The private sector in an economy is made up of all the businesses and firms owned by ordinary members of the general public. It also consists of all the private households in which people live.

The public sector in an economy is owned and controlled by a government. It consists of government businesses and firms, and goods and services provided by the government, such as the National Health Service, state education, roads, public parks and law and order.

If an economy has a private sector and a public sector it is called a **mixed economy**.

Key crosswords

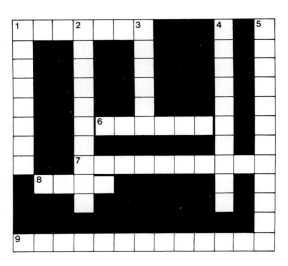

Crossword 1

Clues across

1 Man-made resources, such as machines and factory buildings (7)

6 The producers and consumers wishing to sell and buy a particular good or service (6)

7 Business know how; the ability to make decisions and take risks in a business (10)

8 Natural resources (4)

9 Part of the economy owned by individuals and firms but not by the government (7, 6)

Clues down

1 Person who buys and uses goods and services to satisfy his or her wants (8)

2 Buying of man-made resources, such as machinery (10)

3 Human resources; another name for workers (6)

4 Activity designed to satisfy human wants (10)

5 Part of the economy owned and controlled by the government (6, 6)

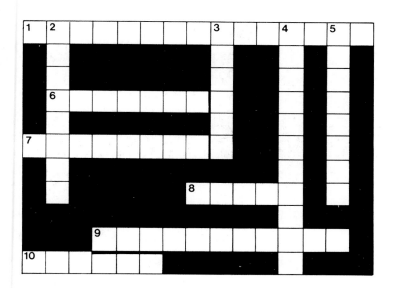

Crossword 2

Clues across

1 The benefit of the next best alternative foregone because of a particular choice (11, 4)

6 Long-lasting consumer goods (7)

7 The central problem in economics (8)

8 Type of goods and services provided by the government because it thinks people ought to have them (5)

9 Products provided by the government, because it is impossible to prevent anyone from benefiting from their provision (6, 5)

10 Stock of accumulated assets (6)

Clues down

2 Person who makes and sells goods and services (8)

3 Money received by households in a period of time from wages and salaries and from unearned sources (6)

4 Using up of goods and services to satisfy wants (11)

5 Things that satisfy a want but do not involve the exchange of a good (8)

25

Chapter 3 | Economic Systems

Unit of Capital, piece of land
The minds of Labour and their hands.
Stir and stir my magic broom,
And answer the questions,
What, How and for Whom?

Aims

At the end of this chapter, you should be able to:

1 Understand the problem of **resource allocation**.

2 Recognize the existence of different solutions to the problem of resource allocation.

3 Describe and explain what is meant by a mixed **economic system**.

4 Evaluate the advantages and disadvantages of mixed economies.

5 Account for differences in the development of different economies.

6 Understand why there is a need for both the public and private sectors in the provision of goods and services.

Section 1 | Coping with scarcity

All countries suffer from scarcity of resources. Because of this, nations cannot satisfy all of their unlimited wants, so they must choose which wants to satisfy and how they will do this. For example, will they satisfy the want for power by producing electricity, and will this electricity be generated by a coal-fired power station or a nuclear power station?

There are a lot of different ways of choosing what to produce with scarce resources. Economists refer to this as the problem of **resource allocation**, that is, choosing what to produce and how much land, labour and capital is needed to produce these things. The allocation of resources therefore refers to the uses factors of production are put to.

Exercise 1   Tropical trouble

Divide into groups of three or four people. Now read on . . . you are part of the crew of a cargo vessel. After weeks at sea a violent storm lashes against your ship. It is forced on to rocks and a group of you are shipwrecked on a desert island. You salvage what little you can from the ship but most of your supplies are lost in the storm.

In the bright tropical sunlight of the next day you take stock of your available resources. You realize that the wreck of the ship provides metal and wood, and the natural vegetation of the uninhabited island provides a valuable source of food.

In your group discuss and provide answers to the following questions:

1   What is the central economic problem facing your group of survivors?

2   What is the best way of using the resources available to you?

Write down how your group has decided to overcome the problems facing it.

| **Section 2** | What, how, and for whom to produce? |

What to produce?

One problem facing people when there is scarcity is deciding exactly what goods and services to make. This involves choosing which wants to satisfy. Every society, no matter what its size, is faced with the same choice. In the case of the desert island the choice may be between food, clothing and shelter. In a more advanced country people may be forced to decide between more nuclear weapons or more hospitals.

How to produce?

Once it has been decided exactly what goods and services to produce there is the problem of deciding **how** to make them. What tools are needed? How many workers? How much land is needed? These questions have to be answered. In addition there are many different ways of making things. For example, when producing wheat a lot of machinery could be used to plough the land, plant seeds and eventually harvest the crop with relatively few workers. Alternatively, a lot of workers could be used to physically plough, plant and harvest, with very little machinery.

For whom do we produce?

When the questions of what to produce and how to produce have been answered a final problem remains. Because of scarcity not every person's wants can be satisfied so it must be decided whose wants to satisfy. In other words, it must be decided **who** gets the goods and services that have been made. Some people are stronger than others, whilst some people may work harder than others – perhaps they should obtain more goods and services? Others may be weak and be unable to work at all – should they get any goods and services? Or should everybody receive an equal share of all the goods and services produced, even if some people are in greater need than others? How did your group decide for whom to produce on the tropical island? The question of who should get the goods and services must be answered by society as a whole. Economists cannot tell us what is best simply because the answer depends on people's opinions, that is it involves making a value judgement.

| Section 3 | Providing answers to what, how, and for whom |

Exercise 2   Problem solving

Remember your solutions to the problems you faced as a group of survivors on a desert island.

1   Copy out the table below and write down your solutions to the problems posed in each column.

2   If you can think of any other ways to solve these problems include these in your table.

3   Compare your answers with another group in your class and make a note of any other ways they have thought of for providing answers to the three questions.

How to decide what to produce?	How to decide how to produce?	How to decide for whom to produce?
Build shelter	Everyone helps using large palm leaves	Everyone shares a shelter

There are many different answers to these three questions. Every society or country must choose and develop its own way of solving these problems. How a country decides what to produce, how to produce and for whom to produce is called its **economic system**. These systems are designed by people, just as you did on your imaginary island. Some people may be very caring and wish to share all their resources with others, whilst some people may want to be rich and powerful by owning all the resources themselves. They may even exploit other people. An economic system will develop from the way people think and behave, but without an economic system no decisions would be made and resources would be left idle.

In Chapter 2 we learnt that the market for any good or service is made up of all the producers willing to sell that particular product and all the consumers willing to buy it. The **market economic system**, often known as the **free market system**, relies on producers and consumers to make the decisions about what, how and for whom to produce.

Exercise 3   An introduction to the workings of a market system

Jennifer Johnson has thirty people working for her business. She owns a patch of land, a factory building and hires fifteen machines. Jennifer wants to make as much money or **profit** as possible for herself. This is the aim of her business. At present she uses her scarce resources to make pairs of bright multicoloured boots.

The latest fashion in the United Kingdom among young people is pastel-coloured shoes and Jennifer notices that sales of her boots are falling. That is, the market for boots is shrinking. Teenagers are no longer willing to use their money to buy brightly-coloured boots, but will instead pay a high price for pastel-coloured shoes. In other words, the market for shoes is expanding.

As her profits begin to fall, Jennifer realizes there is more money to be made from the production of shoes and so switches her scarce resources away from making boots into the production of pairs of pastel shoes to satisfy the wants of teenagers.

Jennifer now faces a problem. There are two ways of making the shoes. The first method only requires twenty of her thirty workers and ten of her machines, and each pair of shoes will cost £6 to produce. The second method requires all thirty workers with only seven machines, and each pair of shoes will cost £10 to produce. Jennifer decides to use the first and cheapest method because she wishes to make as much profit from the sale of her shoes as possible.

After only a short time, Jennifer's profits have increased dramatically and are far greater than her profits when she made boots. Eager teenagers who can afford to pay for the pastel-coloured shoes can now satisfy their wants.

Questions
In a market economy there are many thousands of firms all behaving like Jennifer's.

1   What is the main aim of a business producing goods and services in a market economy?

2   How do firms in this type of economy decide **what** to produce? *Hint* Why did Jennifer decide to produce shoes instead of boots?

3   In a market system how do firms decide **how** to produce goods and services?

4   Once the goods and services have been produced **who** are they for? *Hint* Which teenagers could not satisfy their wants for shoes?

5 In deciding to produce shoes Jennifer chose the cheapest method which meant she needed only twenty of her thirty workers. What will happen to the ten workers who are not needed?

Deciding what, how and for whom to produce

All the resources in a market economy are privately owned by people and firms. Every business will aim to make as much profit as possible. However, a business can only be profitable if it uses the scarce resources to make those goods and services that people will buy.

In a market economic system all firms aim to make a profit and they do this by moving scarce resources away from producing things people will not buy into the production of goods and services that they will buy. That is, firms will move out of markets that are shrinking as people are buying less, into markets which are expanding because people are buying more.

What is produced in the market economy depends therefore on what consumers want and are willing to pay for. Firms will produce what people want in the cheapest possible way so as to make the most profit. The people who are able to enjoy the goods and services produced, however, are only those with enough money to buy them.

How do firms know what is profitable?

If a firm finds that a particular good is selling very well, for example, Jennifer's pastel-coloured shoes, the firm can increase the price charged as they know that people will still purchase the goods and more profits can be made.

If the price of shoes rises it acts as a signal to other firms that there are more profits to be had from making and selling shoes. For example, the Clemence Clothing Company may decide they would be better off using their resources to produce shoes instead of clothing. The Clothing Company and other firms producing many different things will leave what they are currently producing and bring their resources into the production of shoes. That is they enter the market for shoes.

In a market economy high prices are the signal telling firms what people want, that is what will make the most profit. In the same manner, if the price of a product was to fall because people are simply not buying it any more, this will act as a signal to tell firms to move their resources into the production of something more profitable. This is known as the **price mechanism**. In this way **market forces** solve the problem of what, how and for whom to produce. In other words, the profit motive of firms and the changing preferences of consumers determine the allocation of resources, that is, how factors of production are used.

Exercise 4   A problem of resource allocation

BSE sparks mad rush for other meat products

The beef crisis has led to a surge in demand for other 'safe' meat products

Fears about mad cow disease may be disastrous for the beef industry, but for sharp investors they are providing an opportunity for capital gain.

As demand for beef wanes in Britain and Europe one supermarket has reported a 70% drop in sales – other livestock producers and processors are feeling the benefit. Chicken, turkey and pig producing companies have seen share prices surge on the back of rocketing consumer demand.

If the scare continues, resulting in a permanent shift away from beef, then prospects for alternative producers like turkey specialist Bernard Matthews and Cranswick the big breeder and processor look even brighter.

One food expert says "You can assume that consumers will continue to edge away from beef products and more towards white meats, fish and vegetarian foods, providing many business opportunities." With experts warning it could take years to eliminate the risk of human infection from beef, many industry executives are confident demand for non-beef products will steadily rise and prospects for the rest of the meat industry remain good.

But the beef scare also has implications for other less obvious meat producers. The British ostrich-farming industry has been steadily growing since the first farms began breeding in 1990, with the number of farms more than doubling to about 320 in the past two years. The BSE scare has added a new dimension to its expansion plans while some councils are considering introducing kangaroo meat to school dinner menus as they search for a safe substitute for beef.

Research shows that the demand was on a long term downward trend anyway. In 1994 we ate an average of 15.9kg of beef each, compared to 18.5kg ten years earlier. Over the same period consumption of poultry increased from 14.5kg to 20.3kg per person.

The Sunday Times, 31.3.1999

1 From the article, which market appears to be shrinking and which market is expanding?

2 What factors might explain the long term trend in demand away from beef?

3 The article illustrates the problem of resource allocation. Explain in full what this problem involves.

4 What might be the wider social implications of a switch away from the consumption of British beef and towards the consumption of imported meats like kangaroo and ostrich?

Advantages of the market system

1 The free market responds quickly to people's wants.
In the market system if people want a good or service and can afford to buy it, then it becomes profitable to make it and resources are quickly sent to the market to produce such goods and services. On the other hand, if the good is not wanted it becomes unprofitable and resources are directed away into more profitable uses.

2 The market produces a wide variety of goods and services to meet consumer's wants.

3 The market system encourages the use of new and better methods and machines to produce goods and services.

The aim of firms in a market economy is to make as much profit as possible. New methods and machines often reduce the costs of producing goods and services allowing firms to increase their profits. For example, the widespread use of computers in banks has enabled bank workers to make calculations much faster so that more work can be done each day.

4 The market system relies on producers and consumers to decide what, how and for whom to produce and so there is no need to go to the expense of employing a group of people to take these decisions.

Disadvantages of the market system

1 Factors of production will be employed only if it is profitable to do so. If a profitable use cannot be found for some of the scarce resources then they will be unemployed. Labour is just another factor of production, and one reason why some people are unemployed today is that it is not profitable to employ them.

2 The free market can fail to provide certain goods and services.

Some goods and services are consumed by everyone at the same time but some consumers may be unwilling to pay directly for them even though they may enjoy their use. For example, everyone enjoys the benefits of street-lighting at night but no private firm could provide this at a profit because it would be unable to force people to pay for it. Governments may therefore have to provide such goods and services for the general public. You may recall from Chapter 2 that such goods and services are known as Public Goods.

3 The free market may encourage the consumption of harmful goods.

Some people may wish to buy dangerous drugs and if they can afford to buy them then the free market will find it profitable to provide these goods. However, such drugs are harmful and it may need a government to pass laws to stop people from selling them and others from using them.

4 The social effects of production may be ignored.

Factories bellowing smoke into the air can affect us all. Remember how acid rain is destroying plant and animal life around the world. Also the noise from factories, airports and roads affects people who live nearby. Private firms in a market economy may not consider the social effects of these actions.

5   The market system allocates more goods and services to those consumers who have more money than others.

People with a lot of money have the freedom to choose and buy many different goods and services, but for those who have little money, like the unemployed and some old age pensioners, there is much less freedom of choice.

Exercise 5   Freedom of choice in a market economy

The two pictures below show two different groups of people who live in a market economy.

A casino

An unemployment queue

1   Which group of people has more freedom to choose to buy a foreign holiday, a new car and a new home?

2   Explain why this group of people has greater freedom of choice.

There are very few countries in the world today that rely purely on the market economic system. Most countries have a government that makes some of the decisions on what, how and for whom to produce.

Section 5	The mixed economic system

Because of the disadvantages of a market economic system most countries in the world choose to use a **mixed economic system**.

The mixed economic system combines government planning with the use of the free market. In the mixed economy, just as in the market economy, people and firms in the private sector own scarce resources with the aim of making as much money as possible. However, in mixed economies the government or public sector also owns some scarce resources to produce goods and services that they think their country, and its people, need and want. The United Kingdom has a mixed economic system.

1 Market economies experience high unemployment sometimes because it may not be profitable to employ people. In a mixed economy if there is unemployment the Government may be able to create jobs for those people out of work by employing them in their own offices and factories, or by helping private firms to provide jobs.

2 Public goods, such as defence, law and order, and street-lighting, will not be provided by private firms in a market economy as it would be impossible to get people to pay for their use. In a mixed economy a Government can provide these public goods and raise the money necessary to pay for them by taxing people's income and spending. In addition, the government may provide merit goods, such as education and health care, which it feels people should have.

3 Because some people may want to buy dangerous goods like drugs, firms in a market economy may find it profitable to provide them. In a mixed economy a government may be able to stop people consuming harmful goods by making them illegal, for example, hard drugs, or by placing high taxes on them, for example, alcohol.

4 Private firms only take into account their own costs and benefits when producing goods and services. For example, a private firm pouring waste into a river will not consider the cost to the environment. A government may use laws, or high taxes and fines on firms, to try and prevent them polluting the environment (see Chapter 9).

5 One of the main problems of a market economy is that poorer people with little money are unable to buy many of the goods and services that are available. Planning gives the government the power to give goods and services, or more money, to the people that it thinks needs them. For example, in the United Kingdom, the Government provides unemployment benefits and free health care for those who cannot afford to pay.

A mixed economy attempts to overcome the disadvantages of a market economic system by using government intervention to control or regulate different markets. Government ownership of some of the scarce resources allows it to produce goods and services for those people it thinks deserves them. However, if a government provides goods and services it needs to cover the cost of doing so by raising taxes from people and firms. High taxes may discourage people from working hard when some of the money they earn is simply taken away by the Government. Countries can differ in how much government intervention they choose to have.

Opposite is a bar chart for several different countries. Each bar represents 100% of the total amount spent on consumption in each of the economies in 1995 (the figures do not show the amount spent on fixed investment or capital goods). The lightly-shaded area of each bar shows how much the government in each country spent as a percentage of total spending, while the darkly-shaded portion shows how much was spent by the private sector. For example, in 1995 the UK Government accounted for about 25% of total consumption spending in the United Kingdom. That is, out of every £1 spent in the United Kingdom on consumption that year, the Government had spent 25 pence of it.

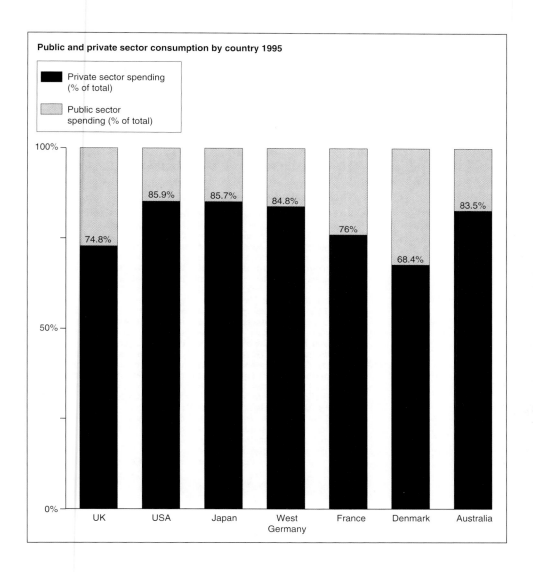

Public and private sector consumption by country 1995

■ Private sector spending (% of total)

▨ Public sector spending (% of total)

UK 74.8%
USA 85.9%
Japan 85.7%
West Germany 84.8%
France 76%
Denmark 68.4%
Australia 83.5%

Planned economies

In the past, in countries like Poland, Hungary, Romania and Russia (as part of the old Soviet Union) governments have tried to plan what to produce, how to produce and for whom to produce, for all goods and services. These countries had **planned economies** and this planning was often known as Communism.

In planned economies government planners decided how all scarce resources were to be used. This involved the government providing millions of instructions to hundreds of thousands of firms on what exactly they should produce, and where people should work. In planned economies firms would not aim to produce what was profitable, instead they would aim to produce what the government wanted.

35

Exercise 6   Mustard

The following newspaper article illustrates how planning often went wrong and how waste occurred in the old planned economy of the Soviet Union.

Soviet mustard glut

Spicy scandal in giant jars

From Christopher Walker, Moscow

The recent acute shortage of mustard throughout the Soviet Union — it was classified as an unavailable product — has been rectified with a vengeance in the Ukrainian industrial region of Krasnadon, where shoppers are now able to buy it only in giant three litre jars

This latest example of the bizarre by-products of the Soviet system has been disclosed by the Moscow weekly *Literaturnaya Gazeta* (Literary Gazette), whose editors explained that they thought protest letters from readers in the Ukraine were a hoax.

As the complaints continued to pour in from many towns in Krasnadon — a region famed for the ferocity of its underground resistance to the Nazis during the Second World War — the magazine questioned Mr G. Stelyanko, the Ukrainian Minister of Trade, who admitted that the Krasnadon food factory had indeed taken to bottling mustard in such impractical jars.

The magazine, the official publication of the Soviet Writers' Union, decided to investigate whose idea it was to sell mustard in such enormous jars.

The results pointed to the very bureaucratic problems in the Soviet system that Mr Mikhail Gorbachov, the Kremlin leader, is struggling to eliminate as part of his campaign to streamline the country's ramshackle administration.

At first it appeared that the answer was simply that the factory had decided to make the change to cut its workload, by reducing from 10,000 to 333 the number of jars produced from each ton of pungent Soviet mustard.

Then the investigators discovered the irony went further. Mr Stelyanko, after further questioning, explained that the Krasnadon factory was suffering an acute shortage of small glass jars because state shops were refusing to refund money on empty jars.

The magazine concluded, with a note of despair, that as a result mustard in the giant jars would soon go off, forcing every family to throw it away. Then, once again, the Soviet Union will have another mustard deficit.

1   How were resources wasted in the economy of the Soviet Union?

2   What is the aim of producing goods and services for firms in:
 a   a market economy
 b   a planned economy?

3   In a market economy why are mustard producers unlikely to make mustard in three-litre jars for the general public?

4   Apart from weight, what other instructions should the old Russian Government planners have given to the mustard producers for them to produce a suitable product for consumers?

5   What problem does the article illustrate about Government planning of production in an economy? Explain your answer in full.

WELL, THEY DID SAY 1000 TONNES OF NAILS !

SOVIET NAIL FACTORY.

The main problem with planned economies was that the goods that were produced were what the government wanted, not what the people wanted. In planned economies like the old Soviet Union, there were often shortages of consumer goods or the goods that were produced were of poor quality. The reason for this was that firms did not have an incentive to do a good job because they were not required to make a profit. Instead their job was to do as the government wanted, and there were just too many firms for governments to provide clear instructions to all of them. This led to the production of a limited range of poor-quality goods. This was one reason why the people of many countries controlled by communist governments wanted change.

Because there were so many disadvantages with planned economic systems, most planned economies have now changed their economic system to that of a mixed economy. Even countries still controlled by communist governments are moving slowly away from a fully planned system – for example, China and Cuba. Firms once government-owned are now owned by the private sector. The advantage of a market system is that firms do not need to be given information by the government on what or how to produce. Consumer demand and spending soon tells firms whether they are producing the right goods in the right way by rewarding them with a profit or a loss. However, many goods and services remain in short supply in these countries. This has meant people in some of the old planned economies are now facing high price inflation and high unemployment for the first time.

Market reforms and structural change in the Russian Federation

Since the break up of the Societ Union, the Russian economy has been changing rapidly. The changes are primarily the result of the demise of central planning, which emphasised heavy industry, especially defence, over light industry, industry in general over services, and repressed the development of the consumer sector. Investment collapsed and crime has become commonplace. To this must be added the effects of the break up of the Soviet Union itself, which severed links between parts of what was once a unified economy. Regional power struggles and military actions have resulted in some areas.

The intention of the Russian government to move towards a stable, market-based economic system has rarely been in doubt. However, the policies and ability of the Russian authorities to bring this about has not always been so clear. Fundamental disagreements over economic policy remain.

Significant moves towards market reform began in 1991 when the right to private property in productive assets was established – the first privatisation law – and in January 1992, when government price controls were removed and prices were able to find their own levels. Due to shortages of many, even basic, goods and services, prices leapt on average by 245% in the first month alone. Price inflation has since fallen but in 1995 was still above 5% per month. Some of biggest price rises were for food items.

During 1992 the government of the Russian Federation cut defence spending by 68%. The size of this cut caused massive shifts in the economy. From 1991 to 1994 light industry and machine builders suffered the largest declines, while electric energy, fuel and metallurgy expanded as a share of industrial production. Given the inefficiency and poor product quality of many industries, their decline following market reforms was not surprising. Instead, there was a rapid increase in imported goods and a collapse in the value of the rouble on foreign exchange markets.

As a result of these and other changes the national income of in Russia fell 50% between 1990 and 1995 according to official figures. Unemployment levels also increased steadily.

Over the same period Russia gradually moved towards a new system of social protection with a mixture of universal and means tested benefits. Some social benefits (maternity and child benefits, disability and old age pensions, and some health benefits) remain similar to their communist predecessors, some are new (unemployment and welfare benefits). Social security financing arrangements were changed; benefits are increasingly paid out of specialised insurance funds reather than from general tax revenues.

Adapted from 'The Russian Federation 1995', OECD Economic Surveys

Developed and less developed economies

The world is commonly divided up into rich countries and poor countries. The terms **developed economies** and **less developed economies** are often used. On the television we can see films, and in the newspapers we can read, about the problems faced by people who live in poor, **less developed countries** (LDCs).

Exercise 7   The characteristics of developed and less developed countries

These pictures depict typical scenes from less developed countries and developed countries. In pairs discuss and list what you consider to be the basic characteristics of:

a less developed economies

b developed economies.

A **developed country**, like the United States or the United Kingdom, is often thought of as one which has large modern farms, many firms producing a wide variety of goods and services, a well-developed road and rail network, and a relatively healthy, wealthy and educated population.

Less developed countries, like Chad or Ethiopia in Africa, are also known as **developing countries**, which suggests that such countries are becoming a little more prosperous. They are nations with problems. Farming methods are very poor, providing scarcely enough food for a growing population to eat, and there may be very few firms producing other goods and services. In general, people are poor, live in poor housing conditions, receive little or no education, do not expect to live to old age, and have no access to clean water, or the modern conveniences of shops and transport.

Some of these characteristics are summarized in the table of figures below. These problems are made worse because the populations of many of these countries are growing fast as more and more babies are born, but the number of deaths has fallen as a result of the increased medical care available nowadays. These countries suffer from **overpopulation**. This situation exists as there are just too few resources to be shared among a large and ever-growing population.

THE GAP BETWEEN DEVELOPED COUNTRIES AND LDCs 1995

	UK	USA	Ethiopia	Mali	Malaysia
GDP per head (US $) 1990 prices	17 471	25 514	186	183	3 582
Life expectancy (years)	74	73	46	45	69
Infant mortality per 1000 births	7	9	119	159	13
Adult illiteracy %	less than 10%		65	69	17
No. of telephones per 1000 people	489	602	3	2	147

* GDP per head (US$): The average income per year of a person in the country measured in US dollars.

* Infant mortality per 1 000 births: The number of babies who die out of every 1 000 babies born in a country.

* Adult illiteracy %: The estimated percentage of people who are unable to read in a country.

Reasons for the underdevelopment of an economy

There are four main reasons why economies remain underdeveloped:

1   High population growth.
LDCs have a large and growing population. This means the available goods and services have to be shared among more and more people.

2   A dependence on the production and sale of agricultural products.
The few natural resources LDCs possess, like coffee and sugar, are bought in vast quantities by developed countries. The developed countries use

their power to pay a low price for these resources, and then use them to make other goods and services for their own people, and for sale to LDCs at very high prices. Many LDCs feel they are unfairly treated by the rich developed nations.

3   A poor infrastructure, that is poor transport and communication networks.

4   A lack of capital.
While incomes remain low and their populations grow quickly, LDCs have found they must use all their money on the purchase of basic necessities, such as food and clothing, leaving little money to invest in the making of new machinery and building of factories. Without these capital goods LDCs will not be able to produce more goods and services than they do at present.

Clearly LDCs will never develop without the help of more machines and factories, that is, without capital goods. To buy goods LDCs need to earn more money. This money can only come from the rich, developed countries. So far the developed world has been unwilling to help. More money for LDCs would mean less money for the developed world. This is a prime example of scarcity and opportunity cost.

Cures for underdevelopment

Self help

Some economists believe that underdeveloped nations should help themselves and not rely on help from the richer developed world.

In order to improve standards of living, underdeveloped countries must invest in new roads, transport networks, systems of communication, power stations and machinery. However, LDCs have few resources. Because of this problem underdeveloped countries receive help from the developed world. This help is called foreign aid.

Foreign aid

There are three main types of foreign aid received by underdeveloped countries:

a   Food aid

The European Union (EU) and the United States of America often produce far more food than they need. Lakes of wine and mountains of butter and meat that will never be used are common in Europe.

The cost of storing all of this food is very high and the food is sometimes given away to underdeveloped countries as food aid.

On a clear day you can see the starving in Africa!

While food aid is necessary when people are starving, it is not always a good thing. If free food is given to an underdeveloped country, people will not need to buy the produce of farmers in that country. Their farmers find they cannot make a living and so leave farming to find work in the cities. This means that in future the country will have even fewer farmers and so will need even more food aid.

b Financial aid

This means giving money to developing countries. Often developed countries give money to developing nations but there are often strings attached.

Exercise 8   No strings?

Look at the cartoon above and pick out as many disadvantages as you can of the way in which financial aid is given to underdeveloped countries.

Financial aid is often given to developing countries on the condition that they spend it on a particular project, for example an airport or a dam. The countries giving aid usually insist that the materials and expertise to carry out the project are bought from them at high prices. Developing countries get little opportunity to decide for themselves how to spend financial aid.

■ OFFICIAL AID: China is the biggest single recipient of foreign aid, according to the OECD's latest report on development assistance. But compared with the size of its economy, China receives relatively little help. Official foreign aid of $2.04 billion in 1997 was worth 0.2% of GDP, one of the lowest ratios among the emerging economies in our chart. Other countries, however, rely much more heavily on foreign aid. In five countries, aid flows are worth more than 10% of GDP. In Nicaragua, official-aid flows reached almost 23% of GDP in 1997, and in Mozambique they amounted to over 37%. Most developing countries have seen foreign-aid flows decline during the 1990s, as rich countries have faced fiscal pressures. Nonetheless, six of the developing countries in our chart—Brazil, Bolivia, Peru, Thailand, Uganda and Vietnam—received more foreign aid in 1997 than in 1994.

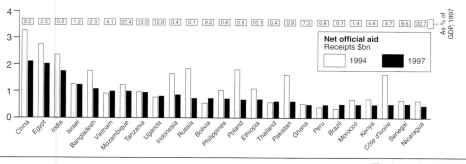

The Economist, 13.3.1999

c Technological aid

To improve living standards aid has been given to developing countries in the form of modern technology, for example, modern power plants and agricultural machinery. The problem with technological aid is that it requires a high level of skill and training to use it and the people of the developing world are very poorly trained. Even if the people were trained, modern technology would employ only a small number of workers.

Technological aid should be simple, for example, instruction on how to use land better to grow food using the labour of people rather than of machinery. This sort of aid employs the most abundant resource in the developing world, people.

Borrowing

Instead of relying on foreign aid, many developing countries have borrowed money in order to improve their economies. However, some developing countries have borrowed so much that they are now unable to repay their debts. For example, in 1997 Mexico owed $150 billion and Brazil owed $200 billion to Western banks. Neither Mexico nor Brazil is likely to be able to pay these sums back.

Trade

If the developing world is to improve its standard of living it must produce more manufactured goods and sell these to the richer developed countries. This would give the poorer developing nations more money with which to develop their economies. However, developed countries are unwilling to buy the produce of developing countries because they fear this would cause unemployment. For example, if people in Britain buy Korean electrical goods, British workers producing electrical goods are no longer needed and so will become unemployed.

More trade may be the only real answer to the problem of the developing world. Trade would also benefit developed countries because as the people of poorer countries become better off they will buy more of the produce of the developed world and so create more employment in developed countries.

Population control

One major problem for developing countries is their high population growth. In 1992 the developing countries contained 77% of the world's population; by the year 2000 this is expected to be 80% (see Chapter 20).

More people in poor countries means less resources per person. Better education about family planning would help to reduce this population growth and improve living standards.

Exercise 9   Why bother with less developed countries?

In groups discuss whether or not the statement made by the shopper is true. Produce a report expressing your feelings.

Many of the UK's manufactured goods are made from imported raw materials bought from Asia, Africa and South America. Without such imported materials as copper, rubber, lead, zinc and tea nearly one half of British manufacturing jobs would disappear.

Developing countries need the developed world, but the developed world needs developing countries just as badly.

Key words

Resource allocation   Planned economy   Developed economy
Economic system   Less developed country (LDC) Price mechanism
Market economy   Overpopulation   Market forces
Mixed economy

Below is a jumble of explanations and definitions for the key words above. Write down the list of key words and find an explanation to match each one.

An economy where some resources are owned by the private sector and some by the public sector.

How resources are used, that is, what they produce.

An economy where resources are allocated by the price mechanism, without government interference.

An economy where a government has the responsibility of allocating resources.

The system according to which resources are allocated and products distributed to people in response to price changes.

A country that has a low level of income, and living standards, few capital and consumer goods.

The influence of producers and consumers on the allocation of resources and thus on the price and quantity of goods and services made.

The method used by an economy to decide what, how and for whom to produce.

A country that has a high level of income and living standards, many capital and consumer goods.

Whereby an area of land has too many people and too few resources.

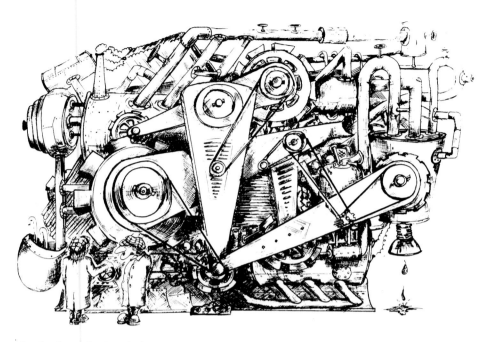

And where do I switch it on?

Aims

At the end of this chapter you should be able to:

1 Identify **production** as any activity that satisfies consumer wants.

2 Distinguish between productive activities that an economist would include in a calculation of the value of output.

3 Classify and identify the stages involved in a chain of production.

4 Analyse the benefits and limitations of **specialization** and the **division of labour**.

5 Recognize and account for the **law of diminishing returns**.

6 Distinguish between **total cost, average cost, marginal cost, total revenue**, and **average revenue**.

7 Calculate **profit** and recognize how important profits are as a motivation to produce.

8 Appreciate how economic decisions are made 'at the margin'.

9 Account for the downward slope of the **average cost curve** and classify **economies of scale**.

10 Appreciate why some firms choose to remain small.

Production and the creation of wealth

Goods and services, or **commodities**, are produced in order to satisfy people's wants. **Production** refers to the making of these goods and the production of services. Firms or businesses are producers. They are responsible for producing goods and services. The firm uses the resources of land, labour and capital (**input**) to make goods and services (**output**).

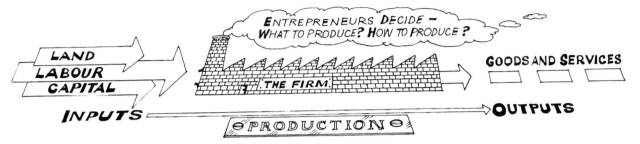

Given the aim of production is to satisfy the wants of people, the process is not complete until the goods and services actually reach the people who want them. Warehouses and shops that sell commodities to consumers, as well as all those people and machines involved in transportation, insurance and many other tasks, are all part of the production process.

Some countries like the United States of America produce a vast amount of goods and services for their people to choose from each year. These countries become very wealthy as a result. For the economist the value of goods and services produced by a country is calculated by how much people will pay for them.

There are, however, some things that cannot be valued in this way. For example, when you help to clean your home, or wash dinner plates, you are probably not paid a wage or salary for these productive services. Similarly, the value of goods and services produced by the keen garden vegetable grower or do-it-yourself enthusiast cannot easily be measured in terms of money.

Exercise 1   How do economists measure the value of output?

You are an economist trying to calculate the total value of production for your country. Using the following list of goods and services produced in your country, copy out those you would use in your calculation.

Oil from the sea	Doing the wiping up	Social Security benefits
A decorating service	Meals cooked at home	Tomatoes sold in a shop
Painting your own room	Old-age pensions from the Government	Employing a gardener
Tickets for a pop concert	Doing your own gardening	Repairing your own car
Coal from the ground	A garage repair service	Meals cooked in a restaurant

Question

How does the economist's view of value differ from a non-economist's view?

(**Hint**: How much do you value the autographs of your favourite pop group? Home-cooking?)

Section 2   The aims of firms

Maximizing profits

Most private sector firms produce and sell goods and services to make as much **profit** as they can. Profit is a reward to successful business owners, or entrepreneurs, for taking the risk of setting up a firm. They will not know in advance how much of a particular product consumers will buy and how much they will be willing and able to pay for it. Even so, entrepreneurs must pay in advance for the services of land, labour and capital in order to make their chosen good or service. In some cases, there may be a very long time between first designing and making a product and selling that product. For example, designing, making and testing a new aircraft takes many years and costs many billions of pounds before the manufacturer is ready to start making them for sale to airlines.

Selling goods and services earns revenue for a firm. Profit is what is left from revenue after all costs have been deducted. A firm that is unable to cover its costs with enough sales revenue will make a **loss** and could be forced to close down if losses continue. A firm may make a loss if it fails to make a product consumers want, at the price or quality they want, or provides a poor customer service. A firm may also make a loss if it is unable to produce products at the same or a cheaper cost than rival firms. It is therefore important for firms to be efficient and continually try to reduce their costs of production.

Profit in economics has a slightly different meaning than in business. This is because in economics we include in costs an extra cost which business owners do not consider. This is the opportunity cost of production, or the cost of the next best alternative foregone (see Chapter 1).

For example, a business executive may earn £100 000 in profit each year from business. The next best alternative use may be to work as a builder for a company and earn £10 000 each year. This is the next best alternative forgone. For an economist therefore **pure profit** is the amount of revenue over and above all costs, including opportunity costs. Thus the economist would argue that the business executive's pure profit is £90 000 because £10 000 a year could be earned if that person was not a business executive.

Exercise 2   Making a profit

Linda has just finished her first year as a bookseller.

In one year Linda has spent £10 000 on wages, £5 000 on materials and £3 000 on advertising.

Linda has converted her house into a shop and so does not pay rent. Although if Linda closed down, she could rent the shop out to somebody else and earn £6 000 per year.

Linda has put some of her own money into the business and this was taken from her building society account where it was earning £600 interest per year.

Linda has total sales for the year of £35 000.

1 List Linda's costs of production from a businessperson's point of view.
2 List the additional opportunity costs that an economist would consider.
3 Calculate profit from a businessperson's point of view.
4 Calculate profit from an economist's viewpoint.

The entrepreneur in exercise 2 would calculate her profit as the value of sales minus her costs, which are wages, materials and advertising costs. An economist would add to these costs the opportunity cost to the entrepreneur of using her own property and money in the business. These are costs because if the entrepreneur closed the business down she could earn interest on her money by putting it in the bank and she could earn money from her property by renting it out to somebody else.

Other objectives

Not all business organizations in mixed or market economies want to make a profit. Some provide a public service or a charity

1. **Providing a public service.** Many organizations owned or funded by Government use resources to provide services people need and might not be able to afford to buy if they were produced for a profit. For example, education and health care are public services.

2. **Providing a charity.** Charitable organizations rely on donations and endowments of money to provide help and care for people and animals in need. Organizations such as the RSPCA and the British Heart Foundation, do not aim to make a profit. All the money they receive is used to cover the costs of providing their services.

3. **Non-profit-making organizations.** Some not-for-profit organizations are not charities. For example, building societies do not aim to make a profit. Any revenue they make in excess of their costs is used to offer their savers better rates of interest or is used to update and expand their operations. Similarly, local clubs may be run as non-profit-making organizations.

Charities do not aim to make profits

Many thousands of different firms in the United Kingdom, and all over the world, are involved in the production of goods and services. For the economist it is useful to try to sort them out, or classify them, according to what they do.

Exercise 3   High power records production

Below is a jumble of pictures and descriptions describing how audio compact discs are produced. Work in pairs to match the pictures to descriptions. Write down the descriptions in order so that they form a flow chart, or chain, to explain how 'High Power Discs' are produced, from their initial stage to their final sale to consumers. Some descriptions can be used more than once.

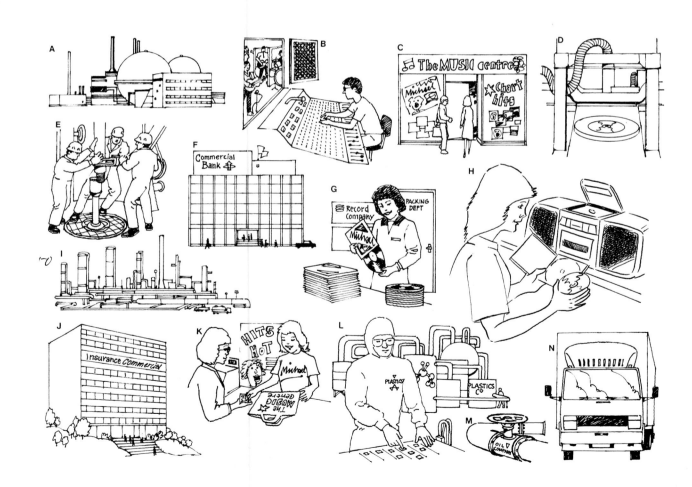

49

Descriptions

1. Recording engineers record pop group in a studio.
2. Coal and oil are used to power electricity stations for use by firms and households.
3. Crude oil is refined.
4. Shops sell CDs.
5. Roads transport goods and people.
6. Consumers buy CDs.
7. Coal and oil are dug and drilled from the ground.
8. Chemical firms use oil to produce plastic.
9. Insurance firm provides insurance to protect firms from risk of damage or theft.
10. CDs are mastered and pressed.
11. Pipeline carries oil to oil refinery.
12. Consumers play CDs on their hi-fis.
13. CDs are packed in plastic cases with paper inserts
14. Banks provide finance for firms.

Producing CDs for sale to consumers is a long and complicated business. In the earliest stages, natural resources, such as coal and oil, need to be extracted from the ground to fire electricity stations. Oil, in turn, is the raw material used to produce plastic for records, which are pressed and shaped by a great many machines. Tape recorders and sound engineers are needed to record the music of a pop group for the CD. The shop is the final destination of the disc before it is sold. Throughout the process a great many banks have probably loaned a lot of money to many firms. Insurance companies have been involved in case of damage or theft, and transport companies ferry raw materials and finished goods to and fro. We can classify all the firms who perform these tasks according to what they do.

Primary industry Those firms which produce natural resources by growing plants, like wheat and barley, digging for minerals, such as coal and copper, or breeding animals, are called **primary firms** and belong to the primary section or **primary industry** in an economy. Primary means it is the first stage of production, as many of the raw materials grown or dug out of the ground are used to produce something else. **Primary industries** are also called **extractive industries**.

Farming wheat is an example of a primary industry

50

Secondary industry

The use of raw materials to make other goods is known as **manufacturing** and firms who engage in this activity belong to the manufacturing or **secondary industry**. For example, the record industry presses records from plastic made from oil. Paper for record sleeves is made from wood. Cars and vans are made from metals.

Car manufacturing is an example of a secondary industry

Tertiary industry

Banking is an example of a tertiary industry

A great many firms do not produce any goods at all. Many sell goods, transport them, or provide financial services, like the banks, building societies and insurance companies. Your school provides an education service, your local hospital a health service. There are also many more personal services, like hairdressers, window-cleaners, tailors, gardeners. All these firms provide a service and belong to the service sector in the economy.

They are also known as the **tertiary industry** because many of these firms provide the final link in the chain of production by selling goods to the consumer. However, it is clear that without services, like transport, insurance and many others, primary and manufacturing firms would find it hard to produce anything.

Exercise 4   Which stage of production?

1   Go back to exercise 3 on High Power Discs; look again at the activities being carried out in each picture and state which are primary, secondary or tertiary.

2   Under three columns headings sort out the following list of industries into primary, secondary and tertiary industries.

Television broadcasting	Health service	Advertising
Film-making	Farming	Shipbuilding
Shipping	Banking	Universities
Decorating	Music	Motor cars
Construction	Furniture	Mining
Fishing	Retailing (shops)	Chemicals
Forestry	Engineering	

Exercise 5   The 'odds and ends' container game

You work in the manufacturing department of the 'Tidy Container Company', which supplies handy size containers for odds and ends, paper-clips, elastic bands and drawing pins all over the world. The aim of the exercise is for groups of four to five students to undertake a production process and organize the use of time, labour and materials to produce containers of the highest quality with as little waste as possible.

Container design

The containers are made following the pattern below, starting with a sheet of plain A4 size paper.

Resources

Each group will be given the following:

Materials	Labour	Capital
20 sheets A4 paper	4–5 students	1 pair of scissors 2 sticks of paper glue 2 pencils 2 rulers

Stage 1
Cut a perfect square.
Do not throw away end paper.

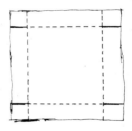

Stage 2
Draw markings as shown. Folds(---) and cuts (—). Now complete these.

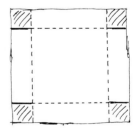

Stage 3
Apply glue to shaded area.

Stage 6
Collect up all end paper pieces for your group and hand them to your teacher at the end of the game.
These can be stapled together to make rough note pads.

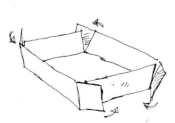

Stage 4
Secure sides of paper.

Stage 5
Check quality of container.

Organization of production

Each group is left to decide how the work will be planned and carried out. You have thirty minutes to reach your target of twenty containers. Your teacher will check all containers for quality or damage. Each container finished is worth £5.00 to your firm, but any rejected container will signify a loss of £7.50. The most successful group is the one which is the nearest to a total output value of £100.00.

After the game

Discuss as a class:

1 Which group was the most successful in terms of the value of containers completed?

2 What appeared to be the best way of organizing the work-force? Give reasons for this.

3 Was the most successful group the most enjoyable to work in?

Your group may have used one of the following methods of production.

Individual production

If you used this method then each person would do everything necessary to produce their own containers. This approach is rather like that of a craftsman making pieces of furniture or pottery. However, it is often a slow process as you probably found out.

Specialized production

Probably a quicker method of producing the containers was to organize the labour into tasks. One member of the group may have been responsible for cutting paper. Another member would fold the paper, another glue, and so on. Each person would **specialize** in one particular operation so that every person would have contributed to the production of all the containers rather than making a few on their own.

Section 5 | From self-sufficiency to specialization |

Most people earn the money they need to exchange for the goods and services they want by doing one particular occupation, such as plumbing, engineering, accountancy, printing or making containers. People do this to take full advantage of their natural talents or the abilities they have acquired from their education or training.

This is a very different situation from that faced by our primitive ancestors who tried to be **self-sufficient**, that is each person or community produced all the things they needed and wanted for themselves, for example, growing and hunting their own food, making their own clothes and shelter. However, people were not always very good at doing everything for themselves and so people slowly started to specialize in doing those tasks they were best able to do. Some people specialized in making spearheads, while others made the spear rods. Others would hunt, while others built shelters and made cooking-pots.

Exercise 6 How specialization began

Below is a cartoon which tells a simple story of how a caveman named Og discovered the benefits of **specialization** over self-sufficiency. Write a story to go with the pictures and include as many advantages and disadvantages of self-sufficiency and specialization as you can think of.

THE TALE OF OG...the first economic caveman!

Section 6   The division of labour

Specialization was the first step towards a wealthier society. A community which practised specialization was able to produce more than enough food, clothes, pots and other things than they needed. The increased production achieved by specialization is the result of the **division of labour**, whereby each worker specializes in doing a particular task rather than being a 'Jack of all trades'. However, with specialization people need to exchange or trade. If people specialized in producing one particular good or service, like Og and his tomatoes, then they must swap any they have left over for goods or services produced by others in order to obtain a variety of goods and services to satisfy their wants.

Specialization and the division of labour means that if people concentrate on doing those tasks they are best able to do, much more can be produced, and more wealth created. This means people's standard of living would improve and they would have greater choice.

54

From trades to operations

The story of Og illustrates how specialization began in early times within a family or tribe of people in a village where the fruits of their labour were shared among the whole family or tribe. As we moved into medieval times people began to specialize in trades. Labour was divided up according to what good or service they produced, and medieval guilds developed. These were groups of skilled trades people, trained to be bakers, engineers, blacksmiths, butchers, carpenters, and so on.

Since then the production process has become broken down into a series of separate operations, each one performed by a separate person or group of people.

In the early days of the motor-car industry one person would put together an entire engine. Then Henry Ford decided to separate the work involved into 84 varied operations. 84 people were needed to build a whole engine instead of just one person. This meant more engines could be built each day. In your own 'Odds and Ends' container game you may have found that the most successful group was the one that practised specialized production and divided labour into tasks.

The organization of labour into a number of divided and specialist tasks has brought a number of advantages to firms and to the economy.

Advantages of the division of labour

1   More goods and services can be produced.
When workers become specialists in the jobs they do, repetition of the same operation increases the skill and speed of the worker and as a result more is produced.

Case study

The Ford Model T

Work on the famous Model T began in 1907, and the production began two years later in 1910 at the company's new plant in Highland Park, Michigan.

As simple as the Model T was, there remained the problem of volume production. Each car was practically hand-built. To boost production Mr Ford and his associates began sub-dividing jobs, bringing parts to workers and scheduling parts to arrive at the right spot at the right time in the production process.

Finally, they devised the moving assembly line, which, with later refinements, pointed the way to mass production. In the beginning it took 12 hours and 28 minutes to assemble a Model T. The time was cut to 5 hours and 28 minutes, then to 93 minutes. Mr Ford set a goal of a car a minute, but eventually Model Ts were rolling off the assembly line at the rate of one every ten seconds of the working day. With increased production, the price came down and the pay of workers went up.

2   Full use is made of everyone's abilities.
With the division of labour there is greater chance that people will be able to do those things at which they are best and which interest them the most.

3 Time is saved.

If a person had to do many different tasks or operations then much time would be wasted switching from one to another.

Time can also be saved when training people. It would take a great many years to train someone to be able to build a complete car, but a person can be trained quickly to fulfil one operation in the process.

4 It allows the use of machinery.

As labour is divided up into specialist tasks it becomes worthwhile to use machinery which allows a further saving in time and effort. For example, today cars are painted by robots instead of by hand. However, many workers are complaining that rather than helping them do their jobs, machines are actually taking them over and making people unemployed.

The disadvantages of the division of labour

1 Work may become boring.

A worker who performs the same operation each and every day is likely to become very bored. To combat this some firms play music to their labour forces, or allow them to have a rest during part of each hour. Longer tea breaks and annual holidays may also result, while the number of hours in the working week may be reduced.

2 Workers may feel alienated.

This refers to workers feeling like a 'small cog in a large machine'. They feel unimportant because they can no longer see the final result of their efforts. Think of the sense of achievement and pride you would have if you could boast 'I built a complete car myself', compared to your disinterest if your job was only to tighten the wheel nuts.

Some firms, for example, car giants like General Motors and Nissan, are trying to reverse this and generate a pride in their work among their workers. They are attempting this by allowing workers to do a greater variety of tasks. Boredom and alienation among workers is often thought to be one of the causes of labour going on strike in developed nations like the United Kingdom.

3 People become too dependent upon each other.

Specialization and the division of labour means that people come to rely on others for the provision of goods and services. For example, people who do not produce food rely on those who do, while the people who produce food rely on others for the provision of tractors, fertilizers and so on. This illustrates how dependent workers in one industry are upon those before them in the production process. A prolonged strike by miners in the coal industry may cause many thousands of other workers to lose their jobs because supplies of raw materials and power stop.

4 Products are all the same.

The goods produced under a system of specialization are usually turned out in vast numbers and share the same design. They are **standardized**.

Whether this is a disadvantage is a matter of people's own opinion. For example, there is probably enough variation in the colour and design of cars and clothes to please most people. However, it is not possible to please everyone because in most factories it would be difficult and expensive to change the production process to suit one person's wishes. This is because most modern factories practise **mass production**. This term is used to describe a production process that aims to use the fewest workers to produce the greatest number of goods, which may often run into millions of articles, at the lowest cost possible.

Section 7 | Worldwide specialization

Cuban cigars

Scotch whisky

Italian shoes

Swiss watch

Japanese hi-fi

With the development of factories in the eighteenth century whole regions of the United Kingdom economy began to specialize. The Midlands became famous for cars, Lancashire for clothing and textiles, Tyneside for shipbuilding. The development of international trade has meant that whole countries began to specialize in producing certain commodities. Japan is now famous for its electronics industry and the production of hi-fis and videos. Swiss watches, Cuban cigars and Scotch whisky are examples of specialization on an international scale.

Section 8 | Production and time

If a firm wishes to increase the amount of goods or services produced, it must employ more resources. If it wishes to do this very quickly it can usually only do so by hiring more labour to work for them or by asking their existing work-forces to work overtime. Obtaining more natural resources, like coal or oil, or land itself, and capital goods, like machinery and new factory buildings, takes a long time.

Economists therefore talk of three time periods:

The **momentary run** is the period of time during which a firm will not be able to increase production. This may be no more than a day.

The **short run** is the period of time during which a firm can increase production only by employing more labour because no more land or capital is available. In the short run, labour is a variable factor of production while land and capital are fixed in supply.

The **long run**, however, is when a firm employs more of all the factors of production.

We cannot say how long the short or long run lasts because the time will vary between different firms. For example, in a matter of weeks both a nuclear power station and a clothing factory could employ more labour, but clearly it would take longer to train a nuclear scientist than a sewing-machine operator. It also takes many years to build a new nuclear power reactor, but would only take a week or so for the clothing factory to obtain some more sewing machines. As for natural resources, cotton plants and wool from sheep can be grown in one season, but it may take a long time to discover uranium and plutonium in the ground for use in producing nuclear power. For the nuclear power station the long run may be a very long time.

Section 9   Changes in inputs and outputs in the short run

The law of diminishing returns

Any business owner or entrepreneur will try to combine the factors of production to obtain the best possible results from their use. There is an important relationship between the inputs of production and the output they produce.

Farmer Scale's fields

Farmer Scale has a very large apple orchard full of apple trees. At the end of the summer the trees were heavy with ripe fruit, ready for picking.

The farmer employed a young apple-picker named Sam who could pick 50 lbs of apples each day in his basket. To enable him to do this, Farmer

Scale had a ladder which Sam would prop against the apple trees so that he could reach the fruit on the high branches. But Farmer Scale was worried that not all the apples would be picked in time before the cold weather arrived. He decided to hire some more units of labour. Angus was the first new employee. He and Sam would climb the ladder together. Sam picked fruit from the highest branches, while Angus picked from the lowest branches. Together they could pick 80 lbs of apples each day. That is, on average, they each picked 40 lbs of apples each day. This is known as their average output or **average product**. Because the ladder had become a little unsteady with both Sam and Angus climbing it, their picking of apples was slowed down.

On his own, Sam could pick 50 lbs of apples each day. With Angus the total weight of apples picked each day increased to 80 lbs. Thus, the employment of Angus raised total output or **total product** by 30 lbs per day. This extra 30 lbs of apples is known as Angus's marginal output or **marginal product**.

Lisa was the second new employee who joined the farm two weeks later. Sam, Angus and Lisa climbed the ladder together. All three could pick 84 lbs of apples each day – an average product of 28 lbs each. This was because the ladder had began to wobble quite a lot and this made picking difficult.

Together Sam and Angus could pick 80 lbs of apples each day, but with Lisa to help the total product of apples increased to 84 lbs per day. Thus, the employment of Lisa increased output by only 4 lbs; her marginal product is 4 lbs of apples.

A fourth unit of labour is employed by Farmer Scale some weeks later. Bob, Lisa, Angus and Sam climbed the ladder together, but they could only manage to pick 45 lbs of apples each day. By now the ladder had become so over-crowded, it was unsafe and it was difficult enough for everyone to cling on let alone pick apples. Clearly, the employment of Bob, the fourth worker, resulted in total product falling from 84 lbs of apples per day to only 45 lbs per day. That is Bob's employment reduced total product by 39 lbs per day. In this case his marginal product is a minus or negative number.

The total, average and marginal products of Farmer Scale's workers are presented in the table below.

| Units of labour | lbs of apples per day | | |
	Total product	Average product	Marginal product
0	0	0	0
1 (Sam)	50	50	50
2 (Angus)	80	40	30
3 (Lisa)	84	28	4
4 (Bob)	45	15	−39

We can plot some of these figures on graphs, with the number of workers employed along the bottom axis, and lbs of apples per day, that is output,

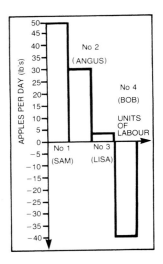

How to calculate the average and marginal product of labour

along the side. The graph on the left shows the marginal product of labour on Farmer Scale's farm.

The graph shows how each new employee or unit of labour produced less than the employee before them until eventually the fourth employee caused the total amount of picked apples to fall.

This example illustrates the **law of diminishing returns**. This states that if one factor of production is fixed in supply (that is, land and/or capital in the short run) and extra units of another factor (that is, labour) are added to it, then the extra output or returns gained from the employment of each extra unit of this factor must, after a time, go down or diminish.

Farmer Scale discovered this when he added extra units of labour to his fixed unit of capital; the ladder soon became shared among too many workers and picking apples became more and more difficult. That is, Farmer Scale experienced diminishing returns to labour.

If 100 workers produce a total output or total product of 4000 compact discs in one week, then clearly on average each worker has produced 40 discs. We therefore use the following equation to calculate the average product of labour.

$$\text{Average product (AP)} = \frac{\text{Total product (TP)}}{\text{Number of workers}}$$

If one more worker is employed and total product rises to 4030 discs then the employment of the extra worker or unit of labour has added 30 discs to total product. This is the marginal product of the worker. We therefore use the following equation to calculate the marginal product of labour.

$$\text{Marginal product (MP)} = \frac{\text{Change in total product}}{\text{Change in number of workers}}$$

Exercise 7 Diminishing returns

Below is a table of figures showing the total product of a number of workers in a micro-computer manufacturing factory using a fixed number of machines, such as soldering irons, plastic presses, and tools like screwdrivers, tweezers, etc.

| | Micro-computers per month | | |
Units of labour	Total product	Average product	Marginal product
0	0	0	0
1	5	5	5
2	12	6	7
3	18	–	–
4	23	–	–
5	27	–	–
6	30	–	–
7	32	–	–
8	32	–	–
9	31	–	–
10	29	2.9	–

1 Copy the table and use a calculator to complete the columns for average and marginal product.

2 Plot the figures you have calculated and join up the points to form three curves which have been started for you on page 60. Plot the total product of labour on the top graph; average and marginal product on the graph below.

You will notice that employing two workers produces more than double the number of micro-computers made by just one worker. This is because two or three pairs of hands working together can be better than one pair of hands. Therefore, at first there are **increasing returns** to labour. This will be displayed on your graphs by the upward slope of the average and marginal product curves up to the second unit of labour employed. However, if there are too many workers the capital goods become shared among too many pairs of hands. Clearly ten workers cannot produce ten times as much as one can. This is the law of diminishing returns which can be seen from your graphs as the downward slope of the average and marginal product curves.

Questions
1 How many units of labour must the firm employ if it wishes to maximize total product each month?

2 What is the value of the marginal product when total product is at a maximum?

3 The ninth worker employed will cause the total product to fall below its maximum, as the capital equipment in the firm becomes shared among too much labour. What happens to the marginal product curve at this point on your graph?

4 How could the entrepreneur who runs the micro-computer firm try to overcome diminishing returns when he employs more and more workers? (**Hint**: What do they need to use to make the computers?)

Section 10 | The costs of production

Just as consumers make decisions about what goods and services to buy, entrepreneurs make decisions about what goods and services to produce and how to do this. Whatever method of organizing production an entrepreneur uses the aim is to reduce costs to their lowest possible level so as to try and make as much profit as possible.

Another concern is the size of the firm, usually measured by how much in total the firm produces per month or per year. A change in the size of the firm will affect costs. As a firm grows in size and as more machines and factory buildings are added to produce more goods and services, we say that the **scale of production** has increased. When we discuss the scale of production we must distinguish between the places in which production takes place.

1 The **plant** or **factory** will be located on one particular site to produce one particular good or service, or perhaps a range of them. Some plants may be very large employing many machines and workers, and occupying a very large area of land, such as a steel plant or a car factory. Other plants may be very small, perhaps no bigger than a shed.

2 The **firm** is the business unit that owns one or more plants. For example, BAE Systems controls 9 different plants in the United Kingdom where aerospace and defence equipment is manufactured and assembled. A firm may be owned and run by one person, a number of people or even a government. We will return to this in the next chapter to consider the ownership and control of firms.

3 The **industry** consists of a group of firms all producing similar goods or services for a particular market. For example, the car industry consists of all firms producing cars. Some industries may be owned and controlled by one very large firm or the government.

Case study

Exercise 8   The Bear Necessities Company

Sue Brennan used to make toys when she was a young girl at school. Her friends and relatives thought that they were so good that they asked her to make some for them to give as presents to others. This gave Sue an idea for the future.

When she left school she went to work in a local furniture-making factory for two years where she gained experience of using cloth to make seat covers. She saved some money and asked her bank to lend her some more so that she could start up her own business under the name of 'Bear Necessities'.

Sue rented a small factory unit on a new industrial estate. The cost of the building, including fittings is £100 per week. She also hired some machinery at a cost of £45 per week. Sue employs her two brothers to help her to make toy bears. Sue pays herself and her brothers £1 for each bear they complete.

Since she started, Sue's toy bears have become very popular and she has many orders for them. She must, however, rely on regular custom from other firms and shops for her bears and so she must try and keep quality high and prices low. The average price she charges for her bears is £10.00 each.

The costs of Bear Necessities
In running her toy-making business Sue has a number of things she has to pay for. These are her **costs**. Some things have to be paid for each and every week no matter how many bears Sue makes and sells. These are her **fixed costs** which do not vary with the number of bears she produces. On the other hand **variable costs** change with the number of bears produced. The more Sue produces the more materials and foam she needs. Wages to herself and her brothers also rise.

Fixed costs per week		Variable costs per bear	
Rent and rates of factory	£100.00	Materials	£6.00
Hire and machines	£45.00	Foam	£1.00
Heating and lighting	£5.00	Wages	£1.00
Repayment of bank loan	£50.00		
	£200.00		£8.00

Sue keeps any profit that is left after she has taken away her costs from the money or **revenue** she earns from selling bears.

Answer the following questions.

1 Write down a definition of fixed costs and give two examples.

2 If Sue produced 100 bears in a week, how much would her fixed costs be that week?

3 If Sue produced 1000 bears in a week, how much would her fixed costs be that week?

4 Write down a definition of variable costs and give two examples.

5 If Sue produced 100 bears, how much would her variable costs be?

6 If Sue produced 1000 bears, how much would her variable costs be?

7 The **total cost** of producing bears is found by adding together the fixed costs (FC) and variable costs (VC).

Total cost (TC) = FC + VC

   a If Sue produced 100 bears in a week, what would her total cost be?

   b If Sue produced 1000 bears in a week, what would her total cost be?

8 Copy the table below and work out the fixed, variable and total costs of producing different numbers of toy bears in a week. The costs of producing 400 bears and 500 bears have already been done for you. We will then plot all this information on a graph. (**Note**: do not attempt to calculate the average cost and marginal cost yet.)

Bears produced in a week	Fixed costs £	Variable costs £	Total costs £	Average costs £	Marginal costs £
0					
50					
100					
200					
300					
400	200	3 200	3 400	8.5	8
500	200	4 000	4 200	8.4	8
600					
700					
800					
900					
1 000					

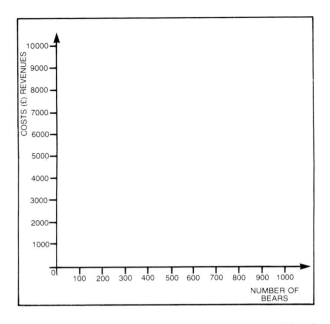

9 Now draw a pair of axes for a graph like the one above on a large piece of graph paper. Use your calculations to plot the fixed cost curve, variable cost curve and total cost curve which show how costs change with the number of bears produced. Do not forget to label each line you plot with its correct name.

10 What is the price charged for each bear?

11 How much money or revenue does Sue receive from the sale of each bear?

You will notice that your answers to questions 10 and 11 are the same.

Clearly if Sue sold five bears for £10.00 each, the revenue per bear is £10.00, while her **total revenue** is £50.00. Total sales revenue is also known as **turnover**.

Total revenue (TR) = Price per bear × number of bears sold

If the total revenue from the sale of five bears is £50, then the **average revenue** for each of those bears is £10, which is the price of each bear.

$$\textbf{Average revenue (AR)} = \frac{\text{Total revenue}}{\text{Numbers of bears sold}}$$

12 If Sue sold 100 bears what would her total revenue be? What would be the average revenue for each bear?

13 If Sue sold 1000 bears what would her total revenue be? What would be the average revenue for each bear?

14 Draw the following table in your books and calculate the total revenue from the number of bears sold. Again, this has already been done for 400 and 500 bears sold.

15 Now look back at the graph you drew earlier and on it plot your figures for total revenue in a different colour and label this line **total revenue**.

64

Number of bears sold in a week	Total revenue £	Total costs £	Profit/loss £
0			
50			
100			
200			
300			
400	4 000	3 400	600
500	5 000	4 200	800
600			
700			
800			
900			
1 000			

16 To calculate the **profit** or **loss** Sue makes from producing and selling bears we take away her total cost (TC) from her total revenue (TR). If her total costs are greater than her total revenue, Sue will make a loss. If she is successful, her total revenue will exceed her total costs and she will make a profit.

Profit (or loss) = TR − TC

On the table you copied in question 14 write in the total costs of producing the different number of bears and calculate the profit or loss. We assume Sue sells all the bears she makes.

On your graph the area between the total revenue and the total cost curve represents the profit or loss. Where the total cost curve is above the total revenue curve the area in between them represents loss. Label this area and shade in one colour. Where the total cost curve lies below the total revenue curve the area in between represents profit. Label this area and shade in another colour.

Where the two curves cross, no profit or loss is made. This level of output and sales is known as the **break-even point of production**. This means that if Sue manages to sell all the bears she makes at this point, she will just cover her costs and be able to remain in business. You should find from your tables and graphs that to do this Sue must make and sell at least 100 bears.

Break-even point of production is where TR = TC

17 Now look again at the total costs of producing a different amount of bears each week. We now wish to calculate for Sue just how much it costs on average to make one bear. This is known as the **average cost** or **unit cost** of production.

We found in question 8 that when Sue produced 400 bears per week her total costs were £3400. Clearly then if 400 bears cost £3400 to make then one bear costs £8.50 to make (£3 400 ÷ 400)

$$\text{Average cost (AC)} = \frac{\text{Total cost}}{\text{Number of bears produced}}$$

Go back to the table you drew in question 8 and calculate the average cost of producing each bear if 50, 100, 200 and so on bears were made.

18 We will now plot the average cost curve on another graph with the number of bears produced along the bottom axis and cost (£) on the horizontal axis. You will need to go up to £12 for your costs axis. When you have done this write down what you notice about the slope of the curve, that is, what happens to the average costs of production as more and more bears are produced? Can you suggest reasons for this? (**Hint**: Even if no bears or 1000 bears are produced what costs does Sue have to pay?)

19 Sue would now like to know how much it would cost to produce one extra bear. The cost of producing one more item is known as the **marginal cost** of production. It is calculated by finding out how much one more bear produced would add to total costs.

$$\textbf{Marginal cost (MC)} = \frac{\text{Change in total costs}}{\text{Change in number of bears produced}}$$

Clearly in this case the cost of producing one more bear must be £8, that is the variable costs Sue must pay to produce an extra bear. This is because Sue will not need to pay out any more fixed costs because she will not need any more machines or factory space. Return to your table in question 8 and calculate the marginal costs of production.

The total costs of any firm are made up of their **fixed costs** and **variable costs**. Fixed costs are those costs which do not vary with the level of output and as a result fixed costs appear as a straight horizontal line on a graph. For example, if a firm rents a factory for £200 per week, this cost is the same whether it produces 100 items or 1000 items. Other examples of fixed costs include machine hire, telephone bills, heating and loan repayments.

Because most of the capital equipment a firm owns wears out over the years, a firm will try to work out how much in value their machinery goes down each week, month or year. This estimate for wear and tear is included as fixed cost and is known as **depreciation**. For example, a construction firm may calculate simply that their mechanical driller has a life of ten years and costs £10 000 as new. Thus each year they may reckon it goes down in value by £1 000.

Fixed costs

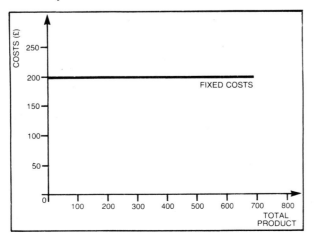

Variable costs are those expenses which do vary directly with the level of output. The buying of materials to make goods will be a variable cost. Wages will also increase if workers have to work longer hours to produce more, or if more labour is hired by a firm. Because of this, variable costs appear as an upward sloping line on a graph.

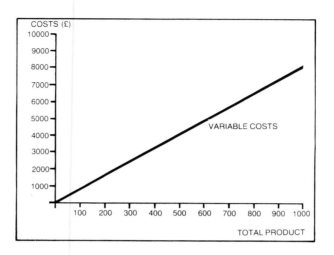

Variable costs

The **total cost** of any level of output is found by adding fixed costs and variable costs together. Because of variable costs, the curve or line representing total costs will slope upwards in a graph. The total cost of producing no items will equal the fixed costs of production.

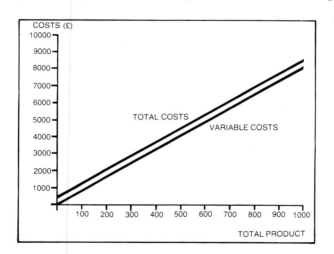

Total costs

The **average cost** of production refers to the average cost of producing each unit of output, that is, each toy, car, pairs of shoes, tin can, video-recorder, etc. When output is low, average costs are high because fixed costs still have to be paid. As output rises, average costs fall because the fixed costs remain the same but their burden is spread over a much larger output.

The **optimum point of production** or best level will therefore be where the average cost of producing each good is at the lowest level possible. At this point the entrepreneur has managed to organize and combine the factors of production in the most cost effective or efficient way.

However, the average cost of production may begin to rise again as more is produced beyond the optimum level of production. For example, in the 'Bear Necessities' business Sue may find that if they attempt to produce 1100 bears each week the shop where they buy the fur material and foam may not be able to supply any more. Sue may then have to buy the extra she wants from another shop where prices are higher. More importantly Sue may have to employ more people to work for her and may have to pay them more money. For example, imagine now that Sue pays herself and her two brothers £100 each week regardless of how many bears they produce. Her total wage bill per week is now £300. If she employs another three workers to help produce bears, wage costs will double to £600 or may more than double if she has to pay them more for them to agree to work for her. The law of diminishing returns tells us that as more labour is added, output will rise but at a diminishing rate. Thus, while wage costs double, the output of bears may not double. Therefore, the average cost of producing each bear will begin to rise. If we plot the average cost of production on a graph it will appear as a flat bowl or 'U' shape curve for many firms, showing that as output rises, average costs fall up to a point and may then begin to increase slowly.

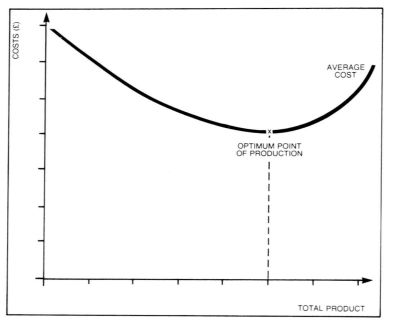

Average cost curve

The **profit** of a business is the income of an entrepreneur and is calculated by deducting **total costs** from **total revenue** (the price of a product multiplied by the quantity sold). Many firms will price their product so that a desirable level of profit is made. For example, Sue Brennan probably calculated that to make a profit of £800 on making and selling 500 toy bears she needed to price each at £10. That is the **average revenue** from selling each bear must be £10.

However, Sue must be careful not to price above other toy bear makers as this competition could cause Sue to lose customers unless she can convince people, by advertising, that her bears are of a better quality than others and therefore should have a higher price.

As a firm sells more of its goods or services, the total revenue from their sales rises and appears on a graph as an upward sloping line. With total cost plotted on the same graph we can mark those outputs that result in a loss or a profit and find the break-even point of production. The area of profit can be found where the total revenue line is above the total cost line (as in the diagram below).

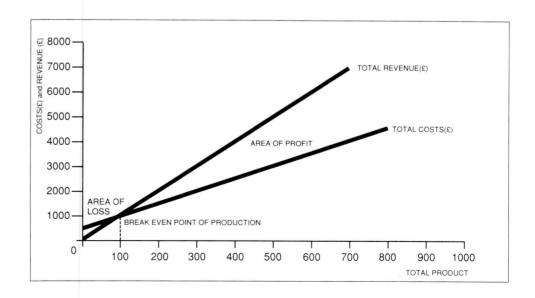

Exercise 9   Costs

1   Below is a set of possible production levels of a new pop magazine to be sold at 50 pence each. Copy and complete the following table of figures for the publishing company if the cost of machinery and factory rental for one month is £1200 and the cost of materials and wages per magazine is estimated to be 10 pence. There are no other costs in this simple example.

Magazines per month	Fixed costs (£)	Variable costs (£)	Total costs (£)	Average costs (£)	Total revenue (£)	Profit loss
0	1 200	0	1 200	0	0	−1 200
1 000	1 200	100	1 300	1.30	500	−800
2 000	1 200					
3 000						
4 000						
5 000						
6 000						
7 000						
8 000						

2   What level of output is the break-even point of production?

3   Plot and label the following curves on a graph with 'magazines per month' along the bottom axis and cost and revenue (£) in £200 intervals along the side axis. This needs to extend up to £4 000.
   a Fixed costs
   b Variable costs
   c Total costs
   d Total revenue

4   Label those areas that represent profit and loss on your graph.

Section 11   Large-scale production

An entrepreneur can consider increasing output in a number of ways:

1   By reorganizing the workforce.
2   By employing more labour.
3   By employing more of all the factors of production.

Reorganizing and employing more labour can take place in the short run, but using more land and capital is only possible in the long run.

If a firm decides to expand the scale of its production in the long run by employing more of all the factors of production what will happen to their returns or output? There should be more output but how much more? Let us consider three different firms all making boxes of chocolates.

Exercise 10   Chewing over a problem?

The following three chocolate manufacturing firms have expanded the scale of their production in two years. All three firms have doubled their inputs or the factors of production they use. But what has happened to their output of chocolate boxes? The figures are given below.

The ACE Company	The BOOM Company	The CRIKEY Company
Year 1		
Labour units 50	Labour units 40	Labour units 60
Number of machines 10	Number of machines 15	Number of machines 5
Number of factories 1	Number of factories 1	Number of factories 1
Total product 10 000	**Total product 12 000**	**Total product 9 000**
Year 2		
Labour units 100	Labour units 80	Labour units 120
Number of machines 20	Number of machines 30	Number of machines 10
Number of factories 2	Number of factories 2	Number of factories 2
Total product 25 000	**Total product 20 000**	**Total product 18 000**

A firm that doubles all its inputs and more than doubles its output of goods or services as a result is said to be experiencing **increasing returns to scale**. This is what happened in the Ace Chocolate Company above. The Boom Company, however, doubled its input but did not manage to double its output of chocolate boxes. Firms like this are said to be experiencing **decreasing** or **diminishing returns to scale**. On the other hand, the Crikey Chocolate Company experienced **constant returns to scale** because as it doubled its inputs it also doubled its output.

Exercise 11   Chewing it over again

Our three chocolate companies have doubled all their inputs and have therefore doubled their total costs. One firm managed to more than double its output, one firm doubled its output while the other did not manage to do this at all. Calculate what has happened to the average cost of producing boxes of chocolates in each company as they moved from year one to year two.

The ACE Company	The BOOM Company	The CRIKEY Company
Year 1 Total cost of all inputs: £10 000 Total product 10 000 **Average cost £1**	**Year 1** Total cost of all inputs: £12 000 Total product 12 000 **Average cost £1**	**Year 1** Total cost of all inputs: £9 000 Total product 9 000 **Average cost £1**
Year 2 Total cost of all inputs: £20 000 Total product 25 000 **Average cost ?**	**Year 2** Total cost of all inputs: £24 000 Total product 20 000 **Average cost ?**	**Year 2** Total cost of all inputs: £18 000 Total product 18 000 **Average cost ?**

Which of the firms above has doubled all its inputs in the long run and experienced:

1   Falling average costs?

2   Rising average costs?

3   No change to their average costs?

So what happens to average costs in the long run?

Falling average costs are an important benefit to a firm. We say that the firm experiences **economies of scale** if it makes cost savings from increasing the scale of production, that is, by raising output. This was certainly the case for the Ace Chocolate Company whose average costs per box of chocolates fell from £1 to 80 pence as it doubled all its inputs and total costs; it experienced increasing returns to scale and more than doubled output. If the average costs of production rise as more is produced then the firm is experiencing **diseconomies of scale**, because the firm is producing too much and has become inefficient. This happened to the Boom Company as it doubled its inputs but failed to double its outputs. Diminishing returns to scale here meant that the firm's average costs increased from £1.00 to £1.20 per box. The Boom Company, like any firm in this situation, would regret taking the decision to expand its scale of production.

So how big should a firm be?

Deciding how large a firm should be is not easy for an entrepreneur. If the firm expands its scale of production it may be lucky and experience falling average costs or economies of scale. If the firm expands too much and watches its average costs rise, like the Boom Company did, it has experienced diseconomies of scale. Clearly then the best size or **optimum size** for a firm is where it can reduce average costs to their lowest point in the long run. Here it can benefit fully from economies of scale. With average costs low, profits will be bigger. The firm could use these profits to improve their factory and their products, and may even lower prices to attract consumers away from competing firms.

The advantages of large-scale production

Economies of scale

When a firm expands the scale of production it has a chance to become more efficient and lower its average costs. This is because it gives the management or owners a chance to reorganize the way the firm is run and financed. Such decisions are taken within the firm and so the advantages or economies they bring are known as **internal economies of scale**. These are the cost savings that result from a firm being large. We shall now look at these in detail.

Exercise 12   Big is beautiful?

Case study

Case 1: Cleaning up their act

A famous detergent manufacturer has recently decided to expand its production plant and install the latest equipment. Studies have shown that they would produce a maximum output more efficiently if they employed several of the new machines. This, the study said, would lower their unit costs compared with their smaller competitors, who could not afford to employ as many machines.

To meet the costs of this expansion the company decided to raise the funds from banks. Banks were only too willing to lend on very reasonable terms, because the firm had offered to put up its premises as security. The banks also noticed that, because of the number of different products the firm had produced for the home and international market, any demand fluctuations would not seriously affect the firm's ability to repay the loan. Its smaller competitors, however, found it hard to raise money for their modernization, and even when funds were secured, the interest rate they were charged was much higher and consequently this meant their average costs were higher.

The large firm has a new soap coming on to the market next week, and they are planning a massive advertising campaign to launch it. The cost of the campaign is around £1 million, but with an output of 10 million, this clearly only adds 10p to the cost of producing each unit of soap. Smaller firms could not possibly advertise on such a scale, because with outputs of around 3 million, it would add 33p to the cost of producing each unit.

Case 2: Blasting off!

The large iron smelting company in Northern Ecoland has recently announced how pleased it is at having achieved a big overseas order, as a result of it being able to offer a lower price than its foreign counterparts in Nomicia.

'Our specialist sales staff were a great help in winning the order,' enthused Mr Justin Time, the Company Director. 'The Nomicians could not afford to employ such specialists.'

He went on to say how his Company had managed to offer a lower price than the Nomicians. He explained that their unit costs were much lower because their plant had managed to employ a large blast furnace, while the smaller Nomician plants had to band together in certain areas to be able to afford such furnaces. Mr Time also added that some Nomician firms incurred higher transport costs as a result of their scale of operations being smaller. The Ecoland Company, however, has been able to purchase large juggernauts which can carry far more tons of iron than could their smaller lorries, but clearly do not require any more drivers and only use fractionally more petrol per journey.

He also told us how his firm's average costs were lower than that of the Nomicians, as a result of their purchase of vast quantities of iron ore. 'You see because we buy 40 million tons of the stuff every year, our suppliers are willing to sell it for £50 per ton,' he said, 'whereas the average Nomician firm only buys 10 million tons a year, but at £60 per ton.'

---

1 Read the two case studies above and with your partner list all the ways that large firms are able to enjoy cost advantages which smaller firms can not.

2 Compare your list with another group's list.

3 Now use your list to try to decide which of the internal economies of scale could be called:

    a Financial economies that is cost savings that arise from the way in which large firms raise money.

    b Marketing economies that is cost savings resulting from the way in which firms sell their products.

    c Technical economies that is cost savings caused by the methods of production used.

    d Risk-bearing economies that is cost savings that result from the way in which firms try to reduce the risk of a fall in demand for some of their products.

Let us now consider the four main types of internal economies of scale.

1 Financial economies
A large firm has several financial advantages because it is large, well known and becomes a more credit-worthy borrower than a smaller firm. This means:

    a A large firm can borrow money from a number of different sources, to buy new machines, etc. Large firms may also be able to raise money from the general public by selling them shares through the Stock Exchange.

    b Large firms have more assets than a small firm, like machinery, deeds to factories and offices, that they can offer to the lenders in case of the unlikely event that they cannot repay the loan. Because this event is so unlikely financial institutions are very willing to lend money to these firms.

    c Because large firms represent such low risk borrowers, financial institutions may not charge them so much for giving them a loan.

2 Marketing economies

The way large firms buy materials, transport and sell their products can also bring them advantages.

a A large firm is able to buy in bulk large quantities of the materials they need and may also be able to store them. Because of this, suppliers will often sell things in bulk at discount prices. They may also offer to deliver the goods to the firm at special low rates to secure their regular custom.

b The large firm is able to afford to employ specialist buyers who have the knowledge and the skills necessary to buy the best quality materials at the best possible prices.

c In large shops specialist sales staff can help customers to buy the things they want, while large manufacturing firms can employ specially-trained staff to visit shops and warehouses to sell the products they make.

d Although large firms spend huge amounts of money on advertising their products to create a want for them, their advertising costs are spread over a very large output.

3 Technical economies

The larger firm can afford to use different methods of production.

a Large firms can afford to employ specialist workers and machines. They can divide up the production process into specialized tasks so that production becomes faster as each worker becomes an expert in their particular job. In small firms there are simply not enough workers or specialized machinery to make this profitable.

b Large firms can also afford to research and develop new faster methods of production and new products. The cost may be high but it is spread out over a very large output.

c The larger the firm the more transport it needs to carry materials and products to and fro. As a firm grows in size it can afford to use large types of transport, like juggernauts, or, in the case of oil companies, supertankers.

4 Risk-bearing economies

Running a firm is a risky business and clearly the bigger the firm the more things can go wrong. Therefore larger firms try to overcome this risk in a number of ways.

a A small firm is likely to need only small amounts of raw materials or components to produce goods or services and so it would probably only obtain these from one supplier. A large firm will, however, need to buy materials in bulk and if they cannot obtain these for some reason, for example, a strike at their suppliers or some transport problems, then their whole operation will grind to a halt. Large firms will try to reduce the risk of this happening by using many different suppliers, buying some of the materials they need from each.

b A small firm is only likely to produce one particular good or service and they could find themselves in trouble if consumers suddenly decided not to buy that product. If a large firm did the same, a fall in consumers' demand for their product would have devastating effects. In order to reduce the risk of a fall in consumer demand damaging the firm, large enterprises often produce a whole variety of goods or services, so that if demand for one falls they still have others they can make and sell. This is known as **diversification** which means producing a diversity or whole variety of products. For example, in recent years the Boots chain of shops and stores have moved away from selling only medicines and cosmetics to a wide range of other goods from video-recorders to garden furniture. Many other shops have done the same along with many manufacturers. For example, Unilever is famous for its soap and detergent products but it also has interests in the production of food, paper, plastics, animal feeds, transport and tropical plantations.

Transport economies

Marketing economies

Section 13 | The disadvantages of larger-scale production

Diseconomies of scale

It seems very beneficial for a firm to grow to a large size so that it may enjoy economies of scale. However, some firms become too large and this can cause inefficiency: production slows down and costs rise. This is caused by **diseconomies of scale**.

1 Management diseconomies
Large firms have to be divided up into many specialist departments, for example, the planning department, personnel, accounts, production, design, sales, etc. Each department will have a manager responsible for running it. For the firm to run successfully all the departments must work together, but with so many departmental managers decisions will take a long time and there may be disagreements.

2 Labour diseconomies
Large firms use very specialized mass-production techniques. Labour is divided up into many specialized tasks but workers may become very bored with their repetitive and often monotonous jobs. The work-force may then become less co-operative or less attentive to their work, so that the quality of the products they produce suffers. Strikes and disruptions may also occur if the workers feel they are poorly treated (see Chapter 11).

Section 14 | The advantages of a whole industry being large

When a whole industry expands, either because the number of firms within it is growing or the existing firms are getting bigger, the firms in the industry may find they can enjoy certain benefits. **External economies of scale** are those advantages in the form of lower average costs which a firm gains from the growth of the industry. They are especially important when all the firms in an industry tend to locate together in one particular place. For example, much of the motor-car industry in Britain centres on the Midlands area of the United Kingdom. In this case external economies of scale are often known as **economies of concentration**.

1 Skilled labour
When firms involved in the same type of activities locate near each other they all employ and train local people in the work skills they need. A large skilled labour force emerges which can benefit other firms who move into the area.

2 Ancillary firms
In areas where similar firms locate other firms may join them to cater for some of their needs. For example, smaller car part-producing firms have set up near the large car factories that dominate the Midlands in the United Kingdom. Similarly, the city of Leicester is known for its shoe-making firms, and to help them other firms who specialize in selling leather and footwear machinery have located nearby.

3 Co-operation
Where firms locate together to produce one particular good or service they tend to help each other even though they are also competing with each other to sell their products. For example, the setting up of specialist magazines for whole industries is the result of co-operation between firms.

However, there may be disadvantages if there are too many firms in an area. This can lead to traffic congestion, pollution and so on. We will consider such damaging effects in more detail in Chapter 9.

Section 15 | So why are there small firms?

Some of the small firms of today could grow to become the large firms of tomorrow, but increasingly small firms face tough competition from larger firms. Before we look at how small firms manage to survive it is important to consider just exactly what is meant by a small firm.

What is a small firm? It is difficult to define exactly what a small firm is. However, economists use a number of guidelines. These are:

1 A small firm has a small share of a market. That is, it only produces and sells a small amount of a particular good or service compared to what is produced and sold in total by all other firms in the same line of business.

2 It is managed by its owners in a very personalized way.

3 It is independent, meaning that the small firm is not part of a large company.

In order to distinguish a small firm from a larger firm easily the committee also suggested that a small firm should be defined as one that employs less than 100 people. But many economists think this is not a very good definition. For example, if a corner grocery shop employed 50 people it would be considered a very large grocery shop. Similarly, a shipbuilding firm may be large if it employed several thousand people to build ships but would be a very small shipbuilders if it employed less than 500 people. However, we do at least have some guide as to what a small firm is.

Exercise 13   Why are there small firms?

Read the following passages and try to list all those factors you think are helping these *small firms* to survive in the economy today.

Mr Granger runs a local newsagent in a small town in Hampshire. It is the only newsagent for some miles around and he stocks a variety of goods ranging from general household items, such as washing-up liquid, to food stuffs. Mrs Scuttle is a regular customer and she comes for the variety of goods the newsagent is able to supply.

'Well,' she said, 'you can pick up most of the things you need here, so why go elsewhere. Old Bill, that's Mr Granger, goes out of his way to provide a good stock of goods and he's only too happy to help you out any time. Me and the other locals get on with Bill like old school pals . . .'

Salisbury Engineering is a small manufacturing firm run by Peter Salisbury making fuse-boxes for a hugely successful, international motor-car manufacturer. Peter started his own business when his previous company collapsed in the winter of 1998. Using a bank loan underwritten by the Government he obtained small premises and some equipment. 'Our initial success was due to the fact that the new type of fusebox I designed was protected by a patent so that only I could produce them,' Peter explained. 'It was then that the car giant got interested.'

Paul and Julie Mallam decided to start up their own business shortly after leaving Art College. Paul had been unemployed for some time but was entitled to financial help from the Jobseekers Allowance for his first 6 months in business.

'The money came in very handy,' Julie explained. 'We had a cash flow problem to start with. We make "exclusive" pattern jumpers that sell for around £100 to £250 each. Our market is limited, our trade coming from the "well to do" 18 to 30 year old age group . . . I suppose it's the very specialized and luxury nature of our sweaters that has kept us going.'

Large firms can enjoy special advantages like bulk buying, receiving loans at low interest rates and employing specialist staff. With lower average costs than smaller firms, large businesses can lower their prices to attract consumers. With such fierce competition why is it that small firms can still survive, and why does there appear to be a growth in their number?

1 The size of the market may be small.

When there is only a small number of consumers willing to buy a product there is no point in a firm growing to a large size. It is better to remain small producing just enough for the relatively small number of people to buy. The size of the market will therefore determine the size of the firm. There may be a number of reasons why the market for a particular good or service is small:

a The market is local.

Mr Granger's newsagent was the only one for miles around and so people would regularly visit to buy the products he sold. Local bakeries, butchers, farms and local newspapers can also enjoy the advantages of regular custom and profits. Where only one small firm is able to supply a good or service to the people of a particular area we call it a **local monopoly**.

b A wide variety of goods and services are wanted.

Some firms face the problem that consumers want a wide choice of products in different colours, styles and designs. Large firms that mass produce goods cannot afford to keep changing the colours and design. Smaller firms, however, can often cater for a variety of tastes. Tailors can make suits to measure, carpenters can make furniture to order.

c Luxury items are highly priced.

The market may be limited by price. That is high prices mean that only a handful of rich people can afford to buy a product. For example, Paul and Julie Mallams' 'exclusive' jumpers of between £100.00 and £250.00. Expensive jewellery, luxury cars and yachts will be produced by small firms for a small number of people.

d People like personal service.

Industries which provide services rather than goods usually consist of a large number of small firms. Mr Granger the newsagent was able to chat and be friendly to customers. In large supermarkets or department stores it is often difficult to get personal attention. In other areas where personal attention is required we find many small businesses. For example, lawyers, accountants, doctors, dentists, hairdressers and many more.

e A large firm requires component parts.

Peter Salisbury's small firm was able to survive because the large car firm required the components he made on a regular basis. Peter also had the advantages of having his fuse-boxes protected by a **patent** which disallows by law any other firm from copying his idea. Many small firms can survive by producing parts for large manufacturers.

2 Small firms can co-operate.

Co-operation between small firms can lead them to set up jointly-owned enterprises which allow them to enjoy many of the economies of scale that large firms have. For example, some small farms have bought large barns for joint storage space together so that they can buy seeds and fertilizers in bulk and store them.

3 The Government helps small firms.

Successive UK governments have provided help to small businesses because they are a key provider of employment and innovations in production processes, customer service and product designs. Over 45% of the UK workforce was employed in firms with fewer than 50 employees in 1999.

UK governments have used a variety of measures to help owners of small and medium-sized enterprises (SMEs). These include:

Business Link

Business Link is a nationwide network of around 240 advice centres. It provides affordable advice and training to all businesses, especially SMEs. Advice covers all aspects of how to start and run a successful business, including how to raise finance, how to market products, and how to comply with health and safety, employment and tax regulations.

Loan Guarantee Scheme

This scheme encourages banks and other financial institutions to lend money for periods between two and ten years to small businesses and business projects which they would normally consider too risky to lend to. The Department for Trade and Industry (DTi) guarantees to repay up to 85% of a loan of up to £250 000 if the small business borrower runs into trouble and is unable to repay.

Enterprise Allowances

Financial help and training is available for unemployed people between 18 and 24 years of age who want to start their own business. They can continue to claim the Jobseekers Allowance during their first six months in business.

The Small Business Service

This acts as a focal point within Government for providing advice to SMEs in England. It also offers an automated payroll service for small employers to make wage payments and collect income taxes using electronic banking.

Tax measures

A 10% rate of corporation tax was introduced in April 2000 on profits up to £10 000. Previously many small companies had to pay up to 25% of their profits in tax. Tax credits were also introduced for spending by SMEs on new research and developments.

Key words

This page is photocopyable

```
M O E C O N O M I E S O F S C A L E
T U R N O V E R S T O C K P O I A R
Y H F C V T V A R I A B L E M A N T
O B R E S E O S Y N J E C C A O D X
M A N U F A C T U R I N G I R O B L
E T R E V E N U A V A R Y A G F R A
T C C A P I T A L L A N D L I G E V
O H O R P I S M S W C O P I N H A E
T I S P R O D U C T I O N Z A T K R
A L I R I R O T O I L O S A L E E A
L S V E M C L A M R E S C T P R V G
P E R I A V E N M I S A B I R T E E
R R R A R L A B O U R S T O O I N C
O V A X Y D I A D N I N E N D A I O
D I M I N I S H I N G R E T U R N S
U C S A B I T C T H I W A N C Y T T
C E N T E R P R I S E E M M T A T O
T S H A V E S S E C O N D A R Y E X
W F I X E D C O S T S I M E M A S S
```

In the jumble of letters above, find and circle, or highlight, the terms that fit the following definition.

Definitions

1 A process that turns raw materials into finished goods.

2 Man-made resources.

3 Costs which do not change with the level of output.

4 The total sales of a firm over a period of time. Also known as total revenue.

5 The service industry.

6 Goods and services.

7 The total output of a firm.

8 Large-scale production of a standardized product.

9 The industry that uses raw materials to produce finished goods.

10 Business 'know-how' or the ability to take the risks and decisions necessary to run a business.

11 All natural resources.

12 Fixed costs plus variable costs.

13 The point of production where total revenue just covers total costs.

14 Costs which vary directly with the amount produced.

15 The cost per unit of a good or service produced.

16 The industry that extracts natural resources.

17 Things that satisfy a want but do not involve a physical good.

18 The addition to total output caused by the employment of one more unit of a factor of production.

19 These refer to factors that reduce average costs for large-scale enterprises.

20 Human resources.

21 This occurs where workers concentrate on producing particular goods or services, or parts of these commodities. Can also refer to whole regions or countries concentrating on one particular line of production.

22 This occurs when the employment of an extra unit of a factor of production, for example, labour, adds less to total output than the unit before it did.

FROM LITTLE ACORNS, BIG OAK TREES GROW...

Aims

At the end of this chapter you should be able to:

1   Give reasons for the existence of different types of business firms.

2   Distinguish between **fixed capital** and **working capital**.

3   Define what is meant by **unlimited liability** and **limited liability**.

4   Distinguish between the main types of business unit in the UK according to how they are controlled, owned and financed.

5   List the advantages and disadvantages of different types of business unit.

6   Explain what is meant by a **multinational** and analyse the various costs and benefits to a country that plays host to such firms.

7   Explain what is meant by a **public corporation** and know how they are controlled.

8   Give reasons why whole industries were **nationalized.**

9   Examine **arguments** for and against **privatization.**

Section 1 — Why are there different types of business firm?

To produce goods and services, the resources of land, labour and capital are needed. These resources on their own, however, will not satisfy our wants. For example, if we want football boots, it is no use just buying leather and hiring workers and land. Something else is needed before these resources can be used to produce boots. Resources need to be organized, and decisions need to be taken in order to manage or control the resources from day to day.

The person who makes these decisions and owns a business is called the **entrepreneur.**

It is the job of the entrepreneur to organize resources in a business or firm. In a modern economy an entrepreneur can choose many different types of business. Each type allows the entrepreneur to organize, manage, control the business and raise money in a different way. A small firm with just one owner will be different in the way it is controlled and financed than a large firm where there are many thousands of owners.

Section 2 — Types of firm

In a mixed economy like the UK there are three main types of firm. **Public corporations** or **nationalized industries** are owned by the Government and are therefore part of the public sector in the economy.

Co-operatives are owned either by shoppers who buy from them or the workers who work in them.

Private firms are owned by ordinary people and can range from very small businesses which are owned by one person to large firms owned by many thousands of people. Co-operatives and private firms are part of the private sector in the economy.

Section 3 — Starting a business

If we trace the growth of a business from a small one-person firm to a large company it will be possible to see the different types of business there are and the reasons for their existence.

Steve Oak is an unemployed school leaver. Steve is good at carpentry and would like to set up a do-it-yourself (DIY) shop as well as doing carpentry jobs. Before starting up his business, Steve, like all entrepreneurs, must ask himself three questions. The answers to these questions will help to decide which type of business is best for him.

Question 1   Will I have enough money?
Starting a business can be very costly. The money put into a business is called **capital**, because it is often used to buy capital goods, such as machinery and buildings. Money spent on capital goods is known as **fixed capital**, while **working capital** is the money used to run a business from day to day, that is, money used to pay wages, electricity bills, telephone bills, heating and so on.

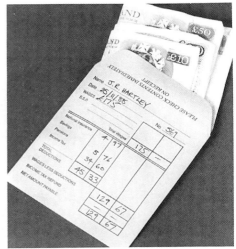

Fixed capital   **Working capital**

Some businesses need more capital than others. Steve Oak must ask himself if he has enough money to set up his business himself, in which case the type of business is called a **sole trader**.

If Steve Oak does not have enough money he may have to find other people who would like to share in the ownership of the business with him. These people have to pay money into the business in order to share in its ownership. This type of business is known as a **partnership**.

If still more money is needed, Steve Oak can turn his business into a **joint stock company** or **limited company**, with many thousands of owners, all paying in order to join.

Question 2   Can I manage the business alone?

If Steve is to start up his DIY business and undertake carpentry jobs he must ask himself if he can manage all of this alone, or will he need to take on partners? Steve is skilled in carpentry only, so this means there are many building jobs he might have to turn down because the work involves other things. However, if Steve was to take on partners with different skills, for example bricklayers, electricians and plasterers, then Steve's business would be able to do many more jobs than just carpentry work alone. All entrepreneurs, including Steve, must decide upon whether or not they can manage alone before choosing the sort of business they are going to start.

Question 3   Will I risk everything I own?

The owner of a business is entitled to a share of any profits made. However, the owner also has the responsibility of finding money to pay for the firm's debts if the business should fail. This financial responsibility is called the **owner's liability**.

Steve must decide before starting up his business if he is willing to risk all his savings and possessions on the venture. The answer to this question will influence the type of business chosen, because some businesses are more risky than others.

84

THEY EVEN TOOK MY CLOTHES!

DEBT COLLECTORS

CLOSED

Some business owners have what is called **unlimited liability**. This means that if a business is not successful and goes bankrupt, the owner, or owners, will have to pay all the business debts. The owners stand to lose all their possessions, like their houses, cars, furniture, and even clothing if they cannot afford to pay off their business debts. However, some business owners may have **limited liability**. This means that if a business goes bankrupt the owners would only lose the amount of money they have put into the business. They will not have to sell their own possessions to pay the company debts. Limited liability reduces the risk of running a business.

Private sector organizations

Section 4 | ## The sole trader

Ownership and control

Steve Oak decides he has enough money to start up on his own and he will be able to manage the DIY and carpentry business without help. He also decides that it is worth risking everything he has, because as his friends keep saying 'Nothing ventured means nothing gained'. Steve's DIY business, like many other small businesses such as newsagents and grocers, is a one-person business or sole trader. A sole trader may have more than one employee but it is always owned and controlled by only one person.

The sole trader is the oldest and most popular type of business in the UK. There are many more sole traders than any other type of business in this country. In fact, many very large and successful businesses started life as sole traders.

Exercise 1   The sole trader

Read the following article and list the advantages and disadvantages of being a one person business.

LOCAL TIMES

OAK DIY OPENS IN HIGH STREET

Steven Oak is now the proud owner of the Oak DIY shop in the High Street. We asked Steve why he decided to open his own shop.

'I was unemployed for a long time,' explained Steve. 'By running my own business I am ensured a job and I get any profits. But to do this I have to work every hour I can and run the business on my own.' Starting your own business is expensive Steve soon discovered. 'I used most of my savings to get the company off the ground, and my bank manager supplied me with a loan. What with the rent of the shop space, hire of machinery, insurance payments, heating and lighting bills I have to make at least £600 a month from the shop before I can break even. And of course if I can't I am out of work again and left holding all the debts.'

With a prime location near to the car-park in the town centre, Steve may be able to look forward to a lot of customers and an expanding business. 'I hope so,' said Steve. 'I can even give other people jobs to do, but I will still be the boss. My own boss. I don't have to answer to anyone. Not bad is it?'

Oak DIY opens at 10 am next Monday with special first week price reductions on many of the tools, paints, wallpaper and other decorations the shop offers. If you cannot get what you want, Steve will be willing to order your requirements. Shoppers can look forward to a personal and friendly atmosphere in the shop. Most of the locals already know Steve and he promises that he will put the kettle on at regular intervals throughout the day for the benefit of callers.

Advantages of the sole trader

1 The sole trader business is a very personal one.
The owner of the business will have personal contact with customers and staff. S/he will be able to find out quickly what people want and then change what the shop sells to suit what customers wish to buy. Furthermore, because anybody dealing with the firm deals with the owner personally this can encourage customers to be loyal to the business.

2 The sole trader is his/her own boss.
Because s/he is the only owner of a business, the sole trader does not have to ask anyone's permission before making a decision. This means they can make decisions quickly. They can decide whether or not to expand the business, what jobs to do and when, who to employ, etc.

3 The sole trader receives all the profits.
Being your own boss and not having to share the profits are important advantages to most people and this, in part, explains why the sole trader type of business is so popular.

4 It is easy to set up a sole trader business.
Sole traders need very little capital to start up with, so it is fairly easy for one person to set up a business alone.

There are also very few legal formalities involved in starting up as a sole trader. Other larger types of business need a lot more capital and legal work before they can begin trading.

Disadvantages of the sole trader

1 The sole trader has unlimited liability.
Unlimited liability means that the sole trader is liable to lose everything s/he has in order to pay off debts in the event of bankruptcy.

Unlimited liability exists because, in the eyes of the law, the sole trader business and its owner are seen as the same. So if the business owes money its owner must pay.

2 The sole trader has full responsibility.
As the sole owner of a business, the sole trader must take all of the decisions. Most people, however, are not good at everything, but sole traders still need to be able to manage the business, do the book-keeping, advertising, buying and selling, and many other things. This means that often the sole trader may work long hours and if they are ill there is no one to take over the running of the business.

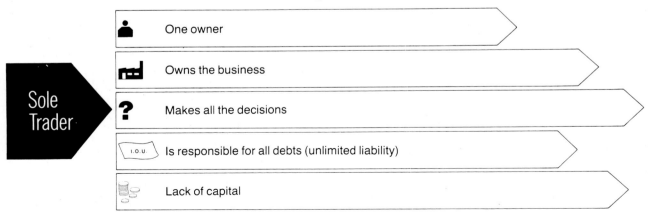

3 Sole traders lack capital.

If Steven's DIY business is successful he may wish to make his business bigger and expand into a second shop. The problem is that enlarging a business requires more money and sole traders like Steven often do not have this extra money.

Steven could use some of his profits to help pay for a second shop but this would leave himself with very little. Bank loans are expensive and banks are reluctant to lend money to sole traders because they often cannot afford to repay the loan.

Section 5   Partnerships

Ownership and control

A sole trader may find that more money is needed to expand the business and that someone else is needed to help run the firm. **Partnerships** can be formed with little formality. Partnerships are common particularly amongst solicitors, doctors, vets, etc.

Let us assume that Steve's DIY and carpentry business is doing well and Steve decides to take on two partners Jan and Bill. And three people, Steve, Jan and Bill, now own the business, control it and share the profit together. The reasons why Steve decided to share his business are explained by the advantages of forming a partnership.

Exercise 2   The partnership

Read the article below and list the advantages and disadvantages of forming a partnership.

LOCAL TIMES

OAK STARTS TO GROW

Today Steve Oak of the Oak DIY shop celebrates over one year's successful trading with the opening of a new DIY shop.

So what is Steve Oak's secret of success?

'Clearly there is a market for DIY products and home improvement centres,' he said, 'but I offer a friendly and personal service that my larger competitors seem to lack. As a result people just come back again and again. I always help them out with their DIY problems if I can.'

Using his own money Steve Oak acquired the premises and equipped his existing store. Banks were unwilling to lend him money for the enterprise because of the obvious risks such an outlet faces from increasing competition from established DIY retailers. With giants such as Sainsburys and W.H. Smiths also expanding into the home improvements market, the fear of competition became more acute. 'The banks are still unwilling to lend I'm afraid,' explained Mr Oak, 'but luckily I have made contacts in my business dealings and have two partners now to help run and finance the business. Not only have they put up a large amount of money but they will also be able to relieve me of some of the responsibilities I've carried for over a year now. For example, Jan is a qualified accountant and can do all the bookwork, and Bill is a trained electrician who will also be looking after the new shop.'

Jan Eversham and Bill Heston are the two new partners in the Oak enterprise. Running a business poses many risks and the collapse of the firm could mean all those personally involved losing their possessions to repay debts. So why did Jan take the risk? 'It's a challenge,' she said, 'I was an accountant, but now I'm a full-time housewife and I wanted something else to keep me occupied.'

What problems, if any, do the partners think may occur?

'Well,' they explained, 'finding the money to decorate and refit the shops is proving a problem, and we had initial disagreements about how to lay-out the two stores. But we're all friends really!'

Advantages of a partnerships

1   Partners bring new skills and ideas to a business.
Steve has taken on Jan and Bill as partners because they have skills which the business needs.

2   More partners means more money for the business.
If other people want to share in the ownership and control of a business then they must pay money to do so. This money can then be used to expand the business.

3   Partners can help in decision-making.
A sole trader has full responsibility for making decisions in a business, whereas in a partnership all decisions are shared.

Disadvantages of partnerships

1   Partners can disagree.
The more partners there are, the more likely are disagreements. If Steve, Jan and Bill find they cannot agree on important decisions affecting the company, the business may suffer.

2   Partnerships have unlimited liability.
Just like a sole trader, in an **ordinary partnership** partners stand to lose everything they have if the business goes bankrupt. Furthermore, each partner is held responsible for the actions of the other partners.

It is possible to have a **limited partnership** where some partners have limited liability. They are called limited partners or **sleeping partners**; like ordinary partners they pay money into the business in return for a share in the ownership and profits. However, unlike ordinary partners they do not play a part in the day-to-day running of the business.

3   Partnerships lack capital.
Because there are more people in a partnership the business will have more money than a sole trader, but it is still difficult for a partnership to have more than twenty partners (with exceptions for firms of solicitors, accountants and stockbrokers). This puts a limit on the amount of money that may be brought into a business.

None of the very large businesses in the UK, or indeed in the world, are partnerships. This is simply because no partnership could raise the necessary capital to expand into a large enterprise.

Other types of business are needed to do this. These other forms of business enterprise are known as **joint stock companies.**

Partnerships

- 2 to 20 partners
- Partners own the company
- Partners are responsible for all debts (unlimited liability)
- Partners make all the decisions
- Lack of capital

Exercise 3   Local businesses

Which of these shops are sole traders or partnerships?

Look around your local area and try to identify businesses that are:

a   Sole traders
b   Partnerships.

In each case try to explain why you think the type of business, and what it does, is suited to that particular form of business organization.

| **Section 6** | Joint stock companies |

Joint stock companies are also known as **limited companies.** These are companies that sell shares to investors in order to raise money.

There are two main types of limited company, the **Private Limited Company** (Ltd.) and the **Public Limited Company** (plc). Most of the smaller Joint Stock Companies are Private Limited Companies; there are around half a million in existence in the UK at present. Public Limited Companies tend to be much larger in size but fewer in number.

The Private Limited Company

After several years of trading the Steve Oak DIY business partnership has become very successful. To build upon this success the partnership now wishes to open up a chain of shops around the country, but to do this they need a lot of money.

To raise this money to expand the business they can form a **Private Limited Company**. These companies can be recognized by the letters Ltd. after their names, for example, OAK DIY Ltd.

Exercise 4   The Private Limited Company

OAK DIY TO BECOME LIMITED COMPANY

Oak DIY, the chain of do-it-yourself stores, has just announced plans to become a Private Limited Company by selling shares in the company. This will raise capital to finance their new expansion programme. Mr Steve Oak, founder of the company, explained how allowing the company to be owned by more people can provide the money he needs to build more stores around the country.

'We simply invite people to buy share certificates in the company,' he said, 'and this allows them to become owners of the business and to share in its profits. These shareholders are also allowed to have a say in how the company should be run.' 'Of course,' he continued, 'I would like to remain as a Director of Oak DIY, but if all the other shareholders decide they don't want me at the head of the company they can vote me out and elect other directors to run the business. Each year they can vote for directors at a special shareholders meeting.' The problem many small companies like Oak DIY face today is one of raising finance. If this is to be achieved through the sale of shares then the additional problem of finding people to buy them arises. Normally shares will be sold to family, friends and workers in the company.

We asked Steve Oak why people would wish to buy shares in his company. 'We are a growing and profitable company,' he replied, 'and the more profit we make the more shareholders receive. This is called their dividend. Also as a Private Limited Company all shareholders would benefit from having limited liability, and so in the very unlikely event of Oak DIY closing down due to bad debts, shareholders would only lose, at the most, however much money they paid for their shares.'

1   How do Private Limited Companies like Oak DIY raise the money they need to expand their businesses?

2   What does the word 'Limited' stand for in Private Limited Company?

3   What is the name given to the people who are elected to run a Private Limited Company?

4   Steve Oak suggests in the article that he would like to remain at the 'head of the Company' and run the business from day to day. Who will decide if Steve can remain in this position, and how is this done?

5   What encourages people to buy shares in the ownership of a company?

How a Private Limited Company raises money

Private Limited Companies can raise money for expansion by selling **shares** to people. A share is simply a piece of paper that states that the person who holds it has paid for part of the company and now has a share in its ownership. (Shares are also known as **securities.**) Below is a share certificate. The value printed on the share, or its **face value**, is the price at which the company first sold the share.

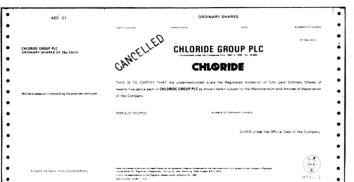

An ordinary share certificate

If Oak DIY Ltd. was to sell 10 000 shares at £1 each then the company would receive £10 000. The people who bought these shares are called **shareholders**. The more shares a person holds, the more of the company they own and the bigger their share of the profits. For example, Oak DIY Ltd. may pay out ten pence of their profits for every share held. The profit paid out on a share is known as a **dividend**. If 1 000 shares are owned then 1 000 times ten pence will be received. That is, a £100 dividend from the profits.

Ownership and control

COMPANY SHAREHOLDERS ANNUAL MEETING 2000

"HE'S THE MAJORITY SHAREHOLDER!"

Oak DIY Ltd. has issued 10 000 shares for £1 each. Imagine that these have been sold to 2 000 different people. All of these people are now owners of the company. However, they cannot possibly all work in the business and manage it from day to day. Such a large group of people would get in each others' way, would not agree with each other easily, and many would just not have the experience needed to run a company.

To overcome this problem the shareholders are allowed to choose a **board of directors** to run the company on a daily basis. This is done by voting at shareholders' meetings. Each shareholder has one vote for each share they hold. The more shares a person holds, therefore, the more votes they can have. In our example, Steve, Jan and Bill, the original partners in Oak DIY Ltd. will wish to keep more shares than anyone else so that they will have more votes than any other shareholders.

This will enable them to vote for themselves to be directors if they wish, or at least give them greater power to choose the directors they want. Ideally, if Steve, Jan and Bill wanted to be directors and have control over the whole company they will need to hold over half of all the shares, leaving all the other shareholders with less than half the shares.

Any person, or group of people, who buys over 50% of the shares in a company is said to have a **controlling interest** in that company. This is because they can out vote all other shareholders and therefore can control the business.

Advantages of the Private Limited Company

1   Shareholders have limited liability.
This means a person who owns a company is only responsible for the repayment of any debts up to the amount of money they originally put into the company. Without limited liability people would be unwilling to buy shares because if the company went bankrupt they could end up losing a lot of money, and even their possessions, to repay large company debts.

2   Shareholders have no management worries.
If shareholders in a company had to run the business, they would have to take on all the worries and responsibilities themselves. However, they can pass on this responsibility and elect directors to manage the business on their behalf. This is done by voting at an **Annual General Meeting (AGM)** of all shareholders.

3   The company has a separate legal identity.
In the eyes of the law the Private Limited Company and its owners are seen as separate bodies. As a result if the company owes money, the name of the company can be sued and taken to court, but the owners cannot. The company can be forced to pay its debts or pay compensation out of

company funds, but the owners, because they have a separate legal identity, are not responsible.

Disadvantages of Private Limited Companies

1   Limited Companies must disclose information about themselves to the general public.
Under the Companies Act of 1981 all limited companies are required by law to keep detailed records of their spending, revenues, profits, etc. and to publish this information so that their shareholders can read about what their company is doing.

This information is published by a company and sent to all its shareholders in the form of a set of annual accounts. These accounts give details of the profits made in the past year, total sales, the money the company owes and the people and institutions that they owe it to. Clearly it is an advantage for shareholders to have information about their company but the writing, printing and postage of such details can be very expensive. In addition, they allow competing companies to know some of the company secrets.

2   Limited Companies must hold an Annual General Meeting of shareholders each year.
An AGM of shareholders must be held each year to allow these company owners to vote on such issues as how the company should be run, and who should run it. This is an advantage for shareholders as it allows them to air their views and reflect them in their votes. However, AGMs are not only expensive to set up but they can result in the original owners of the company losing control over the company.

3   The original owners of the company may lose control.
A Private Limited Company must have a minimum of two shareholders or owners. However, the vast majority of limited companies has a larger number of owners, who can have a say in how the company is run and elect the directors who run it by voting at Annual General Meetings. In this way the original founders of the company may be voted out of their director positions and be replaced by newly-elected directors.

4   Company profits are taxed twice by the Government.
When a company makes a profit, some of this money is paid to the Government as tax. A Limited Company will then use its after-tax profits to pay dividends to its shareholders. When shareholders receive money from dividends they must pay part of this money in tax to the Government.

5   Private Limited Companies cannot sell shares on the Stock Exchange Market.
One of the largest markets in the world for buying and selling shares is the Stock Exchange in London. The shares of Private Limited Companies, however, cannot be traded on the Stock Exchange market (see Chapter 6). Private Limited Companies have to sell their shares privately to people they know, like family, friends and workers. This is a big disadvantage because it is possible to sell many more shares, and raise far more money on the Stock Exchange. This means that these companies are confined to being small to medium-sized firms, unable to raise vast amounts of money to expand.

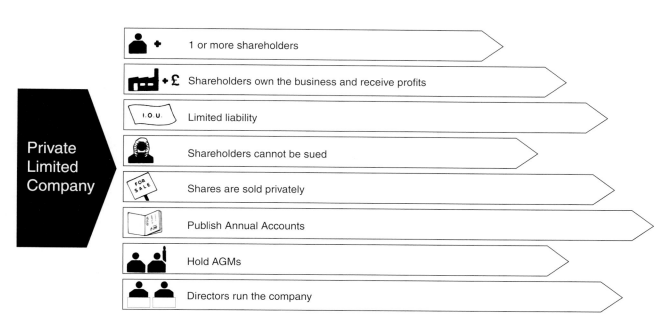

👤+	1 or more shareholders
🏭+£	Shareholders own the business and receive profits
I.O.U.	Limited liability
	Shareholders cannot be sued
FOR SALE	Shares are sold privately
	Publish Annual Accounts
	Hold AGMs
	Directors run the company

Private Limited Company

Exercise 5 The Public Limited Company

CITY TIMES

SEASONED OAK BLOSSOMS

Oak DIY, one of the country's leading do-it-yourself chain stores, has announced plans to sell shares on the Stock Exchange. The Council of the Stock Exchange revealed yesterday that the company has received a full listing which will allow it to float shares on the full stock market and become a Public Limited Company (plc).

'Our plans are to open a chain of discount warehouse stores on a number of sites throughout the United Kingdom, and even one in France!' explained Jan Eversham, one of the original partners in Oak DIY. 'This, of course, requires a substantial injection of cash into the company, but we feel confident that sales and profits will be extremely good.'

Oak DIY, now Oak plc, was founded nine years ago by Mr Steve Oak, an unemployed carpenter from Leeds. The company first sold shares privately to friends and workers four years ago and has gone from strength to strength, with a sales turnover for last year tipping £10 million and a profit of £417,000.

The new issue of four million shares at 100 pence each will be available from next month and with dividend forecasts looking good it is likely that the shares will be snapped up quickly by many thousands of investors, hungry for gain. A major advertising campaign in national newspapers will prepare prospective shareholders for the launch of Oak plc on the full stock market. Clearly, going public by selling shares to the general public is an expensive business, but the financial rewards can be great.

The issue of who controls the large company will be discussed, and subject to vote, at the next AGM where the existing shareholders will be joined by many of the new shareholders. Mr Steve Oak, Mrs Jan Eversham and Mr William Heston, the three original partners, are confident, however, that with their controlling interest in share ownership they can retain positions as Company Directors.

'My only fear,' explains Mrs Eversham, 'is that managerial diseconomies may arise if the company becomes too large. Good managers, who can run the

various departments in the company and can work as a team, are hard to find.'

The application list for the purchase of shares will open on Thursday May 20th. Dealings in the shares are expected to start a week later.

93

1   How do Public Limited Companies like Oak plc raise finance for expansion?

2   How much money will the Oak share issue raise?

3   Why is it easier for a plc to sell shares than a Private Limited Company?

4   What are meant by management diseconomies, and what other disadvantages can plague such a large company?

5   Why are the original owners of the plc more likely to lose their control of the company than if they were in a smaller company?

Forming a Public Limited Company

Public limited companies are the largest and some of the most successful firms in the UK. Examples of plcs include such well known names as HSBC Holdings plc (banking), British Airways plc, Marks and Spencer plc, Commercial Union plc (life insurance services), Dixons Group plc (owners of Dixons, Curreys, PC World and The Link) and Kingfisher plc (owners of B&Q, Comet, Superdrug, Woolworth's, MVC Music Video).

Example of Public Limited Companies

A plc must have a minimum of two shareholders. Plcs will usually offer their shares for sale on the Stock Exchange. Shares can be sold to any member of the general public. Hence the term **going public** is used to describe a company who obtains a **full listing** allowing the company to be listed by the Stock Exchange as a business that is able to sell its shares on this market. The advantage of this is that the Stock Exchange is a worldwide market for shares of plcs, and this allows these companies to attract money from investors all over the world.

Before a Public Limited Company can offer its shares for sale on the Stock Exchange the governing body, or Council of the Stock Exchange will investigate the company to ensure it is a trustworthy business and that it meets certain standards of practice and size, as laid down in the Stock Exchange rules. If a company meets the requirements of the Stock Exchange Council then it will be allowed to sell shares to members of the public through the Stock Exchange. This sale of new shares is known as a **flotation.**

Advantages of the Public Limited Company

The plc has all the advantages of a private limited company but the fact that plcs are often very large and successful businesses means that the plc has important additional advantages.

1   Public Limited Companies can sell shares on the Stock Exchange.
The UK Stock Exchange is one of the largest markets in the world for the purchase and sale of shares. The plc is able to sell its shares on this market to people all over the world and raise far more finance than a Private Limited Company which is only able to sell shares privately.

2 Public Limited Companies can advertise their shares.

Often the plc can attract shareholders by placing advertisements in newspapers and on the television. This can create a want for their shares and enables them to raise more money. Below is an example of a newspaper advertisement inviting people to buy shares in British Steel when it was privatized by the UK Government in 1988.

The UK Stock Exchange

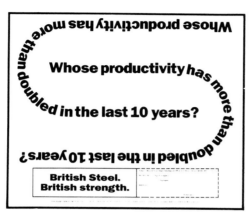

Whose productivity has more than doubled in the last 10 years?

**British Steel.
British strength.**

Disadvantages of the plc

The plc shares some of the same disadvantages of the Private Limited Company. However, owing to the size of many plcs, and the amount of capital they raise, additional disadvantages can arise.

1 It is expensive to form a plc.

Launching a plc is an expensive business. Many legal documents are required. Advertisements in newspapers are needed and a **prospectus** needs to be published either as a pamphlet, or on a couple of pages in a newspaper. The prospectus will tell people and institutions who wish to buy shares in a company such details as how many shares are to be sold, their price, the names of the Company Directors, sales and profits and a brief history of the firm.

2 The original owners of the company may lose control.

The problem of the original owners of a company being voted out of their management position by other shareholders is particularly pressing in a plc. This is because so many shares are sold to other people.

3 There may be a divorce of ownership from control.

Shareholders have the right to attend Annual General Meetings and vote on company policy and on who should be a director to manage the company from day to day. However, many plcs have thousands of shareholders, many of whom do not have the time or inclination to attend such meetings. This is especially true of the small shareholder who has only a limited number of shares, and therefore limited voting power. Only a handful of shareholders actually use their vote and so directors, once elected, act very much on their own. For this reason the majority of shareholders tend to lose control of the companies they own. This is known as the divorce of ownership from control.

Another problem for the small shareholder is the tendency for large financial institutions, like insurance companies and companies who manage pension funds, to use the vast amounts of money they have to buy up huge quantities of shares in plcs. In fact, most shares in the UK are owned by these large financial organizations. (We will consider them in more detail in the following chapter.) As there is only one vote per share, small shareholders have very little influence on their companies' affairs when their votes are set against the thousands of votes made by large financial institutions.

4 plcs may face management problems.

Some plcs may become so large that they become difficult to manage. The more people involved in a business, the more people there are that need to be consulted when decisions are taken. This makes decision-making very slow and disagreements can occur.

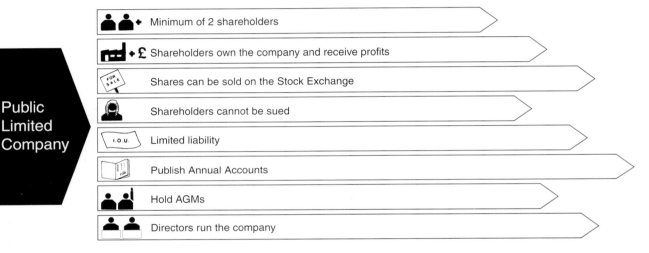

Public Limited Company

- Minimum of 2 shareholders
- Shareholders own the company and receive profits
- Shares can be sold on the Stock Exchange
- Shareholders cannot be sued
- Limited liability
- Publish Annual Accounts
- Hold AGMs
- Directors run the company

Exercise 6   Types of business organization

Below is a list of advantages and disadvantages of the sole trader enterprise.

Sole trader	
Advantages	**Disadvantages**
1 Easy to set up the business	1 Unlimited liability
2 Freedom of being your own boss	2 Owner has full responsibility
3 Owner gets all profits	3 No one else to run the business if the owner is ill
	4 Long hours of work
	5 Lack of capital

Copy the above table and complete for the advantages and disadvantages of:

a   Partnerships

b   Private Limited Companies

c   Public Limited Companies

Section 7 | Co-operatives

There are two main forms of **co-operative enterprise**. One is controlled by workers, and one is controlled by consumers. The aim of a Co-operative business is to provide benefits for its owners. For example, employment for workers, lower prices for consumers. In turn, each of the owners or members of the co-operative has an equal share in the control of the firm. That is, everyone has an equal say in how the company is run, regardless of how much money they put into the business, that is, one person, one vote.

Case study

Exercise 7   Case study

Read the case study below and list as many advantages and disadvantages as you can find for workers forming a co-operative.

NO LONGER OUT IN COLD...

IN many ways Manchester Cold Rollers is probably more like than unlike numerous other small new "entrepreneurial" companies which have struggled into existence over the past few years.

Launched in 1981 by three young engineers who had designed and built an improved machine for the forming of cold rolled steel sections, it came within a whisker of liquidation at the end of the first year.

Now, having survived a protracted crisis and brought a new product in the shape of a heavy duty bicycle lock to the market, its total in-house workforce has grown to eight and it is looking forward with wary optimism.

MCR has been committed to worker ownership since before it started. Upon the successful completion of a probationary period of 12 months all new recruits must purchase not less than £500 of its shares.

For a period of six months its workforce managed in effect to survive on the earnings of wives and girlfriends and to take zero incomes out of the company's cash flow. In this way it was possible, in the current jargon, to "turn the company round." It seems most improbably that a group of conventional wage employees let alone their wives and girlfriends would have been prepared to behave in that way.

Having built the improved machine, the founders based their initial strategy on a two-pronged plan. They would aim to enter the market by securing sub-contract cold roll forming work for their own prototype machine. And they would also seek orders for — and then build — the same machines for specialist steel section fabricators.

At the end of the first year not one single machine had been sold. In the meantime they had found that the market for sub-contract work was difficult, unreliable and unremunerative.

There was, in fact, only one glimmer of hope as MCR ended its first year. They had discovered that they could use their machine to produce galvanised mild steel capping for the domestic electric wiring market.

It was this capping which provided the first key to their survival. Gradually sales were built up. Now, a year after they emerged from the most extreme phase of their crisis, they are supplying several of the country's leading wholesalers.

Equally, or even more "entrepreneurial", has been the development and introduction to the market of its heavy duty bicycle lock. Anyway, for the moment there is no competing British product and MCR, in an English translation of the current French phrase, are "reconquering the home market". Their lock is selling at the expense of imports.

Worker co-operatives These are organizations owned by their workers, such as in a farming co-operative. They pool their money to buy equipment and share equally in decision making and any business profits.

The number of worker co-operatives grew rapidly during the 1970s when many firms were closing down and making their workers unemployed. The UK Government set up the *Co-operative Development Agency (CDA)* to provide advice and financial assistance to help employees to buy the firms they worked for. Most worker co-operatives have been formed by taking over small manufacturing businesses that were facing closure.

There are few worker co-operatives in the UK compared to countries like France, Spain and Italy where this type of business ownership is very popular.

Advantages of worker co-operatives

1 Worker co-operatives are popular with workers because they themselves are in charge and everyone has an equal say. They are also likely to work harder because they can take part in making decisions about how to run the business.

2 The workers receive the profits they make. Profits are paid out as dividends either on the basis of each worker getting an equal share, or according to how much money they put into the enterprise.

Disadvantages of worker co-operatives

1 One of the main reasons why worker co-operatives have not been very successful in the UK is because they find it difficult to raise money. Worker co-operatives must rely on borrowing from banks, workers and local councils. This lack of capital means that worker co-operatives cannot expand easily and so tend to remain small businesses.

2 Worker co-operatives have tended to be badly run in the UK simply because the workers making the decisions usually have little business experience or entrepreneurial ability.

While worker co-operatives presently employ only a small number of workers in the UK some people believe that more worker co-operatives could in the future be one way of encouraging new and innovative small firms. Some people also feel that worker participation in business decision-making can create work incentives. Such participation can, however, take on other forms than full worker co-operative enterprises. Allowing workers to become shareholders in the company they work for is one suggestion, while some people feel that workers' representatives should sit on the Board of Directors of a company. Many foreign firms, like those in Japan, already employ this method of worker participation.

Consumer co-operatives

These are retailing businesses run for the benefit of their customers. The first retail co-operative society was formed in 1844 when a group of workers fed up with low pay and high food prices joined together to buy food direct from wholesalers. Because they were able to buy food in bulk, suppliers would often give them discounts. Today, any profits made in retail co-operatives are given back to their consumers as dividends or by keeping prices low.

The principles of modern consumer co-operatives are unchanged since they were first formed:

- modern co-operatives are owned by their members
- any person can become a member by buying a share for as little as £1
- members elect a board of directors to run the co-operative
- each member is allowed one vote regardless of the number of shares they hold
- profits are shared between members.

Today many of the smaller co-operative shops have closed because of competition with large supermarkets. To compete a number of co-operatives have formed into large superstores selling a wide variety of goods and services, normally located on large sites outside of town centres.

Co-operatives run a travel service and a bank

The co-operative movement has also successfully expanded into other activities such as banking, insurance, travel agents, funeral direction and bakeries. The largest single retailing co-operative is the Co-operative Retail Society based in Manchester.

Worker Co-operatives	Retail Co-operatives
Workers own all the shares	Owned by its members
Managed by its workers	Managers run the organization
Workers have limited liability	Owners have limited liability
Workers share the profits	Members receive profits

Exercise 8   Ownership, control and finance

Below is a table listing how different types of business are owned, controlled, raise finance and distribute their profits. Copy and complete the table by filling in the blank spaces. If you cannot remember all the details then read again Sections four to seven.

	Types of business enterprise					
	Sole Trader	Partnership	Private Ltd. Co.	plc	Worker Co-op	Consumer Co-op
Ownership						Owned by customers and share-holders
Control	Run by the owner					
Sources of finance	Own savings Bank loans			Sell shares		
Distribution of profits						Profits given to customers as stamps or lower prices

| **Section 8** | Multinationals |

A **multinational company** or **corporation** is a firm that operates in more than one country, although its headquarters may be in one particular country. These companies are some of the largest firms in the world, often selling billions of pounds worth of goods and services, and employing many thousands of workers around the globe.

The first multinational on the moon?

Many of the biggest multinational companies in the world are mainly Japanese or US-owned. However, among the world's top 50 global industrial giants in 1998 were key UK companies British Petroleum, British Telecommunications and Shell Trading and Transport (as part of the royal Dutch/Shell Group, one of the largest companies in the world). BP has since merged with the US oil company Amoco and now has business operations in around 100 countries.

The table below illustrates the huge scale of some of the UK based multinationals.

UK Multinationals 1998	Principal activities	Capital employed £ billion	World sales £ billion	Total employees
British Petroleum	Oil & gas exploration, marketing, oil refining, and chemicals	20.5	44.7	53 700
Shell Trading and Transport	Oil & gas exploration, marketing, oil refining, chemicals, coal mining	21.0	32.8	101 000
British Telecommunications	Communications	17.5	14.5	20 250

Other well known UK multinational companies include HSBC Holdings (banking), Bass (brewing), Marks and Spencer (retailing), British Airports Authority (transport and retailing services), Rio Tinto (mining) and Imperial Chemical Industries (chemicals). However, most UK multinationals are small compared to some of the US giants like General Electric (electrical goods) and General Motors (car manufacture), and huge Japanese corporations such as Toyota (car manufacture) and Matshushita (electronics).

Of the world's one hundred largest economic entities in 1998 in terms of annual income, 52 were multinational companies and 49 were countries. Multinationals are responsible for around two thirds of total world trade and entire world industries can be dominated by a handful of these large global organizations. For example, 60% of the world trade in bananas is controlled by just three multinational firms.

Exercise 9 Multinationals

The following chart lists a number of multinational companies. Try to find out the country they originate from and what they produce to complete the table. The first one has been completed for you.

Company	Country of origin	Main products
Sony	Japan	Electronic equipment
Ford		
Esso		
Wal-mart		
Coca-Cola		
IBM		
Union Carbide		
Peugeot		
BP Amoco		
Nestlé		
Unilever		
ICI		

Governments will often compete against each other (see Chapter 7). This is to try to get multinational companies to locate a plant in their countries because:

- They provide jobs.
- They bring business knowledge, skills and technology with them.
- They may pay taxes which boost government funds.
- They bring money to the country by selling goods abroad.

Advantages of being a multinational

1 Multinational companies are able to sell far more than any other type of company.
The ability to set up factories to produce goods in many different countries increases the number of potential consumers of the company's products.

2 Multinational companies can avoid transport costs.
A company that sold goods all over the world would find that it had to pay many transport costs. By producing goods in different countries and selling them in those countries a multinational can reduce its transport costs. It can also locate its factories near to the raw materials it needs.

3 Multinationals can take advantage of different wage levels in different countries.
By locating in a less developed country a multinational can often take advantage of so-called cheap labour. In some countries women and children can be employed for very low wages.

4 Multinationals can achieve great economies of scale.
By having massive production lines and producing millions of goods, multinationals are often able to lower the average cost of producing each good below the average costs faced by companies making fewer goods.

5   Multinationals have less chance of going bankrupt than smaller companies.
Multinationals tend to produce a wide variety of goods so that if demand for one product falls they have other products they can fall back on. Similarly, selling to a large number of countries also reduces the risk of one particular country reducing its demand for the products of the multinational company. These are known as risk-bearing economies of scale (see Chapter 4).

6   Multinationals can carry out a lot or research and development.
In order to improve old products and develop new ones to stay ahead of competing firms, multinationals spend large amounts of money on research and development.

What price multinationals?   Multinationals are big powerful companies employing many people and earning a lot of money. Often their location is welcomed by governments around the world because of the benefits of employment, new technologies and wealth they bring to a country. However, there can be disadvantages for countries who play host to multinationals.

1   Multinationals move their factories to wherever it is profitable to produce.
Multinational companies can move their factories from one country to another to maximize their profits. For example, if taxes on profits are higher in the UK than in Korea, a company might be able to make more profit by closing its UK factory, causing thousands to be unemployed, and opening a new plant in Korea. This means that workers in multinational companies may have little control over their jobs.

Because many countries have high unemployment, governments in these countries do not want multinationals to close their factories in their nations. These governments offer gifts, such as help in the building of factories and lower taxes on profits to encourage multinationals to stay. In fact, different governments often compete with each other over multinationals and this allows such companies to force competing countries to give them more and more favourable treatment.

2   Multinationals may switch their profits between countries.
Often multinationals can avoid paying any taxes to their host nation. This may happen in a less developed country because that country lacks the ability to collect taxes because of a poor tax service and legal framework. Multinationals may also transfer or switch their profits from countries with high taxes to countries with low taxes.

3   They may force competing firms out of business.
The sheer size of multinationals and their great wealth may allow them to force smaller firms in their host country to go bankrupt. If they cause other companies to shut down, unemployment will rise.

4   Some multinationals may exploit workers.
Many multinationals locate in countries where labour is cheap. By locating in less developed countries they are able to keep their wage costs low by paying workers far less for doing the same, or even more work, than a worker in a developed country.

5 Some multinationals may interfere in the government of a country.
Some commentators have suggested that some large powerful multi-national companies have used subversive and illegal activities to try to influence the government of a country, to promote and protect their own interests.

Section 9	Public sector organizations

Public sector organizations are those owned or controlled by government authorities.

Local authorities

Local government organizations include the administrative offices of

- district councils
- county councils (regional councils in Scotland)
- London borough councils

Local authorities provide public services to local businesses and communities such as education, leisure facilities, refuse collection, housing, the maintenance of local roads and parking enforcement.

Central Government

Voters elect members of parliament to form the Central Government to be responsible for taking decisions on national issues and controlling the economy (see Chapter 15). The political party with the most MPs forms the government.

The main decision making body in the Central Government is the **cabinet** which normally consists of around 21 ministers headed by The Prime Minister. Each minister is appointed by the Prime Minister to be responsible for the activities of a government department. There are around 20 **government departments**, including Her Majesty's Treasury, the Home Office, the Ministry of Defence, and the Department of Trade and Industry (DTI). Each department has its own budget to spend on the provision of a range of services and has to submit these spending plans to the Treasury each year for approval (see Chapter 16).

Civil servants are employed by the Central Government in departments to develop and control the economic, social, environmental and foreign policies. The Scottish Executive and National Assembly for Wales are the administrative offices of the Scottish and Welsh parliaments.

Executive agencies

A number of public services, such as the royal mint, prisons, the provision of statistics, passports and benefit payments are run by executive agencies. These organizations are run in a business like way with independent control over how they spend the money paid to them each year by Central Government. Some agencies have been privatized and are now run by private sector organizations.

Quangos

Quango stands for **quasi-autonomous non-government organization**. Quangos are unelected government bodies run by boards of directors to manage a particular government initiative, for example, regional health authorities, research councils, and industrial tribunals. Being 'quasi-autonomous' means they can be run from day to day rather like a private sector business without the direct control of government officials.

Public corporations

Most **public corporations** are responsible for the day-to-day running of industries owned and controlled by Central Government which sell goods or services directly to consumers. These are called **nationalized industries**. For example, the Post Office is run by a public corporation. However, few industries remain nationalized in the UK today. Most industries that were nationalized such as British Rail and British Telecom, have been sold to private sector organizations (see below).

Public corporations also run the Bank of England, which is not involved in trading activities, and the British Broadcasting Authority (BBC) which is neither owned by the Government nor the private sector.

Public corporations have some features in common:

- each is controlled by a government minister. For example, the BBC is accountable to the Home Office minister.
- each has a board of directors which is responsible for the-day-to-day running of the corporation. These are appointed by the government minister responsible for the industry.
- each has a separate legal identity from the government. This means that legal action can be taken against a corporation and but not against the Government.
- each is financed by revenues from the sale of its services to consumers and by Central Government grant (the BBC gets it money from the TV licence fee set by the Government each year and from the sale of its programmes).
- each must publish an annual report and financial accounts.
- they do not have to make an overall profit, although public corporations are expected to earn at least an 8% profit on the value of new investments. For example, if the Post Office invested £100 000 in a new equipment it would be required to earn at least £108 000 in revenue from it.
- public corporations may be allowed by Central Government to retain all or some of the profits made to plough back into improving their services. However, the Government may decide instead to use these profits to finance other public services and help reduce taxes.

The Post Office is run by a public corporation

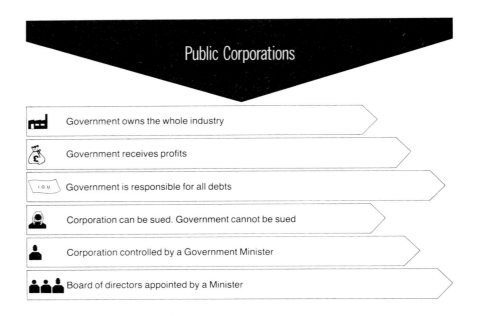

Public Corporations

Government owns the whole industry

Government receives profits

Government is responsible for all debts

Corporation can be sued. Government cannot be sued

Corporation controlled by a Government Minister

Board of directors appointed by a Minister

Section 10 | Nationalization and privatization

Nationalization

Nationalization refers to the transfer of an industry from private to public ownership by the passing of an act of parliament forcing private owners to sell their shares to the government. Between the end of the Second World War and the late 1970s successive UK Governments took over the ownership of all the firms in industries such as coal, electricity, gas and the railways. Each nationalized industry was run by a public corporation.

The Main Nationalized industries in 1982	
British Coal	National Girobank
Electricity (England and Wales)	British Airways
N of Scotland Hydro Electric	British Airports Authority
S of Scotland Electricity	British Rail
British Gas	British Waterways
British Steel	National Bus Company
British Telecom	Scottish Transport Group
Post Office	British Shipbuilders
London Transport	

Why were industries nationalized?

UK governments have in the past taken into public sector ownership entire industries for the following reasons;

To control natural monopolies

In some industries firms need to grow very large in order to take full advantage of the cost savings large-scale production can bring (see Chapter 4). However, this can result in one very large firm becoming the only supplier of a product to a market and, if unchecked, it could take advantage of this market power to charge high prices to consumers. To prevent this, natural monopoly providers of the gas, water, electricity and railway supply networks, were controlled by the Government (see Chapter 10).

For safety
Some industries, such as nuclear energy, are thought to be too dangerous to be controlled by private entrepreneurs.

To protect employment
Some firms were nationalized because they faced closure as private sector loss making organizations. For example, in 1975 the Central Government rescued British Leyland to protect the jobs of car workers.

To maintain a public service
Nationalized industries can provide services even if they make a loss, such as postal deliveries and rail services in rural areas. Private firms seeking to make profit would not operate these services.

Privatization
Since 1979 most nationalized industries, have been returned to private sector ownership. **Privatization** refers to the sale of shares in government-owned nationalized industries to the general public and private sector firms. The first most significant sale was in 1984 when British Telecom was sold. In 1999 only the Post Office, British Nuclear Fuels and the National Girobank remained nationalized organizations.

The UK Government also has plans to privatise many executive agencies (see below).

Those in support of privatization argue:	Those against privatization argue:
• if these industries are forced to compete for profit they will become more competitive, improve their product quality, and lower prices.	• many privatized industries still dominate the markets they supply and have been able to raise their prices and cut services. For example, rail and water companies are local monopoly suppliers.
• whereas there used to be only one nationalized supplier, consumers will be able to choose from a wide variety of goods and services from different producers. For example, there are now many rival suppliers of communication services to British Telecom.	• private sector organizations will not protect public services. Many fear private sector firms providing railway services will cut services and raise fares in the long run. Complaints about rail services are rising all the time.
• the sale of shares in these industries raises revenue for the Government which can be used to lower taxes. For example, the sale of British Gas raised over £6 billion.	• most of the shares in privatized organizations have been bought by large financial organizations such as banks and insurance companies who are interested only in making big profits.
• private individuals can own shares in these organizations and vote on how they should be run.	

The Privatization Programme		

SALES TO DATE:

1979–80	British Petroleum ICL Suez Finance Company and other miscellaneous	1985–86	British Airports Royal Ordnance factories
		1986–87	British Gas
1980–81	Ferranti Fairey North Sea Oil-Licenses British Aerospace Miscellaneous and small NEB	1987–88	British Airways British Airports Authority Rolls Royce Leyland Bus and Truck
1981–82	British Sugar Cable and Wireless Amersham International National Freight Miscellaneous plus Crown Agent and Forestry Commission land and property sales	1988–89	British Steel Trustee Savings Bank British Leyland
		1989–90	Regional Water Authorities
		1990–91	Electricity Area Boards
1982–83	Britoil Associated British Ports Sales of oil licenses, oil stockpiles and miscellaneous	1991–92	Electricity Generation
		1992–93	British Coal
1983–84	British Rail Hotels Cable and Wireless	1994–96	British Rail
1984–85	Enterprise Oil British Gas onshore oil Sealink ferries Jaguar cars British Telecom	Future Sales	National Air Traffic Service British Nuclear Fuels Executive Agencies

Privatization also involves allowing private sector firms to compete with public sector organizations to supply a product or even take over the activity completely. For example, local councils now pay private sector organizations to collect rubbish rather than employing their own refuse collectors to do so.

Exercise 10   Going, going, gone?

'Air traffic sell-off will make passport fiasco look like peanuts'

AIR travellers face a chaotic build-up of delays "that will make the Passport Office queues fiasco look like peanuts" unless the Government drops its planned privatisation of the National Air Traffic Service.

This warning from leaders of 4,800 air traffic control staff comes on the eve of publication of the Government's draft Bill for a £1 billion sell-off.

A campaign of protest against privatisation is to be launched on Thursday by an emergency delegate conference called by the air traffic controllers' union, IPMS.

However, Sir Roy McNulty, the new chairman of the National Air Traffic Service (Nats) argues that privatisation is the only way forward and warns that the European high holiday season will be an air traffic control disaster. "There is going to be one hell of an inquest after this summer," he said.

The Government has already shelved plans to sell off the Royal Mint following widespread objections, but it is set on privatising air traffic control.

IPMS general secretary Paul Noon said: "Privatisation is a bigger threat to air safety over the United Kingdom than the soaring number of flights.

"Key investment decisions are being held up by uncertainty over the Government's intentions while staff struggle to keep up with record levels of growth at airports and air traffic control centres.

The service is responsible for the safety of 1.6 million flights a year over Britain and the number of passengers will rise to 103 million by the year 2000.

Mr Noon added that controllers are having to handle an eight per cent growth in air traffic this year alone with "ageing and often outdated equipment".

The air traffic controllers have logged a record number of "overload" reports but the Civil Aviation Authority claims that British air space is still among the safest in the world.

Travel chaos: air traffic controllers say passengers will suffer more scenes like this after privatisation

Evening Standard, 20.7.1999

1 What is privatization?

2 What are the economic arguments for and against privatizing the National Air Traffic Service in the UK?

3 What other concerns are raised by the privatization? What impact could they have on a. airlines, and b. the travel industry?

Key words

Write definitions for the following terms:

Fixed capital
Working capital
Unlimited liability
Limited liability
Sole trader
Partnership
Ordinary partnership
Limited partnership
Sleeping partner
Joint stock company
Private limited company
Shares
Face value
Shareholders
Dividends
Directors
Controlling interest

AGM
Flotation
plc
Full listing
Prospectus
Consumer co-operative
Worker co-operative
Multinational
Public corporation
Nationalization
Natural monopoly
Quango
Executive agency
Privatization

Now go back to the chapter and check your understanding of these terms.

Chapter 6

The Finance and Growth of Firms

MEANLY, MEANLY & Cº MONEY LENDERS
£ billion

Please sir, can I have some more ?

Aims

At the end of this chapter you should be able to:

1 Suggest various ways a firm can raise finance to expand its operations.

2 Suggest various financial institutions a firm can seek capital from.

3 Analyse the possible risks involved in lending money.

4 Distinguish between **loan capital** and **risk capital.**

5 Understand the various methods by which firms can issue shares.

6 Explain the differences between **preference shares** and **ordinary shares**.

7 Understand how the **stock exchange** works, and the role of **broker** and **market makers**.

8 Distinguish between **bears, bulls** and **stags**.

9 Define what is meant by a **take-over** and **merger**, and distinguish between the various ways firms amalgamate with each other.

Sections 1–4 How do firms get their money?

In the previous chapter we found out how firms need money to buy new capital equipment and expand the scale of their activities.

Such capital for industrial and commercial enterprises may be classified as either **loan capital** or **risk capital**. Loan capital consists of those funds borrowed from a variety of financial institutions and wealthy individuals. Risk capital is raised by the sale of shares in the ownership of a company.

| **Section 1** | Borrowing money |

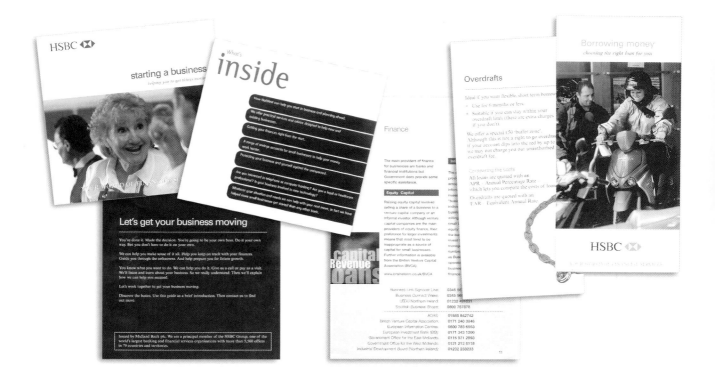

Firms, like people, do not always have enough money to buy what they want. When this happens, firms borrow money. Borrowing money has a cost because banks and other financial companies charge interest on what is borrowed.

The **interest rate** is the cost of borrowing money (see Chapter 19). Firms will only borrow if they expect to use the money in such a way as to generate enough profits to pay for the bank loan and the interest charge. For example, consider a firm deciding whether or not to borrow £100 000 at a 10% interest rate. The total repayment will be £110 000 (that is, £100 000 for the loan plus £10 000 for interest). The firm wishes to use the money to buy a new machine. Clearly it will only do this if it expects the machine to produce enough products to add at least £110 000 to revenue when sold. If not, then the machine is not worth buying and therefore the loan not worth getting.

Why do banks charge interest? A bank or any other company engaged in lending money will charge interest. Exactly how much interest a bank charges for lending money depends largely on how likely the bank thinks it is to get its money back from the borrower. Very large firms like BP have vast sums of money and will be able to repay loans. As a result the interest rate they are charged will be low.

On the other hand, small firms are a much bigger risk and so the interest charged on loans is higher. Smaller businesses often lack the **security** or **collateral** to offer banks to cover the repayment of a loan in case their business fails and they are unable to repay the loan. Banks often accept leases on property, which allow them to sell the property if the loan is not repaid. They also accept the paid-up proportion of any life insurance policies held by the borrower, which the bank could cash in if repayment problems arise.

I hate to hurry you along Mr Smythe but the first payment is nearly due!

Where to borrow money

There are six main ways a firm can borrow money.

1 Commercial banks
The commercial banks or High Street banks like HSBC, Barclays, NatWest., Lloyds TSB and the Royal Bank of Scotland lend money to firms in just the same way as they lend money to ordinary people (see Chapter 19). Banks decide whether to grant a loan by considering such factors as the firm's ability to repay, the firm's reputation, how much money the firm wants, and what it will use the money for. Banks will lend money in the form of a **bank loan** or an **overdraft**.

Exercise 1 Getting a loan

This role-play involves an interview between a bank manager and a person wishing to borrow money to start a new business. On the basis of information provided and what emerges from the interview it is up to the bank manager to decide whether or not to grant a loan.

The customer: Your role
You are Jayne Richards, aged 24. You work as a secretary for a small firm of solicitors. On Saturdays and two evenings a week you help out at a friend's dance and fitness studio. She pays you £80 for your help each week. This sum is in addition to the £15 000 you earn each year, before tax. Tax deductions account for £230 each month.

You live in a rented house and pay £70 each week for your rent and bills. Other outgoings, like food, clothes and entertainment, amount to £250 per month. The remainder is saved in a building society account which totals £2 300 so far.

You want to start your own dance and fitness studio above a supermarket. Rent would total £700 each month, while fittings and decorations have been estimated to be £8 000. You hope a friend will help out in the evenings for £50 per week.

You decide to sell your idea to your bank manager and arrange an interview for a loan.

The bank manager: Your role

Your job is to decide whether or not to loan money to Jayne Richards who wishes to borrow from your bank to start her own dance and fitness studio. To help you make your decision you will need to know:

1 How much money is needed and what is it needed for?
2 For how long does the customer need the loan?
3 Has she any savings she can put into her business?
4 What is her character like? Is she trustworthy?
5 What are her personal incomes and expenditures? Is she a person who is careful with her money?
6 Has she any security to offer against the loan?
7 Will the business succeed? Has she enough experience? Will it generate enough revenue and earn profits? Is there too much risk of business failure?

The following form will help you assess her position in the interview. Assume interest charged on business loans is currently 10% per year.

THE BUSY BANK BB

LOAN DECISION FORM

CUSTOMER DETAILS

NAME:	AGE:
ADDRESS:	SEX:

TELEPHONE:

INCOME (AFTER TAX):   £

EXPENDITURE:	Rent/Board	
	Other outgoings	
	TOTAL	£

INCOME AFTER TAX – EXPENDITURE

LOAN DETAILS

LOAN REQUIRED	PERIOD OF LOAN
£	

PURPOSE OF LOAN

TOTAL INTEREST	MONTHLY REPAYMENTS
£	£

SECURITY OFFERED?

DECISION:
WILL YOU GRANT THE LOAN: YES/NO
WHY? _____

---

2 Specialist banks

While High Street banks lend to both businesses and the general public, there are other institutions that specialize in business loans.

There are also private sector firms like 3i (Investors in Industry), Pi Capital and Paribus, which specialize in lending to new and risky small firms. Money lent to such firms is known as **venture capital**. Venture capital investments in the UK increased from £1.4 billion in 1989 to over £5 billion in 1999.

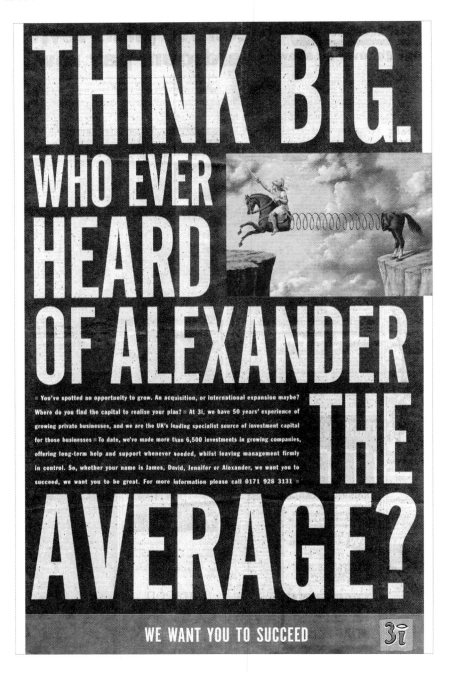

3 International banks and markets

Large businesses, such as Public Limited Companies and Public Corporations, may borrow large amounts of money from banks and wealthy individuals abroad. In return for a loan, a company can issue a piece of paper called a **Eurobond**. This is a promise to pay the holder of the bond a sum of interest each year and to repay the loan in full at a fixed date in the future.

These Eurobonds may also be bought and sold on international financial markets.

4 The Government

The Government also lends money to industry – for example, to safeguard and create new jobs, and promote investments in new technologies.

The Government also offers loans to firms if they move to areas where there are low levels of employment. (Government help is further discussed in Chapter 7.)

5 Hire-purchase and leasing

In recent years hire-purchase and leasing have become very important ways of raising money in order to obtain equipment. With hire-purchase, a firm pays a deposit for a piece of equipment and pays the amount outstanding in instalments over a period of months, or years.

Leasing is another way of obtaining equipment; the firm simply hires the equipment for as long as it needs it and then returns the equipment.

6 Trade credit

Firms often obtain materials and equipment on credit. For example, a firm may order new office equipment and be allowed 30, 60 or even 90 days in which to pay. When the firm eventually pays for the goods it is as if the firm had received a loan for this period. This type of loan is called Trade credit; granting credit is a common practice in industry, especially to big important customers.

Exercise 2   The best way to borrow

In each of the following cases, select the type of borrowing you think would best suit the firms in question. Explain your reasons. (More than one answer may be correct.)

1 A large multinational company wishes to borrow £30 million to finance the construction of a new factory.

2 A corner shop would like £1 000 to improve the decoration of the shop.

3 A private hospital would like to raise £150 000 for a new machine that monitors people's heartbeats.

4 A large British plc is considering the location of a new factory in Northern England, regarded as an area of high unemployment. It requires £15 million for the construction of its factory.

5 A local builder wishes to raise finance for the purchase of a small cement-mixer.

Section 2 — Using retained profits

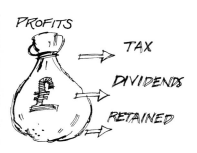

PROFITS
→ TAX
→ DIVIDENDS
→ RETAINED

Profits provide one of the most important ways firms can afford to buy equipment and expand. This is because it is often cheaper for a firm to use its own money from profits rather than borrow from banks and other financial institutions and pay interest.

Some of the profits made by a business are taken by the government in **corporation tax**. Some of the profits are then distributed to the owners of the company. Any profits left undistributed or **retained profits** can be used to invest in new machinery, etc.

Section 3 — Obtaining funds from other financial institutions

Pension funds and insurance companies

Nearly every adult in the country pays money to an insurance company. This may be for one or more of the many types of insurance offered, for example, life insurance, motor vehicle insurance or property insurance. Most working people also pay pension contributions to pension fund management companies. Pension contributions and life insurance premiums are two widely-used forms of saving in the UK. Indeed, just under one half of all savings in the UK are made with pension fund and insurance companies. This means that these companies have vast sums of money to invest to try and make a profit for the individuals who save and contribute to them.

A large amount of this money is used to buy shares in the ownership of Public Limited Companies and to lend to the Government. In fact, these institutions are the largest shareholders in the country. Pension fund and insurance companies are therefore a very important source of capital both for private firms and the Government.

Investment trusts

An investment trust is a company whose purpose is to buy shares in other companies. That is, it buys shares in companies the Trust thinks will be profitable and will pay good dividends on their shares. In turn, the Trust uses the profits or dividends made on the shares it holds to pay their own shareholders who own the Trust.

Unit trusts

Instead of buying shares in just one company, which can be risky if the company fails to make a profit, small savers often buy unit trusts.

Professional investors, who work for unit trust companies, use their savers' money to buy shares in a variety of companies they think will be profitable. The more profit they make, the more interest the unit trust company can pay to its savers.

Unit trusts are different from investment trusts in that the unit trust companies are not limited companies and the saver receives units and not shares in the trust. These units cannot be sold on the stock market and may only be sold back to the unit trust. The value of the units held by a saver is linked to the value of shares held by the unit trust company. If their shares go up in value, this is passed on as interest to the saver in the form of a rise in the value of his or her units.

However, by using these savings to buy shares in companies, unit trusts like investment trusts are an important source of finance for businesses.

Building societies

Building societies are similar to banks but specialise in using their savers' money to help people buy houses, and other property (see also Chapter 19.)

A loan given by a building society for the purpose of buying property is called a **mortgage**, and these are often repayable over a twenty to thirty year period. This money is also made available to industry for the purchase of buildings.

Section 4 — Issuing debentures and shares

Debentures

Public Limited Companies can raise money by issuing debentures or loan stock on the Stock Exchange. A **debenture** is simply an IOU issued by a plc in return for a loan of money.

A person who has lent money to a company and now holds a debenture receives a fixed rate of interest each year for as long as the loan is designed to last, for example 10% per year for five years. At the end of this period the loan is repaid. If the holder of the debenture wishes to get their money back before this, they can sell the debenture to someone else on the Stock Exchange. The new holder now receives the interest and is repaid for the loan when the date to repay falls due.

In the event of the company going bust, debenture holders are the first to be repaid the money they lent the company.

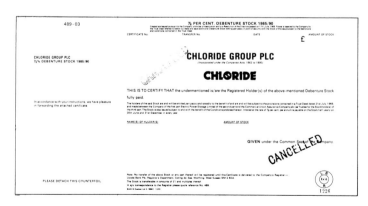

A debenture –
an IOU for a
loan

Issuing shares

The market where buyers and sellers of shares trade with each other is known as the **stock market**. Selling shares in the ownership of a company is the usual way of raising money in limited companies. However, selling shares for the first time can be difficult. If a company charges too much for its shares it will not be able to sell them all. If a company charges too little

117

for its shares it will make less money than it could. Because of this, companies employ experts to help them choose the best price and way of selling the shares. These experts are called **issuing houses** and are often **merchant banks**.

There are five main ways of selling shares:

1 By prospectus
This is an invitation to the general public to buy new shares in a company. The prospectus contains full details of the company's history, future plans, recent results and other financial information, and an application form for shares. This prospectus must be advertised in at least two national newspapers.

2 By offer for sale
With this method the issuing house agrees to buy up all of the shares giving the company an agreed sum of money. The issuing house will then try to sell all the shares itself to the public at a higher price.

3 By placing
When an issue of shares is small the issuing house may arrange for the shares to be sold to its own clients and a number of other financial institutions, like pension funds and insurance companies.

4 By a rights issue
With a rights issue the company offers its new shares for sale to its existing shareholders at a cut price. For example, existing shareholders may be given the right to buy one new share for every five shares they already own at fifty pence less than the price they will be sold to the general public.

5 By tender
This involves inviting the public to make a bid for a number of new shares and then selling the shares to the highest bidders.

Net money for nothing

TENS of thousands of small investors saw the value of their shares jump by nearly 40 per cent yesterday as Britain's first major Internet flotation gripped the City.

Shares in Freeserve, the country's biggest Internet access company, rose from 150p to 215p within seconds of dealing starting, despite warnings that gains might prove short-lived.

The price fell back but closed at 205.5p – 37 percent up – as Freeserve became the heaviest traded share on the Stock Market. Even though the stock was not available until 2.30pm, some 95 million Freeserve shares had changed hands by close of trading, representing nearly two-thirds of the stock on offer.

Freeserve was launched only ten months ago but has already revolutionised the Internet market. It has already enticed hundreds of thousands of Britons to go online by offering 'free' Internet access without a subscription.

Metro London, 27.7.1999

Such new issues of shares by companies issuing shares for the first time, or by companies who have issued shares before and are now seeking additional funds, are traded on the **new issues market**. This consists of the buyers of new issues and their sellers.

Exercise 3 Government share issues

> ## GOVERNMENT SHARE ISSUES
>
> Over recent years the United Kingdom Government has sold a number of public sector enterprises to the private sector. As part of its programme of privatization (a matter considered in much detail in Chapter 5), the Government has sold shares in companies like Amersham International and British Telecom to the general public.
>
> In February 1982, Amersham International, a medical research company, was sold by the Government to the private sector. The shares were sold by prospectus at 142 pence each. The next day these shares were changing hands on the Stock Exchange at 190 pence, at a 33% profit.
>
> Despite expensive advice from Merchant Bankers, the taxpayer lost £23 million from the sale. In opportunity cost terms this represented schools, hospitals and roads given up.

1   Explain how shares are sold by prospectus.

2   What is the role of Merchant Bankers in helping to sell shares?

3   Amersham International shares were being sold one day after the Government first issued them at a 33% profit. What does this suggest to you about the price at which the Government sold them initially?

4   The sale of shares can raise a lot of money for the Government but why was there an 'opportunity cost' ... of 'schools, hospitals and roads' involved in selling the shares at 142 pence each?

> When British Telecom was sold off to the private sector in 1984 it turned out to be greatly underpriced at a 50 pence issue price.
>
> As a result Telecom shares commanded a price of 95 pence on the first day of trading. This meant that the stock market valued British Telecom at £1.3 billion more than the Government did.
>
> If the Government had sold Telecom off in smaller lots of shares it could have adjusted the price of the secound lot after the first lot had been sold of and so on. In this way, the Government may not have lost so much money.

1   a   How much did the Government lose by underpricing British Telecom shares?

    b   What was the opportunity cost for tax-payers of this decision?

2   Apart from the suggestion in the passage, how else might the government have issued Telecom shares to try and raise more revenue from a public clearly eager to buy them?

Types of shares In general there are two main types of shares which can be issued.

1   Preference shares
Preference shares promise to pay their owners a fixed return or dividend.

For example, a preference share issued for 100 pence with a fixed return of 10% will pay its owner 10 pence per year. Every year in which the company makes a profit preference shareholders will receive a fixed dividend.

If, however, no profit is made in one year no dividend will be received.

If the shares are **cumulative preference shares** profits not paid in one year will be paid in the next year in which profits are made.

Even when the company has a very profitable year, preference shareholders receive no more than their fixed rate of interest unless they hold **participating preference shares**. This type of share allows its holder to receive a sum out of profits in addition to their fixed dividend after other shareholders have been paid their dividends.

Companies pay their preference shareholders before any other shareholders, but after debenture holders. This means that if a profit is made preference shareholders face little risk of not getting paid a dividend. Preference shareholders, however, are not usually allowed to vote for Company Directors at Annual General Meetings. By selling preference shares companies can raise capital without the existing owners losing control.

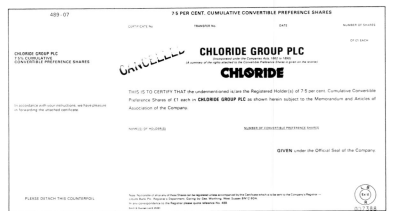

A cumulative preference share

2 Ordinary shares

Ordinary shareholders receive a dividend based upon what is left from profits after debenture holders and preference shareholders have been paid their share of the profits and after some profit has been retained for future investment.

For example, if the remaining profits to be distributed to ordinary shareholders total £10 000 and there are 100 000 £1 ordinary shares in existence then each share will receive 10 pence or 10%.

$$\frac{£10\ 000 \text{ of profits}}{100\ 000 \text{ of shares}} = £0.10 \ (\times 100 = 10\%) \text{ is paid on each share.}$$

If remaining profits are £100 000 each ordinary share will receive a £1 dividend.

$$\frac{£100\ 000 \text{ of profits}}{100\ 000 \text{ of shares}} = £1.00 \ (\times 100 = 100\%) \text{ is paid on each share.}$$

When there are no profits remaining ordinary shares receive no dividends, therefore buying ordinary shares can be a risky way of investing in a business. The payment to ordinary shares may be high or low depending on profits. Ordinary shares carry one vote per share at Annual General Meetings and ownership of these shares is very important when one company tries to take over another.

3 Government stock

When a government or local council wishes to borrow money for its expenditure plans it may sell stocks. These are loan certificates, not unlike debentures, which pay their holder a rate of interest and often carry a date at which they will be repaid. For example, local authority bonds may run for five years, while government stock or **gilt edged securities** may not be repaid for 20 or 30 years. These securities can be bought and sold on the stock market just like debentures and shares issued by firms. The Bank of England acts as Registrar for gilt edged stocks (see Chapter 19.)

Section 5 | The Stock Exchange

Functions of the Stock Exchange

New issues of shares can be made by existing limited companies seeking more funds or when a private company decides to go public by selling shares to the general public.

However, people and firms will only be willing to invest in shares if they know that they can get their money back again later on. This means that they will be unwilling to invest in a company seeking capital in order to expand, unless they are sure of getting it back again. They can do this by selling their shares on the stock market.

Dealing on the Stock Exchange

Stock exchanges run markets for buying and selling new and second hand stocks and shares, or **securities**. The main **Stock Exchange** in the UK is in London but has offices in other parts of the country. It is part of the world stock market and has the following main functions:

- it determines the structure of the markets for different securities
- it makes rules and regulations for the way in which the markets work in order to protect the interest of people and firms who buy securities
- it supervises the conduct of member firms buying and selling shares on the stock market
- it provides up-to-the-minute information on security prices and trading

Without the Stock Exchange it would be difficult for companies to raise capital. It would be difficult and possibly expensive for shareholders to search for other people and firms to sell their shares to. This would mean fewer shares are likely to be sold in the first place.

The markets for securities

1   The UK equity market

The Stock Exchange deals with the buying and selling of securities in thousands of large UK public limited company securities. A listed company is one that has been allowed by the council to sell its shares on the stock exchange (see Chapter 6). Total sales of UK equities reached a record high in 1998 of £1 037 billion. The average daily sales of UK equities was £4 billion with more than 64 390 transactions each day.

2   The international equity market

The London Stock Exchange has an international reputation for its strength in dealing in the shares of international companies. Two thirds of all share trading deals in London are in the shares of international companies. In 1998, international equity sales reached a high of £2 183 billion. On average each share deal was worth £306 701 compared with just over £64 000 for the average UK share transaction.

The buying and selling prices of these shares are available on a computerized database called **Stock Exchange Automated Quotation (SEAQ)** International which is a continuously updated database of share information.

3   The gilt-edged market

The UK Government raises money by selling loan stocks called **gilt-edged securities** (see Chapter 16). During 1998–99 the Government raised around £1.3 billion through gilt sales.

4   UK fixed interest or bond market

Through this market, companies can borrow money directly from the public by selling them fixed-interest securities or bonds. People and firms who buy these bonds get all their money back plus interest, whereas the price of shares can go up and down.

5   The Alternative Investment Market (AIM)

AIM is the London Stock Exchange's market for shares in small and growing companies. The requirements to join AIM are straightforward and there are few rules. There is no minimum size that a business has to be to join and no requirement to show a lengthy business history. The Alternative Investment Market enables small firms to raise capital by having their shares traded widely. Firms wishing to join must employ an advisor from a list kept by the Stock Exchange. The role of the advisor is to ensure that the firm understands and complies with Stock Exchange rules.

Exercise 4   Floating Footballs

Read the article on the next page and then answer the following questions:

1   What is a stock market?

2   Explain how the London Stock Exchange provides a stock market.

3   Why might soccer clubs wish to sell shares on the Stock Exchange?

4   How might smaller clubs sell shares?

5   Why might clubs that are listed on the Stock Market be more careful with their money?

6   What advantages and disadvantages of a stock market listing might there be for the fans?

The days when Europeans sought to copy English football clubs are long gone. But the British fashion for floating clubs on the stockmarket is catching on across the channel. Where Manchester United led, Rome's Lazio and Amsterdam's Ajax have followed. Other big clubs are close behind: Germany's Bayern Munich, Spain's Athletico Madrid and even Italy's mighty Juventus are soon to float.

It looks like a match made in heaven. Investors get a share of the fat returns from ticket sales, television deals and merchandising creamed from diehard fans. Clubs get bundles of cash to buy shiny new stadiums and star players. But many critics are unconvinced. They fret that the fans will suffer. And they argue that the benefits for clubs and investors are often as elusive as winning the European Cup.

Investors in British soccer stocks have had a bad run recently. While the stock market has soared this year, football shares have languished. Some say shareholders may never earn a decent return: few clubs are profitable, even fewer win silverware. Many club directors also have doubts. They welcome the stock markets money, but resent it when investors question extravagant expansion plans and demand more openness and accountability.

But most complaints are wide of the mark. If most football shares have performed badly since floatation, that shows they were initially wrongly valued – as new types of security often are – not that listing on the stock market is a bad thing. That many clubs may be bad businesses is also beside the point. Their share price will reflect that: owners who fear that the market will undervalue their club can choose not to float. And club directors must learn that floatation comes at a price: they should weigh the costs and benefits of listing more carefully.

Listed clubs have more money and are likely to spend it more wisely. Investors who aren't supporters still want success on the pitch: their profits depend on it. And most know enough to realise that clubs like companies have to invest for long-term success.

Buying shares gives fans more say in how clubs are run, by clubbing together fans could even get a seat on the board. Then they wouldn't need to shout from the stands that another awful chairman has let them down. They could sack him.

The Economist, 16.5.1999

How the Stock Exchange works

The Stock Exchange is not open to the general public. This means that if a member of the public wishes to buy or sell some shares they must contact a share dealing firm (or **broker**) which is a member of the Stock Exchange.

The market in stocks and shares is worldwide and growing all the time. This means that share dealers must have very large sums of money in order to be able to buy and sell shares on the stock market. Because of the need for large sums of money, many professional share dealers on the Stock Exchange work for firms owned by banks and other large financial institutions.

Easy does it . . .

Buying and selling shares is now as simple as calling into the local branch of your bank.

Buying and selling shares used to be the preserve of club types who would simply ring up their share broker after lunch and bark 'buy' or 'sell'. Now anybody can simply walk into their nearest bank or ring and snap up Rolls Royce shares or any other blue chip stock that takes their fancy.

Many banks and some building societies offer a comprehensive range of stock-broking services. These include:

- **execution** – you tell them to buy and sell the shares you want.
- **advisory services** – the stockbroker gives some advice on which shares may be best for you, but you still make the final decision.
- **discretionary services** – the stock broker manages your portfolio and makes all the buying and selling decisions.

Usually the bank branch will ring its stockbroking arm and do the transaction for you. But at 290 of NatWest's branches the deal will actually be done in the branch. The prices shown on the screen represent exactly what the shares are trading for at that moment.

A member of the public who wishes to buy or sell shares can either contact a broker for advice on stocks and shares or go to the nearest branch of their bank who will employ their own brokers to buy and sell shares for them. Even some Marks and Spencer stores and large supermarkets offer share-dealing services.

Brokers will buy and sell shares for the public for a fee known as commission. For example, a customer might wish to buy 1000 shares in Manchester United plc at no more than £10 a share. The broker and the customer will agree a commission to be paid to the broker for undertaking the work. For example, this might be a charge of 1% of the total cost of the shares.

The broker will now attempt to buy shares in Manchester United plc at the lowest possible price from other firms of brokers called **market makers**, usually by placing an order on the Stock Exchange computerized share dealing system. Market makers are special broker/dealers who create the market in shares. They do this by always being willing to buy and sell shares with other broker/dealers. These market makers make their profit by selling shares they hold at a higher price than the price they paid for them.

Much of the share trading carried out on the Stock Exchange is done using share information presented on computer screens around the world connected to the London Stock Exchange via the Internet.

Electronic dealing in the shares of the largest companies

Computerized share dealing has transformed the way that leading UK shares are traded. Buyers and sellers of shares place their orders on the computer 'order book' stating which shares and at what price they wish to buy or sell. If the computer system finds a match between buying and selling prices, it will carry out the transaction automatically on screen without anyone having to match up the buyers and sellers. This has greatly increased the speed and efficiency of the share market. This order book system is used for the UK's largest 100 companies and some of the largest European companies.

Four types of order can be placed on the electronic dealing system:

- **a limit** – customers log the number of shares and price at which they wish to buy or sell shares. If the computerized order book finds matches, the order is carried out. If there is no immediate match, it remains on the order book until a suitable match comes along within a given time period, after which it is deleted if no match is made.

- **at best** – customers enter their orders and agree to the computerized system carrying these out immediately at the best price available on the system.

- **fill or kill** – these orders are carried out immediately, or rejected by the system if a price match cannot be found.

- **execute and eliminate** – these are like 'at best' orders, except that limits are placed on the price range that will be accepted by the traders.

By the end of 1998 over half of all share trading was carried out using the electronic order book.

Buying and selling shares in smaller companies

PSSST... WANNA BUY SOME SHARES?

Market makers will display the prices at which they will buy and sell shares and the number of shares that they will trade. Market makers are in competition to offer the best prices and they make their profits by buying and selling shares at a profit.

Share prices are displayed on a continuously updated computer database called the **SEAQ** (**Stock Exchange Automated Quotation**). Up-to-the-minute share prices are available on information services around the world. The SEAQ screen shows a yellow strip which identifies the best bid and offer price for every SEAQ share and it identifies up to four market making firms offering this price.

The buying and selling prices of the stocks and shares of the smallest companies on the Alternative Investment Market are displayed on a computerized system known as the **Stock Exchange Alternative Trading Service** (**SEATS PLUS**). This data is available from information services around the world on the Internet and is updated every minute. The system shows for each AIM stock or share a quote from a market maker giving a buying and selling price, information about the company and a history of recent share transactions.

Share price indices

Like the price of any other commodity, share prices reflect changes in market demand and supply (see Chapter 8). For example, if a company announces poor profits, shareholders may want to sell their shares because they will receive a poor dividend. However, a company that wins a significant customer order or announces a merger with another company to increase market share may cause demand to rise for its shares. Movements in share prices can, therefore, reveal much about how well companies are performing.

The **FTSE 100 Index** (often called the '**footsie**') provides an up-to-date summary of the market prices of shares in the top 100 UK companies. It is recalculated every minute relative to a base value of 1000 in 1984. At the close of trading on 30 December 1999 the FTSE 100 index was 6930 which means the share prices of the top 100 companies had increased by an average of 693% since 1984.

Other share price indices are also available. For example, the Dow-Jones index tracks the prices of shares traded on the New York stock exchange in the USA and the Nikkei tracks the prices of shares traded in the Tokyo stock exchange in Japan.

Speculating on share prices

It is possible for people and financial institutions to make money on the stock market by guessing which way shares prices are likely to move in the future. Attempting to make money from buying and selling shares in the hope their prices will change is called **speculation**.

People and firms who buy shares in the hope there price will rise so that they can sell them at a profit are called **bulls**. The stock market is called **bullish** if share prices are rising in general.

People and firms who sell shares in the hope their price will fall so that they can buy them back later at much lower prices are called **bears**. When share

Economist, 1.11.1997

prices are falling the stock market is called **bearish**. 'Bears' buy the shares back despite their falling prices because they believe their prices will rise again in the long run and that dividend payments from company profits could be good.

People and firms who apply to buy up newly issued shares in the hope their price will rise quickly after dealing begins are called **stags**.

Section 6	The growth of firms

Take-overs and mergers

Firms may wish to become larger for many reasons. In Chapter 4 we learnt how an increase in the scale of a firm can lower its average costs of production through the benefit of such economies of scale as being able to buy in bulk. A firm may also wish to become large and powerful so that it can push up its prices and stop smaller firms from competing with it. (This aspect of growth is discussed further in Chapter 10.)

There are two methods by which firms can grow. The first is by **internal growth** where the firm increases its own size by producing more under its existing structure of management and control.

The second, and more common method today, is by **amalgamation** (or **integration**). This occurs where one or more firms join together to form a larger enterprise.

Firms can amalgamate or integrate in one of these two ways.

1   Take-over
A take-over or **acquisition** occurs when one company buys all, or at least 50%, of the shares in the ownership of another company.

In this way, the firm being taken over by another company often loses its own identity and becomes part of the other company.

Alternatively an entirely new company may be formed for the sole purpose of buying up shares in the ownership of a number of other companies. This is known as a **holding company**. The companies acquired in this way may keep their own names and management but their overall policies are decided by their holding company. For example, HSBC Holdings plc is one of the biggest UK companies and owns many other companies around the world in the banking industry.

2   Merger
A merger occurs when two or more firms agree to join to form a new enterprise. This is usually done by shareholders of the two or more companies exchanging their shares for new shares in the new company.

Types of integration

There are three main forms of integration or amalgamation between firms.

1   Horizontal integration
This occurs when firms engaged in the production of the same type of good or service combine. Most amalgamations are of this type, for example the joining of British Petroleum with Amoco in the oil and gas industry.

This type of integration may provide a number of economies of scale. For example, the employment of more specialized machines and labour, the spreading of administration costs and bulk buying.

The major criticism of firms linking horizontally is that very large firms are formed which are able to dominate the market. They are able to raise prices and see off smaller competing firms. This is one reason why the government often investigates proposed mergers and take-overs (see Chapter 10).

2   Vertical integration
This occurs when firms engaged in different stages of production combine. This would be the case if an oil refinery combined with a chain of petrol stations. This is called **forward integration**. In this way, the oil refinery is assured places to sell its petrol. Firms can also undertake **backward integration**, for example, a bread manufacturer combining with a wheat producers' association. In this way the firm can ensure a supply of materials.

3   Lateral integration
This happens when firms in the same stage of production, for example, primary or secondary production, but producing different products combine. This is often termed a **conglomerate merger** to form conglomerates which are firms which produce a wide range of products. This may be to reduce the risk of a fall in demand for one of their products or to seek out

the profitmaking potential of selling other products in other markets. For example, Unilever is a firm famous for its detergents but with interests in food, chemicals, paper, plastics, animal feeds, transport and tropical plantations.

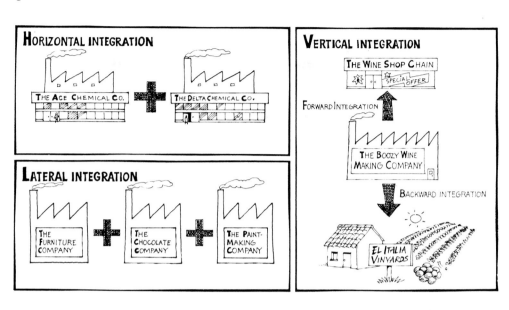

Exercise 5   What type of integration?

From the following amalgamations of firms state which form of integration applies: horizontal, vertical or lateral?

1   A firm producing cars takes over a steel manufacturer.
2   A bank merges with a travel agent.
3   A menswear shop chain merges with a women's fashion store chain.
4   A bus manufacturer merges with a car-maker.
5   A sand quarry merges with a gravel quarry company.
6   A brewery takes over a chain of pubs.
7   A chain of clothes shops takes over a clothing manufacturer.
8   A shoe-maker is taken over by a cigarette manufacturer.

Exercise 6   Cheers!

300 off-licences to close in drink giants' merger

Branches of Thresher, left, owned by Whitbread, and Allied's Victoria Wine, will shut

Drinks giants Allied Domecq and Whitbread are to cut their presence on the High Street by 10% involving the closure of around 300 Threshers and Victoria Wine off-licences and the loss of several hundred jobs.

Allied and Whitbread admitted the reductions would occur as they officially unveiled the merger of their off-licence divisions. Between them Allied and Whitbred own just under 3000 off-licences. Allied's 1488 has outlets trading as Victoria Wine, Victoria Wine Cellars, Haddows, Martha's Vineyard and The Firkin Off-licence. Whiltbread has 1470 outlets variously named Thresher Wine Shop, Wine Rack, Bottoms Up, Drinks Cabin and Huttons. The two drinks groups will each own 50% of the business.

The deal is intended to provide greater muscle so as to compete more effectively against the buying power of the supermarkets. Between them Allied and Whitbread have about 14% of the take-home drinks market, marginally less than the sector leader Tesco. Shop closure and redundancies will take place over the next three years. Staff may be offered jobs in other areas by their respective employers and there is a chance the business will open more shops in the future.

The deal may lead to cheaper drinks but is more likely to mean greater profits and the possibility that prices will be held in future rather than increased. The merger was prompted by the aggressive tactics of the large supermarkets. They have piled into the alcohol market and now account for a substantial proportion of the take-home drinks sector. Sales of the new venture will be more than £1.3 billion and there are combined net assets of £260 million.

Evening Standard, 12.8.1998

1   Why are the two companies merging?

2   What form of integration does the merger illustrate?

3   What impact might this have on
    a   people working for the two firms
    b   customers
    c   rival firms?

Key words

Key crossword

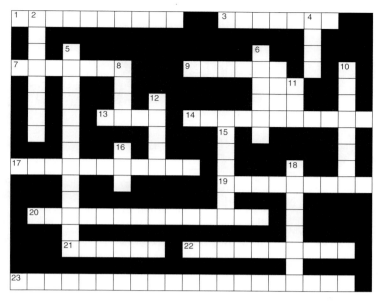

Clues across

1 Taken as security against a loan (10)

3 A grizzly situation if share prices are falling (7)

7 A company must get this from 5 down before it can sell its shares on the UK stock market (4)

9 A specialist firm or person that buys and sells shares for commission (5)

13 Footsie (1,1,1,1)

14 This person or firm will always make sure shares are bought and sold (6,5)

17 Profiteering from the buying and selling of shares you think will change in value (11)

19 Loan stock (10)

20 Money available to finance *adventurous* firms (7,7)

21 Another word for a share in the ownership of a company (5)

22 These shares get repaid first (10)

23 When two firms in different stages of production join together (8, 12)

Clues down

2 Shares with voting rights are hardly this (8)

4 A person who buys new shares in the hope they will rise in price (4)

5 An organization that organizes the markets for trade in securities (5, 8)

6 A bid for new shares (5)

8 This Government stock is edged with security (4)

10 When one company poaches another by buying up its shares (8)

11 Short for the market to target the shares of new and small companies at (1,1,1)

12 Short for the computerized share price database for shares traded on the market in 11 down (1,1,1,1)

15 Buy now, pay later (5)

16 The face value of a share (3)

18 A payment made in return for using another person's or firm's money (8)

MARKET OR MATERIALS

Aims

At the end of the chapter you should be able to:

1 Decide upon suitable locations for a number of different firms.

2 Explain with examples the factors that affect business location.

3 Present a case for and against the location of a business.

4 Explain what is meant by **regional policy** and describe how the Government can influence business location decisions.

5 Understand how the nature of the UK economy is changing and explain what is meant by **deindustrialization**.

6 Suggest reasons for deindustrialization in the UK and the growth of the tertiary industry.

Section 1	Where should a firm locate?

Factors which affect location

The answer to the question of where to build a new plant or factory for a firm may seem simple. Most business owners would wish to choose a place that involves the least cost. However, finding the least costly location is a complicated matter.

Sometimes firms are faced by a limited choice. Building a ship inland and many miles from the sea is not a good idea. A coal-mine can only locate where there are coal deposits. But where should a new supermarket, or nuclear power station, or car factory, or steel plant locate? The answer is not simple.

Exercise 1   Location

In groups of three or four consider the following plans for four new firms. It is your job to make a list of factors that each firm should take into account before deciding upon a final site.

THE SUPERSTORE

The new superstore requires a 15 acre site with ample parking space. A wide variety of goods and services will be sold by a staff of 120 people. Restaurants and customer facilities will also be offered.

THE STEEL PLANT

The large plant will occupy over 75 acres and many of the new materials used will be bought from abroad. For every 1 ton of steel produced, 4 tons of coal, limestone and iron ore are required. A workforce of 300 people is required.

THE MOTOR CAR COMPANY

A 300 acre site of flat land is needed to accommodate a new automated car assembly plant with a proposed staff of 250 people. Car parts will be received from other plants around the country and brought to this assemby plant.

THE NUCLEAR POWER STATION

A large confined 200 acre site is needed to build this new water-cooled reactor which will provide 3 million kilowatts of electricity each year — enough for 500,000 households. A staff of 10 scientists and 40 technicians will be required.

From the above exercise it will have become clear that there are a great many factors which affect the location decision of a firm. For example, your lists may have been similar to these.

SUPA SUPERSTORE	STEELPLANT	MOTOR CAR Co.	POWER STATION
1. Near to large town for workers and shoppers 2. On edge of town for cheap land 3. Near roads for customers and deliveries	1. Near to port for materials 2. Large area of cheap land 3. Near workforce 4. Near coal supplies	1. Near to large workforce 2. Near port to ship cars abroad 3. Large area of cheap land 4. Near car part suppliers	1. Near water for cooling 2. Away from populated areas 3. On cheap land

How many of the above did your group have? Can you think of any more to add?

We will now consider the factors that affect location in detail.

1 Being near to a market
Any firm that makes and sells goods or services will want to be in easy reach of its customers. A shop will wish to locate in or near to the shopping centre of a town. A factory may also wish to be near its point of sale because the goods made may be fragile and will not stand up to transportation over long distances.

The large number of factories, shops, offices and farms that have located in and around London, Birmingham, Glasgow and other cities and towns show just how strong the pull of the market is.

2 Being close to raw materials
A coal-mine will locate where coal is found. An oil drill like those in the North Sea will locate over an oilfield. A steel plant may locate near to a supply of iron ore and coal.

Around these firms other firms like shipbuilders and engineering plants making turbine engines, trains and large machinery may locate to use the coal and steel produced. These materials are very bulky and so transporting them long distances would be expensive. For example, to reduce transport costs the brick-making industry is largely centred around Peterborough where Oxford clay is found.

Today, many raw materials are bought from overseas and so many firms are to be found close to major ports.

Wherever a firm locates it is likely that it will have to pay some transport costs either to receive materials or to send finished goods to market. A

WEIGHT LOSING PRODUCTION

WEIGHT INCREASING PRODUCTION

famous economist long ago called Max Weber argued that entrepreneurs would try to reduce transport costs to their lowest level. This means that if the raw materials used by a firm weigh more than the final products made by them, production is said to be **weight losing** and the firm would locate near to its raw materials. A good example of weight losing production is the making of steel from iron ore. Four tonnes of iron ore, coal and limestone rock are used to produce just one ton of steel in a blast furnace.

If, on the other hand, a firm uses raw materials that are light and small, but the final product is big and bulky, production is **weight increasing**. Firms who are weight increasers are advised to locate near the market. Making footballs involves gaining weight and bulk. Rolls of leather are used to produce round, hard-to-pack, air-filled balls. Beer-making involves adding a lot of water to hops and barley. It then has to be contained in bottles or barrels.

Exercise 2 Production and weight

In pairs try to make a list of as many goods that you can think of that gain weight and lose weight during their production. Try to add to your lists with the help of another pair and your teacher.

3 Being near transport facilities
Transport is an important consideration for many firms. Raw materials and finished goods need to be transported cheaply and with ease. Customers need to reach shops easily, and workers need to get to their place of work.

Many years ago water transport was the only cheap and reliable way of carrying heavy loads and many firms chose to be near canals, rivers and the sea for this purpose. Today, road and rail transport provide good links between locations. Refrigerated lorries can transport perishable goods. Juggernauts can whisk large, heavy loads up and down new motorways. Fast air transport for light loads and large ships have also made international transport much easier.

The case of sunrise industries

This is the name given to firms in modern industries such as computer technology. Many of the firms are regarded as **footloose** because they do not feel the pull of the market or their materials. These factors do not influence them. Finished products and component parts are often light and easy to transport.

However, many of these footloose firms have tended to root themselves near to major motorways especially in the South East of England for good communication links and for a growing body of workers trained in modern work skills.

4 Being near to a supply of labour
Many firms require a large skilled work-force. For example, many years ago when Henry Ford set up a Ford factory in the UK he was influenced by a large housing development in Dagenham, Essex.

5 Being near other firms
Imagine you wanted to set up a sweet shop. Clearly you would want to be near your market but this probably means locating next to other shops so

that consumers who are attracted to the shopping centre will pass, and hopefully call into your shop. Being near to other firms is often an advantage for many firms.

We discovered in Chapter 4 how firms locating together can benefit from economies of concentration. A pool of skilled workers develops, and ancillary firms that supply parts and services to the larger firms locate nearby. A good example of this type of concentration is the large number of car plants that have located in the Midlands. Leicester is famous for shoe-making firms, Sheffield for cutlery firms, Liverpool for chemical plants.

Ford plant, Dagenham

6 Locating on cheap land
A large factory will need much land to locate on. Not only must this land be available, it is helpful if it is cheap to rent or buy. Fords at Dagenham, Essex, occupied 500 acres of land, chosen, among other reasons, for its cheapness.

A large plot of land is unlikely to be found in a big town or city, and even if it was available the cost of it would be very high because so many firms would be competing for its use.

7 Taking advantage of natural factors
Such things as the weather or types of rocks in an area may affect the location of firms.

Many market gardens growing fruit and vegetables have located in the Scilly Isles because of the early spring.

The port of Southampton

The port of Southampton takes advantage of the four high tides a day in the harbour. The oil refinery at Milford Haven in Wales is there because the rock structure there has resulted in a deep water harbour that allows oil container ships to dock.

8 Being near a supply of power
Today most factories and offices use electricity which is readily available all over the country through the national electricity grid. Gas and oil can also be received through pipelines. This means the availability of power is not a very important consideration for business location today. However, many years ago in the eighteenth and nineteenth centuries the burning of coal for steam was the most important source of power. Many firms therefore

located near to coal-mines. Since coal deposits were to be found mostly in Northern England many of the early factories located there. Similarly, firms in the woollen industry moved to Yorkshire to use the power of fast-flowing streams in the Pennine mountains.

9 Traditional locations

Most firms in the clothing and textile industry in the UK are to be found in Lancashire in Northern England.

Originally they located here because the damp air in the area stopped the cotton fibres from becoming too dry and breaking. Nowadays, machines can increase the moisture in air but still new textile firms locate there. Indeed, many firms will locate in an area simply because such firms have always located there as a tradition. Also such areas offer economies of concentration such as skilled labour, ancillary firms, etc.

The tendency for firms to continue to locate in an area, even when the factors that originally brought such firms to the area a long time ago have ceased to exist, is called **inertia**.

10 Being close to their favourite place

Sometimes entrepreneurs may simply locate their new firm near to their favourite town or area of countryside. They may like to be near to their parents or friends, or even their favourite pub!

11 Business location can be affected by other people

Even when an entrepreneur has made the final decision about where to locate there may be further things to consider. For example, will the general public object? Will other firms object? Will local councils or even the Government object?

Exercise 3   Mightyburger comes to town

The Mightyburger chain of American-style fast-food restaurants has applied to the local council of Tanbury to set up a restaurant in the High Street.

The restaurant will serve food and soft drinks between the hours of 11 am and 11 pm everyday to a maximum of 100 people at any one time. It is hoped that the restaurant can be built from a converted supermarket that closed down six months ago.

The Mightyburger chain has sent an application for planning permission to the council, and has published details of the proposal in the local press.

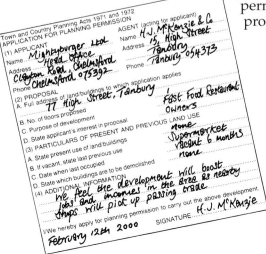

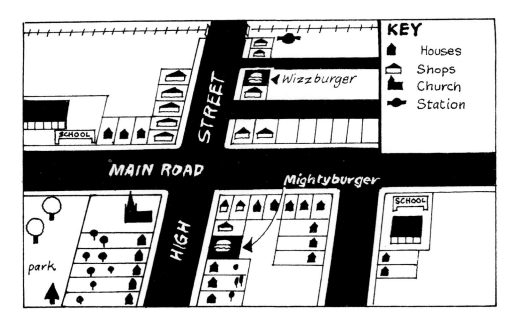

Tasks

1 In groups of six or seven, each person is to take on one of the following roles:

a Owners of the nearby *Wizzburger* restaurant.
b Chief of local traffic police.
c Chairperson of the local residents' group.
d Head of *Youth Aid*, an action group for the young unemployed.
e Representatives from the local Parents/Teachers' associations of two nearby schools.
f Representatives from Mightyburger Ltd.

On your own, compose a letter of support or complaint with regard to the proposed restaurant to the local council. Set out your arguments clearly in the letter.

2 In your group read out your letters and then attempt to argue your case for or against the proposal. Try to reach an agreement as to whether the local council should allow the restaurant to be built or not.

At a local level, the Planning Committee of a local council will influence where businesses are set up. Every council will have a map of their area showing where different types of businesses can locate. Part of a town can only be used for housing. Another area will be used just for shops, and another for factories. It is up to the Planning Committee whether or not a new business is allowed to locate in any of these places. They will take into account the views of all interested parties before they decide.

In the case of large power stations, airports and dockyards, it may be up to the Government to decide where they can locate, because their operation can affect so many people. Often a **Public Inquiry** will be held where everyone who is affected by the location proposal can say whether they agree with it or not, and why. A Government minister will then consider all the arguments and decide whether or not the location of new premises can go ahead.

Exercise 4   Welcome to the UK

'Britain today is very much a pro-business country, and that applies among other things to the level of taxation and labour laws. We as a company found it especially beneficial to be able to operate our factories three shifts a day, seven days a week, basically round the clock, non-stop'

Jurgen Gehrels, Chief Executive, Siemens UK

'Our products can be with our customers across Europe within 24 hours'

John Bennigsen, Managing Director, Toshiba (UK) Ltd.

'Labour costs at (UK plant) are about 50% of what they were at our German plant and about 75% of wages in Italy'

Bob Schwarz, Vice-President of World Manufacturing, Black and Decker

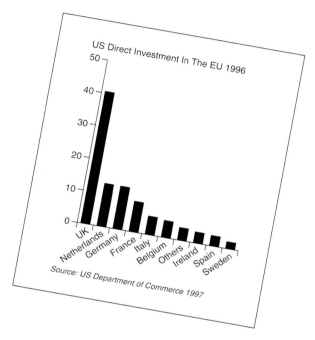

US Direct Investment In The EU 1996

Source: US Department of Commerce 1997

Nissan to invest £250m in UK and create 300 jobs

NISSAN is to create 300 jobs with a £250 million investment in its plant at Washington, Tyne and Wear. The spending – which takes total company investment in Britain to £1.25 billion – will cut further Washington's dependence on Japan and give Nissan one of the most self-contained plants anywhere in the world.

Component suppliers will gain from the plan to end supplies of diesel engines from Japan and build a new turbo-diesel, which will go into the next generation Primera mid-range model.

Washington will also get a new robot welding plant and an assembly shop to make rear axles to help make the plant close to self-sufficient with almost the entire car built with components from Britain and Europe. Up to seventy per cent of the cars will be exported.

Nissan said yesterday that spending on components with European suppliers – including 134 in the UK – would top £400 million a year and help create hundreds of jobs in the supplier network.

Adapted from *The Times*, 19.9.1995

Read the information on this and the next page. It comes from the *Invest in Britain* booklet distributed freely by the UK Government to overseas firms. In addition there is a newspaper article about the decision by the Japanese car manufacturer, Nissan, to increase investment in its UK factories. Use all this information to help you answer the following questions.

1   Why do you think overseas companies like Nissan might be attracted to locate in the UK?

2   How might the decision by foreign firms to locate in the UK benefit the UK economy?

3   Design a poster advertising the key benefits of a business location in the UK.

European opportunities

From Britain you can easily service the whole of the European market. Britain itself is a substantial market, with 58 million consumers, but it is just part of the world's largest free trade area – 377 million consumers in the European Economic Area – the 15 European Union countries plus Iceland and Norway.

A liberal tax environment

The UK offers your company low corporate and personal taxation, economic stability and a regulatory environment designed to encourage growth and profits. The UK has the lowest main corporation tax rate of any major industrialized country and has no additional local taxes on profits.

Fast access to markets

Nine out of ten overseas companies in the UK export worldwide from Britain. UK-based companies are ideally positioned to do business with worldwide markets.

Britain's integrated transport network provides fast, low-cost delivery of raw materials and manufactured products throughout the European Economic Area. A comprehensive toll-free motorway and road network joins all major UK cities and industrial centres to air and seaports.

A skilled and adaptable workforce

The UK has few restrictions on working hours, overtime and holidays. A large number of companies setting up in the UK have negotiated single-union agreements. Many businesses operate shift work and 24-hour, seven-days-a-week schedules for both male and female employees, which gives companies maximum return on capital. Terms of employment are generally agreed directly between companies and their employees. Labour relations in the UK are exceptionally good. Days lost through strikes are among the lowest in Europe, as are absences through vacations, public holidays and sickness.

Staffing costs in the UK are highly competitive, because of the modest level of compulsory social costs on wages.

Europe's financial services capital

London is Europe's business capital. Along with New York and Tokyo, the UK's capital is an essential component of the world's round-the-clock money and investment markets.

Setting up in business

Grants and other financial help may be available to businesses which generate local employment, in designated 'assisted' areas. Investment incentives are especially generous in Northern Ireland.

The UK has seven 'free zones', in which no taxes or charges are levied on goods from outside the European Union until these are released for free circulation. Among other benefits, the zones simplify customs procedures, add security and provide cash-flow benefits. Tax deductions for customs duties relating to the transhipment, handling and processing of goods for re-export are available throughout the UK.

Low-cost utilities

Britain's utilities, including electricity, gas and water, have been privatized – indeed a number of these are owned by overseas investors. Competition between regional suppliers of power gives industrial and commercial users opportunities to negotiate substantial price discounts. The UK's utilities are experienced at installing new facilities and negotiating for high-volume industrial users.

Language

English is the world's business language. Far more people in the European Union speak English as a second language than any other and nine out of ten Europeans consider it the most commercially useful. The UK is also home to speakers of over 190 languages and has a large pool of native and near-native multilingual people.

Section 2 | How Government can influence business location

What is a regional problem?

Some areas suffer higher levels of unemployment than others because industries and major employers in these areas, such as coal mining, iron and steel, and manufacturing, have declined. Unemployment among people can also be high in rural and agricultural areas because of a lack of new employment opportunities.

In addition, there are regional differences in incomes, health and education levels, population growth, migration, and infrastructure provision, such as roads, schools, hospitals, shopping and recreation facilities.

Traditionally, a regional problem exists if an area suffers:

- low levels of employment
- below-average income per head
- a lack of firms in different industries
- underinvestment in new factories, offices and retail outlets
- a lack of basic infrastructure; roads, railways, housing, schools, hospitals
- high outward migration of people

Closure of firms, poor housing and high unemployment are factors in creating a regional problem

Exercise 5   The regional problem

Below is a map of the UK. It is divided up into regions to show how much unemployment there is in each region. For example, in the North East of England 7.5% of the work-force were unemployed in 1999, that is 15 people out of work for every 200 in employment. In contrast in the South East only 5 people were unemployed for every 200 who had a job.

Regional unemployment rates (% 1999)

Tasks

In groups of four you are to be Government officials trying to think up ways you can attract new firms to areas of high unemployment.

1   Which areas on the map do you think require the most help?

2   How will you try to attract new firms to these areas? (Remember, the Government not only taxes firms, it also owns much land and many buildings.)

3   Write up your proposals in a detailed plan to be discussed in class.

Assisted areas   Both the UK and European Union Governments have operated a **regional policy** for a number of years to encourage firms to locate and expand in areas which suffer from high unemployment and industrial decline. These areas are called **Assisted Areas** and firms in, or thinking of moving to, these areas, can apply for financial help called **Regional Selective Assistance (RSA)**. This is a discretionary grant awarded to firms who can demonstrate their projects will safeguard or create jobs, particularly skilled jobs, and increase prosperity.

Assisted areas are reviewed from time to time by the UK Government because of changes in regional employment, investment, population, migration and income patterns. In 1999 assisted areas were redrawn into three different groups as the map below shows.

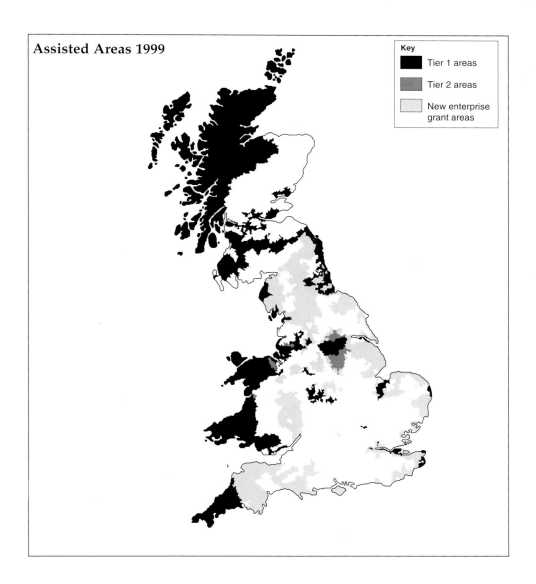

Assisted Areas 1999

Key
- Tier 1 areas
- Tier 2 areas
- New enterprise grant areas

Tier 1 areas include Cornwall, Merseyside, South Yorkshire and West Wales and the Valleys. Northern Ireland is included as an area of exceptional concern. Firms in tier one regions can apply for grants of up to 40% towards new investment projects that safeguard or generate jobs.

Tier 2 areas include the Highlands and Islands area of Scotland, and parts of the East and West Midlands, the North East and West, Yorkshire and the Humber, East Anglia and London. Firms in these areas can apply for grants of up to 20% of the cost of new investment projects.

A third tier of **Enterprise Grant Areas** was introduced to provide assistance to small and medium enterprises employing less than 250 people. These areas include local authority districts with high unemployment, old coalfield areas, and rural development areas.

Regional Selective Assistance is provided through the Scottish Executive, the National Assembly for Wales, the Northern Ireland Office, and eight **Regional Development Agencies (RDAs)** in England.

In 1999–2000 RDAs had a total budget of over £1 billion to spend in their regions on:

- encouraging economic regeneration
- promoting business efficiency, investment and competitiveness
- promoting employment
- developing and improving workforce skills
- improving the environment.

Other UK Government regional initiatives

The assisted areas policy complements other programmes which aim to bring improvements to different areas of the UK. In 2000 these included:

- **The Single Regeneration Budget**, which provides money to help 'regenerate' communities suffering from multiple problems including low levels of employment and skills, a lack of infrastructure, poor health and housing, and high levels of crime and drug misuse. SRB schemes range from employment and training programmes, to community safety and drug abuse projects.
- **Employment Zones**, which target help at improving the employability of the long term unemployed.
- **Education Action Zones**, which aim to raise educational standards in areas where attainment and skills levels are low.
- **Excellence in Cities**, which is a programme aimed at raising standards in run-down city areas, by establishing new opportunities for learning and developing skills in schools.
- **The Coalfields Enterprise Fund**, which targets financial help at small firms with high growth potential in areas blighted by the closure of coal mines in the 1980s and 1990s.

European Structural Fund areas

Many of the assisted areas in the UK also qualify for additional help from the European Union, especially tier one areas which have an average GDP per head of less than 75% of the EU average. These are called 'objective one' areas under the terms of the **European Structural Fund**.

EU Objective	Types of area
1	assisting areas suffering general decline, deprivation and poor infrastructure
2	assisting areas of industrial decline
3	combating long-term unemployment
4	facilitating the adaptation of workers to industrial change
5a	assisting the adjustment of agricultural structures
5b	rural development

Other objective one areas in Europe include eastern Germany, all of Greece, north-west Ireland, central and southern Spain, southern Italy and parts of Austria. Financial help is available in these areas to create jobs, invest in new skills and technologies, build new roads and schools, and improve the environment.

Section 3 | The changing structure of UK industries

Between 1973 and 1980 manufacturing output shrunk by 14% and the output of the construction industry by 23%. In the decade 1971–81 nearly 2 million jobs were lost in the manufacturing and building industries. At the same time services like banking and insurance created 403 000 new jobs. Total employment in service industries rose by 1.8 million people. By 1981 some 61% of the total UK workforce were employed in the service sector.

The shift away from manufacturing towards services in the UK continued throughout the 1980s and 1990s. By 1998 a further 3.1 million jobs in manufacturing had been lost while employment in services had expanded by over 4 million. Over the same period many jobs were also lost from mining, quarrying, energy and water supply as coal mines closed down and following privatization of the electricity, gas and water supply industries (see Chapter 5).

In 1989 manufacturing produced over 23% of the UK GDP. By 1998 this had fallen to just over 20%. In contrast, services generated over 60% of the UK GDP, rising to 68% in 1998.

The table below shows the number of people employed in different industries between 1971 and 1998. It illustrates the changing structure of the UK economy.

Employees in employment: by sex and industry					
United Kingdom					*thousands*
	1971	1981	1989	1993	1998
All industries	22 139	21 892	22 661	21 613	23 237
of which					
Males	13 726	13 487	11 992	10 962	11 699
Females	8 413	9 686	10 668	10 651	11 538
Manufacturing	8 065	7 253	5 187	3 913	4 081
Services	11 627	13 580	15 627	16 219	17 664
Other	2 447	2 340	1 847	1 481	1 492
Employees in employment					
Agriculture, forestry and fishing	450	363	330	326	272
Mining and quarrying; energy and water supply	2 080	1 649	1 176	593	444
Manufacturing of metal goods, equipment, vehicles, etc.	3 709	2 923	2 351	1 878	2 058
Other manufacturing	3 074	2 360	2 125	2 035	2 023
Construction	1 198	1 130	1 082	865	1 003
Wholesale and retail trade; catering and repairs	3 686	4 172	4 730	4 747	5 353
Transport and communications	1 556	1 425	1 362	1 317	1 389
Banking, insurance and financial services	1 336	1 739	2 627	975	1 064
Other services	5 049	6 197	6 908	8 998	9 698

Exercise 6   The changing nature of UK employment

Look at the table above for the years 1971 to 1998.

Questions

1   Distinguish between 'industrial production' and 'industrial employment'.

2   **a**   Name an industry in **i** the primary sector and **ii** the manufacturing sector, in which there has been many job losses in this period.

    b   Give reasons for the loss of jobs in the industries you have named.

3   The table shows that the majority of the job losses have been in manufacturing.

    a   What was the total number of job losses in manufacturing over the given period of time?

    b   Give two examples of such manufacturing industries.

    c   Suggest reasons why manufacturing industries employed fewer workers than before in 1971.

4   **a**   Calculate the increase in employment in the service industries from 1971 to 1998.

    b   Give an example of a service industry which employed more people in 1998 than in 1971 and try to explain why this is so.

Deindustrialization
The UK was one of the first countries in the World to move away from a reliance on farming and other primary industries for jobs and income, towards a new industrial society based upon manufacturing or the secondary industry.

The year 1760 is the date commonly taken for the start of what was called the Industrial Revolution. Since the early nineteenth century the UK industries have grown enormously along with many other countries around the World.

However, since the 1970s many economists in the UK have talked of **deindustrialization**. This refers to the decline of manufacturing industry because:

- The number of jobs in manufacturing industry has fallen.
- The total output of manufactured goods has fallen compared to the total output of all goods and services produced in the UK.
- The UK share in the total output of manufactured goods from all over the World has fallen.
- The UK now spends more on foreign manufactured goods (imports) than it earns from selling its own manufactured goods to foreign countries (exports).

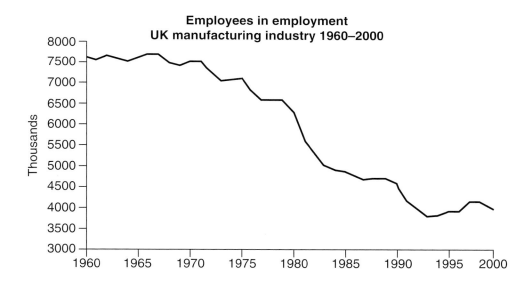

Employees in employment
UK manufacturing industry 1960–2000

What has caused deindustrialization?

Economists have found it difficult to pin-point what exactly has caused the decline of UK manufacturing industry. Many arguments have been put forward:

1 Many of the old industries like shipbuilding, coalmining and textiles manufacture have declined because of competition from overseas producers who have been able to supply these products at a lower cost than the UK. In some cases this has been because foreign governments have given their firms large subsidies so that they could price low and drive existing producers out of business.

2 As incomes have risen people tend to spend more of their money on services, leisure and buying imported consumer goods not traditionally made in the UK. For example, in 1971 UK households spent an average of 23% of their incomes on travel, communications, recreation and entertainment. By 1998 this had risen to 32%. In a market economy this increase in consumer spending will attract more resources into providing services (see Chapter 3).

3 Technological advance and increased capital investment has displaced manufacturing workers. Higher levels of output can be achieved today with far fewer workers than was required many years ago.

4 The strength of the pound on foreign exchange markets has reduced the demand for exports of UK goods overseas. As the pound rises in value the price of UK goods in overseas currencies will go up but the price of goods imported into the UK will go down (see Chapter 14).

5 Wage costs and taxes on profits are lower in many developing countries. This has persuaded some firms to move their production overseas.

Exercise 7 Is it wise to deindustrialize?

Deindustrialization is often seen as evidence of economic decline. On the contrary, it is a natural consequence of economic progress, says the International Monetary Fund.

The word deindustrialization strikes fear into the hearts of many workers, manufacturers and politicians in rich economies. Yet the reason for this is misunderstood. The decline in manufacturing jobs in rich countries has coincided with a rapid increase in manufactured exports from countries such as Brazil and China. This leads many rich country voters to say that these countries are stealing their jobs and that the solution lies in trade barriers. Really?

There is no doubt that manufacturing provides fewer jobs than it used to. The share of manufacturing in total employment in rich economies fell from 28% in 1970 to 18% in 1994. In America less than one worker in six is employed in manufacturing: in the European Union, one in five. In America more than 70% of workers are employed in services and this share will grow. On current trends manufacturing will account for only one in ten American jobs within ten years.

Two explanations are offered for this. One is that as they become richer, consumers want to buy relatively fewer manufactured goods and relatively more services. The other reason suggests that firms are moving their factories to countries where wages are lower. In new research, the International Monetary Fund (IMF) suggests that neither of these explanations is true. A bigger change by far is that productivity is growing much faster in manufacturing than in services, so fewer people are needed to make the same output.

Between 1960 and 1994 argues the IMF, service sector output and manufacturing output grew at the same pace in rich countries. But, productivity in manufacturing grew twice as fast as in services. This naturally shifted employment from the more productive manufacturing sector where fewer workers are needed to produce a given output to service industries where more workers are needed. Productivity improvements in farming caused the same thing to happen in agriculture over the past century. Having made up 50% of all American jobs in 1860, farming now employs only 3%.

As a country gets richer, it is inevitable that a smaller proportion of workers will be needed by manufacturing.

The IMF estimates that fast productivity growth in manufacturing and slower improvement in services could account for two thirds of the drop in the employment share in manufacturing in rich economies since 1970.

The new service jobs, rather than being seen as 'inferior, unskilled jobs', are likely to be in highly skilled areas such as teaching, financial services or information technology.

Deindustrialization can cause problems in economies unable to absorb the workers released by manufacturing. But those who would tackle this by subsidies or trade barriers are missing the point. As manufacturing continues to shrink in an economy, overall growth will increasingly depend on boosting productivity in services. Policy should therefore concentrate on removing obstacles to productivity growth and creating a labour market in which workers can move freely from factories into services. Protection and subsidies will not help this.

Adopted from *The Economist*, 26.4.1997

1 Use your book to help write explanations for the following terms used in the above article; **manufacturing industry**, **deindustrialization**, **productivity**, **subsidies**, **trade barriers**, **labour market**.

2 What evidence is there for deindustrialization in rich countries?

3 Why might deindustrialisation be seen as a sign of economic progress?

4 What reasons are given in the above article by the IMF for deindustrialization?

Exercise 8   The growth in services

Below is a jumbled group of reasons for the rapid increase in the importance of the tertiary industry in the UK and other developed countries. In pairs, pair up each reason for growth with its possible effect on the service sector in the economy.

Reasons for growth

Rise in people's incomes allowing them to spend more on luxury goods, e.g. TVs, videos, cars.

Increase in people's savings as incomes have risen.

Increase in number of tourists as people can now afford to travel more.

Increase in number of people wanting to own their own home.

Reduction in the number of hours people have to work each week (In 1998 the average number of hours per week was 38.6).

More solicitors, building societies, estate agents and insurance services.

Increase in demand for leisure activities, such as snooker, tennis, squash and an increase in the number of leisure centres.

Increase in number of large shops and discount warehouses selling consumer durables.

More restaurants and hotels.

Increase in number of banks and building societies.

Key words

In your own words write down what you understand by the following:

Weight increasing production
Weight decreasing production
Sunrise or footloose industries
Ancillary firms
Inertia
Public Inquiry
Regional policy
Assisted areas
New towns
Enterprise Grant Areas
Regional Development Agencies
Industrial revolution
Deindustrialization

Now go back to the chapter and check your understanding of these words.

Aims

At the end of this chapter you should be able to:

1 Understand the forces of **demand** and **supply** and analyse their effects on the **market price** of a commodity.

2 Draw a **normal demand curve** and a **normal supply curve** and analyse what will cause movements in these curves.

3 Define what is meant by **price elasticity of demand**, **income elasticity** and **cross elasticity**, undertake simple calculations to find their values and understand the importance of these measures.

4 Discuss the effects of a **tax** or **subsidy** on the supply and market price of a commodity.

Exercise 1   Last orders please

WINE SINKS BEER

Vino is most popular drink at home for the first time

Wine has overtaken beer for the first time as our favourite drink at home, a survey revealed yesterday.

Britons are increasingly likely to sip Chardonnay or Bordeaux in front of the TV than a can of bitter or lager thanks to changing tastes and being more helth concious.

Sales of wine have also shot up over the past five years as it has become less snobby, cheaper and easily available.

Wider choice, better advice in stores and off-licences and a less exclusive image have all contributed to its success.

Beer and lager have taken a beating -- except during events like the World Cup -- as Britons become more diet aware.

Sales in supermarkets are they key to the wine revolution. Wines market share there adds up to a massive 33.8 per cent.

In off-licence chains wine is also top with 29.9 per cent.

HOW WINE'S WINNING

Market share by value

	1994	1998
Wine	26.3%	29.5%
Beer	27.9%	29.3%
Spirits	33.1%	26.2%
Fortified wine	6.0%	6.2%
Cider	3.8%	3.8%
Champagne	2.9%	3.5%
Other	0.0%	1.5%

The Mirror, 30.1.1999

1 Who makes up the market for alcoholic drinks?

2 How are consumers' wants changing in the drinks industry?

3 How could the change in consumers' wants affect the allocation of resources in the drinks industry?

4 Why do you think more consumers now want and are able to buy wine?

The article above illustrates the changing patterns of demand in the alcoholic drinks industry. People are now buying less beer while sales of wine are rising. If this trend continues it is likely that entrepreneurs in the drinks industry will move the scarce resources of land, labour and capital into the production of more wines and out of the production of beer. In this way consumers get what they want in a market economy.

Prices act as the signals for producers to show them how to use their scarce resources. If the price of a product is rising they may think they can earn more profits from its production and sale and therefore will use their resources to make this product. If the price of a product falls they may decide not to produce it any more as profits start to fall. This chapter looks at how this **price mechanism** works.

| Section 1 | What is demand? |

Demand curves

Consumers' demand for goods and services plays a large part in deciding how scarce resources are used. **Demand** is the want or willingness of consumers to buy goods and services. To be an **effective demand** consumers must have enough money to buy commodities given a number of possible prices. Producers will only make those commodities if people have money to buy them.

The amount of a good or service consumers are willing and able to buy is known as the **quantity demanded** of that product. Economists measure the quantity demanded of a particular good or service at a certain price over certain periods of time, say the number of oranges bought per week, the number of records per month, or the amount of videos per year.

Individual demand is the demand of just one consumer, while the **market demand** for a product is the total demand for a product from all its consumers.

Exercise 2   What is your individual demand?

1   Imagine your favourite chocolate bar was on offer at a number of possible prices. How many bars of chocolate would you be prepared to buy each month at each possible price?

Possible price of a chocolate bar	Your demand per month
£2.00	
£1.50	
£0.50	
£0.30	
£0.20	
£0.10	
£0.05	
£0.01	

2   Copy and complete the table. You have now completed your **demand schedule** for your chocolate bar, that is, a table of figures relating quantity demanded to price.

Use this information to plot a line graph below to show your individual **demand curve** for the chocolate bar.

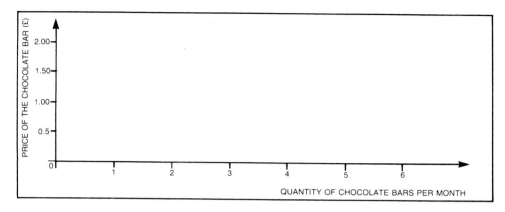

3 Which of the following statements applies to your demand curve?

   a It shows that as price rises, quantity demanded falls, and as price falls, quantity demanded rises.

   b It is roughly downward sloping.

   c Price and quantity demanded move in opposite directions.

Don't be surprised if all three statements apply to your demand curve. For the great majority of goods and services experience shows that quantities demanded will rise as their prices fall. In general, demand curves will be downward sloping when plotted against price.

A demand curve

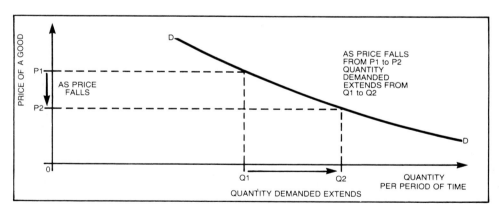

Thus, as the price of a product changes consumers *move along* their demand curve. That is, their demand extends as price falls, or contracts as price rises.

An extension of demand or increase in quantity demanded refers to the way in which demand changes with a fall in price, with no change in any other factor that could affect demand.

A contraction of demand or decrease in quantity demanded refers to the way in which demand changes when price rises, with no change in any other factor that may affect demand.

Why do demand curves slope downwards?

Consumers buy goods and services to satisfy their wants. This satisfaction is called **utility** by economists. We assume that consumers are rational, that is they wish to get as much satisfaction or utility as they can from buying goods and services.

As a person buys more of a good the total satisfaction or total utility s/he gets from it rises, but it does not rise by the same amount. For example, consider eating chocolate bars. One afternoon you feel quite hungry and buy a chocolate bar to eat. It's just what you needed and you feel really satisfied by eating it. You then eat another bar, and then another, and another. By the time you are on your fourth chocolate bar you are feeling a little full and the utility you get from eating it is nowhere near the satisfaction you got from munching your first chocolate bar. If you were to eat another you might even feel sick. The extra utility gained from the consumption of one more chocolate bar is known as the **marginal utility** of the bar, and it is generally accepted that for most people marginal utility goes down as their consumption of any good increases.

The **law of diminishing marginal utility** applies to most people: the more of a commodity they have, the less utility they get from consuming one more unit of it. As the extra utility from each extra unit of a commodity falls so the price consumers are willing to pay for each extra unit falls.

For example, you may have been so hungry that for the first satisfying chocolate bar you buy you may have been willing to pay 50 pence. By the time you ate your sixth chocolate bar and were feeling rather sick it would be unlikely you would pay very much for it.

The market demand curve

The market demand curve for a particular good or service will display the demand of all the consumers of that commodity given a set of possible prices.

Exercise 3 Market demand curve

Producers of orange light bulbs have the following information about the amount of orange light bulbs consumers would buy each year given a number of possible prices. The market demand schedule is as follows.

Prices of orange light bulbs (pence)	Market demand per month
50p	100 000
40p	150 000
30p	200 000
20p	260 000
10p	330 000
5p	400 000

1 With price on the vertical axis, and quantity per year along the bottom axis, plot the market demand curve for orange light bulbs and label it DD.

2 Use the graph to work out how many orange light bulbs would be demanded at a price of:

    a 35 pence
    b 15 pence.

3 If orange light bulb producers together wished to sell the following amount of bulbs each year what price should they charge?

    a   360 000
    b   295 000
    c   180 000

4 Explain why the market demand curve for orange light bulbs slopes downwards.

5 Explain the difference between individual demand and market demand.

In general the market demand curve for any good or service will be downward sloping showing the relationship between quantity demanded and price, assuming that nothing else changes that will affect how much consumers demand.

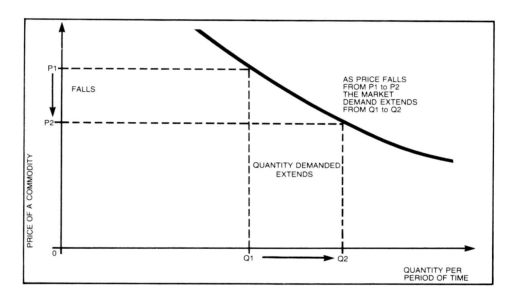

A market demand curve for a commodity

Shifts in demand
An increase in the price of a commodity will normally cause demand to contract. However, this assumes that no other factor that affects consumers' demand changes. Demand curves are drawn based on the assumption that nothing else changes other than price so only changes in the price of the product can be seen to affect demand. This is called the **ceteris paribus** assumption, meaning 'all other things remaining unchanged'.

However, what happens to the demand for particular goods and services when these things do change? For example, will a fall in people's income cause them to demand less of a product whatever its price? What effect will an advertising campaign for a product have on demand, regardless of the price of the product?

An increase in demand

For example, the market demand for chocolate bars:

Possible price (pence) of chocolate bars	Original demand per month	Increased demand per month
50	100 000	200 000
40	150 000	250 000
30	200 000	300 000
20	260 000	360 000
10	330 000	430 000
5	400 000	500 000

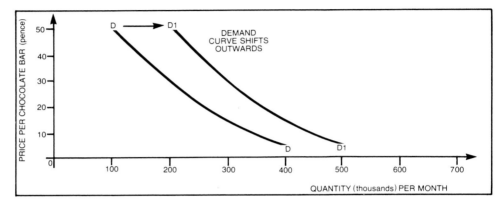

The diagram above shows an increase in demand for chocolate bars, but it could be any other good or service because the same rules apply. At each price consumers are now willing to buy more chocolate bars than they did before. The whole demand curve has shifted outwards from DD to D_1D_1.

An **increase in demand** means that consumers now demand more at each and every price than they did before.

A fall in demand

For example, the market demand for video-cassettes.

Possible price of video-cassettes (£)	Original demand per week	Decreased demand per week
10	10 000	5 000
8	15 000	10 000
6	20 000	15 000
4	25 000	20 000
2	30 000	25 000

156

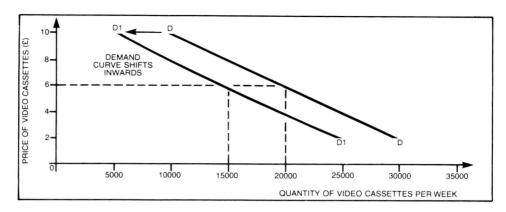

A fall in demand at all prices will cause the demand curve to shift to the left, or inwards, from DD to D_1D_1.

A fall in demand means that consumers now demand less at each and every price than they did before.

Exercise 4   What causes a shift in demand?

Read the following articles and in each case say:

1   What factors have changed that will affect consumer demand?

2   Will demand increase, fall or remain unchanged given the changing factor?

Now draw a demand diagram to show the market demand curves for products before and after the changes described.

Tax Revenue boosts hope of 1 p cut

THE PROSPECT of a 1p cut in the basic rate of income tax in the Budget came significantly closer yesterday as new Treasury figures showed that government finances had been transformed by bulging tax receipts.

Coffee price soars after new frosts

SHOPPERS may have to fork out 20 per cent more for their jars of Gold Blend and other brands over the next few months after more disastrous frosts overnight in Brazil, the world's biggest coffee producer. The price of coffee on the London Commodities Exchange soared from $3076 a tone to $3950 a tonne as reports reached the City that up to half next year's Brazilian crop may have been destroyed.

Evening Standard, 11.7.1999

Consumers 'confident about their future finances'

By Alan Beattie

The UK economy seems set for a steady take-off from its soft landing, according to the preliminary results of a new survey to by the Consumers' Association.

The survey of consumer confidence, due to be launched next month, showed that in April, 64 per cent of consumers reported they were very confident or fairly confident about their household's future circumstances.

Times, 21.6.1999

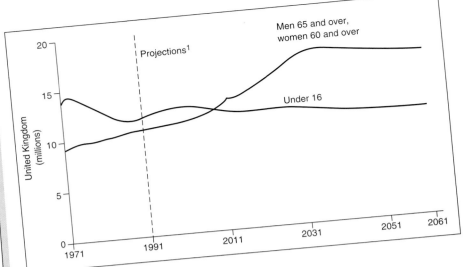

Test fields of conflict

Consumers are concerned, eco-warriors are on the warpath and British agribusiness is on the run. The scare over genetically modified food shows no sign of abating and companies the length of the food supply chain are responding.

The GM food scare, prompted by research which claimed to have found a link between tumours in mice and genetically modified potatoes, and since discredited, is swiftly becoming a huge corporate liability.

David Gamble, director of the risk managers' association Airmic, said that companies should not underestimate the impact GM could have on their business. 'The public perception is that every type of GM food is potentially dangerous. The main risk is a potential loss of sales as pressure from consumers has prompted all big supermarkets to stop stocking GM foods; so anyone out of line could suffer'. It is a lesson that United Biscuits has already learned. When tests revealed that some of its Linda McCartney range of vegetarian foods contained GM soya, sales dropped dramatically.

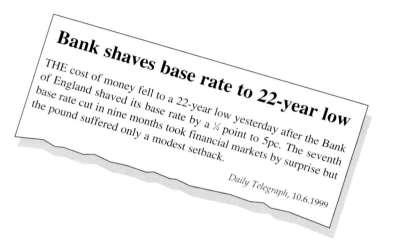

Bank shaves base rate to 22-year low

THE cost of money fell to a 22-year low yesterday after the Bank of England shaved its base rate by a ¼ point to 5pc. The seventh base rate cut in nine months took financial markets by surprise but the pound suffered only a modest setback.

Daily Telegraph, 10.6.1999

Changes in the following factors are likely to cause changes in demand that will shift the demand curve for a commodity.

1 Changes in people's incomes
Clearly the more their income the more people can buy. A rise in people's incomes will therefore cause an increase in demand for many goods and services, while a fall in incomes will cause demand to fall and demand curves will shift inwards.

Rising incomes, however, may cause the demand for some goods to fall. These items are called **inferior goods**. When people's incomes rise they can afford better quality clothes and food, so that basic clothing and foodstuffs can be classed as inferior.

2 Changes in income taxes
If the government wishes people to spend more so that firms will want to produce more and employ unemployed workers to help them do so, they may reduce the amount of income tax people pay. This will give people more after-tax income to spend and demand will increase for many commodities.

Complementary goods

Substitute goods

3 Changes in the population

A rise in the number of people in a country means more food, clothes and many other goods and services are needed. A rise in the population will therefore increase the demand for many commodities and shift their demand curves outwards.

The average age of the population in the UK and many other developed countries is rising as both birth and death rates fall and remain low (see Chapter 20). This can also have an impact on the demand for many goods and services. Older people tend to save more, spend more on household goods and DIY, enjoy more holidays, and prefer wine and spirits to beer.

4 Changes in the prices of other goods

Some of the goods and services we buy need other things, or accessories, to go with them. For example, cars need petrol, compact discs need discplayers, bread may need butter. Goods and services consumers want together, or which are **jointly demanded**, are called **complementary goods** or **complements.**

If the prices of cars rise many people may be put off buying a new car and so the demand for petrol will fall. A fall in the price of compact discs may cause the demand for compact disc-players to increase and their market demand curve to shift outwards.

Some goods and services, however, are **substitutes** for each other. A good or service is a substitute when its purchase can replace the want for another good or service. For example, margarine may be a close substitute for butter for a number of people. An increase in the price of butter may cause people to switch to buying margarine so that the market demand curve for margarine shifts outwards. Similarly a rise in the price of coffee may increase the demand for tea. Different makes of car are also close substitutes; a fall in the price of the Peugeot 206 may reduce the demand for the Ford KA.

5 Changes in tastes and fashion

The demand for goods and services can change dramatically because of the changing tastes of consumers and fashions. Flared jeans and platform shoes were much in demand in the early 1970s, but by the late seventies straight-leg jeans and flat shoes had replaced them. Today, increasing numbers of consumers are demanding goods that are kinder to the environment and animals, and foods that are healthier.

6 Advertising

Carefully-planned advertising campaigns cause consumers to buy more of a product and shift the demand curve for it outwards. Advertising can create wants as we shall discover in more detail in Chapter 10.

7 Other factors

Many factors can affect demand, for example, changes in the weather can shift demand; a hot summer can increase demand for cold drinks, a very cold winter can boost the demand for fuels. A rise in interest rates may cause people to save more and spend less on goods and services. A fall in the value of the pound may increase the demand for UK exports (see Chapter 14).

Change in fashion can cause a shift in demand

Exercise 5 A question of demand

1 How does quantity demanded of a product usually vary with its price?

2 Explain **a** an extension of demand, and **b** a contraction of demand.

3 Make a list of factors that may have caused the following shift in the market demand curve for good X from DD to D₁D₁.

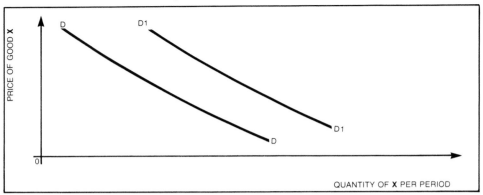

4 Suggest four reasons, other than price, that could cause a fall in the demand for holidays in Spain.

5 The diagram below shows the original demand curve (DD) for a particular commodity Z which is a compliment for another commodity Y.

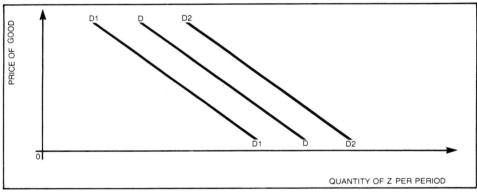

a What is a complementary good?
b Imagine there is a rise in the price of commodity Y. Starting from the original demand curve for Z, which demand curve should now apply? Explain your answer.

6 Below is a list of goods and services. Think of some possible complements and substitutes for each of them.

Goods and services	Possible substitutes	Goods and services	Possible complements
1 Electric cooker		1 Video-recorders	
2 Woollen jumpers		2 Fountain-pens	
3 Gas supply		3 Guitars	
4 DVD players		4 Toothbrushes	
5 Passenger rail journeys		5 Electricity	

160

Supply curves

Supply refers to the amount of a good or service firms or producers are willing to make and sell at a number of possible prices. The amount of a good or service producers are willing and able to make and sell to consumers in the market is known as the **quantity supplied** of that product, measured per period of time, say each week, month or year.

Clearly a firm interested in profit will only make and sell a product if it can do so at a price over and above what it cost the firm to make. The higher the price of the product, the more the firm will supply because the more profits it expects to make. This can be applied generally to the supply of all goods and services. As price rises, quantity supplied rises.

The **market supply** of a commodity will consist of the supply of all the individual producers competing to supply that commodity.

Exercise 6   The market supply curve

The following table represents the **market supply schedule** for silver-plated tankards. Copy the graph axis below, plot this information on the graph axis and label your curve the **market supply curve (SS).**

Possible price (£) of tankards	Market supply per month
20	1 600
16	1 100
12	700
8	300
4	100

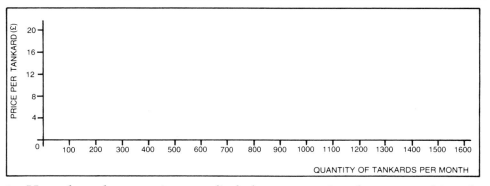

1   How does the quantity supplied change as price changes, making the assumption 'ceteris paribus', that is, that other factors that could affect supply do not change?

2   What will cause an extension in supply?

3   What will cause a contraction of supply?

4   Use your graph to work out how many tankards will be supplied at a price of:

    a   £6

    b   £10

5 a If consumers wished to be able to buy 700 tankards each month how much must they be prepared to pay for them?

b What will be the tankard producers' total revenue?

6 The following table displays the costs and revenues involved in the production and sale of tankards by all the producers in the market. Using the market supply schedule complete the table and explain why the market supply curve for tankards slopes upwards from left to right.

Output of tankards per month	Total cost (£)	Total revenue (price times output) (£)	Profit (£)
100	100	400	300
300	280		
700	420		
1 100	580		
1 600	760		

In general, the supply curve for any commodity will slope upwards, showing that as price rises, quantity supplied rises or extends.

As price falls, quantity supplied contracts. This is because as price falls firms will expect to earn less profits as revenue will exceed costs by a smaller amount.

A market supply curve for a commodity

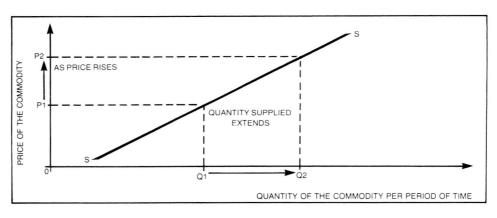

As price rises from P_1 to P_2 the market supply extends from Q_1 to Q_2. That is, a change in the price of the commodity causes a **movement along** the supply curve.

An **extension of supply** refers to how supply changes with a rise in the price of a commodity, given that no other factor affecting supply changes.

A **contraction of supply** refers to how supply changes with a fall in the price of a commodity, without a change in any other factor that may affect supply.

Shifts in supply   A change in the price of a commodity will normally cause its supply to extend or contract. Changes in things other than the price of a good can cause its whole supply to move. A movement of the whole supply curve for a good is called either an increase or decrease in supply.

An increase in supply
For example, the market for disposable razors.

Possible price of razor (pence)	Original supply per month	Increased supply per month
50	10 000	12 000
40	8 000	10 000
30	6 000	8 000
20	4 000	6 000
10	2 000	4 000

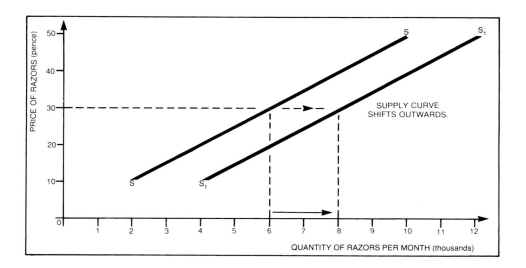

The diagram above shows an increase in the supply of disposable razors, but it could be any other good or service. At each and every price, razor producers are now willing to make and sell more razors than they did before. The whole supply curve has shifted outwards from SS to S_1S_1.

An increase in supply means that producers are now more willing and able to supply than they were before.

A fall in supply
For example, the market supply of potatoes.

Price per lb of potatoes (pence)	Original supply per month (lbs)	Supply per month (lbs)
100	50 000	40 000
80	40 000	30 000
60	30 000	20 000
40	20 000	10 000
20	10 000	0

163

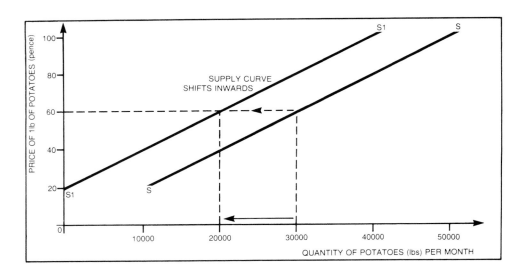

A fall in supply at all prices will cause the supply curve of a commodity to shift inwards from SS to S_1S_1.

A **fall in supply** means that producers are now less willing and able to supply a commodity at each and every price than they were before.

Exercise 7   What causes a shift in supply?

Read the following passage and try to pick out all the factors that have caused a change in the supply of potatoes and cabbages.

Farmer Bumpkin plans to plant five fields of potatoes and three fields of cabbages each year. The price he can usually get for a pound of potatoes is 30 pence, while the price of cabbages is 50 pence. Farmer Bumpkin has estimated that his time, effort, machinery and fertilizer costs add up to an average 12 pence per pound of potatoes and 20 pence per pound of cabbages.

Which crop is the more profitable one to grow?

However, in the following season the price of potatoes rises to 45 pence per lb.

What would you advise Farmer Bumpkin and farmers like him to do? Given your advice what will happen to the supply of cabbages?

In the very next growing season, Farmer Bumpkin discovers a new 'Speedo' cabbage harvester is available, and at a very reasonable price. He used to pay some boys and girls from the nearby village to help pick his crops each year, but now he can pick them all by himself using the machine. He estimates that this saving has reduced the average cost per cabbage grown to only 10 pence.

If the price of potatoes and cabbages have remained unchanged what would you now advise Farmer Bumpkin and farmers like him to do? How will this affect the supply of potatoes and cabbages?

In the very next season the landowner who rents her land to Farmer Bumpkin decides to cut the rent of land from £500 per year to £300. That is from £100 per field to £60 per field. Farmer Bumpkin wonders if he should rent an additional field now that it costs much less to produce potatoes and cabbages. If he decided to do this what will be the likely effect on the supply of his potatoes and cabbages?

A farmer's year is not without its problems. Towards the end of the season an early but very hard frost damages Farmer Bumpkin's entire cabbage crop.

What will happen to the supply of cabbages now?

What factors have caused changes in the supply of potatoes and cabbages?

Changes in the following factors will cause changes in supply and shifts in the supply curve of a commodity.

1 Changes in the price of other commodities
In a free market resources are allocated to those goods and services that yield the most profit.

In the Farmer Bumpkin exercise a rise in the price of potatoes will cause him to move his resources out of the production of cabbages into the production of potatoes. As a result the supply curve for cabbages will shift inwards at every possible price as farmers are now less willing to grow them.

The same will apply to a great many goods and services. A fall in the price of one may cause producers to supply more of another more profitable commodity.

2 Changes in the costs of factors of production
An increase in the wages paid to workers reduces the profits of firms and they may be less willing to supply a commodity at each and every price. Supply will fall. An increase in land rent or payments to capital has the same effect.

However, a fall in these costs will increase profits and the supply curve for a commodity will shift outwards. This would be the case for Farmer Bumpkin as the rent of his land fell enabling him to enjoy lower costs and increase production of his crops.

3 Technical progress
Technical progress means improvements in the performances of machines, labour, production methods, management control, quality, etc. This allows more to be produced regardless of the selling price. For example, the introduction of robots has helped car firms lower their production costs and produce many more cars.

In the case of Farmer Bumpkin his new 'Speedo' cabbage harvester will allow him to shift the supply curve of cabbages outwards.

4 Other factors
The weather is an extremely important factor determining the supply of natural products like cabbages and potatoes. A good summer may bring bumper harvests so that whatever the price supply increases. A bad summer will cause supply curves to shift inwards.

Governments can also influence supply. If the government wants firms to produce more it may give them a **subsidy**, a sum of money, which will lower their costs, boost their profits and increase supply. A **tax** on the commodity, however, will increase their costs and lead to a fall in supply (see section 7). Also if firms are made to reduce their pollution by buying necessary equipment, this increase in costs may reduce supply.

| **Section 3** | Market price |

Reaching an equilibrium

We have now looked at the two market forces that determine price. For each good and service there is a supply schedule and a demand schedule. If the two are combined we will find that the quantity demanded and quantity supplied will be equal at one price. This is the **market price** at which the commodity will be sold in the market. The market price can also be found using the market demand and supply curve.

Exercise 8   Finding the market price

Consider the market demand and supply schedules for chocolate bars.

Possible price of chocolate bars (pence)	Quantity demanded per month	Quantity supplied per month
50	100 000	420 000
40	150 000	300 000
30	200 000	200 000
20	260 000	120 000
10	330 000	60 000
5	400 000	40 000

On graph paper plot the demand and supply curves for chocolate bars on one graph with 'Price per chocolate bar' on the vertical axis and 'Quantity per month' along the bottom axis.

1   Using the above table state at which price demand equals supply.

This will be the market price for chocolate bars because at that price producers are willing to make and sell just as many bars as consumers are willing to buy.

2   **a**   Find the market price of chocolate bars using your demand and supply curves.
   b   What is the quantity of bars traded at this price in the market?

3   When the quantity demanded is greater than the quantity supplied economists say there is an **excess demand**.

Similarly when quantity supplied exceeds the quantity demanded there is said to be an **excess supply**.

State whether there is excess demand or excess supply at the following prices for chocolate bars.
   a   50 pence
   b   10 pence

c 40 pence
d 20 pence
e 30 pence

4 a If there is excess demand what do you think will happen to the price of chocolate bars?
  b If there is excess supply what do you think will happen to their price?
  c At which price will there be no excess demand or supply?

In the above exercise it should be clear that a market price will be determined at 30 pence per chocolate bar. Only here will demand equal supply. Another name for market price is **equilibrium price** because it is the price at which the amount supplied equals or satisfies the amount demanded.

In a graph equilibrium is found where the demand and supply curves cross as in the diagram below. At this market price of 30 pence 200 000 chocolate bars will be traded each week.

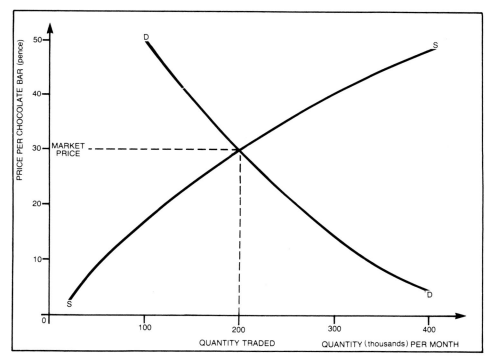

Equilibrium in the market for chocolate bars

At prices higher than the market price (for example 40p) firms will supply more than consumers demand and so there will be an **excess supply**. In order to persuade consumers to buy up this excess supply the price will have to fall.

At prices lower than the market price (for example 20p) the quantity demanded by consumers exceeds what firms will supply. There will be an excess demand. As a result the price will rise.

When demand does not equal supply this is known as **disequilibrium**.

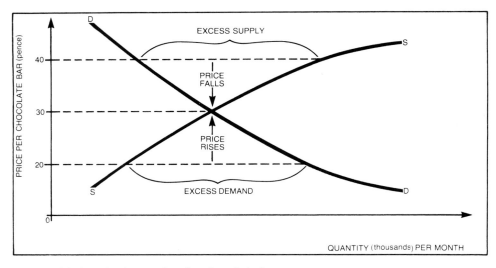

Disequilibrium in the market for chocolate bars

Only in equilibrium where demand equals supply will there be no forces trying to change price.

Changes in market prices

Changes in market prices will occur as a result of changes in demand and/or supply.

1 A shift in demand

An increase in demand for a commodity, because people's incomes have risen, or the price of a substitute good has gone up, will cause the demand curve to shift outwards.

In the diagram below it shifts from DD to D_1D_1. As a result the market price rises from P to P_1.

Producers extend the supply of the commodity to meet the higher level of demand because they are willing to supply more at higher prices.

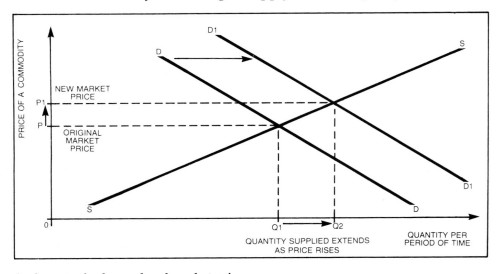

An increase in demand and market price

168

Exercise 9   A fall in demand and market price

Below is the market demand and supply schedule for A4 lined paper in packs of 200 sheets.

Price per pack (£)	Original demand per week	Original supply per week
3	100	500
2.50	200	400
2	300	300
1.50	400	200
1	500	100

Questions

1   Plot and label the demand curve (DD) and supply curve (SS) for packs of paper.

2   Mark in the market price (P) and the quantity traded (Q) at this price.

3   Imagine now that demand falls by 200 packs at each and every price. Draw and label the new demand curve (D_1D_1).

4   What is the new market price (P_1) and the new quantity traded (Q_1)? Show these on your graph.

5   What has happened to supply and why?

6   Suggest four reasons why there has been a fall in demand for paper.

A shift in supply   An increase in supply for a commodity because workers have accepted lower wages, or technical progress has increased the performance of capital equipment, will be seen as a movement outwards in the supply curve from SS to S_1S_1. As a result market price will fall from P to P_1 as a greater supply is available. As price falls so consumers will extend their demand for the commodity from Q to Q_1.

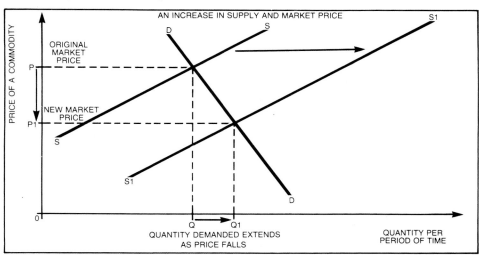

An increase in supply and market price

Exercise 10 A fall in supply and market price

Below is the market demand and supply schedule for wheat (tonnes per year).

The market for wheat

Possible price per tonne (£)	Original demand per year	Original supply per year
500	100 000	500 000
400	200 000	400 000
300	300 000	300 000
200	400 000	200 000
100	500 000	100 000

1 Plot and label the demand curve (DD) for wheat and its supply curve (SS).

2 Mark in the market price (P) and the quantity traded (Q) at this price.

3 Imagine now that supply falls by 200 000 tonnes at each and every price. Draw and label the new supply curve (S_1S_1).

4 What is the new market price (P_1) and the new quantity traded (Q_1)? Show these on your graph.

5 What has happened to demand and why?

6 Suggest four reasons why the supply of wheat may fall.

A fall in the supply of a commodity will cause its supply curve to shift inwards and market price will rise. Consumers' demand contracts along their demand curve as market price rises until demand equals supply once again.

The price mechanism

We have now seen how the price mechanism works in a free market. The forces of demand and supply establish the market price of a commodity. Changes in demand and supply will cause changes in price.

An increase in the demand for a good or service will raise market price. This will be the signal to producers to use more resources and supply more. This way consumers get what they want as firms compete for their custom. An increase in the supply of a commodity lowers market price and enables more people to share the increased supply.

Section 4 Price elasticity of demand

What is price elasticity of demand?

When prices rise we can assume that quantity demanded will contract. However, firms and economists alike would like to know by how much quantity demanded will rise or fall given a change in price. Consider two cases:

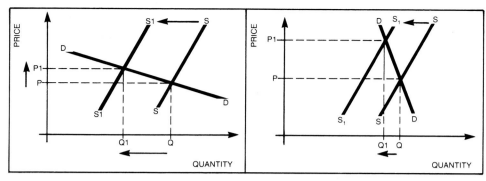

In this diagram the fall in supply has caused market price to rise from P to P₁. As a result demand has contracted rather a lot from Q to Q₁.

In this diagram the same fall in supply has caused market price to rise dramatically from P to P₁ but demand has only contracted a little from Q to Q₁.

The demand curve in the first case has a much flatter slope than the steep demand curve in the second case. As a result a price change in the first case will cause a large movement along the demand curve, while the same price change in the second diagram will only cause a very small contraction in demand.

The responsiveness of quantity demanded, or how much quantity demanded changes, given a change in the price of a good or service is known as the **price elasticity of demand (Ed)**.

If a small change in the price of a product causes a substantial change in quantity demanded, the demand for that product is said to be price **elastic**, that is, quantity demanded *stretches* a lot as the price changes.

If a small change in the price of a product causes only a very small change in the quantity demanded, the demand for that product is said to be price **inelastic**, that is quantity demanded hardly *stretches* at all.

Exercise 11 A problem to 'stretch' you

Assume there is a price rise of about 10% on the following goods. State whether there is likely to be large, small or no change in the quantity demanded. Then state whether you think demand is price elastic or inelastic, and why.

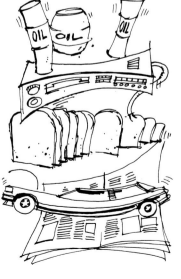

Product	Small or large change in quantity demanded	Price elastic or price inelastic	Why?
Oil			
Video-recorders			
Bread			
Cars			
Newspapers			

171

Products like oil and bread are necessary items for many people. An increase in their price of 10% may only have a minor effect on quantity demanded making demand for them price inelastic. Newspapers only take a small amount of a person's income and this makes them price inelastic. More luxurious, high-priced products like video-recorders and cars are likely to see quantity demanded contract quite a lot as price rises. Demand for them will be price elastic.

How to measure price elasticity of demand

Price elasticity of demand compares the percentage change in quantity demanded with the percentage change in price that caused it. For example, imagine personal hi-fi producers raise their prices from £20 to £25, that is, by 25%. If the quantity demanded contracted from 1 000 per week to 500 per week then this represents a 50% reduction in quantity demanded, which is double the percentage change in price. As demand has changed by a greater percentage than price, demand is price elastic. That is, each 1% change in price will cause a 2% change in the quantity of personal hi-fis demanded.

If, on the other hand, the percentage change in price caused a much smaller percentage change in quantity demanded, demand would be price inelastic.

Demand is **price elastic** when the % change in price is less than the % change in quantity demanded, that is, demand curves will have gentle slopes.

Demand is **price inelastic** when the % change in price is more than the % change in quantity demanded, that is, demand curves will have steep slopes.

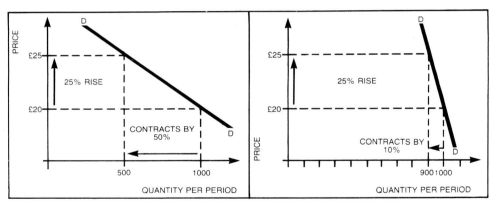

The price elasticity of demand for a product is calculated as follows:

$$Ed = \frac{\% \text{ change in quantity demanded}}{\% \text{ change in price}}$$

Percentage changes are worked out as follows:

$$\% \text{ change in quantity demanded} = \frac{\text{change in quantity}}{\text{original quantity}} \times \frac{100}{1}$$

$$\% \text{ change in price} = \frac{\text{change in price}}{\text{original price}} \times \frac{100}{1}$$

For example, look at the following demand schedule.

Price of the good	Quantity demanded per week
£5	100
£4	110

Taking £5 as the original price and 100 as the original quantity, the change in price is £1 and the change in quantity 10.

1 % change in quantity demanded $= \dfrac{10}{100} \times \dfrac{100}{1} = \dfrac{1\,000}{100} = 10\%$

2 % change in price $= \dfrac{£1}{£5} \times \dfrac{100}{1} = \dfrac{£100}{£5} = 20\%$

3 Ed $= \dfrac{\% \text{ change in quantity demanded}}{\% \text{ change in price}} = \dfrac{10\%}{20\%} = \dfrac{1}{2} = 0.5$

The demand is price inelastic because the % change in price of 20% is greater than the percentage change in quantity demanded of 10%. The Ed is 0.5.

Exercise 12   Using the formula

Below is the demand schedule for tins of baked beans.

Price of baked beans per tin	Market demand per week
40 pence	1 000
30 pence	1 500

1 Calculate the price elasticity of demand. (**Hint** use 40 pence as your original price.)

2 Comment on its value.

3 What will the demand curve for baked beans look like? Draw a simple diagram to show this.

The demand for baked beans in the above example is price elastic because the % change in quantity demanded of 50% is greater than the 25% change in price that caused it (Ed = 2). The demand curve for baked beans will therefore be quite flat.

In general when Ed is **greater than** 1, demand is price elastic. If Ed is **less than** 1, demand is price inelastic.

Price elasticity and total revenue

A firm will wish to know if an increase in price will cause their total revenue to rise. However, if quantity demand contracts a lot, revenue is more likely to fall.

Exercise 13 What happens to total revenue?

Below are two demand schedules, one for bread and one for video-recorders.

Price per loaf	Quantity demanded per month
*25 pence	10 000
20 pence	10 500

Price per video-recorder	Quantity demanded per month
*£500	1 000
£400	1 800

* original price and quantity

1 In each case calculate the price elasticity of demand. Comment on their values.

2 Calculate the total revenue (price × quantity demanded) for bread and for video-recorders, at each price.

3 **a** Would you advise bread-makers to cut the price of a loaf from 25 pence to 20 pence? Explain your answer.
b Would you advise video-makers to cut the price of a video-recorder from £500 to £400? Explain your answer.

4 Using the information above, decide which of the words in italics below does not apply in each case.

a Demand is price elastic when the % change in quantity demanded is *more/less* than the % change in price. A fall in price, will cause a *large/small* extension in quantity demanded so that total sales revenue *falls/rises*. If price is increased, total revenue would *fall/rise*.
b Demand is price inelastic when quantity demanded changes by a *greater/smaller* % than price. A fall in price,will cause a *small/large* extension in quantity demand so that total sales revenue *fall/rises*. A rise in price therefore causes total revenue to *fall/rise*.

Price elasticity of demand and firms' revenues are closely linked.

In the case of bread, because demand is price inelastic (Ed = 0.4), when the price is lowered, there is only a very small extension in demand and so overall total revenue falls. An increase in price would therefore raise revenue. In the case of video-recorders it is advisable for their producers to lower price from £500 to £400. Because demand is price elastic (Ed = 4) sales expand greatly and revenue rises. An increase in price would therefore reduce revenue.

Factors which affect price elasticity of demand

1 The number of substitutes
When consumers can choose between a large number of substitutes for a particular product, demand for any one of them is likely to be price elastic.

Demand will be price inelastic when there are few substitutes. For example, many foods like milk and medicines have few substitutes.

2 The period of time

If the price of a product rises consumers will search for cheaper substitutes. The longer they have, the more likely they are to find one. Demand will therefore be more price elastic in the long run.

3 The proportion of income spent on a commodity

Goods, like matches or newspapers, may be price inelastic in demand because they do not cost very much and any rise in their price will only take a little bit extra out of a person's income. If the price of cars was to rise by 10% this could mean paying an extra £500 or more for a car. This is a considerable part of a person's income. Demand is likely to be price elastic.

Some special demand curves

If a rise or fall in the price of a commodity causes no change in the quantity demanded of that commodity, demand is said to be **perfectly price inelastic**. That is, price elasticity of demand is 0.

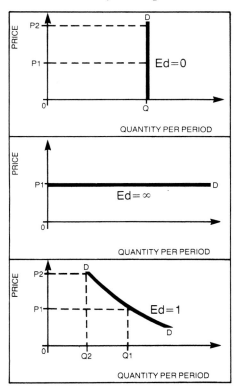

If a commodity is only demanded at one particular price demand is said to be **infinitely price elastic**. That is, a small change in price will cause quantity demanded to fall to zero, that is, quantity demanded will change by an infinite amount.

If the price elasticity of demand is 1 then demand is said to be of **unitary elasticity**. A percentage change in the price of a commodity will cause an equal percentage change in the quantity demanded. The result will be that the total amount spent on that commodity by consumers will remain the same whatever its price.

Exercise 14   Elastic brands

It may be hard to believe but the British high street is now probably the world's toughest battleground for consumer goods brands. For this blame a combination of powerful supermarket chains selling own label products and weak trademark legislation that allows the sales of lookalikes. With point-of-sale scanning enabling competitors to match each others promotions instantly, costly advertising is now often the only way to keep weaker brands on supermarket shelves.

More than half of Britain's top 500 consumer-good brands (including supermarket own label products) have suffered falling sales over the past three years: only 184 saw sales growth. Price has increasingly become the key factor deciding a brand's fate: average prices for grocery items such as baked beans, kitchen towels and sliced bread have fallen by up to a fifth in real terms. But price cutting to gain a market share can often be a losers game with no benefit to overall profit. So what should firms do?

A study by Will Hamilton of Kingston University Business School found the price elasticity of the top 500 brands averaged 1.85. In other words a 10% cut in price should produce an 18.5% increase in sales.

But the study also found wide variations across brands and categories. Thus with an elasticity of 1.01 household cleaning products are less price sensitive than diary and bakery products (elasticity of 1.69). Unsurprisingly across all categories, market leading brands have lower price elasticities than their lesser rivals.

Mr Hamilton's study seems to prove what many marketers have long argued: that it makes sense to support brand leaders with advertising rather than price promotions because their lower elasticity means the increase in sales from price cuts may not add to profits.

1 Explain price elasticity of demand and what is meant by a 'price elasticity of 1.85'?

2 Why do you think that market leading brands might have a lower price elasticity than less well known rivals?

3 Why might it 'make more sense' to improve profits through better advertising rather than price cutting for some brands?

| **Section 5** | Some other measures of elasticity of demand |

Income elasticity of demand

We noted earlier that changes in people's incomes would effect demand. By how much a change in income causes the quantity demanded of a good or service to change is known as the **income elasticity of demand**.

It is measured by the following formula:

$$\text{Income elasticity of demand} = \frac{\%\ \text{change in quantity demanded}}{\%\ \text{change in income}}$$

For most goods and services income and quantity demanded will move in the same direction. A rise in income will therefore bring about an increase in their demand. When this is the case, these commodities are called **normal goods**. For example, if a 10% rise in income causes a 20% rise in the quantity demanded of portable colour televisions we have:

$$\text{Income elasticity of demand} = \frac{20\%}{10\%} = +2$$

It is a positive number because a rise in income causes a rise in demand. Demand for goods like colour televisions is therefore termed **income elastic** because the percentage change in income brings about a much larger percentage change in quantity demanded.

If, however, the percentage rise in income causes only a small increase in demand the demand is **income inelastic**. For example, it is unlikely that a rise in people's incomes would cause them to buy increasing quantities of goods like salt and matches. Demand may only rise slightly. Indeed, it could be the case that demand actually falls for a product as income rises. These are **inferior goods**. For example, a person may now buy a cigarette-lighter and not buy matches any more. In this case income elasticity of demand will be negative. For example:

A 5% rise in income causes a 15% fall in the quantity demanded of matches.

$$\text{Income elasticity of demand} = \frac{\% \text{ change in quantity}}{\% \text{ change in income}} = \frac{-15\%}{5\%} = -3$$

Cross elasticity of demand

Another important factor that affects the demand for one commodity is the prices of other commodities. Cross elasticity of demand measures by now much quantity demanded will rise or fall given a change in the price of another product.

It is measured by the following formula:

$$\text{Cross elasticity of demand} = \frac{\% \text{ change in quantity of good X}}{\% \text{ change in price of good Y}}$$

If the two goods are substitutes, for example, butter and margarine, a rise in the price of one will cause a rise in demand for the other good.

For example, a rise in the price of butter by 8% causes a 24% rise in the demand for margarine.

$$\text{Cross elasticity of demand} = \frac{\% \text{ change in quantity of margarine}}{\% \text{ change in price of butter}}$$

$$= \frac{24\%}{8\%} = 3$$

The cross elasticity of demand for substitutes will always be a positive number as a rise in the price of one causes a rise in the demand for the other commodity.

If, however, two goods are complements, for example, cars and petrol, a rise in the price of one will not only cause a contraction in its own demand but also a fall in demand for the other.

The cross elasticity of demand for complementary goods will therefore be negative.

Exercise 15　How can ice-cream be elastic?

The demand and supply schedules below relate to the price of ice-cream.

Price per ice-cream	Quantity demanded per month	Quantity supplied per month
60p	1 000	8 000
50p	2 500	5 500
40p	4 000	4 000
30p	5 500	3 000
20p	7 000	2 000

1 Plot and label on an appropriate graph the demand curve (DD) and the supply curve (SS) for ice-cream.

2 What is the market price (P) and quantity traded (Q)?

3 Imagine now that the supply of ice-cream increases by 2 500 at every possible price.
    a Draw the new supply curve (S_1S_1)
    b What is the new market price (P_1) and quantity traded (Q_1)?

4 Calculate the price elasticity of demand for ice-cream between the original market price (P) and the new market price (P_1). Comment on its value, and what has happened to ice-cream producers' revenue?

5 The cross elasticity of demand between fruit salad and ice-cream is 7. What types of goods are they?

6 A 20% rise in the total income of the economy has caused the demand for ice-creams to rise by 3 000 at each and every price.
    a Draw in the new demand curve (D_1D_1) on the same graph.
    b What is the new market price (P_2) and quantity traded (Q_2)?
    c Calculate the income elasticity of demand for ice-creams if demand has risen from Q_1 to Q_2. Comment on its value and state what type of good ice-cream is.

Section 6	Price elasticity of supply

What is price elasticity of supply?　We have seen how the price mechanism works whereby an increase in demand will cause the market price of a commodity to rise. As a result, supply extends so that consumers get what they want. However, as economists we would wish to know by how much quantity supplied will change in response to the price change. Price elasticity of supply (Es) is a measure of the responsiveness of quantity supplied to a change in price.

Price elasticity of supply

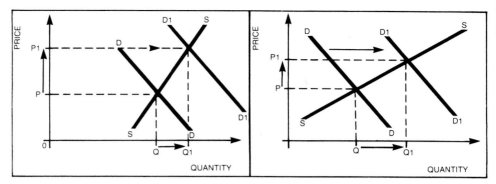

In the above diagram the increase in demand from DD to D_1D_1 has caused market price to rise from P to P_1. However, despite this large rise in price the extension in supply is only small from Q to Q_1. Supply is price **inelastic**.

In this diagram the increase in demand from DD to D_1D_1 has caused only a small increase in price from P to P_1 but a large extension in supply from Q to Q_1. Supply is price **elastic**.

To measure price elasticity of supply we use the following formula:

$$Es = \frac{\% \text{ change in quantity supplied}}{\% \text{ change in price}}$$

If the percentage change in price is greater than the percentage change in quantity supplied, supply is said to be price inelastic and the value of price elasticity of supply will be less than one.

If the percentage change in price causes a much larger percentage change in quantity supplied, supply is said to be price elastic. Price elasticity of supply will therefore be greater than one.

Below is the supply schedule for daffodils in the springtime.

Price per bunch of five daffodils	Quantity supplied per month
£1	10 000
£2	12 000

$$\% \text{ change in quantity supplied} = \frac{\text{change in quantity}}{\text{original quantity}} \times \frac{100}{1}$$

$$= \frac{2\,000}{10\,000} \times \frac{100}{1} = 20\%$$

$$\% \text{ change in price} = \frac{\text{change in price}}{\text{original price}} \times \frac{100}{1}$$

$$= \frac{£1}{£1} \times \frac{100}{1} = 100\%$$

$$Es = \frac{\% \text{ change in quantity supplied}}{\% \text{ change in price}} = \frac{20}{100} = 0.2$$

The price elasticity of supply of daffodils is less than one, that is, supply is price inelastic. This is because even if there is a large rise in price more daffodils cannot be grown very quickly.

What affects the price elasticity of supply

1 Time

The daffodil example illustrates how the price elasticity of supply can vary over time. Supply of most goods and services, including daffodils, will be fixed at any one moment in time. For example, a shop will only have a certain amount of records, books, joints of beef. A market stall will only have a fixed amount of daffodils to sell. It will take time to get more of these things. In this special case the supply curve is a vertical line showing that whatever the price the quantity supplied will be the same.

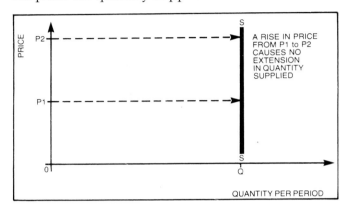

Supply at any one moment is fixed.

In the short run, firms can produce some more goods for sale, but only by using more labour, that is, by working overtime or employing more workers. More daffodils can be picked and sent to the market as price rises. However, supply can only rise a little because the amount of land, seeds and the season needed to grow the daffodils, will soon run out.

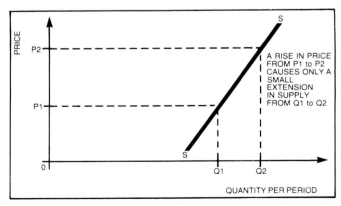

Supply is price inelastic in the short run.

In the long run, firms can obtain more labour, land and capital to expand their scale of production, so in the long run supply becomes more price elastic.

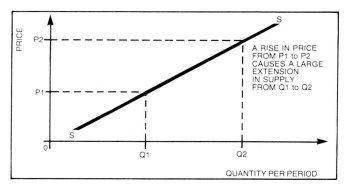

Supply in the long run is price elastic

2 The availability of resources

If a firm wishes to expand production it will need more of the factors of production of land, labour and capital. If the economy is already using most of its scarce resources then firms will find it difficult to employ more and so output will not be able to rise. The supply of most goods and services will therefore be price inelastic.

If, however, there is much unemployment of resources, for example, labour, firms will be able to use them when they want to raise output and supply will be more price elastic.

Exercise 16   Stretching supply

Below are the supply schedules for natural rubber and man-made rubber.

Price per lb	Quantity supplied of natural rubber per month
£0.80p	1 000
£1.00	1 100

Price per 1b	Quantity supplied of man-made rubber per month
£0.80p	2 000
£1.00	2 800

1   Calculate the price elasticity of supply for natural rubber and man-made rubber.

2   Comment on their values and suggest reasons why they differ.

Some special supply curves   If the quantity supplied of a commodity remains the same whatever its price, supply is said to be **perfectly price inelastic**, that is, price elasticity of supply is 0.

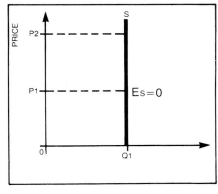

If producers are willing to supply as much as they can at one particular price and supply nothing at any other price then supply is said to be **infinitely price elastic**.

If the price elasticity of supply is 1 then supply is said to be of **unitary elasticity**. A percentage change in price will cause an equal percentage change in quantity supplied. This will be the case for any straight line supply curve that passes through the point of origin of its graph.

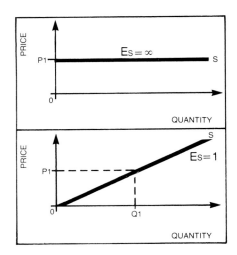

Section 7   Taxes and subsidies

The government may often step into 'free' markets to try and influence the market price and the quantity of goods and services traded.

Tax and supply   Taxes placed on goods and services are known as **indirect taxes**, for example Valued Added Tax, or excise duties which refer to taxes placed on cigarettes and alcohol. These taxes have the effect of increasing market price and reducing the quantity traded in a market.

In terms of a graph the supply curve moves upwards. The vertical distance between the curves SS and S_1S_1 shows the amount of the tax.

The supply schedule below shows how much a producer is willing to supply at each price. For example, if the price was £5 s/he would supply 1 000 articles. The revenue would amount to £5 000. However, if £1 of the price was a tax paid to the government our producer would only be receiving £4 per article, and an after-tax revenue of £4 000. Clearly, if our producer wishes to receive £5 000 of revenue from the sale of 1 000 articles he or she must sell them at £6 each, which after taking £1 away in tax leaves £5 per article for the producer. Clearly, as a result of the tax, supply has shifted up one step. Thus, at each price less is now supplied than before and so it appears that the supply curve has shifted upwards by the amount of the tax.

Price per article (£)	Quantity supplied per month	Quantity supplied after a £1 tax
9	–	1 600
8	1 600	1 400
7	1 400	1 200
6	1 200	1 000
5	1 000	800
4	800	

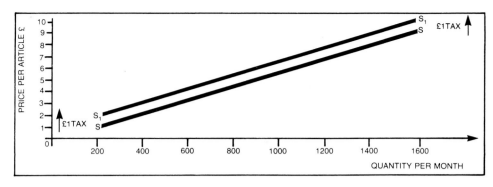

How tax affects the supply curve

But what happens to market price? Let us consider another example. Here are the demand and supply schedules before a £2 tax and the new supply after a £2 tax on a bottle of brandy.

Tax and the brandy market

Price per bottle (£)	Quantity demanded per month	Quantity supplied per month	Quantity supplied after a £2 tax
10	100	900	700
9	200	800	600
8	300	700	500
7	400	600	400
6	500	500	300
5	600	400	
4	700	300	

Before the tax, market price was £6 per bottle with quantity demanded at 500 bottles equal to supply. After the £2 tax we would expect price to become £8 but as supply shifts up by two steps clearly the new market price is only £7 with a quantity demanded equal to a supply of 400 bottles. The tax was £2 but consumers are only paying £1 extra per bottle. This means that brandy producers must be paying the other £1 of the tax. This is because as the introduction of the tax pushes up price, consumer demand contracts, and so the producer is unable to pass on the whole of the £2 to their customers because if they did demand would contract too much. Instead they must pay some of the tax themselves.

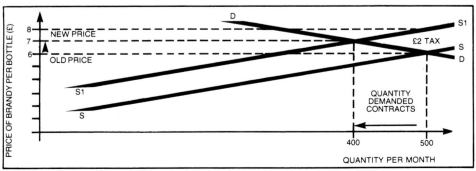

The effect of a tax on market price

Subsidies and supply   A subsidy is a payment made to producers to reduce their costs. As a result producers will increase their supply at every price. As a result of the increase in supply consumers face a lower market price. Subsidies have often been granted to farmers to keep up the supply of essential foodstuffs, like wheat, meat and milk.

Key words

Write definitions for the following terms:

Market forces	Ceteris paribus
Demand	Law of diminishing marginal utility
Supply	Normal goods
Market price	Inferior goods
Price mechanism	Complements
Effective demand	Substitutes
Utility	Excess demand
An extension of demand	Excess supply
A contraction of demand	Price elasticity of demand
An increase in demand	Price elastic
A fall in demand	Price inelastic
An extension of supply	Income elasticity of demand
A contraction of supply	Cross-elasticity of demand
An increase in supply	Subsidy
A fall in supply	

Now return to the chapter to check understanding of these terms.

Aims

At the end of this chapter you should be able to:

1 Distinguish between **private costs** and **benefits**, and **external costs** and **benefits**.

2 Understand that the total cost to society of production, or **social costs**, consists of private and external costs, while the total benefit for society, or **social benefits**, equals private plus external benefits.

3 Realize that the production decisions of firms and consumption decisions of consumers can affect others.

4 Decide whether or not a particular use of scarce resources is **economic**.

5 Understand the ways in which the Government can affect firms' production decisions.

6 Understand what is involved in **cost-benefit analysis**.

| Section 1 | How firms' decisions can affect us |

Case study

RIVER LIFE DEAD!

The river Eden today is a dead river. Over the last year nearly all the fish and plant life in the river has been destroyed. In the past month cattle grazing along the banks of the river have been poisoned. Fears are growing that local children will be next.

A report has found that the river has been highly polluted by the nearby Chemix plastics plant. Chemix has, for the past two years, been dumping chemical waste into the river. The waste is pumped into the river along an underground pipeline from the Chemix plant.

Scientists estimate that it will cost £2 million to clean up the damage caused to the river, but this will only be possible if the dumping of chemical waste is stopped.

Private costs and benefits

In the news clipping above, £2 million to clean up the polluted river is not the only cost of the Chemix plant dumping poisonous waste. Local farmers have suffered the loss of cattle, and their crops have been affected as the

185

waste from the river seeps into the ground. As news spreads of the poisoning, the farmers may not be able to sell their produce. Local fishermen have also lost their livelihood as the fish in the Eden river have died. In addition, rivers attract many tourists, and the towns that grow up beside them are often filled with visitors. A poisoned river like the Eden, however, will drive tourists, and the money they spend, away.

Clearly the costs to the people and area near to the Chemix plant are huge, yet Chemix as a private business is not interested in these costs. Chemix will only be concerned with its **private costs** of producing plastic, that is, the hire of machinery, buying of materials, payment of wages, etc. In fact, no private sector firm is interested in the costs they cause to others.

The Chemix company would, like any other business, try to calculate how much profit they could expect before starting up their own business. How much revenue will they make from their sales? How much will their costs be? Economists call the firm's own costs and revenues or benefits from producing, their **private costs** and **private benefits**.

If Chemix expects £3 million of revenue but only £2 million in costs each year, this would give them £1 million in profits. If this profit was higher than they could expect from doing something else, for example, producing paint, then from the Chemix point of view it was using its resources in the best possible way. The problem is that from society's point of view, the building and running of the Chemix plant has caused widespread pollution, and so may not be the best use of scarce resources.

External costs The costs that have resulted from scarce resources producing plastic, for example, the lost revenue of local farmers and the £2 million needed to clean up the polluted river, are called **external costs** because the rest of society must pay them. Chemix is clearly better off producing plastics, but society as a whole is worse off. This is because while Chemix makes £1 million profit, everyone else bears the external costs, which are at least £2 million, to clean up the damage the Chemix plant has caused.

If the Chemix company had taken into consideration the cost of cleaning up the waste it had dumped then the total cost for society of producing plastic would be £4 million, that is, external costs of £2 million plus private costs of £2 million. If the only benefits from the production of plastic is the £3 million of revenue that Chemix gains, then on the whole society loses £1 million. That is, if the total cost for the whole of society, or **social cost**, of production is greater than the benefits then society is worse off from using scarce resources in that particular use.

Clearly if the Chemix plant had not been built society as a whole would not lose £1 million. In other words, it would be better not to have built the Chemix plant.

External benefits Private firms generally ignore the damaging effects their production can have as long as they make a profit. However, as well as producing external costs, some firms can cause **external benefits**. These external benefits are free. No payment for them needs to be made by the people who receive them.

For example, when Chemix uses its resources to produce plastic it can create external benefits, as well as external costs, for others. Being a large company, Chemix can afford to train skilled workers. These skilled workers can then leave Chemix and work for other companies, which may not be able to afford to train their workers. These firms are getting the benefits of being able to save money on training costs. This is an external benefit provided by Chemix.

The decision to use resources to build the M25 motorway around London has also resulted in external costs and benefits. Noise and fumes from the cars can affect people living nearby. However, houses a few miles away from the motorway have risen in value dramatically because they are near to the new road that offers quick and easy transport around London. Business people have been keen to buy such houses to live in, and this has caused the price of these houses to rise which has been of benefit to the people who already own them.

Just as firms do not have to pay for the external costs they create for others, firms do not receive payment for the external benefits they give to others. For example, Chemix may be saving other companies £250 000 in training costs but has no way of obtaining payment for this benefit.

External benefits must also be taken into account when deciding whether or not a particular use for the resources of land, labour and capital is worthwhile from society's viewpoint. In the case of the Chemix company, private and external benefits now total £3.25 million, but are still exceeded by private and external costs of £4 million. The business is still not worthwhile from society's point of view.

For society the total benefit from the production of any good or service, or **social benefit**, is equal to the private benefits and external benefits from its production. Only when these social benefits exceed the social costs of production will that particular use of resources be worthwhile for all of society.

Case study

Exercise 1

Not painting a pretty picture

The Non-drip paint company is considering whether or not to locate a new factory near the town of Greensville. The company estimates that the new plant will cost £5 million a year to run, but should add £6 million to revenue from the sale of the paint it produces.

The people of Greensville are worried that the new factory will release smoke, containing harmful chemicals, into the air. These chemicals will pollute the air and even get into the soil and water supplies as rain will bring the chemicals down from the air.

The local health authority estimates that over many years this smoke will damage people's health and increase the need for medical care at an estimated cost of £4 million a year.

The local authority believes that the smoke will blacken the walls of historic buildings in the area, and cause their eventual erosion. Regular cleaning will therefore be needed at an estimated cost of £2 million each year.

On a more positive note, it estimates that the paint factory will encourage other firms to locate in the area as suppliers of materials, providers of transport, etc., and that this will reduce local unemployment and help other local businesses. These external benefits are valued at £3 million.

---

1 What does the Non-drip paint company take into account when deciding whether or not to produce paint with its resources?

2 From society's point of view should the firm take other things into consideration?

3 Which of the following statements do you think are correct?
   a From the point of view of the paint company resources are being used in the best way if:
      i   Private benefits are greater than private costs.
      ii   Private benefits equal private costs.
      iii Private benefits are less than private costs.
      iv   External benefits are greater than external costs.
   b From the point of view of society scarce resources are in their best use when:
      i   Social benefits exceed social costs.
      ii   Social benefits equal social costs.
      iii Social benefits are less than social costs.
      iv   Private benefits are greater than private costs.

4 Using the figures presented in the case study calculate:
   a The paint company's estimated yearly profit.
   b Whether or not paint production at the factory is worthwhile for society.

5 A conflict of interest between the paint company and the local community has arisen. How does this illustrate the central economic problem?

Group exercise

Divide into groups of eight or nine. One half of each group will play the role of the directors of the Non-drip paint company, while the other half are local community representatives.

1   The directors of the company prepare a report stating why they feel they are right to go ahead with the paint factory even if it does mean producing smoke. For example, the aim of the company is to make a profit because they have a duty to their shareholders.

2   The local community group prepares a report stating why they feel the paint factory should not locate in their area.

3   The company directors and local community representatives in each group now meet to read and discuss their reports. They must attempt to reach a solution to the conflict. If no solution is reached, the teacher may act as an arbitrator.

4   Each group's recommendations and findings are then reported back to the teacher.

In the above exercise, it can be recognised that the Non-drip paint company ignores any external costs and benefits. The company is only interested in making a profit, or **commercial return**, from producing paint. The result is that because social costs are greater than the social benefits of paint production society is worse off. In fact, private and external costs (£5 million + £6 million) exceed private and external benefits (£6 million + £3 million) by £2 million each year.

Whenever social costs are greater than social benefits, as in the example above, economists say that this represents an **uneconomic** use of resources. Society would be better off if the resources of land, labour and capital were used to make something else.

If social benefits are greater than social costs economists say that this represents an **economic** use of resources. Society would be better off if more resources were put into this use.

| **Section 2** | How the market can fail |

In our earlier example, the Chemix plastics-making company found it profitable to use resources to make plastics near the River Eden. In a market economic system this should be the best use of resources for everyone. Yet because of external costs, society is worse off for using resources in this way. Chemix and the market system have therefore failed to use resources efficiently from society's point of view.

In fact, whenever external costs and external benefits exist, the market system will not make the best use of scarce resources. This is because private firms in the market economic system only decide what, how and for whom to produce simply by looking at private costs and benefits, and their profits.

If production of a good or service results in high social costs, society would be better off without it. If, on the other hand, the production of a good or service results in high social benefits, society is better off by having more. For example, society may benefit from having more parks and open spaces, but a private firm may not find it profitable to provide these in a market economic system. To try and correct the failure of the market system to make the best use of scarce resources from society's point of view, governments often try to affect the way in which private firms use resources.

An uneconomic use of resources?

An economic use of resources?

Section 3 | How can the Government help?

Taxation

It is possible to make firms consider the external costs of their actions by taxing them. For example, an oil refinery may pump smoke and chemical waste into the atmosphere, damaging laundry, plants and buildings. The refinery ignores these external costs because it does not have to pay for the damage. However, a government may be able to make them pay for the damage by taking extra tax from them to cover the costs of repair.

The USA, Hungary and France use pollution taxes, but most countries do not. This is because it is very difficult to work out exactly how much pollution each firm in an area is responsible for. Imagine the problems a government would face trying to put a money cost to a factory that just 'spoilt the scenery'! How much is a nice view worth?

However, the UK Government has been increasing taxes on petrol to discourage car use in an attempt to reduce pollution from exhaust fumes, and has introduced a landfill tax to encourage firms to reduce waste.

Subsidies

Private sector firms are not interested in producing external benefits for others because they are not paid for them. For example, a bus company may find it unprofitable to provide buses for people after the rush hour because not enough people use the service then. However, for those people who do use the buses at these times they benefit from a means of transport. Many old people and schoolchildren travel at off-peak times. To help the bus company provide buses they could be given a subsidy. A subsidy is a payment of money given by a government to a firm. Subsidies are given to firms in order to encourage them to produce goods and services that result in external benefits.

Nationalization

Some industries produce large external benefits. By taking over the ownership and running of a whole industry a government can allow nationalized

industries to act in the public interest, and take account of any external costs and benefits they cause (see Chapter 5).

In the past, the UK national railways were a nationalized industry called British Rail. The UK Government subsidized British Rail to keep loss making lines open for people living in remote areas so that they enjoyed the social benefit of having a rail service. It also encouraged people to commute into cities to work by rail rather than by car by keeping rail fares low.

One difficulty with subsidizing loss making rail services was that British Rail managers and staff had little pressure on them to work efficiently and make a profit. As a result, losses and subsidies may have been even greater than had rail services been run by private sector firms. In order to improve efficiency UK railways were privatized in the mid 1990s. Private sector firms like Virgin Rail and Stagecoach now run passenger rail services in the UK in order to make a profit. However, the UK Government still pays these firms some subsidies to run loss making lines in remote areas.

Legal action   A government can simply pass laws in order to control firms creating external costs. For example, in the UK there are a large number of anti-pollution laws stating exactly which chemicals can be released into the air and which cannot. There are also laws on how high factory chimneys can be, where waste can be disposed of and how it should be done. Firms who break these laws can be fined or their owners can even be imprisoned.

Exercise 2   Lead in petrol

Lead is added to petrol in order to increase the performance of car engines. This lead finds its way into the atmosphere from car exhaust fumes and is responsible for 95% of the lead content in the air.

Studies show that lead is a strong poison which can badly affect the brain, heart and kidneys. Evidence suggests that lead from car exhausts causes most harm to young children in city areas.

Because of this evidence, petrol companies are required by the government to produce lead-free petrol and all cars must run on lead-free fuel.

1   What are the external costs of using lead in petrol?

2   Apart from banning lead in petrol, are there any other means a government can use to encourage petrol companies to stop using lead? Explain your answer.

3   What are the likely effects of requiring cars to be manufactured so that they can run on lead free petrol on

   a   Producers
   b   Consumers?

4   'Banning lead in petrol would be the right decision from society's viewpoint as long as the use of lead is uneconomic.' Explain this statement and say how a government could work out whether the use of lead is uneconomic or not.

Exercise 3

The Mytown Public Transport Corporation

Mytown public transport is owned by the Mytown council. The Transport Corporation has been asked to act in the 'public interest' and to keep fares low.

By keeping fares low the Mytown Transport Corporation cannot cover its costs and loses £100 000 each year. To keep the buses running the Corporation is given a subsidy by the council.

The council raises the money for the subsidy from local rates. Rates are a tax on property, with those people living in large, expensive flats and houses paying more rates than others.

Because fares are low, most people use the buses and very few people drive into the town centre in their cars. This has resulted in great social benefits. Yet trouble is brewing!

Divide into groups of four or five.

You are groups of economists employed by the council to study the costs and benefits of the transport service in Mytown. Study the information provided and together provide reports for the council on your conclusions. Questions are given to guide you when you are preparing your reports. When you have finished, elect a representative to read your reports to the whole class.

Costs and benefits of subsidizing Mytown transport

Income and Expenditure Account Mytown Bus Corporation			
	Costs		**Revenue**
Bus operating costs	£150 000	Bus fares	£150 000
Other costs	£100 000	Subsidy	£100 000
	£250 000		£250 000

Problem 1

The ratepayers of Mytown are angry. Many of them object to having to pay what they feel to be high rates in order to subsidize the losses of Mytown Transport Corporation.

Some of the wealthier ratepayers have formed an action group to put pressure on the council to cut the subsidy and so cut the rates. They claim that there is no valid reason why they should have to subsidize public transport when they get no benefit from it.

A joint committee of ratepayers and councillors has hired an independent team of economists to investigate and report on these claims. The economists' brief is to discuss whether or not the wealthy ratepayers, who mainly use private transport, are correct in assuming that there are no benefits to them in paying for public transport.

Questions for guidance report 1

1 When ratepayers are considering whether or not they benefit from subsidized public transport, what types of cost and benefit are they likely to be thinking about?

2 If the subsidy was removed and fares raised, what effects would this have on the use of private transport?

3 What costs might this involve for people who use private transport? (**Hint** time to get to work, pollution, accidents, etc.)

4 Are these costs considered in question 1? How do they differ?

5 What types of benefit do private transport users receive from subsidized public transport?

Problem 2

The ratepayers are still unhappy. They believe that the council is operating the transport service at a loss and is therefore acting outside its powers. After all, the empowering act says that the service must run economically! The Transport Corporation is losing money, so the ratepayers claim that this cannot be economic. You must meet this time to report on the true meaning of 'economic' and must establish whether or not Mytown Transport Corporation is economic.

In reporting, you have tried to put a money value on the external benefits from public transport. However, like all good economists you disagree! Your team is split in two about the appropriate value of these benefits. The two different views, A and B below, represent the two different bases for the reports.

A(£)		B(£)
20 000	Value of increased road speeds	25 000
15 000	Reduced pollution	30 000
10 000	Better health and fewer accidents	20 000
10 000	Less road maintenance	30 000
55 000		105 000

External costs arising from transport are assumed to be zero.

Questions for guidance report 2

1 The commercial cost of subsidizing Mytown Transport Corporation is £100 000, but what other costs and benefits are involved?

2 Do commercial estimates of the value of a business take these costs and benefits into account?

3 What is the meaning of an economic service?

4 Setting all costs against all benefits, is Mytown transport an economic service?

The Mytown conclusion

The ratepayers who use Mytown transport will only consider the fares they pay and the rates they pay to subsidize the service. The benefit of not having to use their car and paying for parking space will also be in their minds. If fares were raised, however, many of them might be tempted to use their cars instead of the buses. Many more cars on the road will lead to congestion, fumes and perhaps more accidents. Clearly, the ratepayers do not realize the great external benefits of less congestion, faster journey times, less risk of accidents, and less pollution that result from the bus service.

In commercial terms the bus corporation loses £100 000, but if it was closed down the external benefits would be lost. Trying to value these benefits is not easy and the economists have disagreed. One group of economists have agreed that the benefits of less pollution, fewer accidents, etc., save Mytown £55 000. The other group values these benefits at £105 000. The two groups of economists would calculate whether or not the service is economic in the following way.

Group A		**Group B**	
Private costs	£250 000	Private costs	£250 000
External costs	£ 0	External costs	£ 0
Total cost to Mytown	£250 000	Total cost to Mytown	£250 000
Private benefits, i.e., fares	£150 000	Private benefits, i.e., fares	£150 000
External benefits	£ 55 000	External benefits	£105 000
Total benefits to Mytown	£205 000	Total benefits to Mytown	£255 000
– All benefits (social benefits)	£205 000	– All benefits (social benefits)	£255 000
All costs (social costs)	£250 000	All costs (social costs)	£250 000
= Loss for Mytown	–£ 45 000	= Profit for Mytown	+£ 5 000
Answer: Uneconomic use of resources		Answer: Economic use of resources	

For Group B the private and external benefits exceed all other costs and so the transport service represents an economic use of resources for society. It is therefore of benefit to the Mytown ratepayers to pay extra rates to subsidize the transport corporation. Group A, however, suggests that all benefits are still less than all costs and the resources used to run the service would be of more benefit to society if they were used to do something else.

Section 4   Opportunity cost revisited

In Chapter 1 we discovered that because of scarcity we must choose what to do with scarce resources, and in choosing one use we must give up another. The benefit of the next best alternative given up is known as the opportunity cost.

For example, if we use land, labour and capital to build a motorway we may have to go without ten new schools. In Chapter 1 we would have said that the opportunity cost of the motorway is the ten schools given up.

But the real opportunity cost of the motorway is not just the ten schools foregone, it is also the peace and quiet, fresh air and attractive countryside that have also been given up.

The opportunity cost, or the benefit of the next best alternative foregone, therefore, always includes any external costs that occur. If opportunity cost did not include these costs, it would not be a true measure of what has been gone without.

Exercise 4   Car crash

When a person is injured in a car accident it often costs the taxpayer many thousands of pounds. This is because the taxpayer must pay for the injured person's stay in hospital and the medical care they receive. The injured will also receive sickness benefits from the Government.

Look at the picture of the accident and, in pairs, list as many private costs to the injured people, and as many external costs, that is costs to society, that have or will result from the accident. After ten minutes compare your list with another group's.

Exercise 5   Belt up!

Mary Cummings was an economics student at college and now works for a bank. She was injured in a car accident and has just spent six months in hospital. Mary would not have been hurt if she had worn a seat-belt.

Mary decides to work out the opportunity cost of not wearing her seat-belt. She values the wages she has lost over six months at £12 000 and she values her lost social life at £4 000. Mary calculates that the opportunity cost of not wearing her seat-belt is £16 000.

1   What is meant by opportunity cost?

2   What has Mary missed out in calculating the opportunity cost of not wearing her seat-belt?

3   'Wearing a seat-belt is up to me to decide. It's my life and if I get hurt in an accident it affects nobody else.' This is often said by car drivers, but would an economist agree with them? Explain your answer and say whether or not you agree that wearing a seat-belt should be law.

Section 5   How consumers' decisions affect others

So far we have only considered how firms' decisions to produce goods and services can affect society as a whole. However, we will now look at how people's decisions to consume goods and services can affect others. Consider the following examples.

Loud music
The boy in the picture likes playing his records very loudly. The only problem is that his neighbours don't like loud music and are upset by the noise. The boy's decision to consume noisy records has imposed an external cost on other people.

Vaccinations
The girl in the picture is looking forward to her holiday in a hot, foreign country. However, before she can go she must protect herself from some of the diseases she may catch in that country. In the picture she is seen having a vaccination.

This will prevent her from catching a disease. It also protects a great many other people because if the girl had caught the disease she would pass it on to others when she returned from her holiday. Her decision to have a

vaccination has therefore protected the rest of society from the disease. This consumption has resulted in an external benefit.

Litter

The man in the picture has just finished a packet of cigarettes. Instead of placing it in a bin he has carelessly discarded it on the pavement. Litter is unsightly to many people. This is an external cost resulting from others' consumption. Furthermore, society must bear the cost of cleaning up the rubbish.

Exercise 6   Smoking

Look at the picture of a man smoking in a cafe.

1   Give three private costs that a cigarette manufacturer will have to pay.

2   How will the manufacturer calculate the total revenue from the sale of cigarettes?

3   How are other people in the cafe affected by the man's decision to consume a cigarette?

4   In order to protect non-smoking passengers from the external costs that arise from smokers' decisions to smoke on trains, smoking has now been banned by the London Underground authorities. What sort of things will the authorities have to pay for in order to stop smoking?

5   Research has shown that smoking can damage your health.
    a   What is the opportunity cost of increased health spending on treating smokers?
    b   Who will bear the cost of increased health spending?

6   Imagine that the government decides to increase the tax payable on a packet of cigarettes. What affect may this have on:
    a   The number of cigarettes consumed.
    b   The revenue of cigarette-makers.
    c   The workers in cigarette factories?

Exercise 7   Grinding to a halt

> ## London and the Car – facing the 21st Century together
>
> Hemmed in by other traffic, halted by thickening jams and unrelenting roadworks, harried by mounting regulations, harassed by rising costs, hounded by environmental reformers – there are plenty of reasons why the London motorist could logically be considered a threatened species. We all know it, driving in the capital has been getting worse for years.
>
> With 14 million vehicle trips into London every day, London commercial experts calculated that traffic jams put 25p on every London gas bill, 25p on the weekly food bill, 25p on a typical item of clothing, 50p on a typical cab ride and the likelihood of an important letter being 24 hours late.
>
> Firms need 20% more vehicles and 20% more drivers to offset the toll of congestion in the capital, fuel costs are ten per cent higher than elsewhere and total cost penalties related to delivery times are a staggering 30 percent higher within the M25 than outside it.
>
> Six leading companies estimate that serving London with its amazing traffic complexities costs them a total of £30 million a year in extra administrative and delivery costs and London is a fifth more expensive to do business in than any comparable conurbation.

The article above suggests there are significant costs to Londoners caused by heavy traffic congestion.

1 Explain how traffic congestion could put the price of food, clothing and gas up.

2 Given these huge external costs, why do you think that people still use their cars on London roads?

3 Options the UK Government could consider to reduce car use and the external costs it causes include:

- a ban on car use in London

- charging car users in London an additional licence fee

- significantly increasing taxes on petrol.

In groups discuss what impacts (good and bad) these policies might have on:

- car use, congestion and pollution

- use of public transport

- business location

- car manufacturers

- wage demands.

| Section 6 | Cost benefit analysis |

If a particular use of resources is to be economic, then all benefits, private and external, must be greater than all the costs resulting from that use.

The problem is how to value external costs and benefits. Economists do this by using **cost benefit analysis (CBA)**.

Using CBA, economists attempt to change external costs, such as pollution, and external benefits, such as increased employment, into some common measure for comparison. Often this measure is money. For example, in building a new power station private costs and external costs may total £100 million, while the private and external benefits total £10 million. Therefore, this use of resources will be considered economic. However, some economists may disagree on the value placed on the external costs and benefits and, as a result, may find the use uneconomic. Because it is difficult to measure such external costs as 'a spoilt view' and external benefits, such as less traffic congestion because of a bus service, in terms of money, CBA can only really provide a guide to whether or not a use of resources is economic.

In using CBA there are many different ways of comparing costs and benefits. This can be seen in the example below about the costs and benefits of reducing speed limits on roads.

Case study

Exercise 8   Fast living: Lowering speed limits

In 1973 oil prices went up by five times the original price. Because of this the United States (US) Government decided to reduce the speed limit on American highways to 55 mph in order to try to save expensive fuel.

The main result was to reduce the number of deaths on roads from serious accidents. Economists have calculated that the reduced speed limit has saved 7500 lives each year.

However, the slower speed limit has also meant longer journey times. It was found that the extra time taken to travel added up to 456 300 man years.

The job of the economists was to work out whether or not the decision to cut the speed limit to 55 mph was economic. In other words, they had to work out if the benefit of 7500 lives saved was worth more than the cost of 456 300 man years lost.

The economists found that the average age of a US traffic accident victim was 33 years. This meant that each person killed would have, on average, lived for another 42 years. Thus, it was calculated that 7500 deaths worth 42 lost man years each, equals 315 000 lost years in total.

This means that if 7500 lives are saved each year, the US Government is saving 315 000 man years of time. However, by reducing speed limits to 55 mph 456 300 man years are lost each year in longer journey times. On this basis 7500 lives saved are worth less than the cost of the time wasted on journeys because cars must travel at slower speeds. Therefore, the cost of the reduced speed limit is greater than its benefits.

Adapted from Forester, McNown, Singell (1984), Southern Economic Journal

As a class discuss:

1   What is the purpose of cost benefit analysis?

2   What are the main external costs and benefits arising from the reduced speed limit on US highways?

3   How has the effects of a reduced speed limit affected:

    a   Producers
    b   Consumers
    c   Ordinary citizens?

4   How has the study discussed above placed a value on human lives? Can you think of any other ways we can try to place a value on life?

5 'However a person values other people's lives is purely a matter of opinion or value judgement.' Do you agree or disagree with this statement? Explain your answer.

6 If you agreed with the statement in question 5 that the value a person places on life is a matter of their own opinion, is the use of CBA in an example, such as the one above, of any use?

Key words

Write definitions to explain the following terms:

Private costs	**A commercial return**
Private benefits	**An economic use of resources**
External costs	**An uneconomic use of resources**
External benefits	**Subsidy**
Social costs	**Cost Benefit Analysis**
Social benefits	

Now return to the chapter to check your understanding of these terms.

Chapter 10

How Firms Behave and the Interests of Consumers

Aims

At the end of this chapter you should be able to:

1 Distinguish between the ways in which a firm can behave trying to reach a decision on what price to charge for its product and how much to produce.

2 Distinguish between **price** and **non-price competition**.

3 Define what is meant by **market structures**.

4 Understand the characteristics of **perfect competition** and why it gives rise to the best possible use of resources.

5 Define **monopoly** and explain how it differs from perfect competition.

6 Define and describe **barriers to entry**.

7 Understand why, and the ways in which, the government tries to control the behaviour of monopolies.

8 Define **monopolistic competition** and explain its main features.

9 Analyse the use of **advertising** to create demand.

10 Describe the various methods by which the law tries to protect consumers from the behaviour of some firms.

Section 1 | An introduction to competition

Firms will compete with each other to attract customers in a number of ways. Reducing the price of their products below the price of competing firms is one method which can boost sales and profits. This is known as **price competition**.

Firms may also engage in **non-price competition** by creating a want for their products by advertising or by offering free gifts, favourable credit terms when buying by instalments, etc.

Section 2 | Why study types of market structure?

A market consists of all the consumers and producing firms of a particular good or service. Firms will make decisions on what level of output to produce and at what price to sell their product for. The way in which a firm behaves in making these two basic decisions will depend on the type of market in which the firm is operating and the conditions it faces, for example, the number of firms it has to compete with. Some firms have a lot of power over the market charging what price they like for their output.

By looking at **market structures** we can analyse how much competition there is among firms making a particular product in an industry, and try to judge whether there is enough competition to ensure that consumers are not overcharged for the product and that they get what they want with the best possible use being made of resources.

Our job as economists is to look at how scarce resources are being used by firms to satisfy wants and to suggest better ways of doing this in order to try and satisfy more wants.

Before we can suggest improvements, we must find out how well firms are using scarce resources and know what the best possible use for scarce resources would be.

Section 3 | Perfect competition

Perfect competition suggests that the perfect or best use of resources is being made by firms in markets where they face many competing firms. The firms providing the best-quality goods and services at the lowest prices will be the most successful.

Competition between firms encourages them to make a good use of scarce resources, because in order to make profits these firms must produce products that give the best value for money for consumers. The greatest competition between firms in a market is found in a situation of perfect competition.

The characteristics of a perfectly competitive market

1 Homogenous product

All firms produce the same product (known as a homogenous product).

2 Price takers

There are a very large number of buyers and sellers of the product, none of whom can buy or sell enough to be able to influence the price of the product. Because buyers and sellers cannot affect the market price of the product, and have to accept that price, they are known as price takers.

3 Perfect information

All buyers will know all about the prices and products on sale, and all sellers have all the information on the latest production techniques. That is, buyers and sellers are said to have perfect information.

4 Freedom of entry and exit

Firms can freely enter or leave the industry if they wish. That is, there are no **barriers to entry or exit**. If existing firms in the market are making a profit, then other firms will be tempted to make the same products as them in the hope of earning profits for themselves.

There are no perfectly competitive industries in the world. No industry has all of the four features listed above, although certain industries have some of them. For example, in the manufacture of clothes there are a large number of small firms producing products which have the same basic designs. In agriculture, for example, wheat production, there are lots of small farms acting as price takers, where no single farmer can produce enough to be able to charge what price s/he would like. Many industries made up of a large number of small firms have few barriers to entry and exit. There are, however, no industries in the world that have perfect information.

However, simply because there are no perfectly competitive industries in the world does not mean that there is no point studying perfect competition. This is because perfect competition gives the perfect use of scarce resources. If we are to judge how good or bad firms are at using scarce resources we must be able to say how close, or far, they are from being perfect in the economic sense. This is why we must know about perfect competition.

Why does perfect competition make the best use of scarce resources?

1 Low prices

Competition between firms to make profits means that prices to consumers are as low as possible to attract their custom.

2 Efficiency

Only the best firms making the best value-for-money products will survive. Firms using scarce resources to make poor-quality products will be forced out of business so that their resources can be better used elsewhere.

3 Consumer sovereignty

Under perfect competition there is consumer sovereignty, that is, the consumer gets what s/he wants.

Exercise 1   The consumer gets what the consumer wants

Consider the following example of an economy where there is perfect competition among firms producing computers.

1 Imagine there is a rise in consumers' demand for computers. What will happen to the market price of computers? Can you use a market demand and supply diagram to illustrate this?

2 What will happen to the profits of computer-producing firms?

3 Using your knowledge of resource allocation in a free market economy, what will happen to the number of firms in the computer industry?

4 Given your answer to question 3, what do you think will happen to the output of computers and what will be the effect on their market price?

5 Given your answer to question 4, what will start to happen to the profits of computer-producing firms?

6 Given the initial rise in consumers' demand for computers in question 1, have consumers got what they wanted?

7 The answers to the questions above should illustrate how the consumer is sovereign in conditions of perfect competition. However, do you think the market for computers is a good example of a perfectly competitive industry?

If consumers want to buy computers they will attempt to purchase them and the forces of demand will force up their price and as a result will raise profits of firms making these computers. Because of the freedom of entry and exit into the market, some new firms outside the industry will observe that prices and profits are rising for firms in the computer-making industry and will want to enter the market and produce computers to sell and make profits. As the supply of computers increases, the price of them will start to fall again, and so too will the profits of the firms in the industry. Eventually, profits will fall to a level just high enough to keep existing firms in the industry, but not high enough to attract any new firms in search of high profits. In this situation, firms in the industry are said to be earning a **normal profit**.

The result of this is that there are many more firms in the industry and, as a whole, it produces a higher output. Resources have been allocated to the production of computers because this is what consumers wanted.

If, on the other hand, consumers want less of a product, the fall in demand will force prices and profits down. Some firms will leave the industry in search of higher profits elsewhere. As firms leave and the supply of the product falls, so prices and profits will rise again until the remaining firms are earning enough profit to make them stay in the market. That is, they are earning a normal profit once again.

The result is that there are now fewer firms in the industry and, as a whole, it produces a lower output. Resources have moved out of the industry into the production of other goods and services because this is what consumers wanted.

Under perfect competition resources are allocated to the production of goods and services that consumers want. In this way, consumers are sovereign.

| **Section 4** | Monopoly |

We have seen that competition among many small firms to achieve the best use of resources, known as perfect competition, is unlikely to exist in the real world. What is more likely is a number of large firms able to have some control over the price they charge for their product. The opposite extreme to perfect competition is a situation of **monopoly**. A firm is a pure monopoly if it is the only supplier of a particular good or service. For example, Railtrack is the sole supplier of rail network in Great Britain. However, there are very few pure monopolies but many firms have significant market power. Under European and UK law a monopoly is defined as any firm, or group of firms acting together, supplying 40% or more of a market.

A small group of large firms may agree to work together to become a type of monopoly, trying to keep their prices and all their profits high. Their cooperation amounts to the setting up of what is called a **cartel** or price-fixing ring of firms. They will agree not to compete with each other on prices but will use non-price competition, such as advertising or the offer of free gifts, to try and attract consumers away from the other firms.

Where a handful of large companies are able to control the supply of a commodity to a market they are known as **oligopolies**. These type of firms can be found to exist in many markets, for example, oil companies, the banks, soaps and detergents.

Oil companies are an example of an oligopoly

Features of a monopoly

1 No competition
Being the only supplier of a good or service a monopoly faces no competition from other firms.

2 Abnormal profits
Because there is no competition, the monopolist is able to permanently earn high profits, often known as abnormal profits, way above the profits the firm could earn producing another product in a different market.

3 Price makers
A monopolist is not a price taker. Because the monopolist produces all of a particular good or service for a market it can raise the price of its product by supplying less of it.

4 Barriers to entry
In perfect competition if firms earned profits greater than normal profits other firms would want to earn these profits as well. They would enter the market and start up production. Prices and profits would fall back to normal as supply increased.

Monopolists, however, can keep their large profits by preventing new firms from entering their market and taking some of their abnormal profits. Monopolists do this by creating barriers to entry.

5 Imperfect information

Under monopoly there is not perfect information. For example, a firm may hide the price it charges to one group of consumers from another group which is charged a different price.

6 Non-homogenous products

Monopolist firms often do not produce a homogenous product. Usually they will produce different varieties of their product in order to make it difficult for other firms to copy them.

Exercise 2 Fighting for the skies

 # "It won't be a monopoly"
(Pigs might fly.)

In the last few weeks, British Airways (BA) and American Airlines' (AA) intended 'alliance' has been met with considerable criticism from the travel industry and from other airlines.

That's not because the industry is opposed to an airline alliance to manage air passengers and fill up empty seats across their jets. It's because many believe the BA/AA alliance is much more than just an alliance; it is seen as a massive monopoly that could damage the airline industry far more than it benefits from it. And now it seems the Director General of the Office of Fair Trading may also have some concerns. Last week he announced the alliance amounted to a merger and may have to be investigated. If this does take place Virgin Atlantic will be fascinated to see how BA and AA justify their scheme.

But it won't be a monopoly . . .
If BA and AA were to argue this we doubt they would get much joy. BA is the biggest international airline in the world. American Airlines is the world's second biggest.

As the chart shows, together they would exert massive control over flights to and

BA & AA NORTH ATLANTIC MARKET SHARE	
LONDON · NY KENNEDY	70.8%
LONDON · LOS ANGELES	59.76%
LONDON · MIAMI	76.53%
LONDON · BOSTON	60.26%
LONDON · CHICAGO	94.15%
LONDON · DALLAS	100%

from the USA, and over 12 million passengers each year. How then could BA and American deny that they are forming a monopoly when their combined share of key North Atlantic routes is between 60% and 100%?

But it will be good for customers . . .
BA and AA argue that by jointly managing their airline fleets they can increase flight frequencies, in-flight service levels and make savings which they can pass onto passengers as lower fares. But people know only too well that monopolies tend not to be good for the consumer. In the last ten years, competition from smaller airlines like Virgin has brought air fares down in real terms by 40% and has forced other airlines, including BA to improve

their levels of service.

Errr ... it's a monopoly that benefits other airlines
Again we doubt this. BA are claiming that the 'open skies' concession they are making in return for immunity against American anti-monopoly laws will be good for other airlines. 'Open skies' means, in theory, more US airlines will be able to fly into London Heathrow. But London Heathrow is already full and doesn't have the capacity to accept more flights.

BA and American will no doubt argue that their 'alliance' isn't a monopoly. So perhaps the final word on the matter should be given to Travel Trade Gazette, the trade paper of the travel industry who said:

'If BA and AA are allowed to use their massive political strength to railroad through a deal which leaves them in dominant positions, both the travel trade and the travelling public would lose out'

Or in other words, the 'alliance' must not be allowed to fly.

IF YOU WANT AN AIRLINE THAT LOOKS AFTER YOUR INTERESTS FLY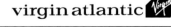

Adapted from a newspaper advertisement placed by the Virgin Atlantic airline in July 1996

Read the above advertisement and discuss with a partner what the advantages and disadvantages of an alliance between British Airways and American Airlines might be for **a** BA and American, **b** other airlines, and **c** air passengers. If you were the UK and US Governments, would you allow the alliance to go ahead? Give reasons for your answer.

How monopolies can prevent competition

Monopolies will try to prevent new firms from entering their market and taking a share of their profits by creating barriers to entry.

There are two main types of barriers to entry: **natural barriers** and **artificial barriers**.

Natural barriers to entry

Some firms naturally become monopolies because of:

1 Control of supply
A firm, or a small group of firms, may own most or all of the supply of a raw material. This means these firms will be the only suppliers; they are a monopoly.

2 Economies of scale
In some industries there are very large economies of scale or cost savings to be gained from increasing production.

If one large firm can produce and sell all of a particular product required in the market at a lower average cost per product than a number of smaller firms put together then this large firm would be a **natural monopoly**.

4 Expense
Some industries, for example, the Nuclear Power Industry, need many millions of pounds worth of equipment. This helps keep the nuclear power industry in the UK a monopoly, because most firms could not afford to start up in the nuclear power industry.

5 Legal considerations
Some firms can stay as monopolies because laws have been passed to make it illegal for other firms to start up in the same industry. This can happen when a firm invents a new product or method of production and prevents other firms from copying it by a patent.

Artificial barriers to entry

While some monopolies occur as a result of natural barriers to entry, other monopolies achieve their powerful position by creating their own artificial barriers to competition.

Exercise 3   Creating a barrier

Divide into groups. Each group should consider one of the following cases based on imaginary firms. You play the role of company directors of different monopolies and your task is to find barriers to entry to stop competition from other firms.

Report your findings to your shareholders (the rest of the class) who will then vote on whether or not to allow the directors to continue to manage the company.

Big Sell Supermarkets plc
You are the board of directors of a large supermarket in a town. There are very few other food shops in the town apart from some very small stores. The supermarket is supplied by a nearby wholesaler and is its single most important customer.

Your monopoly position ensures that the supermarket earns high profits. However, other firms know this and now want to set up large shops in the neighbourhood. The owners of the supermarket are worried about losing trade and profits to these new stores. They have asked the board of directors to find barriers to prevent new shops from setting up nearby. They are not concerned about how you do this.

As directors you must report on what you plan to do before the next Annual General Meeting of shareholders, when they will decide whether or not to re-elect you as directors.

Flyhigh Airlines

You are the directors of a large airline flying to countries all over the world.

A new airline company, Cut Price Atlantic, is about to start up with two planes flying on your route between America and Britain. Cut Price Atlantic intends to undercut your £150 fare by £40 for a one-way flight between the two countries.

Shareholders in Flyhigh Airlines are very anxious. They fear that the new company will make large profits on the route across the Atlantic and will be able to use these profits to buy more planes in order to start up cut-price flights on other routes as well.

Your task as directors is to stop the new airline from taking away custom from your company by devising barriers to entry. (**Hint**, your company operates many profitable routes throughout the world, so what can you afford to do to try and force Cut Price Airlines out of business? Remember, your failure to do so could mean your rejection as directors by shareholders at their next meeting.)

Spreadwell Limited

You are the board of directors of Spreadwell Limited. You hold a virtual monopoly in the market for margarine, producing nearly all of the well-known brands for sale in shops.

Spreadwell Limited relies heavily on television advertising to sell its products and will often help chains of supermarkets to publicize the sale of their margarines.

Because of your near monopoly position, Spreadwell earns high profits and shareholders are keen to protect them from new firms who wish to produce margarine.

As the board of directors you need to stop any new competition. Try to decide how you can set up barriers to entry. Your report must prove favourable to your shareholders.

Artificial barriers to entry
Companies can create artificial barriers to entry to new firms who are potential competitors. These are as follows:

1 Restrictions on supplies

New firms will only enter an industry if they can obtain supplies of raw materials. Monopoly firms can threaten their suppliers that if they supply any new firms, the monopoly will take its custom to another supplier. This is likely to work if there are only a few suppliers and if these suppliers rely heavily on the monopolist for business. For example, in the case of the Big Sell Supermarket, the store could threaten their wholesaler that if they supply any new shops in the area they will lose their largest customer.

2 Predatory pricing

Often monopolies are very profitable and sell a wide range of goods and services. New small companies attempting to compete with large monopolies will not be as profitable and are unlikely to be able to sell such a wide range of commodities.

In the Flyhigh Airlines example, the large company had routes all over the world and made many millions of pounds in profits. A small competitor could not afford to operate so many routes. In fact, Cut Price Airlines could only afford to buy two planes to operate on just one route.

The new company offered fares for £110, being £40 cheaper than Flyhigh Airlines. To stop this competition Flyhigh could afford to cut their flight fares on the Atlantic route even more to force Cut Price out of business. Flyhigh will lose money on this route by offering low fares but can afford to cover these losses from profits on other routes. Once Cut Price has been forced to close, Flyhigh can again raise its prices.

Predatory pricing occurs when a large firm cuts its prices, even if this means losing money in the short run, in order to force new and smaller competing firms out of business. Once the smaller firm has been removed, the larger firm can raise its prices again.

3 Exclusive dealing

Businesses that sell the products made by a monopolist rely heavily upon the monopolist for supplies. If the monopolist produces a well-known and popular good or service it gives them the power to threaten the firms selling its products. In the example of Spreadwell Limited, the firm was the main supplier of popular margarines in the country. Shops would make a lot of profit from selling well-known products like this. Spreadwell Limited can use this fact to threaten shops that if any of them sell any other company's margarine Spreadwell will no longer supply them with its well-established and popular brands. In this way, Spreadwell can prevent competition and maintain its monopoly position.

Refusing to sell to shops that stock other firms' brands of a similar product is known as exclusive dealing. This is often used by firms as a barrier to competition. Raleigh, the famous bicycle manufacturer, was found to be using this barrier to entry when they refused to supply large discount stores with Raleigh cycles in 1981.

Advantages of a monopoly

1 Economies of scale and natural monopolies

Some organizations, for example, the National Grid Company (NGC) which owns and manages the electricity supply grid in the UK, have natural monopolies. That is, average costs of production will continue to fall as output increases so that it is efficient for one large firm to be the only supplier in the market.

Clearly, in the case of the national electricity grid, it would be a waste of resources for each electricity supply company to provide its own network of transformers, pylons and cables to supply electricity to their customers. Imagine if you had five or more sets of cables running down your road and into your house from which you could choose from to buy electricity. Instead, there is just one national supply network through which all the different electricity supply companies sell their electricity.

For example, in the simple diagram below, the National Grid Company is able to move down the industry average cost curve to point A, because it operates the vast network of transformers, pylons and cables to transport generated electricity throughout the UK.

Average costs in the electricity national grid

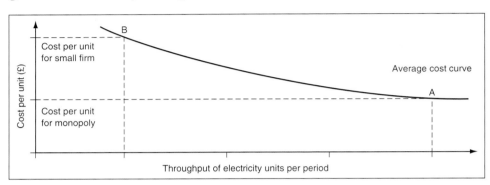

Other examples of natural monopolies in the UK might include Transco, which operates the UK network of gas pipelines, and Railtrack, which owns the national rail network. The gas, electricity and railway industries in the UK were all owned and managed by the government in the past. They have now been privatized but Transco, NGC and Railtrack remain monopolies because they are natural monopolies. Instead the UK Government regulates these organisations to make sure they do not exploit their customers and charge excessive prices.

2 Research and development
A feature of perfect competition is that new firms can freely enter a market in search of profits. Because of this freedom of entry it may not be worthwhile for an existing firm to risk a lot of money on developing new products or new production techniques. This is because any profits that this firm makes will soon be reduced as new firms enter the market and make the product using the new technique, thereby taking customers and profits away from them.

On the other hand, a monopoly may find it worthwhile to spend money on the research and development of new products and techniques, because it knows that it can earn high profits and keep these by using barriers to entry to stop new firms from competing with them and using their ideas.

3 Lower prices
A monopolist produces a very large output and can benefit from economies of scale. As a result, the average costs of production for the monopolist may be lower than a smaller competitive firm producing a lower output, and so

the monopolist can afford to charge consumers a lower price and still earn high profits.

4   The ability to compete in global markets
Some firms need to be large so that they have the financial, technological and marketing resources they need to compete against huge overseas firms.

Disadvantages of monopoly

Monopolies are often large powerful firms and fears are often expressed over their behaviour. While monopolies may give rise to certain advantages, it is the disadvantages of monopoly that have caused concern.

1   Poor levels of service
Monopolies face little competition. This means that monopoly firms do not have to worry very much about losing their customers to other firms. Because of this lack of competition, monopolies can sometimes be very inefficiently run and provide a poor service to their customers. For example, before the UK gas and electricity industries were privatized and competing companies were formed, many customers complained of the poor levels of service provided by these nationalized industries. Economists would argue this was because these industries did not have to compete for customers. Furthermore, because there is little competition, monopolies may not have to work very hard in order to earn their profits. Monopolies may be satisfied with what they are already selling and may not try to develop new ideas and products.

2   Low output and high prices
In order to try and make as much profit as possible, monopolies wish to charge a high price for their products. To do this, it is necessary to restrict the supply of their products in order to force up their market price.

3   Producer sovereignty
One important feature of perfect competition is that consumers decide what goods and services are to be produced with scarce resources. This is known as consumer sovereignty. However, under monopoly, consumers do not control how scarce resources are used. Instead, the monopoly firm will decide what goods and services to produce for consumers. When the producer has control over the use of scarce resources there is said to be **producer sovereignty**. This arises because monopolies prevent consumers from obtaining a wide range of goods and services by using barriers to entry to prevent competition.

Not only can monopoly producers control which goods and services are produced, they can also influence which goods and services consumers want through the use of advertising. Carefully-designed advertising makes people want goods and services that they would not otherwise buy. (The use of advertising in the creation of wants will be considered in section 6).

It is for these reasons that the producer, and not the consumer, is sovereign under conditions of monopoly.

Most goods and services today are produced in markets where the amount of competition is more than under monopoly but less than under perfect competition. This type of market is known as **monopolistic competition**.

The main characteristic of monopolistic competition is that similar, but not identical, goods are supplied by many different firms. For example, soaps and detergents are supplied by a number of different firms, but each firm's soaps and detergents are slightly different in price, smell, colour and, sometimes, quality. When there are lots of similar goods with slight differences between them, like soaps and detergents, we say there is **product differentiation**.

Monopolistic competition has features in common with both monopoly and perfect competition. Monopolistic competition is like monopoly because each firm has a monopoly in the production of its particular product. For example, the Bata shoe company has a monopoly in the production of its shoes simply because no other firm can produce shoes carrying this name. Indeed, every shoe manufacturer has a monopoly simply because no other company can produce shoes with the same name.

Monopolistic competition is like perfect competition because new firms are free to enter and exit from the industry. Freedom of entry and exit of new firms means that although each firm has a monopoly in its particular product, there is a lot of competition from firms producing similar products. Because of this, consumers will face a range of close substitutes to choose from, buying those that offer the best value in terms of price and quality. For example, if Bata shoes increase in price consumers may buy shoes from Barratts, Ravel or Dolcis instead.

Because of this competition, firms in monopolistic competition must find ways of stopping consumers from buying from rival producers. The main way in which firms in monopolistic competition attempt to beat their rivals is through advertising. By advertising, firms can create **brand names** or **brand images** for their products, for example, Dulux paints or Nescafé coffee. Firms try to strengthen their monopoly by creating differences in the minds of consumers between their product and those of other firms. This is achieved by differences in design and packaging of products as well as in the creation of brand names and trade marks. This is known as **branding**.

If, by advertising, a firm can convince consumers that its product is different or better than other products it can increase its sales. The demand curve for its product will shift outwards.

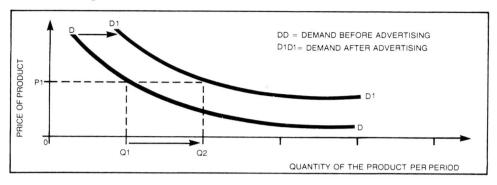

The effect of successful advertising on demand

Some advertising has been so successful that people use brand names of one company without knowing it to describe similar products made by other firms. For example, most people use the brand name SELLOTAPE to describe all types of clear sticky tape, and the brand name BIRO for all types of ball-point pen.

Exercise 4 Spot the trade mark

1 Choosing a name for a product is often as important as what is said about them in an advert, or the price and quality of them. What type of products are these brand names for?

Signal	Domestos	Flash	Cornetto
Bic	Goldenlay	BurgerKing	Radox
Tipp-ex	Horlicks	Crackerbarrel	Old Spice
Uhu	PG Tips	Wispa	Imperial Leather
Heineken	Brillo	Crunchie	Surf

2 Some products have such well-known trade marks or symbols that it is possible to advertise them without using words or pictures. How many of the following symbols can you recognize? What products do they advertise?

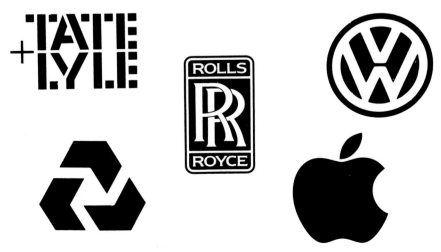

3 Can you think of some good brand names for the following products?

- a new chocolate and peanut bar
- a new perfume
- a new aftershave
- a new toothpaste
- a new car
- a new washing powder.

| Section 6 | Advertising |

One very important difference between monopolistic competition and perfect competition is the use of advertising in monopolistic competition and the absence of it in conditions of perfect competition. In fact, in 1998 a total of £14 308 million was spent on advertising by firms in the UK. The pie charts opposite show how this spending was divided up between the main forms of advertising in the UK.

Total advertising expenditure 1998

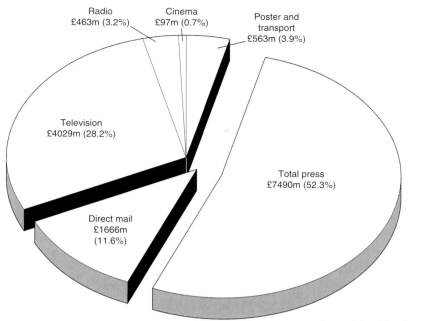

Radio £463m (3.2%)
Cinema £97m (0.7%)
Poster and transport £563m (3.9%)
Television £4029m (28.2%)
Total press £7490m (52.3%)
Direct mail £1666m (11.6%)

Source: Advertising Association

Exercise 5 Advertising – good or bad?

Firms can advertise in lots of ways, such as magazines, posters and even carrier bags, but one of the main forms of advertising is television. So, put your feet up in front of the TV and watch some adverts.

1 Watch a sample of about twenty TV adverts and try to decide whether each advert:

- is informative
- is trying to persuade people to buy
- makes meaningless statements
- promotes a brand image
- seems to suggest that buying the product will improve the quality of life
- is sexist or racist in any way.

Draw a table for twenty or more adverts like the one started below. Tick each one if you think it applies to the advert you are watching.

The product advertised	Inform?	Persuade?	Meaningless?	Exaggerated claims	Brand image	Quality of life	Sexist or racist
Yoghurt							
Soap							

Can you detect any patterns? Do most adverts try to inform or persuade? Do they make exaggerated claims? Promote a brand image?, etc.

2 The statements overleaf list possible advantages and disadvantages of advertising.

215

Statement	Agree?	Disagree?	Reason
Advertising is expensive and puts prices up so the consumer pays in the end			
Advertising informs us about new goods and services			
Advertising is a nuisance on commercial radio and TV			
Advertising helps pay for sports events			
Advertising encourages people to borrow and get into debt			
Advertising informs people about things they should know, e.g., health adverts			
Advertising increases sales and creates jobs			
Advertising helps mass production and so lowers costs			
Advertising makes people want things that they do not need			
Advertising keeps the cost of newspapers and magazines down			
Advertising encourages competition between firms and so the public get a better deal			
Advertising preys on people's weaknesses			

Copy the table of statements and tick whether you agree or disagree with them. Give your reasons why in the fourth column.

3 Compare your thoughts on task 2 above to those of another person in your class. Do you agree or disagree? Try to establish the reasons why. Do you think advertising is good or bad? What does your class think as a whole?

Persuasive and informative advertising

Few people would criticize advertisements that give information about new products or information about health and safety. Advertisements which give information to the public are known as **informative advertising**. Informative advertising increases consumer choice by making consumers aware of the range of goods and services available to them.

However, much advertising tries to persuade people to buy things rather than inform them. **Persuasive advertising** is designed to create a want for a product that consumers would not necessarily buy. However, it is illegal to be misleading in an advertisement.

Advertising: persuasive or informative?

Advertising may be used to persuade people to believe things which may not be true and to buy expensive branded products when cheaper ones are available. It is for these reasons that persuasive advertising is sometimes criticized as being wasteful.

Section 7	Competition policy

Most firms that aim to make a profit compete with rival producers in an attempt to get more customers and become the dominant supplier of a product. As a dominant supplier a firm has more control over the price it can charge to consumers. If a firm, or group of firms acting together, can see off existing competition and establish barriers to entry to new competition, it may then abuse this market power by misleading consumers, cutting product quality and raising prices in order to make huge profits.

Governments can try to protect consumers against **anti-competitive practices** and the abuse of monopoly power by passing laws to control the behaviour of firms and make sure they act in the 'public interest'.

Exercise 6 Colas, cars and controls

Coca-Cola raided by European Union officials

Officials from the European Commission have raided Coca-Cola offices in three countries in an attempt to establish whether the soft drinks group has violated competition rules, it emerged last night.

Commission officials seized internal company documents from Coca-Cola offices in Germany, Austria and Denmark on Tuesday in a series of dawn raids. Authorities also took records from three Coca-Cola bottlers, one of which is based in London.

A Coca-Cola spokesperson said 'We can confirm that the European Commission made unannounced visits to several of our offices and the offices of some of our bottling partners. Their purpose was to review internal files relating to commercial practices with retailers and other customers'.

The Commission is said to be concerned that Coke has been abusing its dominant position by offering retailers incentives to increase sales volumes, forcing them to stock the full range of Coca-Cola drinks and to stop selling competitors' products.

Officials launched the raids after a tip-off, although the Commission refused to confirm reports that Coca-Cola's rivals had launched formal complaints about the soft drinks group's commercial practices. Commission competition investigations are frequently triggered by complaints from rivals.

Coca-Cola was last night adamant that it had done nothing wrong. The company said "We believe we are within full compliance of all competition laws and regulations and we are co operating fully with the authorities."

If the company is found to have abused its dominant position, it could be fined as much as 10 percent of its European turnover.

Volvo admits rigging prices

Volvo has admitted rigging the prices of cars in Britain by restricting the level of discounts offered to customers. An investigation by the Office of Fair Trading (OFT) revealed that dealers were threatened with a loss of bonuses if they offered discounts beyond certain levels.

The secret price fixing agreement between March 1995 and early 1996 was condemned as a 'disgraceful case' by the Director General of the OFT. He said 'This demonstrates a blatant disregard for UK law and an indifference to the exploitation of customers'.

The OFT has accepted an undertaking from Volvo Cars UK, now a subsidiary of Ford, that it will not support price fixing cartels. Volvo said yesterday that the price-fixing was not a company policy but that a limited number of staff had acted against company policy by indicating support for dealer pricing agreements.

The Times, 10.7.1999 and 27.7.1999

1 In both cases describe why the two companies were acting against 'the public interest' and how they were being 'anti-competitive'.

2 What else could be done by governments, in addition to those actions reported in the articles, to control the anti-competitive behaviour of the two organizations?

The control of monopoly

Competition policy refers to any measures that can be taken by a government to control the behaviour of monopolies and dominant firms that are thought to be acting against the public interest:

1 Prohibition
Monopolies can be banned or forced to break up. For example, in the 1980s large UK beer breweries were forced to sell off many of the pubs they owned. This was because smaller brewers were unable to find pubs that would sell their beer. In this way the large brewers were restricting competition and customer choice.

2 Regulation
A government can allow a private sector monopoly to continue but pass laws to make sure it acts in the public interest. For example, in the UK the Office of the Rail Regulator (ORR) exists to regulate the behaviour of Railtrack, and the Office of Gas and Electricity Markets (Ofgem) regulates the prices and services of gas and electricity supply companies.

3 Imposition of fines
Fines can be imposed on firms who are thought to be abusing their market power and overcharging consumers.

Before any of these actions are taken it is important for a government to investigate each case of anti-competitive behaviour and then decide which action is appropriate. A monopoly doesn't necessarily have to be anti-competitive and bad for consumers.

For example, in 1976 Rank Xerox had a virtual monopoly in the supply of photocopiers with 96% of all sales in the UK. For every £1 it invested in its operations it made an extra 40 pence in profit. Rank Xerox was investigated by the UK Government but was found to be acting in the interests of consumers. This is because Rank Xerox was the first firm to develop and mass-produce photocopiers. Its high profits were a reward for the risk the company had taken by investing a huge amount of money in a revolutionary product. Similarly, recent mergers between large UK brewers like Bass and Carlsberg-Tetley were allowed to go ahead because the new larger firms will be able to compete more effectively against huge overseas brewers selling their beers into the UK, and move into rapidly growing markets for beer in Asia and South America.

Competition policy in the UK is put into practice by a number of key organizations:

The Office of Fair Trading
This important office was created by the Fair Trading Act of 1973. It is a Government Agency that watches and investigates the conduct of trade and protects the consumer against unfair or restrictive practices. The Office of Fair Trading (OFT) is run by the Director General of Fair Trading (DGFT).

The OFT collects information on, and makes surveys of, all types of trading practices used by firms. If the information reveals anti-competitive behaviour, the DGFT has the power to fine those firms responsible up to 10% of their annual sales revenues.

The Competition Commission
The Competition Commission was set up by the Competition Act 1998. It came into force in March 2000 and took over the functions of the previous competition watchdog, the Monopolies and Mergers Commission, and Fair Trading Act inquiries into mergers and monopolies. It has the ability to ban behaviour which damages the intere.s of consumers or which abuses monopoly power.

Individuals and firms who are found guilty of anti-competitive behaviour by the DGFT can appeal to the Competition Commission and seek damages in the law courts if they believe that their reputation has been unfairly damaged or that they have been unfairly fined.

Industry Regulators
Following the privatizations of British Telecom, British Gas, the Electricity Area Boards, British Rail and the Regional Water Authorities in the UK the Government created a number of industry regulators. These organizations regulate prices and service quality in these industries because the private sector firms have considerable regional and national market power over the supply of their products. There are few substitutes for their services for consumers. As more competition is introduced into these industries regulation can be reduced.

Industry regulators		Regulate . . .
OfTel	Office of Telecommunications	Telecommunications Industry
OfWat	Office of Water Regulation	Water supply
Ofgem	Office of Gas and Electricity Markets	Gas and electricity generation and supply
ORR	Office of the Rail Regulator	Railtrack plc
SRA	Strategic Rail Authority	Passenger rail services

The European Commission
The European Commission has the power to investigate and take action against companies thought to be operating anti-competitive practices in more than one European Union member country (see Chapter 18).

Section 8 | Consumer protection

Caveat emptor

Consumer protection is about helping consumers to get a fair deal when they buy goods and services.

One hundred years ago, there was very little consumer protection. The basis of the law relating to the sale and advertising of goods and services was known as *caveat emptor*, or 'let the buyer beware'. That is, consumers bought things at their own risk. They could not complain about or return faulty goods, or refuse payment for services they were not satisfied with.

Government protection

With so many billions of goods and services on sale it is impossible for consumers to have all of the technical knowledge needed to inspect goods, such as computers, cars, electrical appliances, etc., or be aware of what standard of service to expect in, for example, hotels or hospitals.

More than ever before consumers must rely on firms for information and advice on what to buy. Because of this, governments have acted to try and protect consumers from dishonest traders.

The Government has passed a number of laws to protect consumers. This has changed the law from caveat emptor to caveat vendor, or 'let the seller beware'!

Consumer protection laws

1   The Sale of Goods Act 1979 (and Sale and Supply of Goods Act 1994)

This act has three main parts:

a   Goods must be in satisfactory condition. This means goods must work properly, not be flawed in any way, and be of a reasonable quality for the price charged.

b   Goods must be fit for the purpose they were made for and this must be made known by the seller. For example, if you asked a shop for a pair of trousers that could be machine washed and not have to be dry-cleaned, then the pair of trousers the shop sells you must be machine washable.

c   Goods must fit the description given of them. For example, if a box of matches is said to contain 250 matches, then it should not contain any less.

If any of these conditions are broken the shopkeeper must refund the consumer's money. The consumer could agree to take a replacement but does not have to accept a credit note. These are notes which allow the consumer to buy another good some time in the future, up to the value of the one bought before, but only in the same shop. Consumers' rights are not affected by notices saying 'no refunds'.

2 The Food Safety Act 1990

The main purpose of this act is to ensure that all foods on sale are pure and wholesome. The act states that all food must be prepared and sold in hygienic conditions. Food must not contain ingredients known to be harmful to people and all pre-packed foods must display a list of contents. The act also forbids advertising that can mislead people about the nature of food.

3 Consumer Protection Act 1987

This is the main act covering consumer safety. The law makes it a criminal offence for producers to supply goods that are unsafe. It also makes it an offence to give misleading information on prices.

4 Weights and Measures Act 1963

This act states that most pre-packaged products should show the quantity of the contents, for example, by weight or volume. It is an offence not to display this information, or to give consumers short weight.

Certain products can only be sold in fixed amounts, for example, milk must be sold in pints, litres, etc.

5 Trade Descriptions Act 1968 (and 1972)

This act provides many different sorts of protection. It is now illegal to wrongly describe a good or service. Spoken as well as written lies break the law. For example, it is an offence to describe a sweater as 100% wool when it has only a 75% wool content. Under this act a number of farmers were prosecuted in 1998 for describing their cattle as coming from BSE free herds.

Furthermore, most goods must be marked clearly with the name of the country in which they were made.

It is also an offence under this act to offer goods at cheaper sale prices if they have not been on sale at the higher normal price for at least 28 days before the sale. For example, a hi-fi shop is offering a stereo amplifier for sale at £90 in its January sales. A week earlier it sold the amplifiers for £100 each, but on this week's price tag it has the previous price stated as £150 and the new sale price of £90 written in its place. This illegal practice tries to make consumers believe they are getting a bargain.

6 Property Misdescription Act 1991

The main legislation for dealing with false descriptions, the Trade Descriptions Act, has never applied to descriptions of land or property, only to goods. So for instance, a house described by an estate agent as being in a quiet secluded area when in fact it was on a main road would not have been covered by the Trade Descriptions Act. Because of concerns about the number of inaccurate descriptions applied to property the Director General of Fair Trading recommended the Property Misdescription Act of 1991.

7 The Unsolicited Goods and Services Act 1971

If a consumer receives a good through the post that they did not want it is an offence for a trader to demand payment for it. If the consumer contacts the supplier and asks them to collect the goods and they fail to do so within thirty days then they become the legal property of the consumer. If the consumer does not contact the supplier then the goods become the consumer's property after six months.

8 The Fair Trading Act 1973

The Fair Trading Act is designed to protect consumers against restrictive trade practices. These unfair practices are investigated by the Director-General of Fair Trading.

The Office of Fair Trading does not deal with individual complaints from consumers, but instead published information on consumer rights, encourages businesses to improve their own standards by publishing codes of practice and suggests new consumer protection laws.

9 The Consumer Credit Act 1974

This act protects consumers when they buy goods or services on credit. It also controls the behaviour of money lenders and debt collectors. These people and their organizations must obtain a licence from the government in order to give credit or lend money to the public. In order to keep this licence, money lenders must always be honest and truthful with the public and not overcharge them when giving credit.

When a consumer enters into a credit or hire purchase agreement, they are allowed to cancel it and return the goods within twelve days.

Consumer aids As well as there being a number of laws that help protect consumer interests there are also a number of consumer aid organizations that can give help.

Local consumer organizations

1 Citizens Advice Bureau
The Citizens Advice Bureau is a national voluntary organization run by the Government.

It gives advice on personal, as well as consumer problems.

2 Local newspapers
These may also give advice and information to consumers.

I ONLY CAME IN FOR A PLASTER

3 Consumer advice centres
These centres give advice on consumer problems and will inform consumers of goods and services available and what prices to expect.

4 Trade associations
If a firm belongs to a trade association, consumers can ask the association for help and guidance. Examples include the Retail Motor Industry Federation and the Federation of Master Builders.

5 Community health centres
These centres deal with complaints against doctors and health treatment in hospitals.

6 Environmental health departments
These departments investigate food-serving conditions in shops, restaurants, canteens, etc. They also investigate safety conditions, the general cleanliness of living and working conditions, and pollution by noise or fumes, etc.

7 Trading standards departments
These are sometimes called consumer protection departments. Trading standards officers in the departments are employed by local councils to enforce consumer protection laws.

National consumer organizations

1 British Standards Institution
This is an independent body, financed partly by a Government grant, which lays down minimum standards of quality, performance, etc., in the manufacture of consumer goods. Where standards are met the BSI will award the product a kite-mark which is a symbol of quality for consumers.

2 Law centres
Law centres provide free legal advice from qualified lawyers.

3 Consumer and Consultative Councils
These are sponsored by the Government to look after the interests of consumers of public services such as gas, water and electricity. It publishes reports that can be used for consumer information.

4 Advertising Standards Authority
This deals with complaints about advertising.

5 Consumers Association

This publishes a number of magazines with the title 'WHICH?'. For example, *Money Which? What Hi-Fi? Which Video? Holiday Which?*, etc.

These provide consumers with information and advice. It is a voluntary body financed by revenue from magazine sales.

Exercise 7 Illegal practices

Work in pairs and decide which of the following situations are illegal trading practices. Explain why they are illegal and which law can protect you in each case.

1 You buy a pair of trousers. You wash them but they shrink. The shop refuses to change them saying you washed them incorrectly.

2 You buy 2 kilogrammes of apples at a local market. At home you weigh them and find that they weigh only 1½ kilogrammes.

3 What you think is a free sample arrives on your doorstep. One week later a payment demand arrives.

4 For a Christmas present you receive a pocket electronic game. The aunt that bought it for you still has the receipt from the shop where she purchased it. The game gives off an electric shock.

5 You buy 1 kilogramme of potatoes from a greengrocer but she gives you 750 grammes instead.

6 You buy a video-recorder on hire purchase, but after one week you decide to return it to the shop and cancel the purchase agreement. The hire purchase company says you cannot do this.

7 A tin of baked beans displays the weight 1 kilogramme. After you have bought it you weigh the tin and contents. It does indeed weigh 1 kilogramme, but the tin weighs 200 grammes!

8 An advert on TV proclaims that a glue can bond together two halves of a car so that it is roadworthy once more.

Exercise 8 Dear Agony...

Imagine you are a consumer Agony Aunt or Uncle. Consumers write to you with their problems. Write replies to the following letters pointing out where they can seek more advice and help, and which laws, if any, can protect them.

Dear Agony, I recently had a meal at a fast food pizza restaurant and I was sure that the food had gone bad. I didn't wish to cause a fuss and I put it down to the taste of some strange topping on the pizza.

That night I was repeatedly sick and had to have three days off work. I cannot be sure it was the pizza but I feel that the restaurant should be investigated. Is there some organization I can contact?

Yours
Upset of Uprey

Dear Agony....

Shortly after starting work I bought myself a brand new pair of black suede boots. They fitted me perfectly and I couldn't wait to show them off.

However, the first time I wore them the heel came away from the bottom of my right boot. I was just walking home from the pictures with my boyfriend.

The next day I took them back to the shop I bought them from. They sent them back to the manufacturer. That was over a month ago now and I don't think this is fair. Is there anything I can do?

Yours

Anxious of Aberdeen

Dear Agony

I wish to buy a new compact disc player but I am overwhelmed by the number available and all the gadgetry. Is there someone that may be able to point me in the direction of the best?

Yours

Bewildered of Brighton

Dear Agony
There are three pubs in my area, the next nearest being over fifteen miles away. I am sure that these pubs have agreed together to push up their prices because they know they are the only ones for miles.

Is there some organization I can get in touch with to complain about this unfair practice?

yours
SKINT OF STILLINGTON

Key words

Write definitions of the following terms:

Price competition

Non-price competition

Market structures

Perfect competition

Price taker

Homogeneous products

Barriers to entry

Consumer sovereignty

Monopoly

Normal profit

Abnormal profit

Oligopoly

Cartel

Predatory pricing

Producer sovereignty

Competition policy

Competition Commission

Office of Fair Trading

Privatization

Monopolistic competition

Product differentiation

Branding

Informative advertising

Persuasive advertising

Now go back through the chapter to check your definitions.

Chapter 11

The Labour Market

Aims

At the end of this chapter you should be able to:

1 Understand why **labour markets** exist.

2 Distinguish between labour markets for different skills and occupations, in different industries, and in different regions.

3 Demonstrate how **wages** are determined by the demand for and supply of labour.

4 Analyse reasons for changes in the **supply of labour** in an economy and to particular occupations.

5 Analyse reasons for changes in the **demand for labour**.

6 Analyse the causes and effects of changes in **productivity**.

7 Describe how a trade union may try to influence wage levels and why.

8 Describe how and why the Government intervenes in labour markets.

Section 1 What is the market for labour?

So far we have used supply and demand 'to examine' the way in which prices are determined when firms sell their output to consumers in the market for goods and services.

In producing, firms must buy the services of land, labour and capital, the factors of production, in order to make the goods and services to sell to consumers. Supply and demand may also be used to examine how the prices of these factors of production are determined.

In this chapter we will examine how the price of one particular factor of production is determined. This price is the price of labour, or **wages**. From the table on the next page it can be seen that incomes from employment and self-employment account for 73% of all income received in the UK.

Factor shares in domestic income 1997		
	£billion	%Share
Income from employment	400.4	62.1
Income from self-employment	69.9	10.8
Gross trading surplus of companies	101.4	15.7
Gross trading surpluses of public corporations and general government enterprises	4.6	0.7
Rent	68.1	10.6
Total domestic income	644.4	100

The market for labour in an economy will consist of all those people willing and able to supply themselves for work and all those people and firms willing and able to employ them. That is, a **labour market** exists when there is a supply of labour and a demand for labour.

There can be many different markets for labour in an economy. Labour markets can be local, national, or even international if people are willing and able to travel overseas to find work. Labour markets will also exist for every different occupation or type of skill. For example, the market for economists, computer programmers, bricklayers, mechanical engineers or hairstylists.

Within each labour market the wage paid to workers will be determined by the forces of labour demand and supply.

Section 2 | The demand for labour

What determines the demand for labour?

The demand for workers in cottage cheese factories depends on the demand for cottage cheese.

1 The demand for labour is a derived demand

The demand for labour is unlike the demand for other goods and services. Consumers demand food, clothing and other goods for the satisfaction that consuming these goods brings. However, firms do not demand labour for the same reasons. Labour, unlike a car or a cake, is not wanted for itself, but is demanded to make the goods and services that consumers want.

If consumers demand more goods and services, more labour is demanded to produce these. If consumers demand fewer goods and services less labour is demanded. Hence the demand for labour is known as a **derived demand**.

2 The quantity of labour demanded depends on the wage rate

Each extra worker employed in a firm will increase the value of total output produced. This addition to output is the value of the worker to the firm and is called the **marginal revenue product of labour**. Each worker must be paid a wage. This wage is the cost of the worker to the firm. A profit-maximizing firm will only employ a worker if the value of output added by the worker is greater than, or equal to, the cost of the worker or the wage rate. For example, if Jack Smith increased the output of lamps by £200 per week and his wages are only £100 then it is profitable to employ him.

229

Imagine a firm produces table lamps. Each lamp sells for £5. At present there are four workers, or units of labour, employed producing a total output of 300 lamps per week. The firm wants to increase output but doesn't know how many extra workers to employ.

Table-lamp production

Number of workers	Firm's total output per week	Extra output per worker per week	Value of extra output of (price × quantity) Marginal revenue product
4	300		
5	350	50	£250
6	390	40	£200
7	420	30	£150
8	440	20	£100
9	450	10	£50

This table shows that the employment of the fifth worker would add 50 lamps to the total output. When these extra lamps are sold, the firm's revenue would rise by £250. If the wage rate was fixed at £150 per week, it is worth employing that worker as well as the sixth and seventh workers. The seventh worker adds £150 to the value of output and costs £150 to employ, but using the rule employed by a profit-maximizing firm, that worker is worthwhile employing. If the firm attempted to employ the eighth worker they would gain £100 in extra output but lose £150 in wage costs. Profits would fall by £50. What we have constructed is the firm's demand schedule for table-lamp makers. Clearly, the only way to increase the quantity of labour demanded by the firm is to raise the productivity of each worker or to cut the wages paid to their workers. For example, if wages were cut to £100 per week even the eighth worker would be worth employing. If we plot the information on a graph we obtain that firm's demand curve for labour ($D_N D_N$) which will slope downwards from left to right. (N is a symbol used to denote labour.)

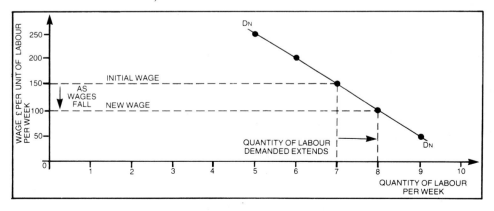

A firm's demand for table-lamp makers

The demand curve for labour for this firm can be more generally applied to all firms. A fall in wages will cause an extension in their demand for labour, while a rise in the wages paid to workers will cause a contraction in demand.

3 The quantity of labour demand depends upon technology

As technology improves, the demand for certain types of labour falls while the demand for other types of labour rises. For example, the introduction of word processors has reduced the demand for typists and, at the same time, has increased the demand for computer service engineers.

New for old

As wages rise and workers become more expensive, employers will replace labour with machines. This substitution of capital for labour can be seen in many modern industries where much of the work is done by machinery. This can be contrasted with less developed nations, such as India and parts of Africa, where labour is relatively cheap and a great deal of labour and little machinery is still used in the production of many goods and services.

Exercise 1 Productivity and changes in labour demand

The figures below represent a demand curve for labour making television parts. It shows how much each additional worker is worth to the firm in terms of the output they produce.

A television assembly line

Units of labour	The value of their output per week
1	£200
2	£190
3	£180
4	£170
5	£160

1 Plot and label the demand curve for labour (D_ND_N) using the information above.

2 If the wage paid to each worker was £180 per week, how many workers would the firm employ?

3 Imagine now that a new machine is introduced which allows each worker to produce more output in the same time. That is, **labour productivity**, or output per worker, increases. This raises the value of output production each worker, as shown in the table below.

Units of labour	Value of their output (after increased production) per week
1	£260
2	£240
3	£220
4	£200
5	£180

    a   Plot this new labour demand curve on your graph and label it D_{N1}.
    b   Explain what has happened to the demand curve and why.
    c If the wage per worker remains at £180 per week, how many workers will the firm now employ?
    d If the firm finds it difficult to find extra workers to employ, what might it do to try and attract them away from other firms?

4   Imagine now that total consumer spending in the economy has fallen. People are now buying less of all goods and services, including television. Explain what may happen to the demand for labour in the firm now.

5 **a**   What may happen to the demand for labour if robots were installed that could do the work of three men?
    b   If workers find themselves out of work as a result of the installation of robots, what do you think will happen to the wages of workers who have kept their jobs, and want to keep them for longer? Explain your answer.

6   If a worker is to become more productive s/he must be trained in the skills necessary to do the work better. Firms train their workers to operate machinery, to file papers, to do book work and many other tasks that are required of them. Colleges also help educate and train workers to be anything from car mechanics to nuclear physicists. How might an increase in training affect the demand for labour?

Changes in the demand for labour

We have learnt that the quantity of labour demanded by a firm varies with the level of wages. Any increase in wages may cause firms to demand workers. However, whatever the wage rate, it is clear that any increase in the demand for goods and services made by a firm, causing their prices to rise, and any increase in the productivity of labour, will cause a firm to increase its demand for labour at each and every wage level. As a result, the demand curve for labour shifts outwards at every wage possible.

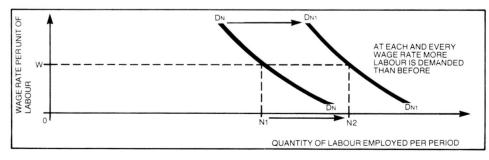

An increase in the demand for labour for a firm

232

On the other hand, a fall in the demand for goods and services, a fall in their prices or any fall in productivity will therefore cause a fall in demand and the labour demand curve would shift inwards. Less labour would be demanded at each and every wage than before. This would also happen if cheaper, more productive alternatives to labour could be employed, like the robots in the last exercise.

Section 3   The supply of labour

How many people are willing and able to work?

Not everyone will be willing or able to supply themselves for work. The **working population** of the UK in 1999 was 28.6 million people out of a total population of about 60 million. This figure is made up of all those people who are employees, the self-employed and the unemployed.

The working population

THE YOUNG	HOUSEWIVES	SCHOOLCHILDREN AND STUDENTS
THE EMPLOYED	SELF EMPLOYED	ARMED FORCES
THE UNEMPLOYED	THE OLD AND SEVERELY DISABLED	

Composition of working population, UK 1999	
Employees	23.7 million
Self-employed	3.2 million
Armed forces	0.2 million
Unemployed	1.3 million
Work related government training	0.2 million
Total	28.6 million

The working population is, in fact, the supply of labour in the UK. This is because the working population represents all those people who are both able and willing to work in the country. Approximately 57% of the working population is male and the other 43% is female.

In recent years the supply of labour has been growing. Between 1976 and 1999 the working population grew by 2 million. One feature of this growth has been the rise in the number of working women.

Why has the labour supply increased?

1 Wages have grown faster than prices. This means that the wages of an average worker will buy more today than, for example, ten years ago. Economists say, therefore, that there has been an increase in **real wages**. Because of this more people want to work.

2 There has been a rise in the number of teenagers entering the working population resulting from the baby boom of the 1960s. There are also fewer people leaving the working population. This is because there are now fewer people of retiring age resulting from the low birth rates sixty to seventy years ago. Both of these factors have increased the size of the working population.

3 There has been a change in social attitudes towards wives and mothers working. This has encouraged more women to join the working population.

How many hours will an individual work?

In Chapter 8 we saw that as the price of a good rises so does the willingness of firms to supply that good. This gives a normal upward sloping supply curve.

In the same way, we would expect that a person would be willing to work more hours the higher the wage rate per hour they receive. For example, for £7 an hour a builder may choose to work 35 hours a week, while at £10 an hour he may work 40 hours. However, it may be the case that as his hourly wage rate rises further he can get more income by working less hours. So, for example, at £15 per hour he may work only 32 hours each week. As a result, the supply curve of the builder, and other workers like him, will be **backward bending**.

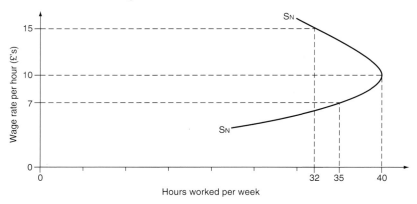

The backward bending supply curve (S$_N$S$_N$) of our builder

When the hourly wage rate rises above a certain level a worker may wish to work fewer hours per week, that is the supply curve of labour becomes backward bending. This is because at higher hourly wage rates it is possible to have both more income and more leisure.

Even though most people do work a fixed number of hours per week, there is still evidence to suggest that the supply curve of labour is backward bending. This can be seen in trade union attempts to reduce working hours as living standards have improved. It may be seen in the reduction of the working week from 60 hours at the start of the century to an average of around 41 hours per week now.

How many people will want to work in a particular job?

The supply of labour to a particular occupation, for example bricklaying, will slope upward from left to right as normal. This is because as bricklayers' wages rise, some bricklayers may want to work fewer hours, but other workers in different occupations will leave their present jobs in order to earn higher wages as bricklayers. More people will wish to become bricklayers and so the total quantity of labour supplied to this occupation will rise as the wage rate rises.

The supply curve of labour for a particular occupation

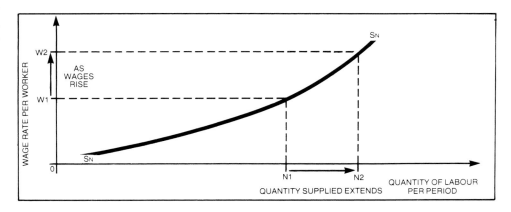

Changes in the supply of labour to an occupation

Exercise 2   What jobs have you in mind?

1   a   Think of a job that you would like to do.
    b   Think of a job that you definitely would not like to do.

2   For each of the jobs in question 1, write down all of the reasons why you do or do not want to do this job after you finish your education.

There are many things other than money that make a job attractive or unattractive.

For example, what other people think of the job, promotion prospects, job satisfaction and job security. In addition, there may be **fringe benefits** or **perks**, such as company cars, free life insurance. These are also important when people decide whether or not to take a job. All of these things that affect the attractiveness of a job are called the **net advantages** of that job. People do not always pick the highest-paid job because there are other things to consider.

It is changes in the net advantages of a job that cause shifts in labour supply curves. For example, a decline in promotion prospects, and in the pay of school teachers relative to other jobs, will cause a fall in the supply of teachers at each and every wage, from $S_N S_N$ to $S_{N1} S_{N1}$ in the figure below.

A fall in the supply of teachers results in their labour supply curve shifting inwards

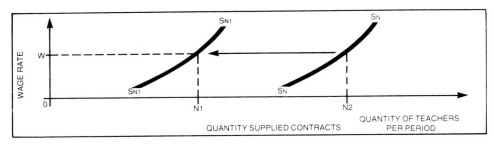

Section 4 The determination of the wage for a job

Equilibrium wage rates

Any labour market will consist of the demand for, and the supply of a particular group of workers. Just as in the markets for goods and services the equilibrium wage, or market price, of labour in a particular job will be determined by the forces of labour demand and labour supply. The equilibrium wage for a particular job can be illustrated graphically. At this wage we find how many workers will actually be employed.

The market for labour

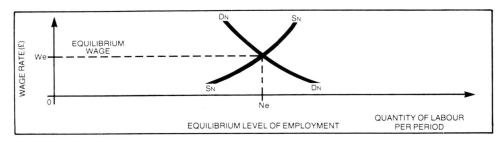

Will the equilibrium wage change?

Like any commodity, the wages of any group of workers will rise and fall given changes in the forces of demand and supply. A rise in the demand for labour, or a fall in its supply, will cause wages to rise. A fall in the demand for labour, or a rise in its supply, will bring wages down.

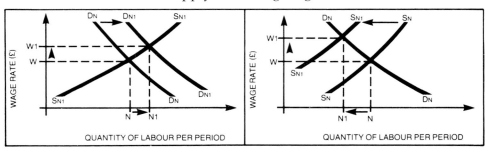

A rise in the demand for labour. Equilibrium wage rate rises from W to W_1 and employment increases from N to N_1.

A fall in the supply of labour Equilibrium wage rate rises from W to W_1 and employment falls from N to N_1.

236

A rise in the demand for labour in a particular job may arise as the demand for goods and services rise, or if capital equipment, that is, machinery, becomes too expensive to employ.

A fall in the supply of labour to a particular occupation may occur as wages rise in other jobs and workers look for higher-paid jobs elsewhere, or if promotion prospects and fringe benefits, like company cars, increase in other occupations.

Methods of payment

In the real world there is a distinction between the **wage rate** for a job, and a **salary**. A worker receives a wage when they are paid an hourly rate and work a fixed number of hours each week. Workers who receive salaries are paid a fixed amount each month, regardless of the hours they work. This is notable in *desk* jobs, like accountancy, banking, teaching and other such professions. Workers on the factory or shop floor usually get paid by the hour or according to their time. These workers can often increase their **earnings**, over and above their wages, by working overtime.

Some workers may even be paid according to how much they produce. This is called **piece-rate working**, whereby workers get a fixed amount of money for each unit of output they produce.

| **Section 5** | Why do people earn different amounts? |

Wage differentials between jobs

Difference in wages between different jobs are called **wage differentials**. An employee of a stockbroking firm in London may earn over £100 000 per year, while an agricultural worker may earn less than £6 000 per year. Such differences in earnings between people are common. In 1998 65% of employees had earnings less than the UK average of £19 494 per year. Only 2.4% of employees had earnings of more than £50 000 per year.

Exercise 3   Why do they earn more than me?

In groups, look at the different job advertisements below.

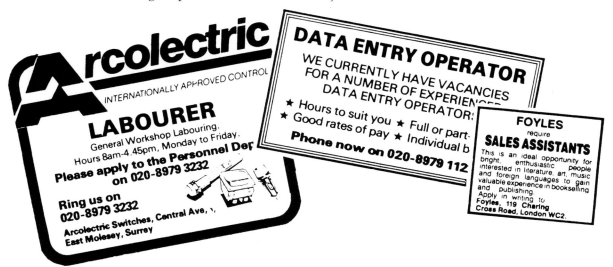

Economist

Shell U.K. Limited is looking for an Economist to join there Business Environment Division, initially on a 2 year contract.

The successful candidate for this unusual opportunity to experience the oil industry at first hand, is likely to have a degree and post-graduate degree in economics; a strong quantitative background including familiarity with PCs and a high level of analytical, written and oral communication skills.

The post can be filled at various levels of previous experience, with a remuneration pack-age to match, but preference will be given to those whose understanding of the U.K. economy within a global environment can be readily acknowledged.

The planning team is responsible for analysing the U.K. economic scene and for identifying economic trend and developments in particular those relating to energy demand and supply.

Please telephone or write for an application form, quoting reference 8/067 to:

Shell U.K. Limited
(UKPR/5)
Shell-Mex House
Strand
London WC2R 0DX

PART-TIME SECURITY PERSON

We require a part-time security person for the reception area at our Group Head Office on Kingston Road, New Malden.

The hours of work involved are Monday to Friday 5pm to 7.30pm and duties include dealing with all visitors and deliveries to the building, whilst maintaining an effective security presence.

Applications are invited from mature persons who are confident and alert, and of a smart appearance.

We offer a good rate of pay for this responsible position.

Interested applicants should telephone for an application form or write to: R.J. Howard, Group Personnel Manager, Higgs and Hill PLC, Crown House, Kingston Road, New Malden, Surrey KT3 3ST. Telephone 0208 942 8921 and ask for extension 2267.

WAREHOUSE STAFF

You could be earning instead of looking!

WAREHOUSE STAFF – We've found the way to make temporary assignments more interesting for YOU.

You'll have the opportunity to select from a variety of assignments locally or in London offering excellent rates of pay, holiday pay and other benefits.

If you're available for a week or more we can put you to work.

For details call Charlotte Ellyatt.

0208 549 5046
6–12 Eden Walk
Kingston
Surrey (above Sainsbury's)

Kelly Temporary Services

Call us right now

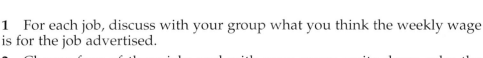

1 For each job, discuss with your group what you think the weekly wage is for the job advertised.

2 Choose four of these jobs and with your group write down why the higher-paid jobs pay more than the lower-paid ones.

1 Different abilities and qualifications

Workers do not all have the same education, training and ability. For example, an accountant is a more skilled worker than a cashier. If both workers were paid the same amount, very few people would be willing to undertake the many years of study necessary to become an accountant.

Because the training period is so long for some jobs the supply of these particular workers may be very low and as a result their wages may be very high. For example, it takes doctors over six years to qualify to do their job.

People with skills that are in very short supply relative to the demand for those skills will tend to be offered very high wages. This explains why skilled footballers like David Beckham, and actresses like Julia Roberts, are able to command huge salaries (see also Chapter 2 on 'economic rent').

2 'Dirty' jobs and unsociable hours

Some jobs are dirty or dangerous and so workers must be paid more in order attract a supply of labour. Some people have to work nights or other unsociable hours and may be paid more to compensate for this.

3 Satisfaction

Certain jobs, for example, nursing, are thought by some people to give a lot of job satisfaction and some people may be prepared to do them without very high pay.

4 Lack of information about jobs and wages

Sometimes workers work for less than they could earn simply because they do not know about better-paid jobs elsewhere. Lack of information about jobs is one reason for differences in earnings.

5 Immobility

People may earn different amounts because some workers may not wish to leave their families and friends in order to move to a better-paid job elsewhere. At the same time, other workers would like to be able to move to a better-paid job, but may not be able to do this because they cannot afford housing in the new area.

The ease with which workers can move between jobs and different parts of the country is known as **labour force mobility**. If workers are very mobile, they will move to the jobs that offer them the most pay, and they will also move from places with high unemployment to areas with job vacancies. High labour mobility or willingness to move can help reduce differences in unemployment and wage rates in different parts of the country.

6 Fringe benefits

Some jobs may offer lower wages than others because they offer more perks, such as company cars, free life insurance, cheap travel. However, it is the higher-paid jobs that tend to offer the most perks.

People in different occupations can earn different amounts of money, but even people in the same jobs can earn very different amounts. The table on the opposite page gives the average weekly pay of construction workers in the UK. Even though these workers are doing the same jobs all around the country, there are large differences in their earnings. For example, there is a

£154 difference between the average weekly earnings of construction workers in London and in Wales.

Industrial Relations Survey	
Construction industry pay April 1998 (Male manual workers' average weekly earnings)	£
London	448.3
South-East (non London)	350.2
Scotland	341.1
East Midlands	342.3
Eastern	343.9
York & Humberside	329.2
North-West	335.4
South-West	304.7
West Midlands	338.4
Wales	294.5

New Earnings Survey

Differences in earnings between workers doing the same jobs happen because of the following:

- **Shortage of workers**

There may be shortages of particular types of workers in parts of the country. If there is a shortage of skilled labour in the South-East of England then employers in the South-East will pay more to skilled labour in order to attract a greater supply of skilled labour.

- **Length of service**

Many firms have salary scales that automatically add to workers' pay, the longer they have worked for the firm. This extra pay is both a loyalty bonus and a payment for having more experience and skill.

- **Local pay agreements**

Workers and managers often agree their pay locally. This means pay may differ for the same job simply because of different arrangements around the country. For example, some workers might promise never to strike in return for extra pay, while other workers will agree on different bonuses for good performance at work.

What is productivity?

Productivity refers to the amount of output that can be produced from a given input of resources. For example, a firm that uses 10 units of labour, land and capital to produce 40 units of output is twice as productive as a firm that uses 10 units of resources to produce 20 units of output.

The aim of any business will be to combine its resources in the most efficient way. That is, it will attempt to maximise the productivity of its resources in order to produce as much as it can it can at the lowest cost possible. For example, a construction firm that employs ten carpenters and yet supplies only one hammer, drill and chisel between them has clearly not combined labour and capital in the most efficient way. By increasing the input of capital – i.e. more hammers and drills etc. – the firm will increase productivity.

In general, productivity in a firm will increase if more output can be produced with the same input of resources, or if fewer resources can be used to produce the same amount of output.

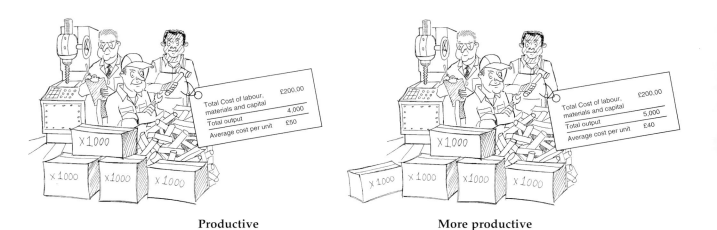

Productive   More productive

The decision on how best to combine factors of production will depend on a number of things:

1   The nature of the product
Products in high demand, in national and international markets, will tend to be mass produced using a large input of automated machinery.

2   The relative prices of labour and capital
If wages are high, a firm may decide to use more capital instead of labour.

3   The size of the firm.
As a firm grows in size, it tends to employ more capital relative to labour.

241

Measuring the productivity of labour

Labour productivity in an organization can be calculated by dividing total output in a given period of time (for example, each day, week or month) by the number of workers employed.

$$\text{Average product of labour} = \frac{\text{Total output}}{\text{Number of employees}}$$

The **average product** of labour is a useful measure of how efficient workers are. For example, if a company employs 10 workers to produce 200 DVD players per day, the average product per employee per day is 20 players. If output rises to 220 DVD players per day without the company employing any more workers, then productivity will have increased to 22 players per worker per day.

However, this measure tells us nothing about the quality of work. Productivity is also about increasing the quality of work and outputs – because consumers demand quality.

Why do firms want to raise productivity?

If the same amount of labour, land and capital employed can produce more output for the same total cost, then the cost of each unit of output will have fallen. Increasing productivity can therefore lower business costs and increase profits.

A firm that fails to increase productivity at the same or a faster pace than its competitors will face higher costs and lower profits. It will be unable to cut prices to compete for consumer demand without reducing profits or even making a loss. If a firm is unable to offer quality products at competitive prices, then demand for its products will fall. In the long run the firm will face closure and workers will be made redundant.

Business organizations in the UK and other developed countries are facing increasing competition from firms in developing economies such as China, Malaysia and Taiwan in South East Asia. Wages in these countries are generally lower than wages in developed countries for similar work. It is therefore vital that firms in the UK increase productivity, lower their average costs, and improve product quality in order to compete with overseas organizations. This should ensure their survival.

How can firms raise the productivity of labour?

A firm can attempt to raise the productivity of its workers through a combination of the following:

- training workers to improve their existing skills and learn new skills.
- rewarding increased productivity with performance-related pay and bonus payments.
- encouraging employees to buy shares in their organization. Improved productivity will help to raise profits and pay higher dividends on shares.
- improving job satisfaction – for example, by improving the working environment, making jobs more interesting, teamworking, involving workers in business decision making and giving regular feedback on performance.
- replacing old plant and machinery with new, more efficient machines and tools for workers to use.

- introducing new production processes and working practices designed to reduce waste, improve quality and increase output – for example, computer-aided design and manufacturing, robotic assembly lines and recycling.

Many of the above will tend to raise the cost of employing labour in the short run. However, if productivity improves, average costs will fall and profits will tend to rise. Lower costs can be passed on to consumers as lower prices in an attempt to increase consumer demand and generate more sales revenues. If consumer demand expands, then the demand for labour may also increase.

Exercise 4   The competitiveness of UK industry

Annual Percentage changes in

Country	Real unit wage costs							Average labour productivity						
	1992	1993	1994	1995	1996	1997	1998	1992	1993	1994	1995	1996	1997	1998
UK	−1.3%	−2.6%	−1.7%	−0.7%	−0.7%	−0.2%	1.1%	1.6%	3.6%	3.6%	1.3%	2.0%	1.9%	1.2%
USA	−0.4%	−0.4%	−0.6%	0.4%	−0.2%	0.2%	1.3%	2.9%	0.5%	0.5%	0.9%	1.4%	1.5%	0.8%
Japan	−0.4%	0.2%	1.1%	0.9%	−2.0%	0.5%	0.4%	0.0%	−0.1%	0.5%	1.3%	3.4%	0.0%	0.0%
France	0.2%	0.4%	−2.2%	−0.1%	0.1%	−0.9%	−0.7%	1.9%	−0.2%	2.9%	1.1%	1.5%	2.5%	1.8%
Germany	0.7%	−0.3%	−2.3%	−0.4%	−1.1%	−2.4%	−1.8%	4.1%	0.6%	3.4%	2.1%	2.6%	3.7%	2.7%
European Union (average)	0.0%	−1.0%	−2.4%	−1.3%	−0.6%	−1.0%	−0.9%	2.4%	1.4%	3.3%	1.8%	1.7%	2.3%	1.9%

Look at the information on changes in average labour productivity and unit wage costs for different countries.

1 Explain how average productivity and unit wage costs are calculated. Why are they useful measures?

2 Which countries have become more competitive over time? Which have become less competitive?

3 What might explain these differences?

4 Plot four graphs, each one showing changes in unit wage costs and labour productivity for the UK, Europe, the USA and Japan. When unit labour costs are rising faster than productivity, firms profits are likely to be falling. If productivity rises faster than unit wage costs, profits are likely to be rising. Describe what is happening in each graph.

5 Suggest ways in which firms could try to increase labour productivity.

Section 7 | Employee and Employer Associations

What is a trade union?

Many workers do not negotiate their wages individually with their employers. The wages of many workers are decided by **collective bargaining**, or negotiations, between worker and employer representatives.

A **trade union** is an organization that represents the interests of workers in negotiations about improving wages and working conditions with employers and government. In 1998 around 31% of people in employment in the UK were members of around 238 trade unions. In some countries union membership is much higher.

Types of trade union

Trade unions can be grouped into four main types:

1 **General unions** represent workers from many different occupations and industries. For example, the Transport and General Workers Union (TGWU) represents all sorts or clerical, manufacturing, transport and commercial workers.

2 **Industrial unions** represent workers in the same industry – for example, the Communications Workers union (CMU) and the Iron and Steel Trades Confederation (ISTC).

3 **Craft unions** are often small and few in number today. They usually represent workers with the same skill across several industries, such as the Graphical, Paper and Media Union (GPMU) and the Amalgamated Engineers and Electrical Union (AEEU).

4 **Non-manual unions** and **staff associations** represent workers in professional and commercial jobs – for example, the National Union of Teachers and the Royal College of Nursing. UNISON is the largest union in the UK with 1.4 million members representing local government, health-service, and other public-sector workers.

The Trades Union Congress

Around 70 different unions belong to the **Trades Union Congress (TUC)** representing over 6.7 million workers in the UK. The TUC allows the union movement to speak with one voice to employers, the media, and the UK and European Union Governments. It has a keen interest in protecting employee rights, education and training, and improving working conditions.

A meeting of the Trades Union Congress

Union membership

Membership of trade unions in the UK has been declining. In the late 1970s over 50% of people in work belonged to a union. By 1998 this had fallen to just 31%. Union membership has declined as employment in manufacturing industries has fallen. Participation in unions is now highest in professional occupations with around 44% of male employees and 62% of female employees in unions. Membership is lowest in sales occupations with fewer than 14% of sales employees in unions.

How can trade unions influence wages?

If a trade union wishes to raise the wages of its members, it must influence the supply or demand for labour.

A trade union can try to raise their members wages by restricting the supply of labour to an occupation or place of work by

- negotiating a **single union agreement** with an employer. This means one union will represent all the workers in a particular place of work. Employers benefit by having to negotiate on wages and working conditions with only one union rather than many.

- restricting their membership to only those workers who have served long apprenticeships and undertaken a long period of training to develop their skills.

A trade union may also try raise wages by agreeing to improve productivity. The demand for their labour may increase if labour productivity rises.

245

Exercise 5   A single-union agreement

Read the two interviews below and then answer the questions.

Ken Yomoto,
Head of Toyota UK

'We opened our new factory in Derbyshire in 1991. It was important for us to achieve levels of productivity at our new car plant equal to those in Japan. This required training our workforce to use our new machines and to be flexible so that each person could undertake many skilled tasks rather than just one or two. We also had to make sure production was not disrupted by strikes and any other industrial actions. These are costly and reduce profits.

We offer our workers training, stable employment, high wages, a friendly and safe working environment, and the opportunity to have representatives on the company board to help make decisions. In return, our workers must be very productive, work 39 hours each week, and agree not to undertake industrial actions without a full ballot. Our single union agreement with the Amalgamated Engineering Union (AEU) secured these commitments from our workers. It is also far easier to negotiate on wages and conditions with one union rather than several or with individual workers.'

'The AEU represents all the workers at the Toyota plant in Derbyshire. This gives us a seat on the company board where we are able to influence decisions which may affect the wages and employment of our members. We were one of five unions who competed for the right to represent the Toyota workers. Any new worker that joins must become an AEU member.

The management chose the AEU because it offered them the best deal. And the lowest unit labour costs. We agreed to meet productivity targets, work a 39-hour week (even though we had previously campaigned for 37 hours), not to take industrial actions without a full ballot of our members, and to participate fully in the training programme. We are keen to make sure all our members are highly skilled because in return Toyota has offered us very good terms and conditions.'

Ron Duin,
Shop Steward of the
Amalgamated Engineering
Union (AEU) at Toyota

1   What is a single-union agreement?

2   What are the advantages and disadvantages of a single-union agreement for **a** the owners of a firm, and **b** the workforce?

3   Why is it important for Toyota to raise labour productivity levels in their Derbyshire plant to those achieved in their Japanese plants?

4   What are the benefits to Toyota of locating within the UK and the European Union? If necessary, use Chapter 18 to help you.

Industrial disputes

If a union demands a wage increase that is not matched by an increase in productivity, business costs will rise and profits will fall. Demands for reduced working hours, increased holiday entitlements, better pensions, healthcare and other benefits will also raise the cost of employing labour. For this reason disputes can occur between unions and employers.

Sometimes it is necessary for industrial disputes to be settled with the help of an organization set up by the Government called the **Advisory, Conciliation and Arbitration Service (ACAS)**. The staff of ACAS are trained in negotiating skills and can be asked by unions and employers in dispute to 'conciliate' (be a channel of communication between the two sides), 'mediate' (propose a solution), and 'arbitrate' (help the two sides reach an agreement).

Ford machinists on strike for equal pay and skill recognition

A delegation of health workers meeting an MP to protest at cuts in the National Health Service.

What are employer associations?

These organizations exist to provide employers with help and advice for example, on legal matters and calculating tax, and to represent their views in discussions with trade unions and Government. For example, the National Farmers Union (NFU) represents the views of farm owners and managers. Other examples include the Society of British Aerospace Companies and the Federation of Small Businesses.

The Confederation of British Industry

Many employers associations belong to the **Confederation of British Industry (CBI)** along with many trade associations and over 250 000 different companies. The CBI is a very influential national organization representing the interests of many different employers in discussions with unions and governments. It also collects and publishes up-to-date information on industrial trends, such as productivity and unit costs, and on how well UK firms are performing.

The UK Government is a major employer demanding the services of teachers, nurses, doctors, civil servants and other public sector workers.

However, the Government is also active in the labour market for many other reasons. These are:

1   to protect the rights of employees and employers

Employment Laws and Health and Safety Regulations have been introduced in the UK and across the European Union not only to give employers and workers certain rights, but also to make them responsible for observing the rights and responsibilities of each other.

Key legal responsibilities and rights

Employees	Employers
• to comply with the terms and conditions of their employment, for example, on hours of work, holidays, dress codes, maternity leave, disciplinary procedures, etc.	• to comply with the terms and conditions of their contract with an employee
• to comply with health and safety regulations, such as observing no-smoking signs and wearing protective clothing	• not to discriminate against any worker because of their sex, marital status, race, religion, disability, union membership, or because they work part-time
• to receive at least the legal minimum levels of sick and maternity pay, and redundancy compensation	• to provide a healthy and safe working environment and any necessary equipment
• to receive at least 4 weeks paid holiday per year and take minimum rest periods each day	• to comply with the legal rights of employees to minimum daily rest periods, paid holiday entitlements, maximum weekly working hours, payments for sickness, maternity and redundancy
• not to have to work more than 48 hours each week, except for jobs involving the driving of goods and public service vehicles	• the right to legally terminate employment and to defend their actions at ACAS, an employment tribunal and the European Court of Justice
• protection from unfair dismissal and the right to defend their actions at ACAS, an employment tribunal and the European Court of Justice	

2   to outlaw and regulate the restrictive practices of powerful trade unions and employers

In a free market wages will be set by the forces of supply and demand. However, a powerful employer may be able to pay wages that are too low while a trade union may seek wages that are too high and not matched by productivity.

Laws have been introduced by UK Governments to control the power of employers and unions over wages and working conditions. For example, employers must observe the legal rights of their employees, and trade unions no longer have the right to strike without first conducting a full ballot of their members. A trade union may also be liable for any damages or losses suffered by an employer from industrial action.

3 to raise the wage levels of workers on very low pay

In April 1999 the Government introduced **national minimum wage** legislation. This ensures no employee over 21 years of age can earn less than £3.60 per hour, or less than £3 per hour if they are between 18 and 21. These rates will be raised from time to time. Some employers have argued this will raise costs and reduce their demand for labour.

4 to increase the competitiveness of UK firms by raising skill levels and productivity

The Government is encouraging more people to undertake 'lifelong learning' i.e. learning new skills and updating their existing skills by undertaking more education and training throughout their working life.

5 to reduce unemployment

Benefits are paid to many people who are unemployed. Some economists argue these benefits may reduce some people's willingness to find work. Others argue they reduce the costs of searching for employment and therefore help the unemployed to look for work. The 'Jobseekers Allowance' (JSA) replaced unemployment benefit and income support in October 1996. JSA is only paid to unemployed people who can show they are actively seeking work, and who participate in the Jobseekers Direction programme run at local offices of the Employment Service. A 'Jobseekers Direction' consists of interviews and training to help unemployed people find and apply for jobs suited to their skills.

Regional Selective Assistance (RSA) is made available to some firms to create new jobs and protect existing ones in areas of high unemployment (see Chapter 7). RSA provides money to help start new projects and provide training.

Exercise 6   The minimum wage debate

Minimum wages do create some jobs – for economists. In America and the UK economists have been studying whether setting a floor under pay destroys jobs or reduces poverty.

A recent study by the OECD suggests the policy is ill suited to dealing with the problem of poverty. In most countries, many low earners have well-paid partners or affluent parents. Since most low paid workers are not in poor households, most of the income gains that might come from a minimum wage would benefit families which are not poor.

Critics of minimum wages frequently argue that a government-mandated pay level reduces total employment because firms will scale back hiring rather than adding employees who must be paid more than they are worth. Those in favour argue an imposed wage minimum could have an opposite effect where the employer is large and powerful in relation to the pool of suitable workers. A powerful employer may be able to hold down wages by restricting its demand for labour. If a government sets a higher minimum wages, the employer no longer has this incentive. Because the employer must pay the higher wage there is no point any longer in restricting its demand for labour.

The OECD study – which considers data from nine countries, including America, Japan, France and Spain – finds that a 10% rise in the minimum wage reduces teenage employment by around 3% in both high and low minimum wage countries.

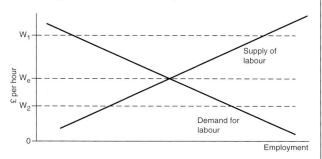

249

1 From the article, what are the arguments for and against a minimum wage. Does it matter what level the minimum wage is the set at? Explain your answer using diagrams where possible.

2 How could you try to monitor the impact of a minimum wage in the UK over time?

3 In the diagram, what will be the impact of a minimum wage set at **a** W_1, **b** W_2?

4 Calculate the wage elasticity of demand for teenage labour suggested by the findings of the study.

Key words

Write a few sentences to explain each of the following terms:

Labour market	Labour force mobility
Marginal revenue product of labour	Average product
Real wages	Collective bargaining
Salary	Trade unions
Wage differentials	TUC
Fringe benefits	Single-union agreement
Working population	ACAS
Productivity	Industrial action
Performance-related pay	Employers Associations
Piece rates	CBI
Wage differentials	A national minimum wage

Aims

At the end of this chapter you should be able to:

1 Understand the **circular flow** of output, expenditure and incomes in an economy.

2 Distinguish between **injections** and **withdrawals** from the circular flow of income.

3 Define **aggregate demand** and **national income**.

4 Explain the characteristics of **booms** and **recessions**.

5 Explain, using a simple illustration, what the **multiplier** effect of a change in expenditure is.

6 Calculate national income like a Government statistical expert.

In this and the following chapters we are concerned with the way in which the whole economy works, not just parts of it such as individual labour markets, or how prices are determined in different goods markets. The study of how an economy works, and the problem it faces, such as price inflation and unemployment, is called **macroeconomics** – because 'macro' means 'big'.

In a macroeconomy, the total amount of output produced is known as the **national output**. Factors of production – land, labour and capital – are used to produce the national output. Workers, and the owners of natural resources and capital receive incomes from their use. The total amount of income earned in an economy is therefore its **national income**.

The **circular flow of income** is a simple way of showing how output, income and expenditure circulate and change in an economy over of time.

Exercise 1   A circular flow of income

1   Look at the pictures above. Explain what is happening at each stage.

2   Explain why one person's spending is another person's income.

3   Draw a simple flow diagram to show the exchanges made between each picture.

4   Using the diagram suggest one reason why workers become unemployed.

5   What would happen if the Government placed a tax of £1 on the goods on sale in the picture?

Section 1   A simple model of an economy

Let us assume that an economy has no government and is closed to trade with foreign countries. There is only a private sector consisting of **house-holds** and **firms** in our simple model of the economy. The people who live in the households own the factors of production: land, labour and capital. These resources are organized into firms in return for income. Firms produce the goods and services households can buy. We will assume for the moment that prices do not change. The income households spend on firms' output is known as **consumption expenditure** (given the symbol C). Thus, we have a simple circular flow of output, expenditure and income.

A SIMPLE MODEL OF THE CIRCULAR FLOW OF INCOME IN AN ECONOMY

If all income is spent on consumption, then it is clear that national income national expenditure and the value of national output are all equal.

National income = National expenditure = National output

In the real economy this is still true, but things are rather more complicated.

The circular flow of income in an economy

In our simple model we assumed there was no government, no foreign trade and firms only produced goods and services for consumers. We will now drop these assumptions, but still assume that prices do not change.

Money can leak out from the circular flow. Households and firms pay taxes (**T**) to the government. They may also save some of their incomes (**savings = S**). Money may also leak out of our economy and go abroad to pay for **imports**. Indeed, households, firms and governments can all buy imported goods and pay for services abroad. (Expenditure on imports = **M**.)

Taxes, savings and imports are all known as **leakages** or **withdrawals** from the circular flow of income, because they do not represent payments made for goods and services produced in our economy.

It should be clear, therefore, that the national income (given the symbol **Y**) in an economy is divided between what we pay in tax, what we save and what we spend on imports and domestic goods and services.

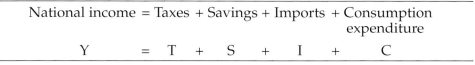

National income = Taxes + Savings + Imports + Consumption expenditure

$$Y = T + S + I + C$$

Flows of money can also be added to the circular flow of income. At any given time firms, as well as producing goods and services for consumers also produce capital goods. Their spending on these goods is terms **Gross Capital Formation** or **Investment (I)**. Governments can also spend money on many goods and services in their public expenditure programmes on education, health care, welfare benefits, roads, defence, etc. (**Government expenditure = G**). Foreign countries can also inject money into our economy by buying UK **exports (X)**.

Investment, Government spending and expenditure on exports are known as **injections** into the circular flow of income in an economy.

It is only the spending of consumers, firms, governments and foreign countries that generates outputs and incomes in an economy. If nothing was ever bought, nothing would be produced, no factors of production would be employed and no income would be earned. One person's expenditure is another person's income. The total amount spent in an economy on its

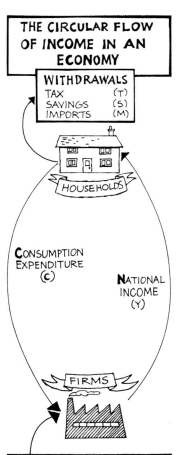

THE CIRCULAR FLOW OF INCOME IN AN ECONOMY

WITHDRAWALS
TAX   (T)
SAVINGS   (S)
IMPORTS   (M)

HOUSEHOLDS

CONSUMPTION EXPENDITURE (c)

NATIONAL INCOME (Y)

FIRMS

INJECTIONS
INVESTMENT (I)
GOVERNMENT EXPENDITURE (G)
EXPORTS (X)

output over a given period of time represents the **aggregate demand** for goods and services.

Aggregate	=	Consumption	+	Investment	+	Government	+	Exports
demand		Expenditure		Spending		Expenditure		
AD	=	C	+	I	+	G	+	X

An economy in equilibrium

An economy in **equilibrium** will be in a state of balance or rest. That is, the total amount of output, expenditure and income flowing around the economy will be the same week in, week out. As a result, prices and employment should also be stable. This situation will exist only if the total amount of goods and services firms produce is bought by all the people, etc., who spend. That is, if aggregate demand equals total output.

If, however, firms produce more output than there is demand for, some will remain unsold. Firms will learn by their mistake and produce less next time, but this means they do not need to employ so much land, labour or capital. Resources will become unemployed and, as a result, incomes will fall. Because the level of output, employment and income starts changing, the economy is said to be in a state of **disequilibrium**.

On the other hand, aggregate demand may be greater than the value of national output. Firms will want to increase the production of goods and services and will therefore require more factors of production. Output, employment and incomes will rise.

Equilibrium occurs only when these things remain the same.

For the amount of output, expenditure and income passed around the economy to remain the same, flows of money in and out of the circular flow, that is injections and withdrawals, must be equal. In other words, investment, government expenditure and spending on exports must be balanced by a flow of taxes, savings and spending on imports.

For the economy to be in equilibrium
injections must equal withdrawals
$$I + G + X = T + S + W$$

Therefore

$$C + I + G + X = T + S + M + C$$
Aggregate demand = National income

If they are not equal the amount of income in the economy will change. This can be likened to the amount of water in a bath. If water runs out of the bath (withdrawals) faster than water runs into it (injections) then the total amount of water in the bath will gradually fall (national income falls).

254

WHEN WITHDRAWALS EXCEED INJECTIONS OUTPUT, EMPLOYMENT AND NATIONAL INCOME FALL

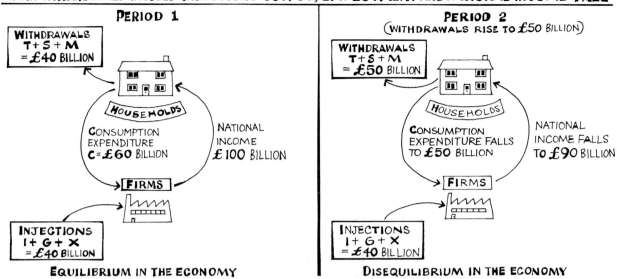

If, on the other hand, injections push more money into the circular flow than leakages withdraw, total spending in the economy will be rising and firms will increase output, employment and income.

IF INJECTIONS EXCEED WITHDRAWALS OUTPUT, EMPLOYMENT AND NATIONAL INCOME RISE

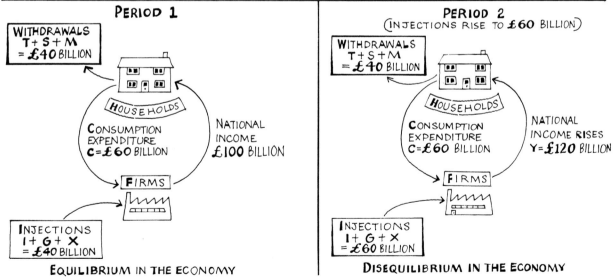

Changes in the value of injections and withdrawals cause changes in aggregate demand or expenditure. As the total demand for goods and services changes firms will either raise or lower the total output of goods and services, with consequences for employment and income.

Exercise 2 Plotting some changes

The graph below shows the annual percentage change in national income in the UK, assuming prices are constant, that is, they have remained the same, since 1990. In some years national income fell as the negative percentage changes show. The other graphs relate to changes in the components of aggregate demand in the UK.

Expenditure on the Gross Domestic Product

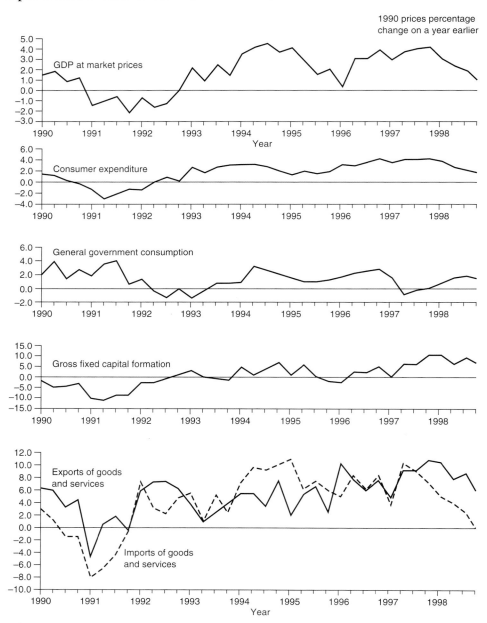

1 Look at the graphs. Is there any relationship between the changes in aggregate demand and changes in national income? If so, explain how they are related.

2 Which component(s) of aggregate demand appear to display the most changes?

3 What effect are the following changes likely to have on output, employment and income in the UK?

   a An increase in firms' investment.
   b An increase in taxes on income.
   c A rise in the interest rate causing a rise in savings.
   d An increase in Government spending on unemployment benefits.
   e A fall in the price of imports.
   f An increase in spending by consumers.
   g Firms become optimistic and predict a rise in demand in the near future.
   h A fall in the interest rate stimulates more industrial borrowing for investment purposes.
   i A cut in public spending on roads and defence.

   j A fall in the value of the pound compared with other currencies. (This will make exports appear cheaper and imports dearer in price.)

4 Look at the pie chart of shares in total expenditure in the UK. Which forms the largest component of aggregate demand?

5 Calculate how much expenditure was on consumption, investment, exports and Government activities in 1998.

Total final expenditure 1998 (£1 036 billion)

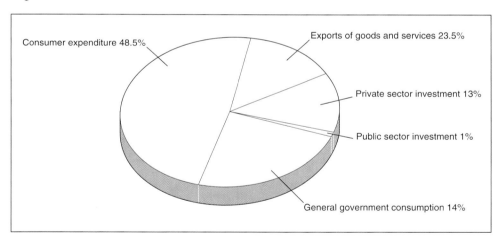

Consumer expenditure 48.5%
Exports of goods and services 23.5%
Private sector investment 13%
Public sector investment 1%
General government consumption 14%

Section 4   Booms and recessions

If the total amount of goods and services, or **real output**, an economy can produce increases over time there has been economic growth. (See Chapter 13.) As a result, the national income will grow in real terms (i.e., incomes can buy more goods and services). Plotted against time it should look like a steadily rising line. However, even if there is a tendency for growth in the long run, national output and income can display many ups and downs in the short run.

The ups and downs of national income

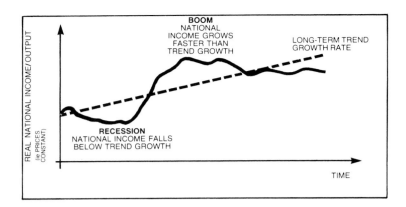

These continuous ups and downs in national income are displayed in many economies and have been labelled the **business cycle**. When an economy experiences a **boom**, real output and national income appear to grow faster than normal, while in **recessions** or **slumps** they tend to fall. That is, real output and national income shrink or experience negative growth rates. Just why economies experience booms and slumps in a continual cycle is the cause of much debate amongst economists. No one is absolutely sure, but the circular flow of income we have just explored may provide some clues.

In periods of boom there is a high level of spending. Investment in new machines by firms also tends to be high as they try to increase output. That is, aggregate demand is high and exceeds national output. Firms try to increase output by employing more factors of production but they eventually reach a position when all the available scarce resources in their economy are fully employed. No more suitable land, labour, capital or even entrepreneurs are available. As a result, the prices of goods and services will tend to rise. There will be an increase in the general level of prices, or an **inflation**, as firms cannot meet demand. Therefore, booms tend to be associated with a high level of spending, low unemployment, rising prices and profits and a high level of output.

As people in the economy cannot buy domestic goods and services they will tend to buy more imports. In turn, rising prices make our exports expensive and foreign demand for them will start to fall. Rising prices at home will also serve to reduce consumers' expenditure after a while, as they become unable to afford to buy so much. As aggregate demand starts to fall so the boom breaks.

Falling aggregate demand can result in a recession. Firms no longer wish to invest and this causes a further fall in spending. They try to cut back output and therefore employment falls as demand falls. Unemployment rises and national income falls. The rate at which prices rise will slow down.

In fact, prices may even fall as firms try to increase the demand for their products. Profits fall and many firms may even go out of business. However, falling prices may cause an increase in demand for exports. Firms producing exports will start to increase output and employment. Slowly incomes start to rise and this causes a rise in spending. Eventually the economy is lifted out of recession and on to the road of recovery. And so the cycle goes on, powered by changes in the level of demand in the economy.

Section 5 | Why do booms get bigger and slumps get deeper?

The multiplier

A change in aggregate demand whatever its source, be it consumption expenditure, investment, Government spending and/or spending on exports by foreign countries, can have widespread effects in the economy. Once started, a change in expenditure will tend to carry on. Booms become bigger, and slumps tend to get deeper once they have begun. Why is this so?

We will now discover what the **multiplier** in an economy is.

Exercise 3   The rise and rise of unemployment

A small fall in demand in an economy can have widespread effects. This is known as the multiplier effect.

Here is an example of how unemployment can spread. Suppose the demand for motor cars falls.

TYRES –150 JOBS

WINDSCREENS –100 JOBS

CAR PANELS –250 JOBS

LIGHTING + WIRING –70 JOBS

GEARBOXES –100 JOBS

FORDS CAR ASSEMBLY –400 JOBS

UPHOLSTERY –110 JOBS

ENGINE PARTS –180 JOBS

Imagine there is a car manufacturer called Fast Cars UK. It has a plant in the south-east of England that assembles cars from parts made all over the UK at different sites. As people buy fewer cars Fast Cars UK has no need to make so many. Thus, 400 people are made redundant (i.e. lose their jobs). Now see how this spreads.

1   How many jobs are lost immediately as a result of the fall in demand for cars?

2   How many jobs are lost in Fast Cars UK in total?

3   All the factories use electricity. As they now produce less cars they do not need as much electricity? What will happen to workers at power stations?

4   Power Stations run on coal and oil. What will happen to the demand for coal and oil? What will happen to coal-miners and oil-drillers?

5   All the people who have lost their jobs now have less money to spend on clothes, records, entertainment, food and many other things. What will happen to the level of demand for all other goods?

In the example the fall in demand for cars caused Fast Cars UK to reduce production and employment in many of its factories. Fast Cars UK buys materials and uses power produced by other industries which reduce their output as demand for their commodity falls. The workers who find themselves out of work have less money to spend. Shops suffer and have to reduce their orders from wholesalers and manufacturers. The fall in demand for goods and services is general now and causes many more firms to reduce their output and employment. As unemployment rises so aggregate demand falls. Firms reduce output and employment further. This is known as the **multiplier effect** whereby a small change in spending can cause large changes in income, output and employment.

In May 2000 Ford UK announced it was to cease assembly of its cars at Dagenham in Essex and that many workers could be made redundant. It is likely that this decision could also have a negative multiplier effect similar to the example above.

In the past, UK governments have often increased public spending during recessions in an attempt to boost aggregate demand and reduce unemployment through a multiplier effect. However, recent UK governments have been persuaded by economists that this policy simply resulted in higher price inflation and little or no change in unemployment in the long run. They now believe there is no multiplier for public spending, and if there is it may even be negative. Governments must borrow more or raise taxes to pay for higher spending. Both of these ways reduce the amount of money available to the private sector to spend. So as public spending rises, spending by the private sector falls. This is called **crowding out**. Private sector expenditure may fall by even more than public spending rises if, for example, higher taxes on incomes reduce incentives to work so that output and incomes fall. As a result, national income may fall despite an increase in public spending. We return to this discussion in Chapter 15.

Section 6   What influences aggregate demand?

Exercise 4   Changes in demand

Look at the following articles and list as many factors that influence the four components of aggregate demand as you can.

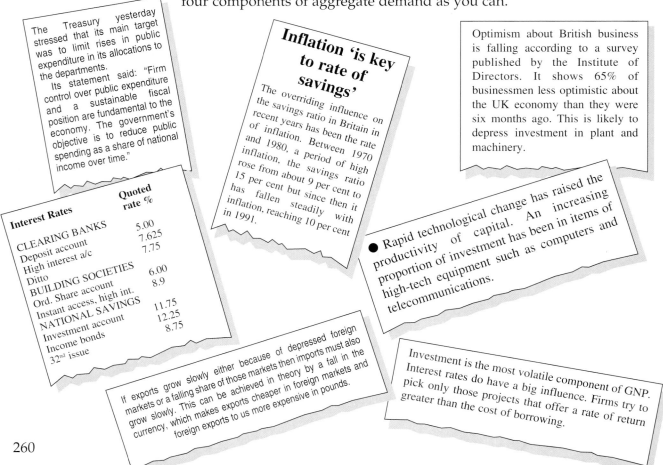

The Treasury yesterday stressed that its main target was to limit rises in public expenditure in its allocations to the departments.

Its statement said: "Firm control over public expenditure and a sustainable fiscal position are fundamental to the economy. The government's objective is to reduce public spending as a share of national income over time."

Inflation 'is key to rate of savings'

The overriding influence on the savings ratio in Britain in recent years has been the rate of inflation. Between 1970 and 1980, a period of high inflation, the savings ratio rose from about 9 per cent to 15 per cent but since then it has fallen steadily with inflation, reaching 10 per cent in 1991.

Optimism about British business is falling according to a survey published by the Institute of Directors. It shows 65% of businessmen less optimistic about the UK economy than they were six months ago. This is likely to depress investment in plant and machinery.

Interest Rates	Quoted rate %
CLEARING BANKS	5.00
Deposit account	7.625
High interest a/c	7.75
Ditto	6.00
BUILDING SOCIETIES	
Ord. Share account	8.9
Instant access, high int.	
NATIONAL SAVINGS	11.75
Investment account	12.25
Income bonds	8.75
32nd issue	

● Rapid technological change has raised the productivity of capital. An increasing proportion of investment has been in items of high-tech equipment such as computers and telecommunications.

If exports grow slowly either because of depressed foreign markets or a falling share of those markets then imports must also grow slowly. This can be achieved in theory by a fall in the currency, which makes exports cheaper in foreign markets and foreign exports to us more expensive in pounds.

Investment is the most volatile component of GNP. Interest rates do have a big influence. Firms try to pick only those projects that offer a rate of return greater than the cost of borrowing.

What affects consumption and savings?

1 The level of income

The amount of income people earn is the largest influence on consumption and savings. The higher a person's income the more they can save and spend.

2 The Government

The Government can affect the amount of income a person has to spend or save. By lowering taxes people can afford to spend and save more. Increasing benefits for the unemployed or old-age pensioners will give them the ability to consume more.

3 The availability of saving schemes

People can save in a wide variety of forms nowadays. Bank deposits, building societies, unit trusts, life insurance, national savings, even stocks and shares. The more forms of savings available the more people tend to save, and the less they spend.

4 The rate of inflation

People tend to save more of their incomes when inflation rises to protect the real value of their savings.

5 Personal factors

Some people like to spend their money, others are more cautious and save some. People save as a precaution, or for a special purchase like a car or holiday, or even for a wedding, or for their old age in the form of a pension.

6 Interest rates

People may save more if the interest rate on savings rises.

What affects investment?

1 Business optimism

If firms believe sales of their goods and services will rise in the future they will want to buy new machines and build new factories to produce their commodities for sale. If, however, they think future sales look bleak it is unlikely they will invest large amounts of money in new capital to produce goods they think will not be wanted.

2 Interest rates

Many firms who wish to invest in new machines and factories, etc. need to borrow the necessary money. High interest rates mean that borrowing is expensive and it may put off many firms.

3 Technological advance

New improved machines and new faster production techniques can reduce the costs of production and increase profitability. Not surprisingly firms will want to invest more when new developments take place.

4 The Government

Cheap loans, tax allowances and cash grants are offered by the UK Government to a number of firms especially in regional problem areas, to try to encourage investment.

What affects the demand for exports?

1 Incomes in foreign countries

The higher the incomes of people in foreign countries, the more able they are to buy goods from abroad.

2 The value of the pound

If the value of the pound falls, foreigners will find it cheaper to buy British goods and so there may be an increase in demand for them.

3 Interest rates

If UK interest rates are high, foreigners may find it more profitable to save their money in Britain than in their own country where interest rates may be lower. As a result a lot of money from abroad flows into the UK economy (see also Chapter 14).

Section 7   Measuring national income

As economists we would like to measure the total output or national income of a country. The value of the total output of goods and services can be measured by how much people pay for them. That is, total or national output should be the same as total or national expenditure.

Another view of national output is to recognize that goods and services are produced by factors of production. The payment made for their work is a cost for firms but an income for the owners of the factors of production. Thus, the value of national output should also be the same as the total value of incomes earned in a period of time, or national income.

In our model of the economy we discovered that one person's spending is another person's income, and people spend their incomes on goods and services or output. It should therefore be clear that all three measures of the total output of an economy are the same.

National output = National expenditure = National income

Government experts collect figures on all three of these measures. In practice, however, their values do not always add up to the same amount. Government experts must therefore make some adjustments in the figures they use.

From GDP to GNP   The total value of output produced by all domestic firms in the UK is known as the **Gross domestic product (GDP)**. We have used this term in earlier chapters as an approximate guide to the national income in a country. However, this does not give us the final total of goods and services available to people in the country as some income is also earned by them in the form of interest on loans made abroad, rent from property abroad, profits from companies owned abroad, and dividends on shares held in foreign companies.

These incomes from abroad must be added to our calculations of GDP.

On the other hand, some of the UK's output is produced by resources owned by foreigners and held in the UK. This means incomes flow out of the UK to people and firms abroad. As this does not represent work done for the UK it should be deducted from GDP.

The difference between the flows of income coming into the UK and those being paid abroad is known as **net property income from abroad**.

If we add net property income from abroad to Gross Domestic Product we obtain a figure for **Gross National Product (GNP)**.

Gross national = Gross domestic + Net property income
product (GNP)   product (GDP)   from abroad

GNP is therefore the total value of output from resources owned by people who live in the UK, wherever these resources are located.

From GNP to NNP   Machines, cars, trains, boats, cranes, typewriters, screwdrivers and hammers become worn out as they are used, or rust over a number of years. Buildings too can become old and in need of repair. Many of these capital goods will therefore need repair or even replacing. The amount spent on the repair or replacement of old, worn-out capital is known as **depreciation**. It is also known as **capital consumption** which tells us that capital is being used up. However, a country will never be able to enjoy more goods and services if its resources are used just to repair or replace old, worn-out capital goods.

If the total output of resources owned by a country was ten computers each year, this would be its Gross national product. If the computers never wear out, GNP after two years will be the value of twenty computers. If, however, each computer only lasts one year, then the GNP every year will only be the value of ten computers. If computers are produced solely to replace old ones, the economy has gained no extra capital goods.

If, on the other hand, only four computers need replacing after one year, the economy will gain six new computers.

This gain in the numbers of computers available for use is called the country's **Net National Product (NNP)**. It is calculated by deducting the value of capital goods replaced, that is, depreciation, from the total output of the economy, that is, GNP.

263

Net National Product =	Gross National Product – Depreciation	
(NNP)	(GNP)	

The net national product of an economy consists of all the goods and services becoming available plus any additions to the total amount of capital goods in existence. This is the total generally known as **national income** that is, the money value of the total new output of an economy in a period of time. In 1998 the UK national income was around £800 billion.

Exercise 5 Calculating national income

The figures below set out the value of output in different industries in the imaginary economy of Zetaland for the years 1990 and 2000.

Zetaland Output of industry (£ millions)	1990	2000
Agriculture, forestry and fishing	10	12
Mining and quarrying	15	12
Manufacturing	57	65
Construction	20	30
Transport	13	18
Insurance, banking and finance	18	25
Distributive trades	25	40
Other services	22	32
Gross domestic product (GDP) =		
*Net property income from abroad	5	10
Gross national product (GNP) =		
*Depreciation	20	28
Net national product (NNP) =		

* Be careful – do you add or take away?

1 Calculate GDP, GNP and NNP in Zetaland for 1990 and 2000.

2 Define GDP, GNP and NNP and explain why these figures differ.

3 **a** What has happened to national income in Zetaland between 1990 and 2000?
b Assuming all prices have not changed since 1990 explain what may have caused this change in national income.
c Still assuming prices have not changed in Zetaland, what possible advantages may the change in national income bring its people?

A note on real national income and money national income The measurement of national income is carried out in terms of money values. Output values are measured in terms of what is paid for them in terms of money. But using money as a measure can give rise to problems when prices rise and, as a result, the value of output, spending and incomes change. Just because the value of output, spending and incomes has risen in terms of money, due to higher prices, people may be no better off. Indeed, they may even be worse off, because what matters is how much, in terms of the amount of goods and services, incomes can buy. The amount of goods and services the national income can buy is known as the **real value of output** or **real national income**. For example, assume the national income in Zetaland in 1998 was £200 million and bought 100 million goods, each one sold for £2 each. By 1999 the price of each good had increased to £3. National income in Zetaland had also increased to £300 million in terms of money, but in real terms people were no better off because the national income still only bought 100 million goods. Clearly, if prices had remained the same and real output had increased to 150 million goods instead, Zetaland would be better off!

As economists, therefore, it is important to know, when measuring national income from year to year, how much of its increase is due simply to rising prices and how much is due to an increase in the number of goods and services available for the people in a country to enjoy. We return to this comparison in Chapter 13.

Using national income figures

In early times no one was very interested in national income figures. However, in the Second World War many governments realized there was a need to know how much their nations could produce for the war effort. Since then, the Government has collected and published figures on income in their National Income and Expenditure publication or 'Blue Book' every year.

These figures help the Government and economists in a number of ways.

1 If the Government knows how resources are being used, and what they are making, it is more able to try and change the allocation of resources. For example, if the Government finds the economy is producing too many consumer goods, like personal stereos, it may try to encourage the production of capital goods instead.

2 It allows comparison to be made of the standard of living in one year compared to the next. If the amount of goods and services produced in an economy has increased over time, and therefore national income is higher, we can assume most people are better off.

3 The figures allow us to compare our standard of living with other countries. Dividing national income by the population in a country gives an indication of how much each person on average earns in a country.

Key words

Write definitions for the following terms:

National income	Recession	Net property income from abroad
Aggregate demand	Trade cycle	Gross Domestic Product
Circular flow of income	Boom	Gross National Product
Injections	Depreciation	Net National Product
Withdrawals	Crowding out	

Now check your understanding of these terms by returning to the chapter.

Chapter 13

Macroeconomic Problems (1): Inflation, Unemployment, and Growth

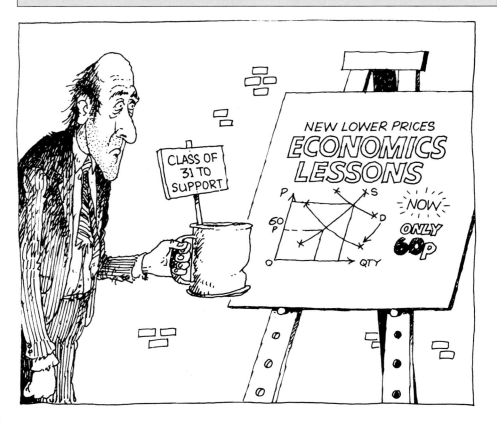

Aims

At the end of this chapter you should be able to:

1 Define what is meant by **inflation** and describe how it is measured.

2 Calculate a **weighted price index**.

3 Analyse the causes of rising inflation.

4 Assess the costs of inflation.

5 Calculate the **unemployment rate**.

6 Understand the problems defining unemployment.

7 Analyse possible causes of unemployment in the UK.

8 Examine the personal costs and economy-wide costs of widespread unemployment.

9 Describe and explain the nature and desirability of **economic growth**.

10 Calculate **real GDP per capita**.

Inflation on target to hit 35-year low of 1pc

INFLATION fell to a five-year low of 1.3 per cent last month – and is on course to fall to just 1 per cent later this summer.

If it does break the one-point barrier, it will be the first time since February 1964, when Reginald Maudling was Chancellor of the Exchequer in the Tory Government of Sir Alec Douglas-Home.

Then, a loaf of bread cost the old money equivalent of just over 5p, a pint of beer 11p, and a pint of milk just over 3p.

Yesterday's figures will prompt further pressure for another cut in interest rates. Only a few days after the bank base rate was slashed to 5 per cent – a 22-year low – new figures show prices are rising at the slowest rate since October 1994.

According to the Office for National Statistics, the annual underlying rate of inflation in May was 2.1 per cent, down from 2.4 per cent the previous month, and well below the official Government target of 2.5 per cent.

Headline inflation, which includes mortgage interest repayments, also continued to decline in May, from 1.6 per cent to 1.3 per cent – the lowest level since 1993.

At the same time, the euro zone measure of inflation, the so-called harmonised index of consumer prices, also showed a fall from 1.5 per cent to 1.3 per cent.

Conversion chart

Pre-decimal money	Decimal money
£1 (= 20s)	£1 (= 100p)
1s	5p
1d	Less than ½p

Just look at what things cost in 1957!

Item	Price in 1957	Price in 1999	How inflation would boost 1957 price
Average price of a house	£2,170	£96,600	£28,932
1lb of potatoes	3d	30p	40p
1lb of New Zealand butter	4s 1d	90p	£2.79
Large white loaf	7½d	79p	£1
Pint of milk	7d	50p	93p
20 cigarettes	2s 11d	£3.95	£2.13
Electric kettle	£4 16s 11d	£17.20	£64.64
Toaster	£6 14s 11d	£19.50	£89.91
Cinema ticket	2s 6d	£5.50	£2.00
Return air fare London/Paris	£15 10s	£284.40	£206.15
Electricity per kW hour	1½d	9.9p	20p

Daily Mail, 16.6.1999

The article above tells us that price inflation in 1999 had fallen to a very low rate. This does not mean prices had fallen. It means that the general level of prices in the UK in 1999 was not rising as fast as it had done in the past. Not all prices need go up at the same rate. For example, if all prices had increased at the same rate since 1957, the average price of a house in 1999 according to the table should only have been £28 932 not £96 600. On the other hand, the price of an electric toaster should have been nearly £90 instead of £19.50. Some prices may even fall over time due to the impact on costs of more efficient production methods and technological improvements. So what exactly is inflation?

Inflation refers to a general and sustained rise in the level of prices of goods and services. That is, prices of the vast majority of goods and services on sale to consumers just keep on rising and rising. Prices change over time so inflation is always given per period of time – per month or per year. In 1998–99 the inflation rate in the UK was 2.9%. That is, on average the prices of all goods and services rose by 2.9 pence in every pound over that year. However, compared to 1975 this increase in prices appears quite low. In 1975 the inflation rate in the UK stood at approximately 25%: a good that cost £100 at the start of 1975 would have cost £125 by the start of 1976. But even this inflation rate is low in comparison to the increase in prices some countries have faced at different times in history. In the mid-1990s Brazil experienced a rise in prices by an average of 2 300% in one year while Bolivia faced an inflation rate of 20 000% during the 1980s! This type of run-away inflation during which prices rise at phenomenal rates and money becomes almost worthless has been named **hyperinflation**.

Exercise 1   UK inflation since 1960

The graph below shows how the rate of inflation in the UK has changed since 1960.

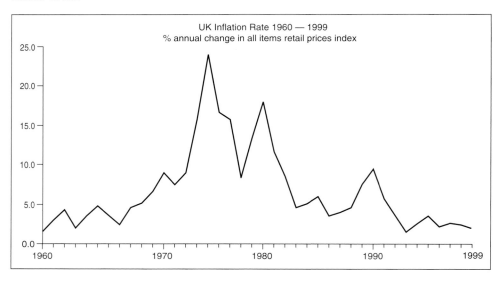

UK Inflation Rate 1960 — 1999
% annual change in all items retail prices index

Annual increases in the general level of prices during the 1950s averaged about 3%. In the decade that followed prices in general rose at the slightly higher rate of 3.5% each year on average. Throughout this period recorded annual inflation rates were in a narrow range of between 1% and 5.5%.

However, from 1969 onwards UK price inflation gathered pace, rising from 4.6% in 1968 to a peak of over 24% in 1975 following the dramatic fivefold increase in world oil prices in 1974. Between 1968 and 1979 the general price level more than tripled reducing the purchasing power of £1 in 1968 to just over 30 pence in 1979. The rapid rise in inflation during the 1970s was accompanied by rising unemployment. The term **stagflation** is used to describe the situation when prices and unemployment rise together.

Despite a climb to 18.1% in 1980 the annual inflation rate during the 1980s and 1990s has remained in single figures. Between 1981 and 1999 annual inflation has averaged 4.3%.

1   Which year on the graph was UK inflation at **a** its highest, **b** its lowest?

2   Over which ten year period was UK price inflation at its highest?

3   Explain the passage 'between 1968 and 1979 the general level of prices more than tripled reducing the purchasing power of a pound in 1968 to just over 30 pence in 1979'. (Try to find out how much £1 in 1968 would be worth today.)

Exercise 2 Hyperactive!

Living with 24,000% Inflation

● The great inflation of 1920-23, which blighted the birth of Germany's ill-fated Weilmar Republic, started in a relatively stately way — 36% in the first year, 63% in the second, and then rocketing to 3,300% in 1922. The first month in which prices (in paper money) actually doubled was September 1922. After that the country went currency-mad. A first desperate drive for stability, based on linking the value of money to the price of rye-flour, collapsed in April 1923. After this inflation recorded a 100% rise in May, 390% in June, 1,456% in July, 2,460% in August, an unbelievable 24,300% in September, and a further 17,800% in October.

It could not last. The real purchasing power of all those barrow-loads of billion-mark notes was less than Germany's money supply would have bought in 1914. When Dr Hjalmar Schacht, later Hitler's finance minister, invented a new token the "rentenmark", (later the Reichsmark) on October 20, 1923, and fixed its value at 100,000,000,000 old marks or 24 US cents, to everyone's amazement it stopped the rot almost overnight.

Peter Wilsher

Sunday Times

1 What distinguishes hyperinflation from the type of inflation experienced in the UK?

2 If the price of a good was £1 in German money in April 1923 calculate what price it would have been by the end of October 1923. Plot a graph of this price increase over time.

3 Stories have been told of how the people in Germany took barrow loads of money to local shops just to buy bread. In some cases unsuspecting people browsing in shop windows would have their barrows stolen and all their money dumped on the ground. Other people used the currency to paper their walls.

What had happened to the functions German money was supposed to perform?

4 How did Germany stop its hyperinflation?

Section 2   How to measure inflation

The rate of inflation is measured by calculating the percentage price increase in goods and services, usually over a year.

Percentage price rises are usually shown by a **price index**. In this case, index numbers or indices are simply a way of expressing the change in prices of a number of items as a movement in just one single number. The average price of all the items selected in the first year, or **base year**, is given the number 100. If on average all the prices of the selected items rise by 25%

over the following year the price index for the second year will be 125. If in the next year price rises average 10% the price index will now stand at 137.5 (that is, 137.5 − 125 = 12.5 which is 10% of 125).

Thus on average prices have risen by 37.5% over years 1 and 2.

In the UK official attempts to measure changes in the prices of a range of goods and services began in 1914. In 1947 it was given the name the **Retail Price Index (RPI)**.

The RPI calculates the average price increase as a percentage for a basket of 600 different goods and services. Around the middle of each month it collects information on the prices of these commodities from 120 000 different retailing outlets.

Total household expenditure on groups of commodities 1998

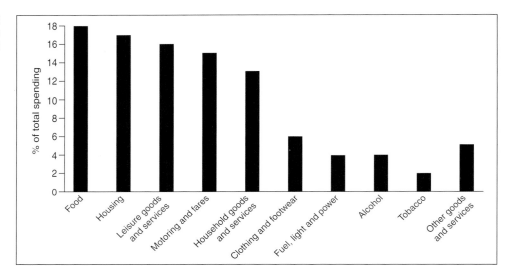

But some people spend more on some goods than on others. (See chart above.) A rise in the price of food is likely to matter much more to people than a rise in the price of tobacco.

Somehow the RPI must take this into account and average out price rises and their effect on households' spending patterns. To help them with their research the government selects 7 000 households each year to take part in the Family Expenditure Survey. Every two weeks these families record how much they have spent and on what items.

Using this information government experts decide how much a rise in the price of one good matters to people compared to another. For example, spending on food represents about 18% of households' spending, whereas spending on tobacco only accounts for 3% of total spending. Thus, food price rises are given more importance in the RPI. This would be achieved by **weighting** the price rise on food six times more than the price rise on tobacco. The RPI calculates the weighted price index for all 600 goods and services. A base year is chosen and the average level of prices in this year is given the number 100. The base year chosen is a typical year in the sense that there is neither very low or very high inflation, or any extraordinary occurrences like wars or general strikes by workers which can distort prices.

Taking the base year as 1990 (RPI = 100) the index of retail prices stood at 132.4 by 1999. That is, on average the prices of the basket of goods and services used to calculate the RPI had risen by 32.4% over this nine-year period.

The Retail Prices Index 1990–99

Year	RPI	% Increase on previous year
1990	100.0	9.4
1991	105.8	5.8
1992	109.8	3.8
1993	111.5	1.6
1994	114.3	2.5
1995	118.2	3.4
1996	121.1	2.4
1997	124.9	3.1
1998	129.1	3.4
1999	132.4	2.0

As the pattern of consumer spending changes over time so the RPI will have to change to weights it attaches to different commodities. The chart shows how spending categories and weights have changed between 1963 and 1997.

Weighting of main groups in RPI in 1963 and 1997

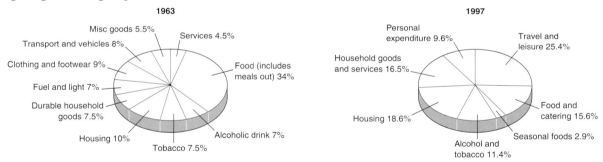

The RPI must also take account of new goods coming on to the market, for example, consumers are now devoting more of their spending to mobile phones and digital camcorders, goods which only ten years ago were not available.

RPIX is also an important measure of price inflation in the UK. It is simply the RPI excluding changes in interest rates charged on money loaned to buy flats, houses and business premises. When mortgage interest rates are rising fast the RPI will also be rising rapidly even if the prices of other goods and services are not changing. Also, there are more people in the UK without a mortgage than there are people with mortgages to pay. Taking out mortgage interest payments from the RPI therefore provides a better measure of the rate of price inflation in the UK. When interest rates are stable or changing only very slowly the RPIX and RPI will be very similar or even the same.

Inflation and the supply of money

Economists today tend to agree that the main cause of inflation is 'too much money chasing too few goods'. This means people are able to increase their spending on goods and services faster than producers can supply the goods and services they want to buy. The rise in spending causes an excess of aggregate demand for goods and services and their prices are forced upwards.

The Government can allow the supply of money to rise in the economy by issuing more notes and coins or allowing the banking system to create more credit, that is, lending more to people and firms to spend (see Chapter 15). The Government may expand the money supply

• to increase aggregate demand in the economy in an attempt to reduce unemployment.

• in response to an increase in demand for goods and services from consumers and firms.

• in response to workers demands for higher wages, or a rise in the other costs of production.

Exercise 3   The money supply and prices

The graph below shows the rate of inflation as measured by the retail prices index, and the rate of growth in the money supply from 1970 to 1999. (The money supply here is defined as all notes and coins in circulation plus money held by private sector individuals and firms in deposit accounts with banks and building societies. This measure of the supply of money in the UK economy is known as M4 (see Chapter 19).

RPI and UK money supply, 1970–1998
(% annual change)

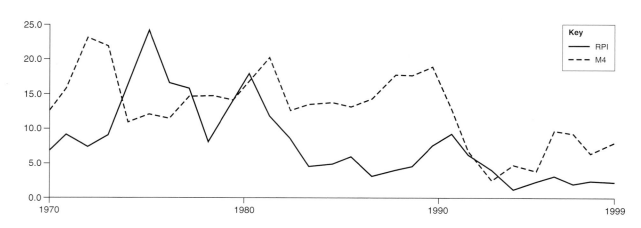

1   If the supply of money rises, how will this affect the amount of spending on goods and services?

2 Given what is likely to happen to spending, what effect will this change in demand have on the prices of goods and services?

3 If people try to spend more on goods and services but there are no more available, suggest what will happen to their prices and why.

4 Does the graph suggest that an increase in the rate of growth in the money supply causes higher inflation one year or so later? Give examples from the graph to support your view.

If the money supply expands people will have more money to spend. As they spend this money the increase in demand forces up the prices of the goods and services they buy. To understand why increases in the rate of growth in the money supply cause inflation let us consider a very simple example.

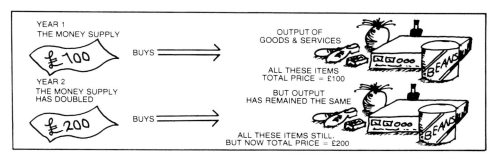

In year 1 the money supply stood at £100 and bought six items for a total cost of £100. In the second year output has remained the same. The simple economy can only produce six items. There are no more resources available to make any more each year. Now suppose the growth in the money supply is 100%. That is it doubles to £200. As consumers try to spend this money they find there are no extra goods and services to buy. With a fixed supply prices must rise. Indeed, they double. Inflation is 100%! Clearly, if output could have risen prices need not have gone up by so much, if at all.

The non-accelerating inflation rate of unemployment (NAIRU)

How much more inflation there will be depends on how near the economy is to the **non-accelerating inflation rate of unemployment** or **NAIRU**. If resources, such as labour, are unemployed, they can be employed to raise output as aggregate demand for goods and services increases. As firms increase the supply of goods and services to meet demand, prices will tend to rise only very slowly over time. That is, the economy is below its NAIRU because resources are unemployed. However, if resources are hard to come by or fully employed, firms will not be able to expand output as quickly as demand is rising, and so they will tend to raise their prices instead. As a result, the rate at which prices rise will tend to accelerate because the economy is above its NAIRU.

A monetary rule

Economists argue that what is true in the simple example above is true for a highly complex economy. Any increase in the supply of money will cause inflation to accelerate if there is no growth in real output. Only if the output of goods and services rises should the money supply rise so that people have enough money to buy up these extra products.

273

This means there is a **monetary rule** the Government can follow if it wants to keep inflation low and stable in the economy: it should only allow the supply of money to expand at the same rate as the increase in real output or real GDP over time. Increases in the money supply over and above increases in output simply cause inflation to rise. However, this can take time. It may take a year or more before prices increase faster after a rise in the money supply. It takes time for consumers' spending to rise, firms to realize demand has increased, and for firms to raise their prices.

Government policy and inflation

Some economists argue that different UK governments over time only have themselves to blame for the high inflation rates the UK experienced during the 1970s and 1980s. This is because they tried to boost demand to reduce unemployment in the economy in periods when labour unemployment was high and rising. They did this by allowing the money supply to expand faster than output was growing. For a time the increase in demand would reduce unemployment as firms took on more resources to produce more goods and services. However, inflation soon began to rise as aggregate demand increased faster than output. Eventually the high inflation would reduce the purchasing power of people's incomes and demand for goods and services would begin to fall. Workers would demand higher wages to keep pace with the rising cost of living and so unemployment would rise again as firms reduced their demand for labour. As a result, Government policy was responsible for **stagflation** – a situation when inflation and unemployment were high and/or rising together.

Demand-pull inflation

Inflation caused by an increase in aggregate demand is called **demand-pull inflation**. Aggregate demand in an economy will rise if spending by governments, consumers and/or firms increases (see Chapter 12). Consumers will be able to spend more of their incomes if they reduce saving or if a government cuts income taxes.

An increase in aggregate demand will cause prices to increase and inflation to rise if firms are unable to increase the supply of goods and services at the same rate as demand because the economy is at or above its NAIRU.

To finance an increase in aggregate demand consumers and firms may borrow more from the banking system and/or the government can issue more notes and coins. Both of these ways of financing an increase in demand involve increasing the supply of money in the economy.

Cost-push inflation

Inflation caused by higher costs feeding into higher prices is called **cost-push inflation**. The cost of producing goods and services can rise because workers demand increases in wages not matched by increased productivity (see Chapter 11). Firms may pass these higher costs on to consumers as higher prices so that they do not have to suffer a cut in their profits. However, as wages rise the demand for labour will tend to fall and workers could be made unemployed. To prevent a rise in unemployment the government may expand the supply of money to boost aggregate demand.

Continual increases in prices may take place if workers demand more and more wages time and time again. This will cause a **wage–price spiral**. As prices rise, workers will want more wages so they can buy the more expensive products. However, these higher wages simply add to firms' costs and so prices rise even further prompting even higher wage demands. And so it goes on.

Increases in the cost of materials, transport, power and other costs of production can also cause inflation if the higher costs are passed on to consumers as higher prices. Inflation rose rapidly in the UK in 1974 and 1979 following significant increases in the world price of oil.

Economists who believe in cost-push theories of inflation argue that most firms simply calculate how much it costs to produce a product and then add on a **mark-up** for profit to obtain a price to sell it for. This is known as **cost plus profit pricing**.

Imported inflation Many materials and finished goods and services are imported from overseas. An increase in their prices will also boost inflation in the UK. This **imported inflation** can occur if the value of the UK pound falls against foreign currencies like the US dollar or French franc (see Chapter 14). As the value of the pound falls the price paid for imported products will rise even if the prices of those goods in US dollars, French francs or other foreign currencies have not changed. The reverse is also true: if the value of the pound rises the price paid for imported products will fall.

It has been argued that in the late 1990s the government was able to keep inflation low by keeping the value of the pound high.

275

Exercise 4 Pushing or pulling?

The graphs below display changes in import prices, changes in average earnings, changes in aggregate expenditure and changes in the UK inflation rate as shown by the Retail Price Index.

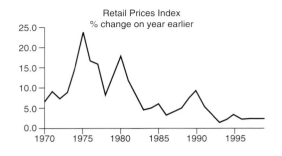

Retail Prices Index
% change on year earlier

UK Import Prices
% change on year earlier

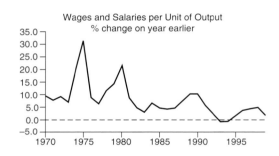

Wages and Salaries per Unit of Output
% change on year earlier

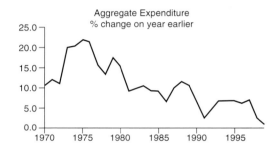

Aggregate Expenditure
% change on year earlier

1 From the graphs in which year was:
  a inflation at its highest,
  b the largest increase in, unit wage costs,
  c the biggest rise in import prices,
  d the greatest increase in total expenditure?

2 Explain how the following may affect inflation:
  a an increase in import prices,
  b an increase in wages.

3 What is the wage–price spiral?

4 What is likely to happen to the level of employment if wages rise without an increase in workers' productivity?

5 What effect may an increase in total expenditure have on:
  a inflation
  b employment?

6 Look carefully at all the graphs. Is there evidence of:
  a cost-push inflation
  b demand-pull inflation?

Use figures from graphs to support your arguments.

7 What effect do you think inflation has on the total demand for goods and services in the UK?

People are always moaning about rising prices. But why is inflation thought to be so bad?

Exercise 5   How inflation affects . . .

THE GREAT DIVIDE: How we spend our money

The diagram above shows how different income groups allocate their spending among different commodities.

1   How does inflation affect the amount of goods and services one pound of money can buy?

2   Which income group displayed above will be the most affected by a rise in the price of:
    a   food, heating fuel and housing costs?
    b   household goods and transport?

3   Are people always worse off if prices rise? Explain your answer.

4   Which income groups above are probably the:
    a   most able
    b   least able to increase their incomes?

5   Low-income earners include pensioners and many students. Who decides the level of their incomes?

6   If prices rise and people cannot afford to buy as many goods and services as before what effect will this have on unemployment?

7   If the prices of British goods go up faster than foreign goods what is the likely effect on:
    a   foreign demand for UK exports
    b   UK consumers' demands for imports?

The personal costs of inflation

Rising prices reduce the **purchasing power** of people's incomes. That is, their **real income**, in terms of what it can buy, falls. For example, if a person's income in terms of money, or their **money income** (also called **nominal income**), was £100 it could buy ten goods at £10 each. If each one of those goods goes up in price to £20 their money income of £100 will now only buy five of those goods. That is, real income has fallen. Clearly, if that person could increase their money income to £200 they will be no worse off. However, many people will face hardship if they are unable to increase their money incomes.

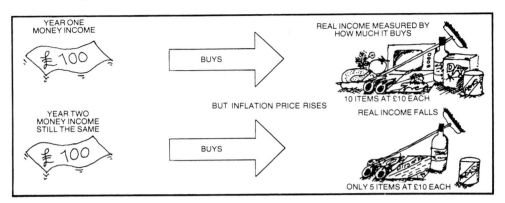

People like pensioners and students are on fixed incomes decided by the Government. If the prices of the goods and services they buy rise they may not be able to afford as much food and heating as before. Their real incomes and therefore their living standards will fall. For example, if the general level of prices rises by 10% in one year real incomes will have fallen by 10%.

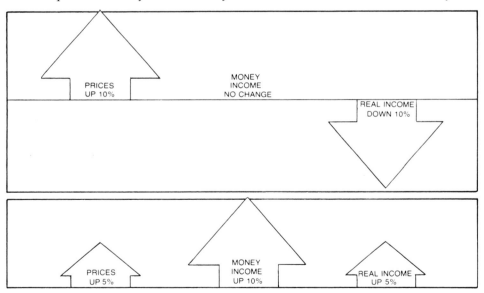

Professional people and workers in strong trade unions may be able to ask for wage or salary increases that match price rises to protect their real wages or incomes. Indeed, they may be able to secure a rise in their money incomes that exceeds the rate of inflation. For example, if inflation is 10% in one year and money incomes rise by 15%, then in real terms they will be 5% better off. However, many workers, especially the low paid and non-unionized workers, may not be able to do this. As prices rise they become worse off.

People who save or lend money may also be hurt by inflation. If they find the interest rate received on money they have saved or lent is lower than the inflation rate the real value of their money will fall. They will be worse off. On the other hand, people who borrow money will benefit by repaying less in real terms than they borrowed.

Pensioners, and other people on fixed incomes, can be protected from inflation by increasing their money incomes in line with inflation as measured by the Retail Price Index. This is known as **index-linking** or indexing. Indeed, state pensions and most other welfare benefits in the UK are already index-linked. Some savings schemes also offer index-linking so that the money value of people's savings can go up with inflation. Workers wages could also be index-linked.

In demand-pull inflation increased spending tends to boost company profits. However, in cost-push inflation their profits are squeezed. Rising prices may also yield the government more tax revenue as the tax paid, as a percentage of the price of goods and services, rises as their prices rise. However, the government will also have to pay more for the goods and services it buys.

The costs of inflation to the economy

Some economists argue that inflation causes unemployment. As prices rise, people cannot afford to buy so many goods and services and so demand falls. In addition, some people save more in times of high inflation to protect the real value of their savings. This again means less spending on goods and services. As a result firms may cut their output and make resources, including labour, unemployed. Thus, the three million or more workers unemployed in the mid-1980s was the result, it is argued, of the high inflation of the 1970s.

If the UK rate of inflation is higher than the rate of price inflation in other countries it becomes more and more difficult for UK firms to sell their increasingly expensive goods and services abroad. In addition, UK consumers may increase their spending on cheaper imports and buy fewer domestic products.

The argument continues as follows. If the UK can reduce its inflation rate it will become more competitive and be able to sell more goods and services. If this is so, more workers will be needed and unemployment will fall.

Section 5   Measuring unemployment

Unemployment rises to 3 million

During the 1950s and 1960s no more than 300 000 workers in the UK were unemployed in any one year on average. Throughout the 1970s unemployment began to rise and by 1979 stood at 1.3 million. During the 1980s the rise in unemployment gathered pace and in 1986 had reached 3.3 million people, some 11.1% of the total UK workforce. Between 1986 and 1990 total unemployment fell back to under 1.7 million workers but within 3 years the number of people out of work had once again grown to nearly 3 million as the economic recession of the early 1990s bit deep into UK economic activity. Unemployment has since fallen every year and in mid 1999 was just under 1.3 million.

The amount of time any one person spends unemployed has also increased over time. That is, on average, the duration of unemployment has risen. In 1971 about 15% of the unemployed work force had been out of work for more than a year. By 1987 46% of the unemployed work force had been unemployed for over a year. By 1999 25% of the unemployed workforce had been unemployed for over a year, and 12%, or 300 000 people, had been out of work for over two years! 31% of people who have been out of work for over three years were over 40 years of age.

UK Unemployment 1950–98

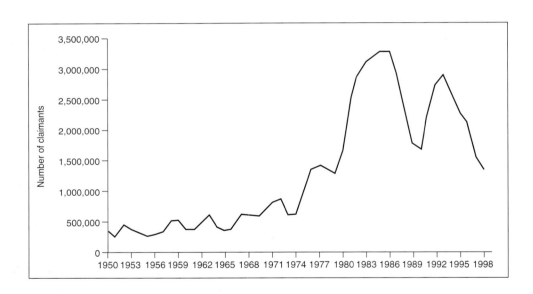

Unemployment among young people aged between 18 and 24 years of age has remained high over time. Young workers lack work experience and are often the first to be laid off when firms are cutting back staff for this reason and because their redundancy payments will be small or zero. In May 1999 22% of the unemployed in the UK were aged between 18 and 24 years.

The number of people unemployed in the UK is measured by the government each month. The **Jobseekers Allowance (JSA) claimant count** is a count of all those people who are claming unemployment related benefits at Employment Service local offices and who have declared they are unemployed, capable of, available for, and actively seeking work during the week in which their claim is made. People claiming unemployment benefits

Claimant Unemployment: by duration, sex and age, May 1999

UK   *Percentages and thousands*

	Duration of unemployment (percentages)					
	Up to 13 weeks	Over 13 weeks and up to 6 months	Over 6 and up to 12 months	Over 12 and up to 24 months	Over 24 months	Total (=100%) (thousands)
Males aged:						
18–24	50.9	25.1	19.0	3.9	1.2	203.5
24–49	31.0	17.8	19.0	16.8	15.3	597.2
50 and over	28.3	15.6	16.1	15.5	24.4	162.4
All ages	35.1	19.0	18.4	13.7	13.7	972.1
Females aged:						
18–24	51.2	24.8	19.2	3.6	1.2	83.0
24–49	39.1	20.0	18.2	13.3	9.4	146.4
50 and over	32.5	17.9	17.7	15.3	16.5	54.1
All ages	42.2	21.0	18.1	10.6	8.1	290.3

Labour Market Trends, Office for National Statistics, July 1999

must enter a Jobseekers Agreement setting out the action they will take to find work and improve their prospects of finding employment – for example, with the help of the Employment Service training courses in writing job applications and interview techniques.

The claimant count is compared with the total working population in the UK and expressed as a percentage to give the unemployment rate. In May 1999 the unemployment rate in the UK was just below 5%. That is, around 5 out of every 100 workers were unemployed in the UK.

Exercise 6   Calculating unemployment rates

Overleaf is a table of figures for the working population in the UK and the total number of people officially out of work for selected years from 1975 to 1999. Using the figures calculate the unemployment rate (%) in the UK and then plot these figures on a suitable graph.

$$\text{Unemployment rate \%} = \frac{\text{Number unemployed}}{\text{Working population}} \times \frac{100}{1}$$

Year	UK Working population (000s)	UK Unemployed (000s)
1975	25 894	978
1980	26 972	1 665
1985	27 891	3 271
1990	28 775	1 665
1993	28 249	2 919
1996	27 977	2 122
1999	27 667	1 276

Because unemployment figures are calculated only for the number of people who register to claim benefits many people argue that the official government statistics understate the true level of unemployment in the UK. For example, many married women may be looking for work but cannot claim benefits. Some workers are forced to take early retirement but may want to carry on working. Many people work in part-time jobs when what they really wish to be is full time. Also excluded from official figures are young people who stay on in the sixth form at schools and colleges because they fear they will not be able to get a job. Young people on government training schemes are also not counted in unemployment figures.

Groups of people like these are said, to be the **hidden unemployed**. That is, official figures conceal the fact that many more people are looking for work than the official unemployment record suggests.

Section 6 | Why do workers lose their jobs?

Exercise 7   The rise and rise of unemployment again

Look at the extracts opposite. What do they suggest causes unemployment? In groups, write a report for the government expressing a summary of your thoughts on the causes of unemployment and what action you would take to reduce it.

There will always be some unemployment in an economy. **Frictional unemployment** occurs as workers change jobs and spend some time looking for a new one. Workers may become unemployed for relatively short periods as they leave jobs they dislike, move to higher paid jobs, move their homes, are made redundant or are sacked. People who are 'in-between jobs' do not tend to remain unemployed for long.

Seasonal unemployment occurs because consumer demand for some goods and services is seasonal. For example, the number of jobs in the tourist industry tends to expand during the summer because that is when most people want to take holidays. However, during winter months many workers in hotels and holiday camps are not required. The building industry also tends to be very seasonal.

FIRMS REDUCE OUTPUT AS CONSUMER SPENDING FALLS

700 JOBS LOST IN SWITCH TO NEW TECHNOLOGY

At least one quarter of a major newspaper's workforce are to be made redundant this week in a plan to introduce new computerised typesetting machines.

LORDS CALL FOR HELP FOR MANUFACTURING INDUSTRIES

A report of the House of Lords select committee has found that Britain's poor export performance and high import penetration is the result of low levels of investment and the high level of the pound. This has caused a serious decline in the fortunes of the British manufacturing industry.

Minimum wage is no route to maximum employment

Minimum wages hit the young hardest

PEOPLE SEEKING WORK FACE NATIONAL INSURANCE TRAP

A recent report has urgued that the present structure of employer's national insurance contributions has reduced the demand for labour. Employers pay no national insurance contributions for an employee earning less than £56 per week but will have to pay 4.6 pence in every pound for every employee earning from £56 to £95 each week.

A FAMILY MAN ON OR BELOW AVERAGE EARNINGS MIGHT JUST AS WELL BE ON THE DOLE

Frictional and seasonal unemployment are not a big problem. The Government is, however, concerned with unemployment that is long-lived and due to more serious problems in the economy.

Falling demand

In Chapter 12, Exercise 3 we saw how falling demand for goods and services can have a downward multiplier effect on output, employment and incomes. If the demand for cars fell it would not just be the car industry that suffered job losses.

Unemployment in the UK may also be triggered by a fall in demand for UK exports to other countries. The price of UK goods on a world market may be too high because of high UK inflation or because the value of the UK currency sterling is high.

Cyclical unemployment occurs when there is too little aggregate demand for goods and services in the economy during an economic recession. Falling demand during a slump in the business cycle will mean falling spending on goods and services. In response firms will reduce production and workers can become unemployed. The mass unemployment experienced in many countries during the 1930s was blamed on a very severe world recession.

Structural change

If the fall in demand, for some goods and services is permanent because of a change in peoples tastes, for example, in favour of new goods and services or cheaper sources of supply from overseas firms, the change in demand is called structural.

Structural unemployment arises from long-term changes in the structure of the economy as entire industries close down because of a lack of demand for the goods or services they produce. As a result, many workers are made unemployed and have skills which are no longer wanted. That is, they are occupationally immobile. Re-training in new skills may help them become more mobile and find new jobs.

There are many examples of structural change in the UK economy. Many years ago shipbuilding, coal mining, iron and steel making, and textiles employed many thousands of workers. Today, these industries produce very little in the UK and employ very few workers. Instead, most workers are employed in the service sector of the economy (see Chapter 7).

Technological advance

Technological progress has meant machines have become smaller but are able to undertake much more work. Computers and microchip technology have revolutionized the production of many goods and services, and in some cases labour has been replaced by machines giving rise to what some people term technological unemployment. However, as economists we should recognize the potential benefits of being able to reallocate these unemployed resources to other uses. For example, there has been a rapid growth in employment in technologically advanced industries such as electronics, computers and communications.

Imperfections in the labour market

In a free labour market the forces of demand and supply will determine the wages workers are paid for different jobs and how many workers are employed (see Chapter 11). However, it is often argued that labour markets in the UK and many other countries have imperfections. That is, there are factors that interfere with the way markets work and reduce the number of workers employed.

1   Powerful trade unions demand wages that are too high.
Trade unions may attempt to increase the wages of their members which are not matched by improvements in productivity – for example, by threatening to take industrial action (see Chapter 11). As wages rise, employers may not be able to afford as many workers and so reduce their demand for labour. Reducing the power of trade unions, it is argued, may allow wages to fall and employment to rise.

2   Benefits paid to the unemployed reduce the incentive to work.
The UK Government provides cash benefits to workers who become unemployed. However, many people believe this simply causes unemployed workers not to bother to look for work because they are better off 'on the

dole'. They would only be willing to work at much higher wages. The supply of labour falls and less people will be in employment.

Those people who decide not to work (**voluntary unemployment**) may be forced back to work by cutting the benefits they receive. However, this may be unfair to those people who are out of work through no fault of their own because of a fall in the demand for the good or service they produce (**involuntary unemployment**).

3 Employers' national insurance contributions make it too expensive to employ workers.

For every worker a firm employs it must pay the government a tax in the form of employer's national insurance. This increases the cost of employing workers and so reduces firms' demands for their services. Cutting employers' contributions may give them the incentive to employ more workers.

4 A lack of job information prevents people from finding jobs.

Workers who leave their jobs to search for better ones are probably never fully aware of all the possible jobs, and the wages, conditions and other factors involved in these jobs. As a result, it is unlikely that a worker will take the first job offered to him or her and will therefore be unemployed for some time as he/she searches for work. Improving information on jobs available is one way of increasing workers' knowledge of jobs and reducing the likelihood of them spending a lot of time searching for jobs. To this end the government has invested in the opening of many high street Job Centres.

5 The minimum wage has been set too high and reduced the demand for labour.

Since April 1999 workers between 18 and 22 years of age must be paid a minimum of £3 per hour, and workers over 22 must be paid at least £3.60 per hour. Workers on lower rates of pay have benefited from the minimum wage legislation. However, some employers argue this will reduce the demand for labour, especially for low skilled workers with low levels of productivity.

6 The immobility of labour prevents workers from finding new jobs

When economists talk of labour **immobility** they refer to the inability of workers to move to other jobs.

If workers are unable to move to a different job requiring different skills they may be unable to do so because they are not qualified. This is known as **occupational immobility**. In some cases re-training in the skills required will allow them to take on different jobs. However, in some cases a trade union closed shop may prevent non-union members taking on a particular job. Professional associations of solicitors or architects, for example, may act in the same way and prevent people entering their occupation unless they have taken certain examinations.

Some employers may even refuse to employ some people because of their sex or colour, although this is illegal if it can be proved.

Other workers are immobile if they are unable or unwilling to move to another area to take up a job. In this case a worker is said to be **geographically immobile**. Regional differences in house prices, ties with family and friends, children's schooling and many other factors may prevent people from moving in search of work.

When workers are immobile they will tend to stay unemployed for longer periods of time.

Section 7 | The costs of unemployment

Unemployment has been described as one of the 'greatest evils of our times' and a 'drain on the nation'. In this section we will try to discover the consequences of unemployment.

Exercise 8 A sorry tale to tell

1 How does the article on page 287 suggest unemployment can affect family life?

2 What other personal costs can an unemployed person face?

3 'The unemployed are just a bunch of scroungers. They should be forced to do national service in the army!'

This is one view of unemployment expressed in the letter page of a local newspaper. Using information from the article and drawing on your own experience of people who are unemployed, pretend you are the following three people in turn. Write a reply to the newspaper expressing how you feel about being unemployed as

    a a person in their late teens living with their parents,
    b a person in their late thirties with children to support,
    c a person in their late fifties.

Compare your views on how these people would feel with the views of others in your class.

Unemployed drown their sorrows

Beneath the national aggregates for disposable income and consumer durables, modern Britain is fostering an underclass of unemployed and unskilled workers, afflicted by family breakdown and also alcoholism. David Walker, Social Policy Correspondent, describes the two nations disclosed by the new edition of Social Tends.

In recent years a network of advisory and counselling services has grown up, among them Alcoholics Anonymous. In the 6 years before 1983. AA's clients increased from 13,4000 to 30,000 and the organization expanded from 895 to 1880 branches, a reflection of growing alcohol abuse and Social Trends shows how for men of all ages serious alcohol problems are much more prevalent in Ulster and Scotland and among the un-employed. In spite of the fact that the unemployed usually have less to spend on drink and everything else there is a considerably higher proportion of heavy drinkers among unemployed men.

About 43% of unemployed men aged 25 to 46 are counted as heavy drinkers, compared with 28% of men of the same age in work.

This pattern of drinking reflects a cultural habit: most working class men have manual working class backgrounds, and it is the manual socio-economic groups which include relatively high proportions of drinkers.

Unemployment's effects are more evident than in previous editions of Social Trends. Divorce rates among couples where the man is jobless are noticeably high. There is a link with chronic illness.

Blacks are more likely to have experienced joblessness than white workers, likewise young people. Surveys show that about 94% of professional people and those in management jobs have not been unemployed in the past year. But 77% of manual workers have experienced no unemployment in the past year.

Men experiencing joblessness in the year prior to interview % experiencing 1 or more spells out of work

Age group
18–24	35
25–39	16
40–59	16
All men aged 18–64	18

Colour
White	17
Non-white	29

Social type
Professional/managerial	6
Skilled	
Non-manual	11
All non-manual	8
Skilled manual	17
Semi-skilled/unskilled manual	32
All manual	23

Men's drinking habits
Age Group/Employment type of Drinker as % employment group

	Abstainer	Occasional	Frequent	Heavy
Age 18–24				
Working	4	11	49	35
Unemployed	7	19	36	38
Economically inactive (eg student)	9	11	52	27
Age 25–44				
Working	3	19	51	28
Unemployed	7	13	36	43

The cost for people in work

The unemployed receive support from the UK Government paid from taxation, but Government revenue from taxes on incomes and expenditures will be lower than they would have been had fewer people been unemployed and more people were in paid employment instead. People in work may therefore have to pay more taxes to pay for the rising cost of Jobseekers Allowances and other forms of support for unemployed people. As unemployment rises and tax revenues tend to fall, the government may be forced to cut back public spending in other areas, such as on schools, health care and roads. The standard of living of many more people may fall as a result while cuts in public spending may mean even fewer jobs and more unemployment in the long run.

The cost for the whole economy

As economists we should realize that leaving labour unemployed is a waste of resources. With unemployment rising total output falls and people have fewer goods and services to share. That is, the opportunity cost of having so many workers unemployed is the goods and services they could have produced. In addition, there is the opportunity cost to tax-payers. The tax revenue used to pay for the Jobseekers Allowance could have been used to fund other projects in the economy, like roads and new hospitals.

Section 8 | What is economic growth?

An increase in real output

People's demands for higher living standards have made governments try to achieve faster rates of **economic growth**. When economists and politicians talk of economic growth they refer to the increase in the amount of goods and services the whole economy can produce over and above what it produced in the last year. That is, there has been economic growth if there is an increase in the **real output** of the economy over time.

How can we measure growth?

The production and sale of commodities generates incomes for people: wages, rents, interest and profits. Economists therefore measure the rate of economic growth by how much national income, or **Gross Domestic Product (GDP)**, has increased each year in a country.

However, as prices rise, the sale of goods and services raises firms' revenues, and therefore people's incomes, without any more goods and services being produced. When prices rise there may be no real growth in output or incomes. Economists say this represents a rise in nominal or money GDP but without growth in real GDP. To find out by how much real output has changed, if at all, the effects of inflation must be taken into account.

Let us consider an example. In 1999 the small island of Costas produced 1 000 tonnes of oranges. This is the real output of that country. If each tonne of oranges sells for £50, the value of this output is £50 000, and therefore the country's income will be £50 000. In the following year inflation increases the price of one tonne of oranges to £60. Their real output remains the same at 1 000 tonnes, but the money value of this output has been inflated to £60 000. It appears as if there has been growth, but this growth is only in money terms and not in real terms. This is because £60 000 in 2000 can buy no more oranges than £50 000 did in 1999. There has been no increase in real output or GDP.

If, however, Costas can produce more than 1 000 tonnes of oranges, say 1 020 tonnes in 2001, then there will have been economic growth.

For economists people are only better off if **real GDP per capita**, that is, real income per head, increases. This is calculated by dividing the real GDP of an economy by the size of its population.

Does economic growth really make us 'better off'?

If there is an increase in real output, there has been economic growth. However, whether people have higher living standards really depends on which goods and services have increased in supply. If, for example, the Government builds more nuclear weapons, total output would have increased but most people would not view themselves as being better off.

Incomes and wealth in many economies are very unequal. If an increase in real output is simply shared out among a few rich people, the vast majority of the people in the economy will be no better off.

People might even become worse off if the population of the economy increases and goods and services become shared among more and more people. In this case real GDP per capita will fall. There will have been negative growth.

Exercise 9 Has there been growth?

Economists judge whether or not an economy has experienced economic growth by seeing if real income or real GDP has increased over time per head of the population (per capita).

1 For each of the economies below calculate the real GDP per capita in each year. (By dividing real GDP by population.)

2 Which economy, Alphaland or Betaland, has experienced economic growth?

3 Comment on your results.

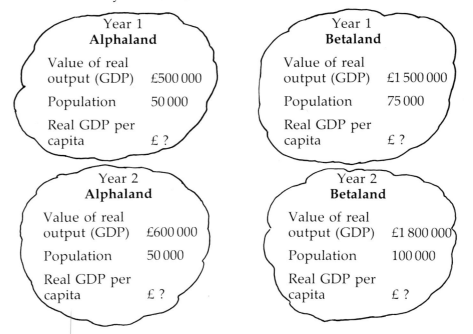

Year 1
Alphaland

Value of real output (GDP)	£500 000
Population	50 000
Real GDP per capita	£ ?

Year 1
Betaland

Value of real output (GDP)	£1 500 000
Population	75 000
Real GDP per capita	£ ?

Year 2
Alphaland

Value of real output (GDP)	£600 000
Population	50 000
Real GDP per capita	£ ?

Year 2
Betaland

Value of real output (GDP)	£1 800 000
Population	100 000
Real GDP per capita	£ ?

The graphs below display how real output, or real GDP, has changed in the UK since 1975. The graph immediately below shows the percentage change in real GDP compared to money GDP. It shows that over the periods 1974–75, 1979–81 and 1990–92 real GDP experienced negative growth rates. That is, real output in the UK fell and the people of the UK had less goods and services to enjoy.

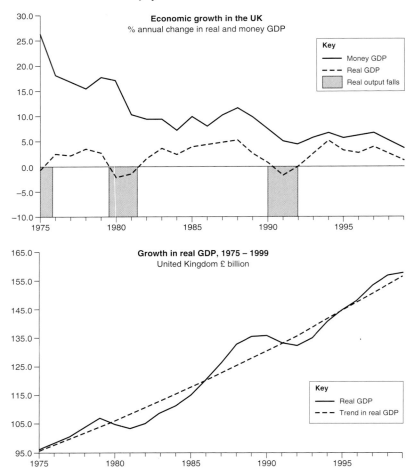

The graph above shows clearly how real GDP has risen and fallen in the UK between 1975 and 1999, from around £96 billion to just under £160 billion assuming prices have not changed since 1975. If real output grew by the same amount each year, it would have followed the trend line in the graph. When real GDP is rising above trend the economy is experiencing fast growth, or a boom. When growth in the real GDP falls below trend, the economy is said to be slowing down and possibly in recession (see Chapter 12).

The growth 'league' table

The table below shows growth rates in the value of real output or real GDP in a number of countries. For example, in the UK the economy grew by an average of 1.8% each year over the period 1990–98. That is, the economy as a whole produced 1.8% more goods and services each year. Some countries, however, experienced negative economic growth, or falling real output.

Economic growth rates 1990–98 (*1988–94)

Country	Real GDP (Average annual growth%)	Country	Real GDP (Average annual growth %)
UK	1.8	Korea	5.4
USA	2.5	Mexico	3.0
Sweden	1.2	Hungary	3.3
Japan	1.4	Turkey	4.9
Germany	2.4	Albania*	−1.6
France	1.7	Belarus*	−3.0
Australia	2.8	Somalia*	−3.0
Thailand*	9.4	Vietnam*	6.3

Section 9 — How to achieve economic growth

As economists we would wish that scarce resources are used as fully as possible, in the best possible way, to produce as many goods and services as possible. This will satisfy the most wants.

If resources are unemployed, that is, if labour is out of work, land disused or capital lying idle, then an increase in the amount of goods and services can be achieved simply by using these available resources more fully. The problem of economic growth, however, is how to increase output when all resources are fully employed. Clearly economic growth will be achieved if these resources can be used more efficiently to produce more.

Ultimately, because the scarcity of resources places a limit on how much an economy can produce, economic growth can only really be achieved by an increase in the resources of land, labour and capital.

The following are ways in which economic growth can be achieved:

The discovery of more natural resources

The discovery of North Sea gas and oil gave the UK the ability to increase her total output. Indeed, the discovery of more natural resources, like coal, gold or even new varieties of fruit or cereals, would help any economy to increase output.

An offshore North Sea oil field

291

Searching for new natural resources, however, costs a lot of money. Some countries, particularly those in the less-developed world, do not have enough money to do this.

Investment in capital

Investment, or the production of new capital equipment, that is, tools, machinery and factories, is often said to be the key to growth. People can produce much more if they have tools and machines to help them, and buildings to make things in. Investment can come from private sector firms and the government.

By lowering interest rates, the government can make it less costly for private sector firms to borrow money to buy new machines.

Technical progress

New inventions, better production techniques that produce more efficiently, better organization and management of firms, better training, better transport and communications all come under the banner of technical progress.

All these things allow a country to increase output. Progress and investment often go together when old machines are replaced by new, more sophisticated machines that can work faster.

The development of robotics and information communications technology has helped stimulate economic growth

The government may help firms to research and develop new machines and techniques by giving them cash grants (see Chapter 7).

Increasing the amount and quality of human resources

Education and training are often called 'investments in people' or 'human capital'. A more skilled and knowledgeable workforce, able to produce more, and better, goods and services, will result from better education and training.

Improving health care and medicines can improve the health of the workforce in a country and help them to have less days off sick. As a result, a healthier workforce is a more productive workforce able to raise output.

While the quality of human resources can be improved with education and health care, the actual amount of human resources or labour can also be increased in a number of ways. Longer hours and less holidays is one way, but would probably prove unpopular with the vast majority of workers. Government tax cuts may encourage people to work harder.

In recent years, more women have gone to work to help produce more. This has the effect of increasing the working population which could only be further increased by reducing the school-leaving age, which can harm growth, raising the retirement age, which would be very unpopular, or waiting for a natural increase in the population and waiting for the newly born to grow up. As long as real output rises faster than the population, real GDP per capita will rise.

A re-allocation of resources

As a country develops, resources tend to move out of primary production and into manufacturing and services where large increases in output have occurred. This has led to economic growth (see Chapter 7).

Section 10 | ## The benefits and costs of economic growth

The benefits of growth

The benefits of economic growth and increased output can be enjoyed in a number of ways.

1   Higher levels of consumption for all to enjoy, providing they have the money to buy these goods.

2   Higher levels of output can probably be achieved using less labour. People may benefit from shorter working weeks and longer holidays.

3   Rising incomes means more tax revenue for the government. They can use this money to spend on schools and colleges, hospitals, roads and many other services that may benefit us all.

The costs of growth

Despite the benefits growth can bring, there are always costs to be considered.

1   There is an opportunity cost of growth. Economic growth may be achieved by producing more capital goods but at the expense of less consumer goods, like televisions, fashionable clothes and compact discs.

2   Economic growth may mean we use up scarce resources more quickly. Oil, coal, metals and other natural resources are limited and may soon run out. When they do, there can be no more capital goods, food supplies may diminish and the population of the world may suffer.

3   An increase in the number of factories producing goods and services will mean less land available for parks and other recreational activities. Noise, fumes, river and scenic pollution may increase as economies strive to produce more. These too can destroy plants and animals.

4   Technical progress may replace workers with machines so that many people find themselves without work and unemployed for long periods of time.

Because economic growth has costs as well as benefits, many governments are now concerned with using their policies to achieve **sustainable growth**. This means using policy to minimize the costs and any harmful effects of economic growth – for example, by placing restrictions on emissions of

PROGRESS AT ANY PRICE?

harmful pollutants from power stations and vehicle exhausts, raising taxes on petrol to reduce car use, limiting developments of large superstores in out of town locations.

Exercise 10   Trying to breathe

1   What does the article shown below blame as a possible cause of the increase in asthma among children?

2   Suggest how increased car ownership and road use has helped economic growth, but may now hinder economic growth in some areas.

3   In groups discuss the possible impacts the introduction of each of the measures suggested in the article could have on **a** business location, **b** the market for new motor vehicles, **c** other transport markets, such as bus and train travel, **d** labour markets, **e** price inflation, and **f** economic growth.

Asthma and wheezing in children under five almost doubled in less than a decade, it was disclosed yesterday. In 1990 only 12% of children in this age group were diagnosed with asthma, but by 1998 this had risen to 21%, according to figures from the National Asthma Campaign.

The figures included in the National Asthma Campaign's annual asthma audit emerged from research by scientists who questioned the parents of 2 600 pre-school children in the Leicester area.

Health and environmental groups argue the increase is due to increasing road use and congestion in many towns and cities.

Exhaust emissions are at their peak in slow moving traffic.

'Children living in areas where traffic has become congested are particularly at risk from respiratory problems' argued a spokesperson for a local lobby group.

'We are asking the local authority and the government to look seriously at a number of measures they could introduce to help reduce the problem: for example, placing limits on new parking spaces, banning car use in cities on certain days, introducing additional charges for car use in congested areas and increasing taxes on vehicles and petrol.'

The Mirror, 30.1.1999

294

Key words

What key words in this chapter fit the following definitions?

1 A sustained increase in the general price level.
2 Runaway inflation at very high rates.
3 When inflation and unemployment occur together.
4 A measure of price inflation in the UK based on the change in the average price of 600 different goods and services.
5 A measure of price inflation excluding interest payments on mortgages.
6 A level of unemployment in an economy below which price inflation is relatively low and stable and above which it rises rapidly.
7 The type of inflation caused by rising aggregate demand.
8 The type of inflation caused by rising costs.
9 Inflation from overseas or caused by a falling exchange rate.
10 The official count of the number of unemployed in the UK.
11 The number of people unemployed as a percentage of the working population.
12 A situation when workers find it difficult to change jobs.
13 The type of unemployment that arises from a permanent change in the pattern of demand.
14 The type of unemployment that occurs in a recession.
15 The change in the value of GDP after the effect of price inflation on money values has been removed.
16 A sustained increase in the real output of an economy.
17 The amount of real national income per head of the population in a country.
18 Economic growth achieved with minimum social costs.

Chapter 14

Macroeconomic Problems (2): International Trade

AND NOW FOR MY FAMOUS BALANCING TRICK...

Aims

At the end of this chapter you should be able to:

1 Explain the main reasons for **international trade** including the principle of **comparative advantage**.

2 Describe and explain the main forms of **protection** against trade and the arguments for and against free trade.

3 Identify the main **visible** and **invisible exports** and **imports** of the UK.

4 Describe and explain the structure and meaning of the **balance of payments accounts**.

5 Calculate the **current balance** on the balance of payments.

6 Analyse factors that affect **foreign exchange rates**.

7 Describe the differences between **fixed** and **floating exchange rates**.

Section 1 ## Why countries specialize and trade

In Chapter 4 we discovered that people and whole regions of a country specialize in particular industries. They do this because they have skills and resources suited to the production of certain goods and services.

For the same reason, whole countries tend to specialize in the production of certain goods and services. For example, Japan is famous for her electronic industries, France for her wine, Italy for her shoes. Countries that specialize then trade their goods and services for a variety of other commodities from other countries.

Why do countries trade?	**1** Countries trade in order to get goods and services that they cannot produce themselves. For example, the UK must import zinc and copper because there is none in the UK.

1 Countries trade in order to get goods and services that they cannot produce themselves. For example, the UK must import zinc and copper because there is none in the UK.

2 Countries trade for goods that they can produce themselves but which are more cheaply made elsewhere. For example, the UK could grow tropical fruits, but only at great expense. It is cheaper for the UK to buy these goods from abroad.

3 It can pay to specialize and trade even when two countries can produce the same good at the same cost. Through trade, each country is able to sell to a larger market and benefit from economies of scale caused by mass production.

Exercise 1 Something special

1 There are many goods which the UK cannot produce herself that have to be imported. Name six such goods.

2 List at least ten goods the UK is able to produce but which we choose to import.

3 Arrange the following words, so that each country is paired up with the product in which it specializes.

New Zealand	Coffee
Brazil	Wine
India	Lamb
France	Beef
Argentina	Manufactures
West Germany	Fish
Norway	Timber
Iceland	Tea

4 List the benefits each country may gain from specialization and trade.

Section 2	The theory of comparative advantage

Case study

Absolute advantage

Music centres and wheat – will there be a gain from trade?

We will now discover in a simple exercise how countries can increase their output and their standard of living through specialization and trade.

Assume that the UK and the USA both produce just two commodities, wheat and music centres. Each country we assume will have 100 workers, half devoted to wheat production and half to the production of music centres. The total output per year of both countries is shown below.

Before specialization

	Music centres produced by 50 workers	Wheat (tonnes) produced by 50 workers
USA	40	35
UK	50	30
Total output per period	90	65

In this example, the USA is better than the UK at producing wheat. With the same number of workers the USA can produce five more tonnes of wheat than the UK. That is, they have an **absolute advantage** over the UK in wheat production. When one country is better at producing a particular commodity compared to another it is said to have an absolute advantage. The UK has an absolute advantage over the USA in music centre manufacturing. If each country specialized the USA would produce only wheat and the UK only music centres. Total output of both would rise as shown below.

After specialization

	Music centres produced by 100 workers (in UK only)	Wheat (tonnes) produced by 100 workers (in USA only)
USA	0	70
UK	100	0
Total output per period	100	70

The example assumes that 100 workers can produce twice as much as 50 workers, that is, there are no diminishing returns to labour.

If the UK now agrees to trade 40 music centres for 30 tonnes of wheat from the USA, each country after trade is better off.

After specialization and trade

	Music centres	Wheat (tonnes)
USA	40	40
UK	60	30
Total output per period	100	70

Comparative advantage

Case study

It still benefits countries to specialize and trade even if one does not have an absolute advantage in the production of a commodity. Look at the examples of Germany and Japan. We assume for simplicity that each country devotes half its 100 strong workforce to the production of cars and televisions.

	Cars	Televisions
Japan	100	400
Germany	80	160
Total output per period	180	560

Japan has an absolute advantage in both goods. However, in Japan they would need to give up four televisions to produce one extra car. In Germany only two televisions would have to be given up to produce one extra car. So Germany is relatively better at producing cars than Japan. That is, Germany has a **comparative advantage** in car manufacturing. While Germany is less efficient than Japan in producing both goods, it is least inefficient in car production.

By concentrating on the production of cars, a country like Germany can export cars and import other goods like televisions with their export earnings. Japan should, in our example, concentrate on the production of televisions. Both countries can gain from specialization and trade.

Exercise 2   At an advantage

The table below displays the monthly output of clocks and peanuts in two countries, A and B. Each country devotes half its work-force to the production of each commodity.

Country	Clocks	Peanuts (lbs)
A	2	21
B	4	7

1 What is the total output of clocks and peanuts?

2 Which country has an absolute advantage in **a** clock production, **b** peanut production? Explain the reasons for your answer.

3 Draw a table to show the output of the two countries after they have specialized in what they are best able to produce. (Assume no diminishing returns to labour.)

4 What are the total output figures now? By how much have they increased?

5 If the countries now agree to trade three clocks for twelve pounds of peanuts, show in a new table what they have gained from trade.

Section 3	Exports and imports

The UK, in common with other countries, needs to trade in order to survive. Each year the UK sells many millions of pounds worth of goods and services to other countries. These goods and services sold to other countries are known as **exports**. An export is represented by a flow of money coming into the country. At the same time, the UK buys many millions of pounds worth of goods and services from other countries. Goods and services bought from other countries are known as **imports**. An import is represented by a flow of money leaving the UK and going abroad.

Many of the UK's imports are essential foodstuffs and raw materials that allow UK firms to make their own goods and services, many of which are, in turn, sold abroad.

Without exports and imports, UK consumers would have far fewer goods and services to choose from, UK workers would find it harder to get jobs and many UK producers would go out of business.

Visible trade

Visible trade involves trade in goods, such as oil, machines, food, chemicals, etc. Trade in goods is called **visible trade** simply because exports and imports of goods may be seen, touched and weighed as they pass through UK ports.

By finding which goods the UK has a comparative advantage in, it should be possible to discover her main exports and imports.

Exercise 3   Resourceful trading

Look at the following two lists of resources.

	List A	List B
Land	Coal, oil	Zinc, copper, tin
Labour	Skilled work-force	Cheap work-force
Capital	Factories, machinery	Robots, computerized machines

1 Which list represents resources which are plentiful in the UK and which list represents resources in short supply?

2 Which exports might the list of plentiful resources allow the UK to produce?

3 Which imports does the list of resources in short supply suggest to you that the UK needs?

Visible exports

Oil

Machinery

You may have found from the exercise that because the UK has a large supply of oil and natural gas its visible exports include fuel and raw materials. The UK, as one of the most developed countries, is also well equipped with factories and a skilled work-force. These things allow Britain to export manufactures, chemicals and machinery. (The table below gives the percentage of total exports accounted for by each of the UK's main exports.)

UK Visible trade by commodity, 1997

	Exports % share of total	Imports % share of total
Food, drink and tobacco	6.5	9.3
Crude materials	1.5	3.3
Oil and other mineral fuels	6.0	3.4
Chemicals	12.7	15.2
Manufactures classified by materials used	13.1	9.5
Machinery, transport, equipment and other finished manufactures	58.9	58.3
Miscellaneous	1.3	0.9

Visible imports

You may have found from exercise 3 that the UK is short of raw materials and has to import these. Yet the UK is not short of the resources needed to produce manufactures. However, the UK still imports large numbers of these. The table shows that in 1997 over 73% of imports were manufactured items.

The fact that the UK exports and imports manufactures can in part be explained by comparative advantage. Other countries, for example Japan, are more efficient at manufacturing consumer goods, such as videos and compact disc players, than the UK is. So consumers benefit from buying imports of such goods because by buying them consumers get a wider choice and lower prices. The UK on the other hand, is efficient at manufacturing machinery and equipment and so it is sensible for the UK to concentrate on these and export them.

Yet the UK also imports and exports the same goods, for example, cars. This is done because some consumers in the UK may prefer foreign cars, while some consumers in other countries may prefer cars from the UK. Consumers like variety.

The balance of trade   When the UK sells visible exports, such as oil and manufactures to foreigners, it earns money. When the UK buys visible imports, such as video and TVs, it pays out money.

The **balance of trade** measures how well the UK does overall on visible trade.

Balance of trade (£) = Value of   − Value of
                        visible exports   visible imports

For example, if the UK sold £10 000 million worth of visible exports and bought £8 000 million worth of visible imports from abroad, it would have a balance of trade **surplus** of £2 000 million. This would mean that the UK would be earning £2 000 million a year on visible trade. If however, the UK was spending £15 000 million on visible imports, the balance of trade would be in a **deficit** of £5 000 million a year. This would mean that the UK was losing £5 000 million each year to foreign countries. This is said to be an **unfavourable** balance of trade for the UK.

The UK balance of trade or **visible balance** in recent years is given in the table on page 303.

The table shows that in most years the UK has had a balance of trade deficit. That is, the UK spends more on visibles from foreign countries than they buy from us. The minus numbers in the last column of the table show how much the UK loses to other countries each year because of visible trade. The UK had surpluses on visible trade from 1980 to 1983. These were largely due to the export of North Sea oil. Before this the UK had to import all her oil.

While the UK has an overall deficit in visible trade, it has traditionally done well in one particular visible good, manufactures. The UK has, in the past, exported more manufactures than it has imported. In 1970 exports of manufactures were 50% higher than imports of manufactures. However, this comparative advantage in manufactures has fallen, and in 1983 the UK had a deficit in manufactures for the first time in its history. This has continued.

UK balance of trade

Year	Visible exports £m	Visible imports £m	Balance of trade £m
1980	47 147	45 794	+1 353
1985	77 991	81 336	−3 345
1990	102 313	121 020	−18 707
1995	153 725	165 449	−11 724
1996	167 403	180 489	−13 086
1997	171 783	183 693	−11 910
1998	163 704	184 302	−20 598

(How did the economic downturn in the UK in the 1990s affect the demand for imports?)

Invisible trade
Invisible trade involves the exchange of services. Exports and imports of services, such as insurance, banking and tourism, cannot be seen or touched at ports, hence the name invisibles.

If a British person buys a foreign holiday s/he is paying for a foreign service which takes money out of the UK and so is an **invisible import**. If a foreigner buys insurance from the UK, s/he is buying a UK service which brings money into the UK and so is an **invisible export**.

How well the UK does in invisible trade is measured by the **invisible balance**.

Balance of invisible trade (£) =	Value of visible exports	−	Value of visible imports

303

Exports and imports of services, such as insurance and tourism, are examples of invisible trade

Year	UK invisible balance £m
1980	+1 487
1985	+6 136
1990	+4 010
1995	+8 915
1996	+8 897
1997	+11 842
1998	+12 678

The UK has a large comparative advantage in invisible trade and had an invisible surplus in nearly every one of the last 200 years. UK insurance, banking and shipping services in particular have a worldwide reputation and earn the UK a great deal of money. The main UK invisible exports are shown in the table below.

UK invisible earners

£ million	1991	1997
Transportation	7 207	10 911
Travel	8 330	13 805
Communications	1 004	998
Insurance	1 276	3 552
Financial services	3 040	6 283
Computer and information services		1 186
Royalties and licence fees	1 887	4 215
Other business services	6 339	13 865
Personal, cultural and recreational services	208	733
Government services	1 535	1 125

Invisibles also include flows of **interest, profits** and **dividends**. The UK earns interest on money saved or loaned abroad, profits from UK-owned businesses abroad, and dividends on shares held in foreign companies. On the other hand, the UK pays interest, profits and dividends on savings, loans, and investments made abroad.

A number of **transfers** are also made between countries. For example, the UK not only gives foreign aid to less developed countries but it also pays contributions to the European Union (see Chapter 18).

Exercise 4   Now you see them, now you don't!

1   Pick out from the following list:

Visible exports   Invisible exports
Visible imports   Invisible imports

a   Oil sold to Germany

b   Wine bought from France

d   Italian insures his ship in the UK

c   UK tourist takes a holiday in the USA

e   UK resident uses foreign bank

f   Foreign company uses UK advertising agency

h   UK car dealer buys Japanese cars

g   UK sells guns to Saudi Arabia

2 Calculate the balance of trade and the invisible balance from the following figures:

	£ million
Invisible imports	= 10 000
Visible exports	= 15 000
Invisible exports	= 20 000
Visible imports	= 17 000

3 Taking visible and invisible trade together state whether the country above is gaining or losing money. What effect will this have on output, employment and national income in the country?

Section 4 | **The balance of payments**

The balance of payments shows all the payments and receipts between one country and all the other countries it trades with. In the UK the balance of payments is split into three main parts: the current account, the capital account, and the financial account.

The current account

The main purpose of the balance of payments on **current account** is to show how well the country is doing in international trade in goods and services. It measures all the money paid by the UK for imports of goods and services, and all the money received by the UK for her exports of goods and services.

The current account also includes wages received by people from the UK working temporarily overseas and paid out to workers from foreign countries working temporarily in the UK. It is also records flows of money into and out of the UK for interest payments, profits and dividends (**IPD**) on loans, investments and shares. The balance of incomes received and paid out for cross-border employment and IPD is recorded in the income balance.

Central Government payments overseas, such as taxes and payments to the European Union are recorded as current transfers. Any money received by the Central Government from the European Union, such as farming subsides, are balanced against these.

The balance on current account is therefore equal to the balances of visible trade, invisible trade, income and current transfers.

306

UK balance of payments current account

£million	1991	1997
Visible exports	*103 939*	*163 704*
Visible imports	*114 162*	*184 302*
Balance of trade in goods (A)	**−10 223**	**−20 598**
Invisible imports	*31 346*	*61 777*
Invisible exports	*26 955*	*49 099*
Balance of trade in services (B)	**+4 471**	**+12 678**
Income balance (C)	**−1 953**	**+15 782**
Current transfers balance (D)	**−669**	**−6 388**
Current balance (A+B+C+D)	**−8 374**	**+1 474**

The balance of payments on current account between 1986 and 1997 is summarized in the following graph.

UK balance of payments on current account, 1986–98

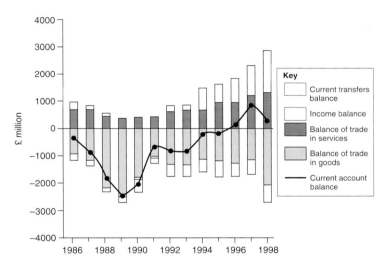

The capital account Flows of money into and out of the UK to pay for a change of ownership of fixed assets (such as houses, machinery and factories), the sale of fixed assets, or the cancellation of debts, appear in the **capital account** of the balance of payments. By far the largest amounts are due to the transfer of fixed assets belonging to overseas firms and workers moving to the UK, and money received from the European Union from the regional development fund (see Chapter 7). Money brought into the UK by immigrants, for example, are recorded as credits to the capital account, while money sent abroad by UK residents and firms emigrating to other countries are recorded as debits. The size of capital account transactions are small compared to the current and financial accounts of the balance of payments.

The financial account The financial account records flows of money into and out of the UK to pay for investments in capital, shares and loans. Any profits, dividends and interest payments (IPD) resulting from these investments are recorded as incomes in the current account.

Direct inward investment is received whenever a foreign firm sets up a factory, office or retail outlet in the UK. For example, the location of Japanese car manufacturers like Nissan and Toyota in the UK are examples of direct inward investment. Any profits reinvested in their UK operations, rather than paid to their shareholders overseas, will also score as a direct inward investment.

Portfolio investments received from overseas by the UK are purchases of shares in UK companies (equity) and loans of money (debt). When the UK Government, residents or firms buy shares in overseas companies or lend money overseas these are portfolio investments abroad.

The financial account also records government drawings on (+) or additions to (–) their reserves of foreign currencies.

UK investment overseas creates **external assets** because someday they will be repaid to the UK or provide a stream of income into the future from overseas, for example, as dividends on shares or interest on loans. Investment in the UK from overseas creates **external liabilities** because the UK may one day have to repay these investments or pay dividends and interest overseas.

If UK investment overseas exceeds investment in the UK, the financial account balance will be in deficit. This is often the case when the balance of payments on current account is in surplus because this extra money allows the UK to invest more overseas. When the current account is in deficit, however, the UK cannot invest as much abroad. The UK may even try to attract more loans and investments from overseas to pay for a current account deficit. In this case the financial account balance may be in surplus.

UK Financial Account, 1997

UK investments overseas (net debits)		Investments in the UK (net credits)	
	£m		£m
Direct investment overseas		**Direct investment in the UK**	
Equity capital	18 820	Equity capital	11 859
Reinvested earnings	16 620	Reinvested earnings	6 911
Other capital transactions	904	Other capital transactions	4 487
Portfolio investment overseas		**Portfolio investment in the UK**	
Equity	–5 508	Equity	3 123
Debt	57 497	Debt	26 498
Other investments	170 271	Other investments	195 257
Reserve assests	–2 357		
(drawings on +/additions to –)			
Total investment overseas	**256 247**	**Total investment in the UK**	**248 135**

Financial account balance (net credits *less* net debits) = –£8 112 million

Movements in 'hot money' can often cause large changes in the financial account balance. Hot money refers to short-term investments or large sums of money that are moved by investors from country to country in search of the best interest rates. High UK interest rates will attract flows of hot money from abroad.

Hot money will appear as part of UK investments overseas in the table above which summarizes the flows of UK investments in 1997.

When the total amount of money flowing out of the UK exceeds the amount the UK receives from overseas from the sale of exports and/or from borrowing, investments, etc., there is a deficit which must be paid for. For example, the Government can draw on its own reserves of gold and foreign currencies, or as a last resort can borrow from the **International Monetary Fund** and from other countries' central banks.

If there is a surplus the Government can repay foreign loans and even keep some to add to its reserves of gold and foreign currencies.

The UK balance of payments must always appear to balance. If the current account is in surplus then the financial account will usually be in deficit. However, the two need not match each other precisely because overseas trade and financial transactions figures are compiled from a great many sources by a large number of people over a long period of time and things are often left out and errors made. The **net errors and omissions** are therefore included to balance the accounts. The table below summarizes the three main sections of the balance of payments accounts and net errors and omissions in 1991 and 1997.

UK Balance of Payments, 1991 and 1997

£million	1991	1997
Current account balance (A)	−8 374	+8 006
Capital account balance (B)	+290	+262
Financial account balance (C)	+9 990	−8 112
Overall balance (A+B+C)	+1 906	+156
Net errors and omissions	−1 906	−156

How to correct a balance of payments deficit

A balance of payments deficit, resulting from imports exceeding exports and/or because the UK financial account is in deficit, is said to be unfavourable. However, a government has a number of *weapons* available to it to try and correct the imbalance.

1 Deflation

A government can use its tools of public expenditure and taxation to reduce aggregate demand in the economy (see fiscal policy in Chapter 16). Raising taxes and reducing public expenditure means there is less money being *pumped* around the circular flow of income in the economy. People will have less to spend on imports. However, a fall in aggregate demand will also affect UK industries. As people buy less UK goods this may mean more are available for export, but it is also likely to mean firms cutting back on their production and making some of their workers unemployed.

2 Interest rates

By raising interest rates in the economy the Government may attract flows of hot money into the UK as foreigners search for good returns for their money. However, high interest rates in the UK make borrowing expensive. Consumers may borrow less to spend, and firms less to invest (see Chapter 16).

3 Protectionism
This refers to policies designed to prevent trade between countries. These will be discussed in detail in the next section.

4 Devaluation
This refers to lowering the value of the pound to make UK exports cheaper for foreign countries to buy and, at the same time, to make imports more expensive. This policy is discussed in detail in section 7.

| Section 5 | Barriers to trade: Protectionism |

Exercise 5   Made in Japan

Read the article below and then answer the questions that follow.

1   Explain the 'trade barriers' the Japanese were using to 'protect' Japanese business from foreign competition. Many of these are still used today.

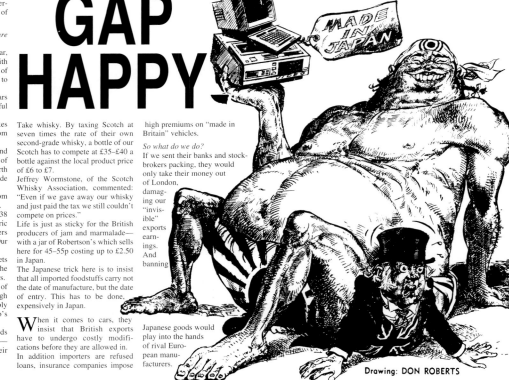

£3,700 million problem that's got Britain talking tough to Japan

Britain looks like getting tough with Japan over our ever-widening trade gap with the Land of the Rising Yen.

How crushing is the Gap? Here are the facts.
It rose to £3,700 million last year, from £600 million in 1985—with the Japanese selling us £4 worth of goods for every £1 worth we sold to them.
• We bought 214,452 Japanese cars last year. We sold them a pitiful 4,109.
• We bought 74,808 motor-bikes from them. They bought 1,550 from us.
• They sold us 485,676 TV sets and 582,001 videos. Our exports of those items to Japan are not worth recording in Department of Trade statistics.
• We bought 557,617 cameras from Japan, and exported only 164,721.
• British workers switched on £638 million worth of Japanese electric typewriters, cash registers, copiers and office machines last year. Our sales to them: £20 million.
Japan's success in world markets has nearly doubled the value of the yen against the pound in five years. That should have priced a lot of Japanese goods out of our High Streets and made ours irresistibly cheap along the Ginza, Tokyo's Oxford Street.
The Japanese use all kinds of tricks to stop our goods—however good—reaching their shops.

Take whisky. By taxing Scotch at seven times the rate of their own second-grade whisky, a bottle of our Scotch has to compete at £35–£40 a bottle against the local product price of £6 to £7.
Jeffrey Wormstone, of the Scotch Whisky Association, commented: "Even if we gave away our whisky and just paid the tax we still couldn't compete on prices."
Life is just as sticky for the British producers of jam and marmalade—with a jar of Robertson's which sells here for 45–55p costing up to £2.50 in Japan.
The Japanese trick here is to insist that all imported foodstuffs carry not the date of manufacture, but the date of entry. This has to be done, expensively in Japan.

When it comes to cars, they insist that British exports have to undergo costly modifications before they are allowed in. In addition importers are refused loans, insurance companies impose high premiums on "made in Britain" vehicles.

So what do we do?
If we sent their banks and stock-brokers packing, they would only take their money out of London, damaging our "invisible" exports earnings. And banning Japanese goods would play into the hands of rival European manufacturers.

Drawing: DON ROBERTS

adapted from *Sunday Mirror*, 5.4.1987

2 What effects could these trade barriers have on UK exports to Japan and consequently output, employment and income in the UK?

3 Imagine you are a government economist who has been asked to write a report for the Government on trade with Japan. In your report:

    a Outline the problem using information from the article.

    b Say what possible action the UK could take to try to stop or retaliate against this unfair competition.

    c State the problems involved if such action was taken.

We have seen how it can benefit countries to trade with each other, yet often countries attempt to prevent trade. In this section we will investigate the possible **barriers to trade** used to protect a country from foreign competition.

Trade barriers

You may have discovered from the exercise above that one or more of the following can be used to reduce trade between countries.

1 Tariffs

A tariff is a tax on the price of imports. Tariffs are used to raise the prices of imports to make them more expensive than home-produced goods to stop people buying them.

Tariffs, however, can encourage retaliation from other countries.

As a member of the European Union, the UK has no tariffs between itself and other members. However, all EU members charge a tariff, known as the common external tariff, on goods imported from non-members of the EU (see Chapter 18).

2 Subsidies

A subsidy is a grant given to an industry by the Government so that the industry can lower its prices. Subsidies are used to stop consumers from buying foreign imports by making UK goods cheaper.

Subsidies have the advantage that they can be given secretly and are less likely to encourage a reaction from foreign competitors than tariffs would.

The disadvantage of subsidies are that consumers must pay for the lower prices in higher taxes to raise the money for the subsidy.

3 Quotas

A quota is a limit on the number of imports allowed into a country per year. A quota reduces the quantity of imports without changing their prices.

4 Embargo

An embargo is a complete ban on imports of certain goods to a country. An embargo may be used to stop imports of dangerous drugs, for example, heroin, or to punish a country for political reasons by refusing to buy its goods.

Recently, exports of beef from the UK were banned in Europe and many other countries because of health fears about BSE, the 'mad cow' disease.

1   Protection of a young industry

New and small firms, known as **infant industries**, will be unable to benefit from the economies of scale enjoyed by larger foreign competitors. These infant industries will have higher prices than foreign firms and so will be unable to sell their goods. Tariffs or other forms of protection can be used to make foreign goods dearer and so allow infant industries to grow.

The danger with this is that infant industries may continue to demand protection from foreign imports even when they have *grown up*.

2   To prevent unemployment

In the example in section 2 we found that both the USA and the UK could be better off if one specialized in agricultural production, the other in manufactured music centres, and then trade took place between them.

Yet although specialization and trade can benefit a country as a whole, it can still cause hardship for some. For example, if the USA produced all of the agricultural produce for both the USA and the UK, this would mean cheaper farm produce for UK consumers, but unemployment for farmers in the UK. At the same time, if the UK specialized in manufacturing this would mean cheaper manufactured goods for consumers in the USA, but unemployment for US manufacturing workers.

So free trade will always hurt someone. If those hurt are rich or powerful enough the Government involved may be persuaded to prevent free trade by using barriers to trade.

3   To prevent dumping

Dumping is when one country sells goods in another country below their cost of production. For example, a foreign country may produce jeans at £8 a pair, but sell them in Britain for £6 a pair. This will give foreign producers a foothold in the UK market and help to weaken UK producers. Once the UK producers are removed, foreign competitors might raise their prices again.

4   Because other countries use barriers to trade

Before any country removes barriers to trade on foreign goods it needs to be sure that foreign countries will remove barriers to trade on their goods. With many dozens of trading countries, it is very difficult to get agreement on removal of barriers to trade.

Because of this the **General Agreement on Tariffs and Trade (GATT)** was set up by trading countries in order to try to get countries to agree on removing their trade barriers. 117 countries are members of GATT, including the UK. In 1993 they agreed to cut tariffs on industrial products traded between them by one third. The **World Trade Organisation** was set up to make sure this agreement was acted upon and to encourage free trade in international markets.

5   To prevent over-specialization

Free trade encourages countries to specialize in the goods in which they have a comparative advantage. Yet specialization in one or two products can be dangerous in the modern world.

The demand for goods and services is always changing and if a country relies on just one or two goods it risks a huge fall in its income if demand moves away from these goods to others.

Protectionism allows a country to keep a wider range of industries alive and so prevents the dangers of over-specialization.

Section 6 | Exchange rates

Why do we need foreign currencies?

When firms import goods and services they must also use foreign currency to pay the country they bought them from. In the same way, UK firms will want UK currency in return for any commodities they export.

International trade, therefore, not only involves the exchange of commodities but also the exchange of currencies beforehand.

The foreign exchange market

The UK currency, **sterling**, and all other countries' currencies can be viewed just like any other commodity, like video-recorders, wheat or insurance services. Foreign currencies can be bought and sold all over the world. The market for foreign currencies or foreign exchange consists of all those consumers, firms and governments wishing to buy foreign exchange and all the suppliers of foreign currencies.

When any commodity is bought and sold it is done so at a price. The price of a foreign currency is known as its **foreign exchange rate**. That is, its value in terms of other countries' currencies. For example, the value of the pound is quoted as so many Swedish krona per pound, so many US dollars to each pound, and so on. The table below shows the price of a UK pound in terms of it value in other currencies on 3 August 1999.

Sterling exchange rate against other major currencies

Currency	Value of £1 sterling
Dollar	1.6139
Deutschmark	2.9606
French Franc	9.9292
Yen	184.961
Lira	2 930.92
Swiss Franc	2.4197
Peseta	251.858
Guilder	3.3358
Punt	1.1922
Krona	13.2486
Euro	1.5137

Exercise 6 The value of the pound

Using the table of exchange rates on page 313 try to find out which country uses (or used to use) each currency. Also try to find up-to-date statistics on the value of the pound using the daily newspapers.

Foreign exchange rates

The foreign exchange rate of a currency is its price in terms of other currencies. Like any commodity, the price of a currency will be determined by the forces of demand and supply.

1 Why are pounds demanded?

Foreign countries buy UK currency to pay for their imports of goods and services from the UK. They may also want to save money in UK financial institutions or invest in UK companies.

2 Why are pounds supplied?

The UK sells pounds in return for foreign currencies to pay for imports from abroad. UK consumers, firms and governments may also wish to save and invest abroad.

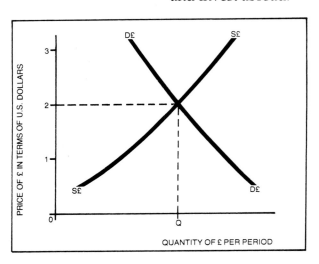

Equilibrium in the foreign exchange market

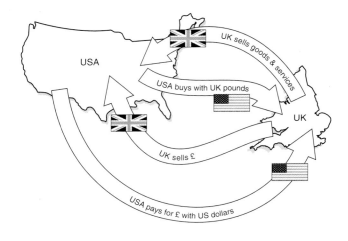

The demand and supply for UK sterling

The diagram shows the demand for UK pounds (D£D£) and their supply (S£S£) on the foreign exchange market. The price of the pound is expressed in terms of US dollars for simplification, but it could be in terms of any other foreign currency you care to think of.

The higher the price of pounds, the more are supplied but the less are demanded. The market price or equilibrium price of the pound is determined where demand equals supply in the diagram at an exchange rate of $2 = £1. Given this, a car sold for £10 000 in the UK, when exported to the USA, will sell for $20 000.

The value of the pound can be expressed in the terms of any currency, for example £1 = $2 or £1 = 200 Japanese yen. However, the value of currencies can change. For example, the price of the pound may fall to £1 = $1.5. At the same time the price of the pound may go up in terms of francs to £1 = 240 yen. Because the value of a currency can move in different directions

Sterling exchange rates (rates to the £–log scale)

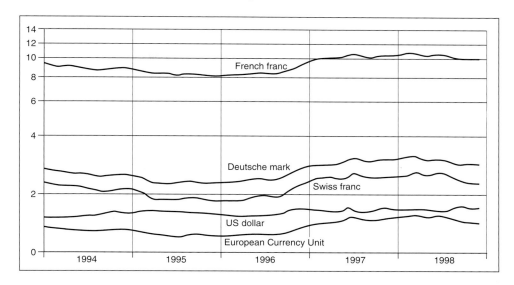

against different currencies it is difficult to judge whether the pound has increased in value or not on the whole foreign exchange market.

To overcome this the Government calculates the average value of the pound against the currencies of the countries we trade with the most. The average value of the pound is calculated as an index number like retail prices. This is known as the **sterling exchange rate index**. The graph below shows the average value of the pound over the period 1980–98.

UK sterling exchange rate index

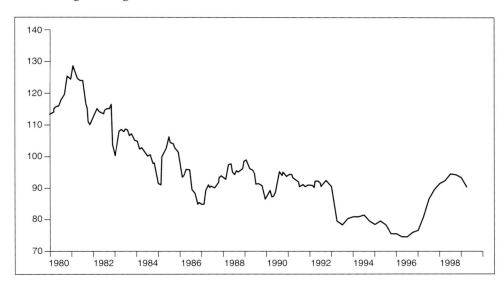

Section 7 Floating and fixed exchange rates

Floating exchange rates If an exchange rate, the price of a currency, is allowed to *float* it means that it will be determined freely by the forces of demand and supply without interference by governments. Changes in the forces of demand and supply will therefore cause changes in the value of a currency.

When the value of a currency falls it is known as a **depreciation** of its value. On the other hand, a rise in the price of a currency is known as an **appreciation** of its value. We will now examine what may cause the value of the UK pound to appreciate or depreciate.

Exercise 7   Floating up and down

Look at the cases below. For each case:

1   State what factor has changed that may affect the value of the pound.

2   State whether you think the pound will depreciate or appreciate against the US dollar.

3   State what effect the changing factor will have on the demand and/or supply of the pound.

4   Copy the diagram of the foreign exchange market between the pound and US dollars below. Show in the diagram the shift in the demand and/or supply curves of £s which best illustrates what is likely to happen (or has happened).

Case 1

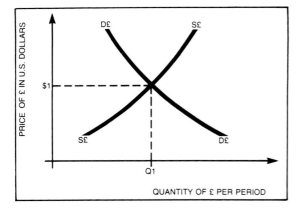

Exports slump sparks record deficit in goods

Slowing growth in Europe and the faltering euro have sent Britain's quarterly deficit on trade in goods ballooning to the highest level recorded, official figures showed yesterday. Imports outstripped exports by £7.1bn in the January to March period, according to data from the Office for National Statistics.

This beats the previous record for the visible trade deficit of £6.3bn set in the last quarter of 1998 and is the largest shortfall in the 300 years that the government has been collecting figures on imports and exports.

Most of the deterioration resulted from falling goods exports to European Union countries. The deficit with EU countries reached £1bn in March, the highest monthly level since July 1990.

The Guardian, 27.5.1999

316

Case 2

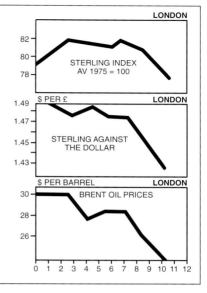

PRICES COLLAPSE ON OIL MARKETS

THE POUND fell sharply yesterday for the second consecutive day as oil prices weakened, prompting the Prime Minister to rule out an early cut in interest rates.

The fall in oil prices since Monday's decision by the Organisation of Petroleum Exporting Countries to defend its share of the oil market has created uncertainty about the scope for tax cuts in the next year's Budget.

Case 3

Pound surges as traders bet on interest rate increase

The pound powered to a two-month high against the dollar on foreign exchanges yesterday after government figures showed that the pace of economic recovery is accelerating.

Sterling hit $1.6243 shortly after the Office for National Statistics said that the UK economy grew by 0.5% in the second quarter – a much bigger rise than the markets expected.

Currency traders are betting on an early rise in interest rates which would push up yields on sterling holdings. They believe there will be a 0.75% increase in the base rate of interest by March 2000.

'The GDP figures today and yesterday add weight to the view that the Bank of England has finished cutting interest rates and this is supporting sterling,' said Jane Foley, currency strategist at Barclays Capital in London.

But the rebound in sterling might persuade the Bank's monetary policy committee to hold off from raising rates. At last month's meeting the committee welcomed signs that the value of the pound had peaked which had priced British goods out of world markets, contributing to a record trade deficit in the first three months of this year.

The Guardian, 31.7.1999

There are a number of reasons why the value of a currency changes or fluctuates. With specific reference to the value of the pound, the main factors are:

1 Changes in the balance of trade in goods and services
If the UK imports a greater value of goods and services than it exports there is said to be a current account deficit. If the deficit increases further it means the UK is buying more imports, or losing its export trade. As a result, more pounds must be supplied to pay for the imports, while less pounds are demanded by foreigners because they are buying less of our exports. As a result, the price of the pound will depreciate.

If, on the other hand, the UK earns more from its exports than it pays for its imports its current account will be in surplus. More pounds will be demanded to pay for UK exports while the UK will not supply so many pounds as it buys less imports. The value of the pound will appreciate.

2 Inflation

If the UK's inflation rate is higher than that of other countries the price of UK goods and services will be rising faster than foreign prices. As a result UK goods will become uncompetitive. Demand for UK exports, and therefore for pounds, will fall. On the other hand, imports become more competitive and more will be demanded in return for more pounds being supplied to pay for them. High UK inflation will tend to reduce the value of the pound.

3 Changes in interest rates

When UK interest rates are high or rising, foreigners may be keen to save or invest money in UK banks and other financial institutions. The demand for pounds rises, increasing the value of the pound. The Government can use interest rates to affect the value of the pound and the price of imported goods and services (see Chapter 16). A rise in other countries' interest rates may lead to the withdrawal of foreign investment from the UK with a depressing effect on the value of the pound.

4 The price of oil

Since 1979 the UK has become a major exporter of oil. It earns much money from its oil trade, and so changes in the price of oil on the world oil market will have a large effect on the UK's oil export earnings. A fall in the price of oil will mean foreign countries will not have to pay so much for UK oil and the demand for pounds will fall. As a result the price or value of the pound will fall.

5 Speculation

A **foreign currency speculator** is a person or firm, for example, a bank, that tries to make money by buying and selling foreign currencies to try to make speculative gains.

For example, if speculators think the value of the pound is going to fall, because, for example, UK interest rates have gone down, they may sell pounds and buy other currencies. This increase in the supply of pounds reduces their value. The speculators can then buy back pounds at a cheaper price. The difference between the price they sold pounds for and the price they buy them back for is their profit. The following diagram illustrates how this is done.

If speculators believe the value of the pound will rise, as a result of a balance of payment's surplus for example, they will buy pounds now and try to make a profit out of a rising pound. Of course, their increased demand for pounds helps its price to rise.

Current account deficit hit by rise in imports

Britain's current account deficit widened last month to its highest figure since April after the effects of sterling's devaluation led to a sharp rise in the imports bill.

The rise in the deficit to £1.1bn from £891m in September came as imports increased by 5 per cent between September and October to £10.2bn, the highest monthly figure since mid-1990.

The widening deficit was in spite of a strong rise in exports in October compared with September, which indicates UK exporters are holding their own in difficult trading conditions caused by the international economic slowdown.

Much of the large rise in the value of imports was due to the 13 per cent devaluation in the pound since it left the European exchange rate mechanism in mid-September. This had the effect of pushing up unit prices of imports by 3.4 per cent between September and October.

The increased imports suggest that underlying economic demand may be picking up as part of a recovery. However, any large increases in the prices of imports in the coming months could increase inflationary pressures, making it more difficult for the government to keep its target of maintaining underlying inflation at beneath 4 per cent.

The increase in exports to a value of £9.1bn in October from £8.7bn in the previous month helped sentiment on the stock market, where a burst of buying support saw the FT-SE 100 index of leading shares reach a new trading high of 2,745.2.

The Financial Times, 24.11.1992

The article points out how a fall in the value of the pound against other currencies (either through depreciation or devaluation) can have far reaching effects on the UK economy.

A fall in the value of sterling will cause a rise in the price of imports. For example, if the exchange rate is £1 = €2 euros then a bottle of french wine priced at €4 euros would cost the UK £2 to import. A fall in the value of the pound to say £1 = €1.6 euros would cause the price of the bottle of wine to rise to £2.50. Rising import prices means rising inflation. Consumers will not be able to afford to buy as much as they could before and less wants will be satisfied.

The fall in the value of the pound should, however, boost the demand for UK exports abroad. A falling pound means falling prices for UK goods in foreign countries. For example, at an exchange rate of £1 = €2 a UK computer costing £500 will sell for €1 000 in Germany. If the exchange rate then falls to say £1 = €1.8 the price of the computer in Germany will fall to €900. A boost in demand for UK exports will mean more money flowing into the UK. Exporting firms will raise their output and jobs may be created. However, many UK goods exported are made from imported materials. A fall in the price of exports following a fall in the value of the pound is not so clear cut.

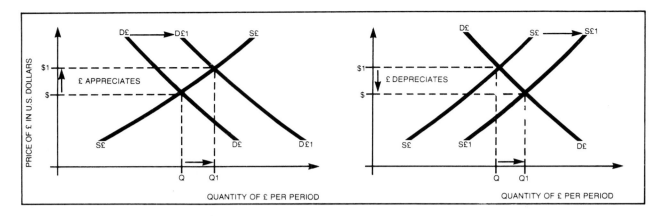

A rise in demand for sterling causes its value to appreciate
Thus, a fall in demand for pounds causes their value to depreciate.

A rise in the supply of sterling causes its value to depreciate
Thus, a fall in the supply of pounds causes their value to appreciate.

Fixed exchange rates

Why fix exchange rates?
In spite of the fact that floating exchange rates appear to be able to correct balance of payment's problems, some countries' governments have intervened in the foreign exchange market to fix their own value for their currency for a number of reasons.

First, if the value of a currency falls imports become dearer and this can cause home prices to rise leading to inflation. Secondly, a rise in the value of a currency makes a country's exports much dearer and so exporting firms may lose orders, cut production and lay off workers. Freely floating exchange rates can also cause uncertainty. If the value of currency is constantly changing then the prices of exports and imports will also be constantly changing. Traders will be uncertain about the prices they must pay in the future and this may mean they trade less.

How to fix exchange rates
Governments of the UK have at many times tried to fix or *peg* the value of the pound. For example, in 1967 the value of the pound was fixed at £1 = US $2.4.

The Bank of England holds the Exchange Equalization Account on behalf of the UK Government. It can use there funds or reserves of gold and foreign currencies to buy or sell sterling when it is asked to intervene in the foreign exchange market.

If the Government thinks the pound will fall in value it instructs the Bank of England to buy more pounds with its funds. This increase in the demand for pounds pushes up their price. If, on the other hand, the value of the pound is about to rise the Bank of England sells more pounds. This increase in supply stops the price of sterling rising.

In practice, the value of any currency when fixed is allowed to undergo slight changes either side of its fixed value before the Government intervenes to buy or sell its currency.

The graphs below show how the movements of a fixed exchange rate differ from those of a freely floating exchange rate over time.

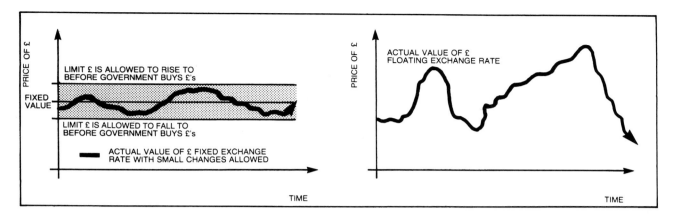

Fixed exchange rate

Floating exchange rate

Devaluation

The problem with fixed exchange rates is that as a result of the changing pattern of international trade changes in the value of currencies are necessary.

The UK Government, for example, may have fixed the value of the pound at £1 = $3. This means that a UK export to the USA costing £1 000 would sell for $3 000 over there. Similarly, a US export to the UK valued at $1 800 would cost us £600.

Because of the high value of the pound Americans will face high prices of UK exports. As a result, demand for UK exports may fall. On the other hand, imports coming into the UK may appear good value and our demand for them will rise. With export demand falling and import demand rising the UK balance of payments is plunged into deficit. If the exchange rate was allowed to float the value of the pound would fall, exports would become cheaper and imports dearer. The balance of payments should be corrected. However, as long as the value of the pound is fixed too high the deficit will persist. For this reason the Government may have to abandon the existing fixed exchange rate and adopt a new lower one, for example £1 = US $2. This is known as **devaluation**. This will make exports cheaper and imports dearer. The demand for UK exports should rise and the demand for imports fall.

The diagram overleaf shows what happens to the prices of goods traded between the UK and the USA after a devaluation of the pound and what is hoped would happen to the balance of payments on current account. The same principles apply for trade between any two countries following the devaluation of one country's currency.

By far the usual state of world affairs this century has been a system of fixed exchange rates between countries.

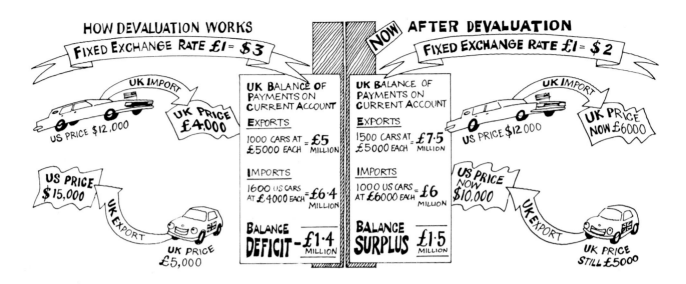

HOW DEVALUATION WORKS
FIXED EXCHANGE RATE £1 = $3

UK IMPORT
US PRICE $12,000
UK PRICE £4,000

US PRICE $15,000
UK EXPORT
UK PRICE £5,000

UK BALANCE OF PAYMENTS ON CURRENT ACCOUNT

EXPORTS
1000 CARS AT £5000 EACH = £5 MILLION

IMPORTS
1600 US CARS AT £4000 EACH = £6·4 MILLION

BALANCE
DEFICIT − £1·4 MILLION

NOW

AFTER DEVALUATION
FIXED EXCHANGE RATE £1 = $2

UK BALANCE OF PAYMENTS ON CURRENT ACCOUNT

EXPORTS
1500 CARS AT £5000 EACH = £7·5 MILLION

IMPORTS
1000 US CARS AT £6000 EACH = £6 MILLION

BALANCE
SURPLUS £1·5 MILLION

UK IMPORT
US PRICE $12,000
UK PRICE NOW £6000

US PRICE NOW $10,000
UK EXPORT
UK PRICE STILL £5000

Until 1918 the price of a pound was fixed at $3.7. After the First World War the pound was allowed to float. The period 1918 to 1921 saw the value of the pound depreciate sharply, but from 1921 to 1925 its value went up, or appreciated, until in 1925 it was fixed once more at $3.7. From 1931 until 1941 sterling like many world currencies at that time was floated again.

Following World War II the value of a pound was fixed at $4.03. Under the system of fixed exchange rates that lasted until 1972 the UK has devalued only twice. The first devaluation in 1949 fixed the pound at $2.8, while in 1967 its value was lowered to $2.4.

Since 1972 the pound has mostly been allowed to float on the world currency markets, except for the period October 1990 to September 1992 when the UK belonged to the European Exchange Rate Mechanism (ERM). The ERM fixes the exchange rates of the members of the European Union (see Chapter 18). The UK withdrew from the ERM when the UK Government was unable to stop the pound from plunging in value despite spending £10 billion of foreign currency reserves to buy UK pounds and raising interest rates from 10% to 15% in one day. The UK had still not rejoined the ERM in early 2000.

4 Dirty floating

Despite allowing the exchange rate to float in many countries, the buying or selling of a country's currency by their governments has often been carried out if they felt the value of their currency had fallen or risen by too much. This has been nicknamed **dirty floating**, or is known as **managed flexibility**. For example, this would mean the value of the pound is allowed to float or find its own value for most of the time, but if the Government thinks it is falling too low it will instruct the Bank of England to buy some pounds to keep up its value or raise interest rates.

Similarly, if the price of the pound rises too high the Government may ask for a sale of pounds or reduction in its interest rates, to reduce its value.

Dirty floating is a characteristic of many countries exchange rate policies.

Key words

**This page is
photocopyable**

Clues across

1 To fix the value of the pound at a lower level. (7)

3 A tax on imports. (6)

4 A floating exchange rate that is not allowed to float too far before the government is up to these *tricks*. (5)

6 You can't see these exports and imports. (9)

8 Represented by a flow of money into the UK. (6)

9 The account that takes account of the flows of export receipts and payments for imports. (7)

11 This money searches the world for high interest rates. (3)

13 A complete ban on a particular import. (7)

14 This is the name given to a practice whereby a country floods another with low cost imports. (7)

16 A country has this advantage if it is better at producing a particular commodity than any other country. (8)

17 These young industries may need protection from foreign competition. (6)

Clues down

1 When the pound floats down in value. (10)

2 Those exports and imports which can be seen. (7)

4 The balance of payment's position when imports exceed exports. (7)

5 An exchange rate system where a currency is free to find its own value. (8)

7 Italian currency (before the euro) (4)

10 A limit placed on the number of a particular import allowed into a country. (5)

12 The discovery of this boosted the UK visible balance in the early 1980s. (3)

15 Japanese currency. (3)

Aims

At the end of this chapter you should be able to:

1   Describe the objectives of government macroeconomic policies and understand possible conflicts between them.

2   Distinguish between demand-side policies that attempt to influence the level of demand in the economy and supply-side policies that try to boost the total output of the economy.

3   Use simple diagrams to show how changes in **aggregate demand** and **aggregate supply** can affect the general level of prices, output and employment in an economy.

4   Describe the instruments of **fiscal policy** and analyse the possible impact of changes in fiscal policy on the economy.

5   Describe the aims and instruments of **monetary policy**.

6   Explain various **supply-side policies**, including **competition policy**, changes in **taxation**, **privatization** and **deregulation**, and how they can help to raise output and employment, and reduce price inflation.

Exercise 1   Economic management

Overleaf are two letters from opposing political party members expressing their concern over the state of the economy. The letters are addressed to their economic advisers asking them to write a report outlining a number of policies each party should pursue to manage the economy.

In groups of three or four pick one of these letters and write a report outlining the economic policies you propose given the view of the economy expressed by your party leader.

When you have finished your report compare your policies to those of the opposition party. Do you agree or disagree?

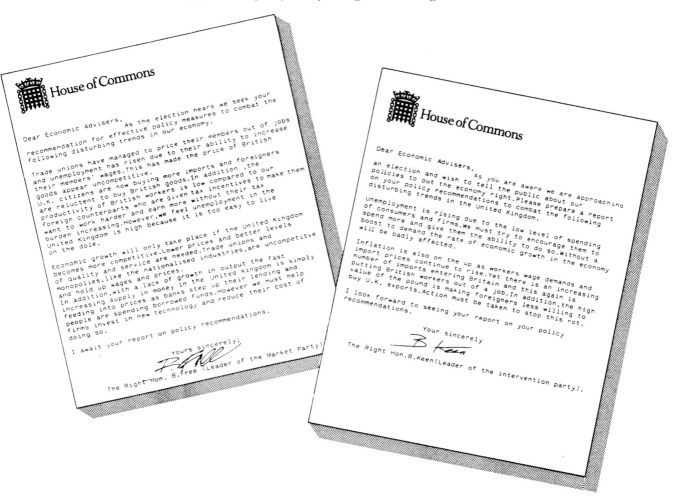

House of Commons

Dear Economic Advisers,
As the election nears we seek your recommendation for effective policy measures to combat the following disturbing trends in our economy.

Trade unions have managed to price their members out of jobs and unemployment has risen due to their ability to increase their members' wages. This has made the price of British goods appear uncompetitive.

U.K. citizens are now buying more imports and foreigners are reluctant to buy British goods. In addition, the productivity of British workers is low compared to our foreign counterparts who are given tax incentives to make them want to work harder and earn more without their tax burden increasing. However, we feel unemployment in the United Kingdom is high because it is too easy to live on the dole.

Economic growth will only take place if the United Kingdom becomes more competitive. Lower prices and better levels of quality and service are needed. Trade unions and monopolies, like the nationalised industries, are uncompetitve and hold up wages and prices.

In addition, with a lack of growth in output the fast increasing supply in money in the United Kingdom is simply feeding into prices as banks step up their lending and people are spending borrowed funds. However we must help firms invest in new technology and reduce their cost of doing so.

I await your report on policy recommendations.

Yours sincerely,
The Right Hon. B.Free (Leader of the Market Party)

House of Commons

Dear Economic Advisers,
As you are aware we are approaching an election and wish to tell the public about our policies to put the economy right. Please prepare a report on your policy recommendations to combat the following disturbing trends in the United Kingdom.

Unemployment is rising due to the low level of spending of consumers and firms. We must try to encourage them to spend more and give them the ability to do so. Without a boost to demand the rate of economic growth in the economy will be badly affected.

Inflation is also on the up as workers wage demands and import prices continue to rise. Yet there is an increasing number of imports entering Britain and this again is putting British workers out of a job. In addition, the high value of the pound is making foreigners less willing to buy U.K. exports. Action must be taken to stop this rot.

I look forward to seeing your report on your policy recommendations.

Your sincerely
The Right Hon. B.Keen (Leader of the intervention party).

| **Section 1** | Macroeconomic objectives |

The UK Government, like most governments of developed economies, has four main economic aims. These are:

a to achieve low and stable inflation in the general level of prices (see Chapter 13)

b to maintain a high level of employment and a low level of unemployment (see Chapter 13)

c to encourage economic growth (see Chapter 13)

d to encourage trade and secure a favourable balance of payments (see Chapter 14).

Has the UK reached its objectives?

Year	Annual change in RPI % (Inflation)	Claimant unemployment rate %	Annual change in real GDP % (Growth in total output)	Balance of payments (Current account £m)
1980	18.0	5.8	–2.2	+2 843
1985	6.0	10.9	3.7	+2 238
1990	9.4	5.8	0.4	–19 513
1991	5.9	8.0	–2.0	–8 374
1992	3.8	9.8	–0.5	–10 082
1993	1.6	10.4	2.1	–10 618
1994	2.5	9.4	4.3	–1 458
1995	3.4	8.1	2.8	–3 745
1996	2.4	7.4	2.3	–600
1997	2.8	5.6	3.5	+6 303
1998	2.6	4.7	2.1	+1 474
1999	2.0	4.3	0.8	–10 000

Section 2 | The demand side and supply side of the macroeconomy

We can draw some simple diagrams to help examine how the Government can use different policies to help manage the macroeconomy and achieve its objectives. These diagrams show aggregate demand and aggregate supply in the economy.

Aggregate demand

Recall from Chapter 12 that aggregate demand is the total demand for all goods and services in the economy – i.e., demand from consumers, firms, the government and overseas for exports.

From Chapter 8 we know that demand tends to rise as prices fall. If we add together all the individual demand curves of consumers, firms and government for all the different goods and services produced in the economy, we can plot an aggregate demand curve (AD). It shows what happens to total demand as the general level of prices of all goods and services change.

Aggregate supply

Similarly we can add up all the individual supply curves of all producers in the economy to develop an aggregate supply curve (AS). The aggregate supply curve shows what happens to the total output of all the goods and services in the economy (or Gross Domestic Product – see Chapter 13) as the general level of prices changes. It slopes up because as prices rise producers will tend to expand the amount they are willing to supply (see Chapter 8).

However, to expand output producers will need more resources; land, labour and capital. Recall from Chapter 2 that resources are limited in supply and have alternative uses. At some point, therefore, resources will become fully employed. Producers will be unable to expand output further however

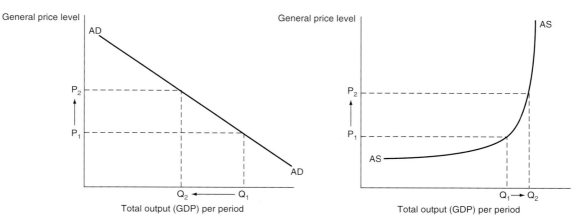

The aggregate demand curve shows total demand for goods and services tends to fall as the general price level rises.

The aggregate supply curve shows total output tends to rise as the general level of prices rises, but after a point all resources are fully employed and output cannot expand any further.

much the general price level rises. At this point the aggregate supply curve will become a straight line pointing up showing that aggregate supply cannot expand any more.

Macroeconomy If we plot an aggregate demand curve and aggregate supply curve in the same diagram, we can find the general price level at which the demand for all goods and services equals their supply. At this point the macroeconomy has reached an equilibrium. The general level of prices is stable, at point P_e in the diagram below. That is, there is no price inflation (see Chapter 13). However, there may be unemployment if resources, namely labour, are not fully employed at the level of total output Q_e in the diagram.

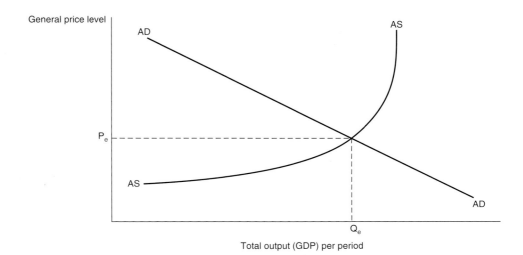

Equilibrium in the macroeconomy.

Demand-side policy   In an economic recession aggregate demand, output and employment all tend to fall (see Chapter 13). If the Government wants to increase employment in the economy, it can attempt to do so by increasing aggregate demand. If successful the aggregate demand curve shifts outward to the right, from AD_1 to AD_2 in the diagram below. As aggregate demand increases the level of output or GDP rises from Q_1 to Q_2. However, this will be at the expense of some price inflation as the general price level increase from P_1 to P_2.

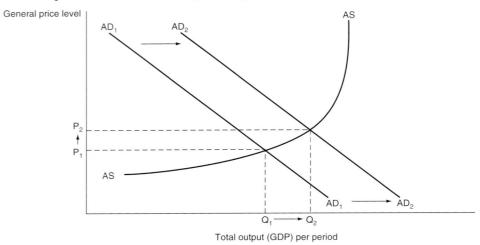

An increase in aggregate demand can boost output and employment if resources are not fully employed.

In contrast, if the Government thinks inflation is too high it might try to reduce aggregate demand, from AD_1 to AD_3 in the next diagram. As a result, the general level of prices falls from P_1 to P_3.

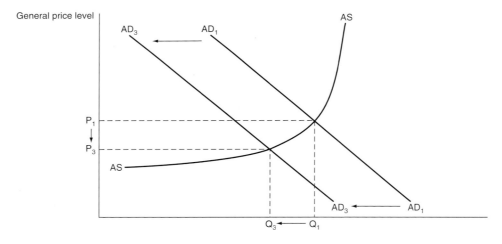

A decrease in aggregate demand can help reduce inflation but may also contract GDP.

Government policies that aim to control price inflation and unemployment by influencing aggregate demand in the economy are called **demand-side policies**. They include **fiscal policy** which uses public sector spending and taxation to control demand, and **monetary policy** which uses the interest rate to control spending by consumers and firms.

Supply-side policy   Increasing aggregate supply can raise output and employment and reduce inflationary pressure in the economy. For example, if the aggregate supply curve shifts out from AS_1 to AS_2 in the diagram below, the general price level falls from P_1 to P_2 as output rises from Q_1 to Q_2.

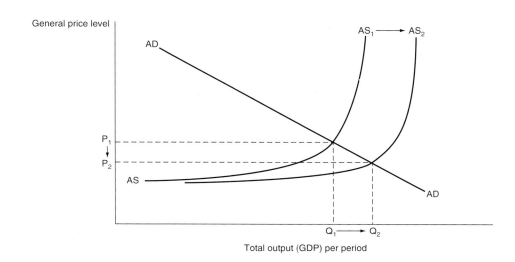

An increase in aggregate supply can raise output and employment in the economy and help reduce inflation.

Government policies that aim at raising aggregate supply in the economy are known as **supply-side policies**. These policies attempt to remove constraints on the productivity of resources, for example, by reducing taxes to encourage people and firms to work harder, and encouraging competition to expand output and keep prices low.

Section 3   Demand-side policies

What is fiscal policy?   Fiscal policy involves changing the level of public spending and/or taxation to affect the level of aggregate demand.

During an economic recession increasing the aggregate demand for goods and services can help boost output and reduce unemployment. If private sector spending is too low, then the Government can increase its own spending (see Chapter 16). This can be combined with cuts in taxes on people's incomes and firms' profits. This will give them more money to spend. However, there is a risk they will simply save this extra money or spend it on imported goods and services.

Increasing public spending and/or cutting taxes to boost aggregate demand, output and employment is known as **expansionary fiscal policy**.

Fiscal policy can be used to influence prices, output and employment if ...

INFLATION IS CAUSED BY TOO MUCH AGGREGATE DEMAND *Some agree it is also due to increasing costs*

UNEMPLOYMENT IS CAUSED BY LACK OF DEMAND.

Exercise 2   Can increased public expenditure create jobs?

The diagram below shows how the building of a new hospital by the Government can help create jobs and incomes. In your own words explain what is happening in the diagram, and how an expansionary fiscal policy can boost demand, output and jobs in an economy. How might the impact of the policy on the economy and your explanation change if the increase in public expenditure is paid for by **a** raising taxes, or **b** raising interest rates to encourage people and firms to lend the money to the Government?

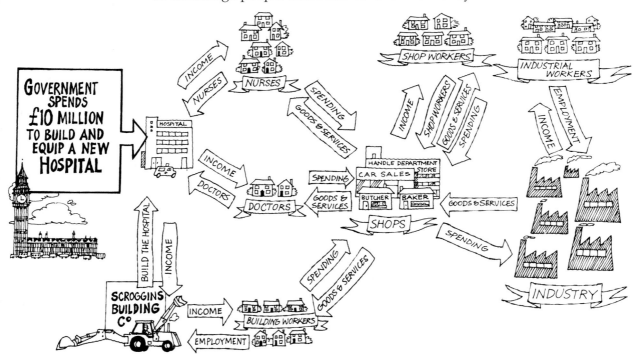

During a period of high demand-pull inflation fiscal policy may be used to deflate the economy by reducing aggregate demand. This involves reducing public spending and/or raising taxes. However, a deflationary fiscal policy may reduce employment and growth in real output.

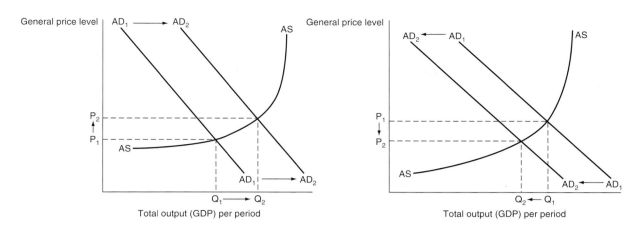

An expansionary fiscal policy involves increasing public sector spending and/or cutting taxes to boost aggregate demand.

A deflationary fiscal policy attempts to lower demand-pull inflation by cutting public sector spending and/or raising taxes.

Problems with fiscal policy

The use of fiscal policy to influence the level of demand in an economy has been criticized by many economists. They argue fiscal policy has not worked in the past. Instead inflation and unemployment got much worse in many countries, for example, in the UK during the 1970s and 1980s when the rate of price inflation climbed as high as 25% over a 12-month period and more than 3 million people became unemployed (see Chapter 13). This is because

1 Fiscal policy is cumbersome to use.

It is difficult for a government to know precisely when and by how much to expand public spending or cut taxes in a recession, or cut spending and raise taxes during a boom.

Boosting aggregate demand by increasing public spending and/or cutting taxes may cause an economy to 'overheat'. That is, demand may rise too much and too quickly. If the amount of goods and services to buy does not rise as quickly as demand there will be demand-pull inflation. On the other hand, the Government may cut spending and raise taxes by too much following a period of high inflation and cause unemployment to rise.

2 Public spending crowds out private spending.

To finance an increase in public spending and/or cut in taxation the Government may borrow the money from the private sector. The more money the private sector lends to the Government the less it has available to spend itself. This is called **crowding out**.

To encourage people, firms and the banking system to lend money to the Government it may raise interest rates. However, higher interest rates may discourage other people and firms from borrowing money to spend on consumption and investment. Reducing investment in modern and more productive equipment can reduce economic growth (see Chapter 13).

3 Raising taxes on incomes and profits reduces work incentives, employment and economic growth.
If taxes are too high, people and firms may not work as hard. This reduces productivity, output and profits. As productivity falls firms' costs increase and they are less able to compete on product price and quality against more efficient firms overseas. As a result demand for their goods and services may fall and unemployment may rise.

4 Expansionary fiscal policy increases expectations of inflation.
As a result, people will push for higher wages to protect them from higher prices in the future. Rising wages increases production costs and reduces the demand for labour (see Chapter 11). This in turn causes cost-push inflation and rising unemployment.

Fiscal rules In recent years, successive UK governments have accepted these arguments and no longer use fiscal policy to try to boost aggregate demand in recessions and cut demand in booms. Instead, they have adopted a number of **fiscal rules** which govern public spending and borrowing. These are:

- current and capital expenditures are managed and controlled separately. This is so that the costs and benefits of long-term capital investments (e.g. in new roads, hospitals and school buildings) can be easily identified.

- the Government should only borrow money to pay for public investment and not to fund current spending on public sector wages and consumables, such as stationery.

- public sector debt as a proportion of GDP should be kept at a low and stable level, so that debt interest payments do not become a burden.

These fiscal rules help to keep public spending and borrowing under control so that interest rates and taxes can be lowered.

What is monetary policy? **Monetary policy** refers to actions taken by a government to try to control either the supply of money in the economy or the price of money. Interest rates are the price of borrowing money, or the reward for lending money.

Why use monetary policy? **1 Growth in the money supply can cause inflation**.
If the supply of money increases people will have more to spend on goods and services. If the output of goods and services available to buy does not rise as fast as the money supply, the increase in demand will cause demand-pull inflation (see Chapter 13).

2 Changes in interest rates cause changes in aggregate demand
Interest rates are the price of money. If interest rates fall, people and firms will find it cheaper to borrow, while others will be less willing to save money and will spend it instead. That is, as interest rates fall more people will want to spend more money.

Consumer expenditure and firms' investment in new machines and buildings will rise. Increased aggregate demand helps to create jobs and reduces unemployment. Increased investment helps to create economic growth as the economy will be able to produce more output in total.

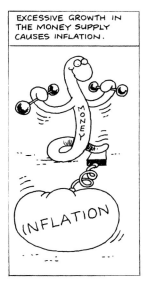

EXCESSIVE GROWTH IN THE MONEY SUPPLY CAUSES INFLATION.

MONEY

INFLATION

3   Interest rates can be used to affect the value of the pound

Interest rates can be raised to help increase the value of the UK currency sterling compared to other countries' currencies (see Chapter 14).

If interest rates are higher in the UK than in other countries, wealthy foreigners will prefer to keep their savings in the UK and so earn high rates of interest on their money. However, to put their money in the UK foreigners must buy UK pounds with their currencies. This increase in demand for pounds will cause their price, or value, to rise in terms of other currencies.

This can help to reduce imported inflation but will also increase the foreign currency prices of UK exports. As a result, consumer demand overseas for exports of goods and services from the UK may fall.

Monetary policy therefore involves influencing the supply of money and interest rates to control the level of inflation, unemployment, economic growth and the value of sterling, or its exchange rate.

What to control? Money supply or interest rates?

Control of the money supply can influence the aggregate demand for goods and services and the rate of inflation, while control of interest rates can also influence aggregate demand and the exchange rate for sterling.

It would be very convenient if a government could control both the price of money and the supply of money at the same time. However, it can only control one at a time.

Exercise 3   The market for money

The price of money, or interest rate, like the price of any good is determined by the forces of demand and supply. The equilibrium rate of interest in the economy is where the demand for money and the supply of money are equal.

Equilibrium in the money market

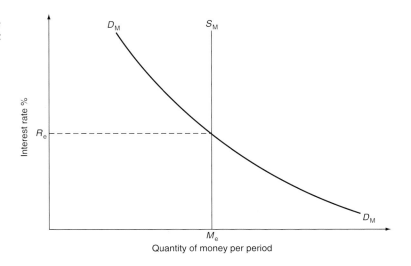

Note: The demand for money (D_M) shows that as interest rates fall people and firms want more money to spend. As interest rates rise people prefer to save and borrow less, rather than hold money.

The supply of money (S_M) is assumed to be fixed. That is, the stock or quantity of money cannot change in the time period under consideration. If the interest rate is too high and above its equilibrium rate (R_e) there will be an excess supply of money. Banks, building societies and other financial institutions will have a lot of money to lend but not many people will want to borrow it. To encourage them to do so they will lower their interest rates.

1 Explain what will happen if the rate of interest is too low and below its equilibrium (R_e).

2 a Copy the diagram showing the market for money and show the effect of a reduction in the quantity, or supply, of money available in the economy.

  b What will happen to the interest rate and why?

3 a Now show on the diagram the effect of an increase in the supply of money.

  b What will happen to the interest rate and why?

4 Assume that the Government now wishes to reduce the money supply to lower inflation and also wishes to reduce the interest rate to encourage firms to borrow money to invest. Will it be able to do both? Use supply and demand analysis to explain your answer.

If the Government wishes to reduce the supply of money it must let interest rates find their own level. If the supply of money falls, banks, building societies and other money lenders find they have less money to lend to people and firms. To try to obtain more money they will increase their interest rates to attract savers to put their money in deposit accounts. On the other hand, if the supply of money rises banks and building societies, etc., will lower their interest rates to try to encourage people and firms to borrow all this money. That is, the Government cannot choose to keep interest rates stable or the same if they want to change the money supply.

If the Government wishes to increase interest rates, for example, to protect the value of the pound, then clearly it cannot leave the money supply alone. To engineer a rise in interest rates they must reduce the amount of money banks and building societies, etc., have to lend.

Therefore, the Government must choose which to control: the money supply or interest rates. It cannot control both at the same time. In the UK the Government has given the job of controlling interest rates to the central bank.

The role of the central bank

The **central bank** in an economy is the bank of the government and will help support its fiscal and monetary policies. A central bank is responsible for looking after tax and other revenues received by the government, managing payments for public spending, and holding gold and foreign currency reserves. A central bank will also oversee the operation of the banking system and will make loans to high street and other banks in the economy.

The Bank of England is the central bank in the UK (see Chapter 19). In 1997 it was given independence by the new UK Government to set the level of interest rates required to meet the Government's inflation target of no more than a 2.5% increase in the general level of prices each year. That is, the

Bank of England has to decide when, and by how much, to raise or lower interest rates in the economy in order to keep price inflation low and stable. It does this with the help of a **Monetary Policy Committee (MPC)**. The Governor of the Bank of England is head of the MPC.

Controlling interest rates

The MPC is a panel of economists who meet each month to help the Bank of England make its decision on interest rates using up to date information and forecasts of movements in the general price level, wages, real output, exchange rates and other economic variables.

If the information and forecasts suggest price inflation could rise the MPC will tend to raise interest rates. Raising interest rates will tend to reduce the demand for borrowing from consumers and firms. If they borrow less money, they will have less money to spend and aggregate demand will fall or rise more slowly. Higher interest rates will also tend to raise the value of the UK exchange rate and hold down the prices of imported goods and services (see Chapter 13).

If, on the other hand, the MPC thinks inflation is likely to fall and the economy is in danger of sinking into an economic recession, it may cut interest rates to encourage borrowing.

The Bank of England is able to change interest rates in the economy by changing the interest rate it charges on the loans it makes to the banking system when it is short of money. The rate of interest charged on loans from the Bank of England to other banks is called the **base rate** of interest in the economy. If the Bank of England wants interest rates to rise it will raise the base rate. If it costs financial institutions more to borrow money, then to cover this cost they will tend to raise the interest rates they charge their customers for loans. In this way an increase in base rate causes a general rise in interest rates throughout the economy.

Bank of England base rate of interest, 1969–99

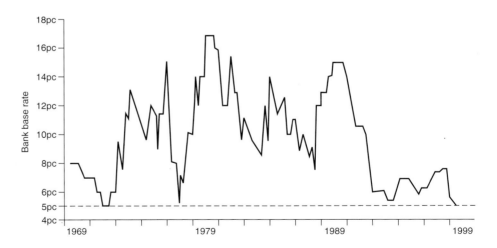

335

If the Bank of England wants to reduce interest rates it will lower the base rate on loans to the banking system. As the cost of borrowing from the Bank of England falls, financial institutions can lower their interest rates.

Exercise 4   Interest rates and the Monetary Policy Committee

---

Interest rate held as growth picks up

Interest rates were put on hold yesterday amid signs that seven cuts in the cost of borrowing since October 1998 have fuelled a boom in the housing market in the south and a resumption of economic growth.

With sterling showing signs of weakness against the dollar on the foreign exchanges, threatening to increase import prices, the Bank of England's monetary policy committee voted to leave its base lending rate at 5%.

The City believes that having succeeded in stimulating activity the MPC will eventually switch its attention to heading off a rise in inflation, which it is charged by the government with keeping at 2.5%.

But most economists say it is premature to conclude that the next move in borrowing costs will be up. Despite rapidly rising house prices in London and the south-east, prices overall remain relatively subdued. The latest Halifax house price index shows prices rising nationally at an annual rate of 6.6%, compared with a peak of more than 30% in the late 1980s.

Moreover, sterling's persistent strength against the euro – which cuts import prices and restrains export sales to Britain's largest market – and weakening wage growth suggest that borrowing costs may have further to fall.

The Guardian, 9.7.1999

---

1   What is the role of the Monetary Policy Committee in the UK?

2   Describe what has happened to interest rates in the UK since the MPC was formed, and why the MPC made these decisions.

3   How is the Bank of England able to change interest rates in the UK economy?

4   Draw a simple diagram of the UK economy using aggregate demand and supply curves. Show the impact of an increase in interest rates in the diagram on the general price level and output. Describe what has happened.

Controlling the money supply   In most countries deposits of money in banks and building societies make up the bulk of the money supply. For example, in the UK in 1999 only 3.4% of the money supply was notes and coins (see Chapter 19). Therefore, when a government attempts to control the supply of money it will concentrate on the creation of bank deposits rather than on the amount of notes and coins in circulation.

1   Open-market operations
Open-market operations refer to the borrowing and repayment of public sector debt to private sector individuals and organizations.

In the UK the Bank of England can borrow money from the private sector by selling 'promises to pay' called Government Securities. **Treasury Bills** issued by the Government are loans that are repaid after around 3 months.

For example, Mrs Save buys a £100 000 treasury bill from the Bank of England. They allow her to pay £95 000 for the bill with the promise to repay her the full £100 000 (that is, the £95 000 loan plus £5 000 interest) after

3 months. Mrs Save pays for the bill with a £95 000 cheque drawn on her Lloyds TSB bank account. Lloyds TSB bank must now pay the Government this sum of money. As a result, government borrowing has reduced banks' deposits of money. With less money available banks cannot lend out as much money as before.

Selling treasury bills to the private sector, therefore, reduces the supply of money. Selling more treasury bills to raise more money than the Government needs is called overfunding and can help reduce bank deposits and the supply of money even further.

2 Special deposits
The Bank of England can reduce the money supply by calling for special deposits. The Bank of England orders commercial banks to deposit money with it for a certain period of time. Calling in special deposits automatically reduces the amount of money that the banks have available to lend to their customers.

3 Funding
From above we know that the Government can borrow money and reduce the money supply by selling 'promises to pay' to the private sector in return for a rate of interest. Treasury bills are repaid within 3 months. In contrast, gilt-edged securities issued by the Government are repaid after 25 years. Therefore, by selling gilt-edged securities instead of treasury bills the Government is able to raise money that does not have to be repaid to the private sector for a much longer time. So, 'funding' government borrowing by selling gilt-edged securities can help keep down growth in the money supply over a longer period of time.

Section 4 | Supply-side policies

What are supply-side policies?

Supply-side policies are those which attempt to promote jobs, low inflation and economic growth by removing barriers to increased productivity and competition in domestic and international markets. Barriers to trade can reduce output, require fewer people to be employed and help to force up prices. If the prices of goods and services from the UK are too high, this will

337

ECONOMIC GROWTH IS STIMULATED BY COMPETITION - LOWER TAXES, REDUCING THE POWER OF THE UNIONS AND MONOPOLIES, HELPING SMALL BUSINESSES.

reduce the demand for exports and increase the demand for cheaper imported goods and services.

Supply-side policies include:

1 Reducing the tax burden

High tax rates on incomes may make workers less inclined to work hard and achieve higher levels of productivity. Also, high tax rates on profits can reduce the incentives of firms to invest in new products and production methods if any additional profits they make are simply swallowed up by tax.

The UK Government recognizes that cutting taxes on incomes and profits can have a direct effect on the efforts of workers and firms to produce more output and be more competitive. As such, rates of tax on incomes and profits in the UK have been reduced over time (see Chapter 16).

2 Labour market reforms

Laws have been introduced in the UK which curb the power of trade unions to call strikes and for other disruptive actions. Some powerful unions were able to use these actions to force firms to pay their members high wages. This could reduce the demand for labour and raise unemployment. Now all union members have to take a vote on strike actions and unions can be fined if they disrupt output and cause firms to lose revenue (see Chapter 11).

3 Competition Policy

Competition Policy concerns the removal of barriers to free competition which in turn forces consumers to pay higher prices by restricting output and therefore employment. Anti-competitive behaviour by powerful monopoly firms, such as predatory pricing and price-fixing agreements, can be investigated by the competition authorities in the UK. They have the power to fine firms by up to 10% of their revenue if they are found guilty (see Chapter 10).

4 Privatization

Privatization involves the transfer and sale of public sector activities to the private sector (see Chapter 5). This has involved the sale of state owned organizations such as British Gas and regional water boards to private shareholders, and the contracting out of services such as catering, cleaning, computer maintenance in hospitals and government departments.

It has been argued that many public sector activities were overmanned and inefficient because they faced no competition and did not have to make a profit. Competition to supply these services for profit is argued to have improved their quality and lowered their costs. Others argue that privatization has created private monopolies that have increased their profits by cutting quality and making excessive profits by not passing on costs savings to their consumers as lower prices.

5 Deregulation

Deregulation involves removing old and unnecessary rules and regulations on business. For example, the Deregulation and Contracting Out Act 1994 removed some 450 statutory regulations on business, including restrictions on opening hours, the sale of methylated spirits, the licensing of employment agencies etc. The removal of these restrictions should reduce business costs and help to increase output and lower prices.

6 Improving education and training

In order for UK firms to be successful when competing in international markets it is essential to have a highly trained and skilled workforce. Skill needs in industry are rising as the pace of change in competition and technology increases.

A well-trained workforce can raise labour productivity and will be better able to adapt its skills to new products, technology and production processes. Because of this the UK Government is investing more in education and training facilities, encouraging more people to attend universities and colleges, and introducing new courses to teach modern skills.

7 Encouraging new research and development (R&D)

The Government provides funds to help firms invest in new research and the development of better products and production methods. It can also encourage firms to invest in R&D by giving them tax relief on the money they spend on it.

Exercise 5   Expanding the supply side of the economy

1 Find examples of current supply-side policies in newspapers and from the internet.

2 Draw a simple diagram of an economy using aggregate demand and supply curves. Show the impact of a successful supply-side policy in your diagram and explain the impact it has on the general level of prices, output and employment, and potential overseas trade.

Section 5 | Policy conflicts

Some economists argue there will often be conflicts between government macroeconomic policy objectives.

In times of rising aggregate demand unemployment will be falling and output rising leading to economic growth. However, rising demand may cause prices to rise and people may spend a lot of their money on imported goods causing balance of payments problems. On the other hand, they point to the early 1980s when falling aggregate demand caused rising unemployment and stunted economic growth, but brought lower rates of inflation, while the export of North Sea oil helped improve our international trading position. UK consumers also bought fewer imports as aggregate demand fell.

However, not all economists accept there is a **trade-off** between objectives. That is, there is no reason why low rates of unemployment and high economic growth should be associated with high rates of inflation and an unfavourable balance of trade.

Similarly, low inflation and a favourable current account balance on trade need not be experienced at the same time as high unemployment and slow growth.

If price inflation in the UK could be reduced to a low level then low rates of unemployment, high economic growth and a favourable balance of trade on current account would follow.

Reducing inflation will make UK goods and services more competitive. Demand for UK goods and services will rise at home and abroad. Increased demand for UK exports will improve the balance of trade. Firms will need to increase output to meet this demand. Jobs will be created for the unemployed. Firms will also wish to invest in new machines and factories. This will boost economic growth.

Exercise 6   Conflicts

1   Look at the graphs below. In what years were the following at their highest?:
    a   The rate of inflation.
    b   The rate of unemployment.
    c   The rate of economic growth.
    d   The surplus on the current account on the balance of payments.

2   In what years were the following at their lowest?:
    a   The rate of inflation.
    b   The rate of unemployment.
    c   The rate of economic growth.
    d   The deficit on the current account on the balance of payments.

3   Using your information from questions 1 and 2 is there evidence to support the view that economic policy objectives conflict? Explain your answers.

4   From the information presented in the graphs has the UK Government been successful in achieving both low inflation and unemployment, and high rates of economic growth and a favourable current account on the balance of payments? Explain your answer.

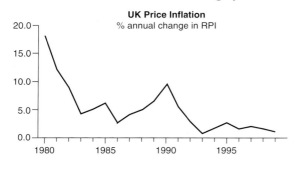

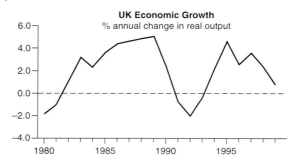

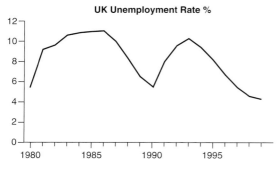

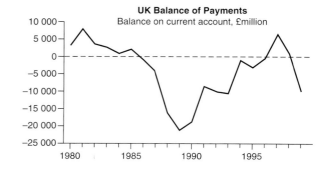

Key words

In your own words write down what you understand by the following:

Demand-side policies	**Monetary Policy Committee**
Supply-side policies	**Base rate**
Fiscal policy	**Treasury bills**
Fiscal rules	**Gilt-edged securities**
Monetary policy	**Competition policy**
Crowding out	**Privatization**
The Bank of England	**Deregulation**

Now check your understanding of these terms by reading through the chapter again.

THE CHANCELLOR GIVETH AND THE CHANCELLOR TAKETH AWAY.

Aims

At the end of the chapter you should be able to:

1 Understand the size of, and trends in, government spending and know the main types of government expenditure in the UK.

2 Explain the main reasons for government spending.

3 Identify **transfer payments**.

4 Understand the purposes of taxation.

5 Identify **progressive**, **regressive** and **proportional taxes**.

6 Describe the main **direct** and **indirect taxes** in the UK.

7 Understand the purposes of the **budget**.

8 Analyse the meaning and importance of the **public sector borrowing requirement** and the **national debt**.

9 Understand the services provided by the **local authorities** and their main sources of revenue.

Section 1 Public sector organizations

Some examples of Central Government services	Some examples of Local Government services
Major road building and maintenance	Street lighting
Tax assessment and collection	Parking enforcement
National Health Service	Refuse collection
Armed services	Libraries
Social security payments	Parks
Collection of economic and social statistics	Schools
Consumer protection	Cutting grass verges
Immigration services	Local road building and maintenance
Air traffic control	Council housing
Law and order	Housing benefits
Post Office	Fire service

What is the public sector?	The public sector in the UK is made up of organizations which are funded by, and accountable to, Local and Central Government (see Chapter 5). These organizations affect our daily lives by the way in which they raise money and through the services they provide and rules they make.

Local Government

This consists of the decision making bodies and administrative offices of district councils, county councils (regional councils in Scotland), and London borough councils. Local voters elect council representatives, or councillors, to make decisions that affect their communities every four years. The decisions of local councils and the day-to-day running of their offices are carried out by paid employees known as local government officers.

Central Government

The Central Government is the elected body responsible for macroeconomic policy and taking decisions on other national issues (see Chapter 15). The administrative offices of Central Government are government departments, for example, the Department for Education and Employment (DfEE) and the Northern Ireland Executive.

Other public sector organizations

A number of organizations are also accountable to Central Government.

- **Executive agencies** such as the Royal Mint and Passport Office
- **QUANGOS (Quasi-autonomous non-government organizations)** such as Regional Health Authorities, research councils, and employment tribunals
- **Public Corporations** such as the Post Office, Bank of England and BBC.

In 1999–2000 public sector organizations in the UK spent over £330 billion on the provision of goods and services, and on capital investment, and raised over £340 billion in revenue from taxes and other sources.

Section 2 |  The pattern of public expenditure

Public expenditure can be broken down into a number of different categories. One method is to distinguish between **current expenditure** and **capital expenditure**. Current expenditure is on public sector workers' salaries, benefits paid to the unemployed, the sick and pensioners, and spending on consumable goods, like medicines in the health service and all other materials that can be used up. It can be thought of simply as the day-to-day running expenses of the public sector. Capital expenditure refers to the Government's investment in new roads, school buildings, hospital buildings, weapons, etc.

Examples of current and capital expenditure

On health		On education	
Current	**Capital**	**Current**	**Capital**
Nurses' pay	Heart monitors	Teachers' pay	Computer equipment
Doctors' pay	Kidney machines	Photocopy paper	New school blocks
Uniforms	Other equipment	Exercise-books	Swimming pools
Medicines	New laboratories	Heating	New schools and
Bandages	Hospital extensions	Lighting	colleges
Heating	New health centres	Chalk	
Lighting		Pens	

Another way is to distinguish between that public spending made in return for goods and services, and that which is not. Much of this spending constitutes payments made to people who are not productive in the economic sense. These payments are known as **transfer payments**.

Many millions of pounds of spending included in total public expenditure are not really spent by the Government at all. Instead, the Government gives the money to people in the form of pensions, unemployment and social security benefits and other payments. The people who receive these payments may then spend the money on goods and services. They are called transfer payments because the Government is simply transferring money from those in work who produce goods and services to those who do not. People in work have to pay taxes to pay for these benefits.

Because the number of people of pensionable age has been rising in the UK means that public spending on transfer payments has been increasing.

Public expenditure as a percentage of GDP, United Kingdom 1901–99

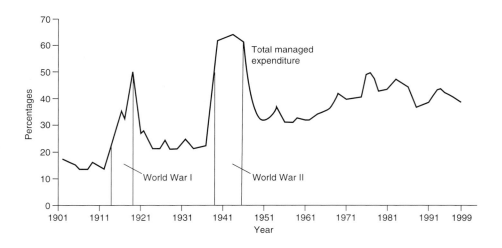

The graph shows that in 1999 general Government expenditure by Central and Local Government accounted for 40% of total spending in the UK. That is, the Government created 40 pence of every £1 of national income. Out of this amount half was spent on goods and services and the other half on other payments, including transfer payments. The graph clearly shows that public spending has remained at over 40% of Gross Domestic Product in most years since 1970.

This figure may seem high, but government spending of over 40% of GDP is common among countries in Western Europe. For example, government spending as a proportion of GDP was 59% in Denmark and 50% in France in 1998–99.

The left-hand side of the diagram below shows the main items of public expenditure in the UK are social security, health, education and defence.

The right-hand side shows that 70% of public spending is undertaken by the Central Government, and just over one fifth of total public spending is by local authorities.

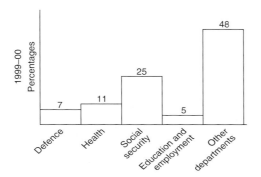
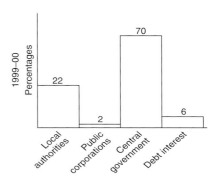

Exercise 1   Trends in public expenditure

As the charts on the next page show, public spending, as measured by Total Managed Expenditure, moved on to a rapidly rising trend during the 1960s, both as a percentage of Gross Domestic Product (GDP) and in real terms. In the 15 years from 1963–64 to 1978–79 public spending grew significantly faster than real GDP. As a result public spending as a proportion of GDP rose from around 35% in the early 1960s to 48.5% in 1982–83, having reached a peak of just under 50% in 1975–76.

By 1988–89 public spending as proportion of GDP had fallen back to 39.2%, and then increased again to peak at 44.2% in 1992–93, since then public spending increases have been held back, and spending had fallen to just under 40% of GDP by 1999–2000.

1   If national income (as measured by GDP) grows faster than public spending, what will happen to public expenditure as a percentage of GDP?

2   Describe what has happened to public spending over time as a percentage of GDP in the UK.

3   Why does the Government spend so much money in the UK? Write down as many reasons as you can for public spending.

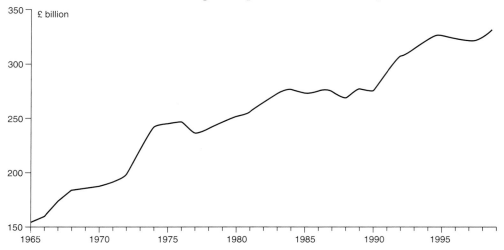

Real Total Managed Expenditure (1997–98 prices)

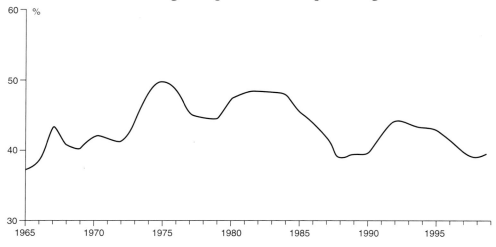

Real Total Managed Expenditure as a percentage of GDP

| Section 3 | Reasons for government spending |

1 Public goods   You may remember from Chapter 2 that some goods, known as public goods, cannot profitably be provided by private firms. For example, it would not be profitable for private firms to provide the services of defence or street-lighting, but these things are of great value to the public. Because of this the Government provides these and many other public goods.

2 Merit goods The Government also spends money on the provision of merit goods. These are goods that the Government feels everybody should have, whether or not they can afford them. For example, the Government provides state education and health care so that everyone can benefit from them.

Government spending by Department (£ billion)

	£ billion					
	Outturns		Estimates		Plans	
	1996–97	1997–98	1998–99	1999–00	2000–01	2001–02
Current Budget						
Education and Employment	13.4	14.0	13.7	14.5	15.8	16.8
Health	33.4	35.1	37.6	39.9	42.7	45.5
of which: NHS	*32.8*	*34.5*	*36.9*	*39.2*	*41.9*	*44.5*
DETR – Main programmes	4.2	4.1	4.1	4.4	4.6	4.8
DETR – Local Government and						
Regional Policy	31.2	31.1	32.4	33.9	35.4	36.9
Home Office	5.9	6.2	6.6	7.4	7.5	7.6
Legal Departments	2.5	2.6	2.6	2.7	2.7	2.6
Defence	20.7	20.1	20.9	20.8	21.3	21.4
Foreign and Commonwealth Office	1.0	1.0	1.0	1.0	1.1	1.1
International Development	1.9	1.9	2.1	2.0	2.5	2.7
Trade and Industry	2.8	2.7	2.7	2.9	3.1	3.1
Agriculture, Fisheries and Food	1.8	1.4	1.2	1.1	1.0	1.0
Culture, Media and Sport	0.9	0.8	0.8	0.9	0.9	1.0
Social Security (administration)	3.4	3.4	3.5	3.3	3.4	3.4
Scotland	11.4	11.5	11.7	12.2	12.8	13.3
Wales	5.4	5.6	5.9	6.3	6.7	7.0
Northern Ireland	4.8	4.9	5.2	5.3	5.5	5.5
Chancellor's Departments	2.7	2.7	2.9	3.0	3.1	3.1
Cabinet Office	1.0	0.8	1.2	1.2	1.1	1.1
Welfare to Work		0.0	0.4	1.2	1.0	1.0
Invest to Save Budget (unallocated)				0.0	0.0	0.1
Capital Modernisation Fund (unallocated)				0.0	0.0	0.0
Reserve				1.1	1.7	2.2
Allowance for shortfall			–1.5			
Total Current Budget	**148.3**	**149.8**	**155.1**	**165.3**	**174.0**	**181.6**
Total Capital Budget	**13.0**	**12.6**	**12.9**	**14.0**	**15.8**	**18.1**
Departmental Expenditure Limits	**161.3**	**162.3**	**168.0**	**179.2**	**189.7**	**199.5**

Financial Statement and Budget Report, March 1999

3 Social reasons Today most people feel that it is unacceptable for the old, unemployed and sick to be left to starve if they cannot earn an income for themselves. Because of this, the Government spends large sums of money in order to provide a safety net, so that nobody in this country need go without food, shelter or health care. All of the goods and services provided by the Government for social reasons, like health care and social security, are often called the **welfare state.**

4 Control of the economy The Government receives many billions of pounds in taxes each year and also spends many billions of pounds on the provision of goods and services. In fact, the Government spends and receives so much money that a change in either government spending or taxation can have important effects on output, employment, prices and national income. The Government uses its spending and taxation to influence the economy. This is known as **fiscal policy** and is discussed in detail in Chapter 15.

5 Overseas spending Some public spending is made overseas to help countries in need because they have suffered droughts, earthquakes or war. **Foreign aid** can help provide food and medicines and pay for new infrastructure like roads and railways. The UK also pays money into the European Community budget because it is a member of the European Union (see Chapter 18).

Section 4 | Financing the public sector

With central government spending of over £300 billion each year the Government must find some way of paying for it. There are six main sources of government finance:

1 Public sector borrowing.

2 Interest payments on loans of money made by the public sector.

3 Rent from public-owned land and buildings.

4 **Gross operating surpluses** (or profits) from executive agencies and publicly owned industries selling goods and services.

5 Proceeds from the sale of government-owned industries and assets (see privatization in Chapter 5). For example, privatization proceeds in 1990–91 and 1991–92 were around £5 billion and £8 billion, mostly from the sale of the water and electricity industries.

6 Money paid into the national lottery distribution fund by the organization running the national lottery.

7 Taxes on incomes, wealth and expenditure. By far the most revenue is raised from taxation. Taxes are compulsory payments backed by law. Non-payment of tax or **tax evasion** is a punishable offence.

Taxes, however, can be avoided. For example, wealthy people, pop stars, etc., can move out of countries that impose high taxes to those with lower taxes. People can also avoid some taxes by avoiding the purchase of some goods and services which the Government has taxed.

Exercise 3   Why have taxes?

In pairs, read the statements below and then write down as many reasons as you can think of for government taxes.

'British Government needs to raise £2 billion for new motorway.'

'Smoking and alcoholism cause record number of deaths.'

'The rich are getting richer and the poor are getting poorer.'

'Imports of foreign electrical goods are causing rising unemployment among workers in British electrical industries.'

'Record spending boom causes prices to rise.'

| Section 5 | Why do we pay taxes? |

There are six main reasons for having taxes.

1   Taxes are the main way of raising money for the Government.

2   Taxes can be used to raise the prices, and reduce the consumption, of harmful goods such as alcohol and tobacco.

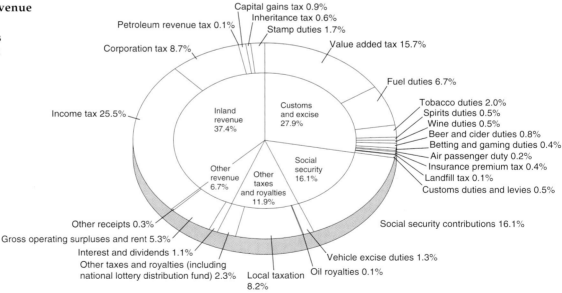

Sources of revenue 1999/00

Total receipts £344.3 billion

Capital gains tax 0.9%
Inheritance tax 0.6%
Stamp duties 1.7%
Petroleum revenue tax 0.1%
Corporation tax 8.7%
Value added tax 15.7%
Income tax 25.5%
Fuel duties 6.7%
Tobacco duties 2.0%
Spirits duties 0.5%
Wine duties 0.5%
Beer and cider duties 0.8%
Betting and gaming duties 0.4%
Air passenger duty 0.2%
Insurance premium tax 0.4%
Landfill tax 0.1%
Customs duties and levies 0.5%
Inland revenue 37.4%
Customs and excise 27.9%
Other revenue 6.7%
Other taxes and royalties 11.9%
Social security 16.1%
Other receipts 0.3%
Gross operating surpluses and rent 5.3%
Interest and dividends 1.1%
Other taxes and royalties (including national lottery distribution fund) 2.3%
Local taxation 8.2%
Oil royalties 0.1%
Vehicle excise duties 1.3%
Social security contributions 16.1%

3   In the UK wealthy people tend to pay more in tax than poorer people. Taxation can help to reduce differences in incomes between people and gives the Government money to spend on providing goods and services for the less well off.

4 Taxes can be used to make foreign goods more expensive. By taxing foreign goods their prices increase and this makes UK consumers more likely to buy UK goods and services.

5 If people try to spend too much at once, this can cause prices to rise. Raising taxes can reduce the amount of money consumers have to spend. In this way taxes can be used to affect the economy. Lowering taxes may help to boost employment opportunities.

6 Taxes can be used to protect the environment. For example, taxes on petrol have been increased in an attempt to reduce car use and air pollution. A landfill tax has been introduced to encourage firms to recycle more of their waste by making dumping at landfill sites more expensive.

Exercise 4   What is a good tax?

Look at the proposed imaginary tax changes below. Do you think they are good or bad changes from the point of view of:

a   The tax-payer

b   The Government

c   The whole economy?

- Height tax to be introduced on all people under 5 feet and over 6 feet tall, says Chancellor, who is 5 feet 6 inches, in his Budget speech.
- Overtime to be taxed at 95 pence in the pound.
- Pay-as-you-earn income tax to be abolished. Tax-payers will receive bills every two years.
- Tax system to be simplified!
  All taxes to be abolished and to be replaced by equal tax payment of £2 000 per person per year over the age of 18 years.
- New tax office set up at an annual cost of £15 million to administer tax on pet cats. The Government expects its cat tax to raise £7 million in revenue each year.

Section 6 | What is a good tax? |

A good tax must possess the following qualities:

1   Fairness   Taxes must be fair. If most people think that a tax is unfair, they are unlikely to pay it. For example a tax based on height would be very unfair.

2   Must not discourage people from working   A tax should not discourage people from working. If taxes are too high, then people may decide that it is not worth trying to earn more.

3   Cheap to collect   There is little point introducing a tax if it costs more money to collect than it earns in revenue for the Government. For example, a tax costing £10 million to collect but only bringing in £3 million in revenue would be pointless and a waste of public money.

4 Convenience Imagine how inconvenient it would be if tax-payers were expected to work out their own tax bills and then had to keep enough money back to pay them once every two years. People who are not very good at managing their own money would find themselves in trouble when called to pay their taxes. For this reason it is important that taxes are easy to pay and easy to understand.

Exercise 4   Window tax: Good or bad?

Chancellor proposes new tax

Only a month after the last budget, the Chancellor of the Exchequer last night announced plans to once again broaden the existing tax base in the economy. Such plans include imposing a flat rate tax on the number and size of windows in a property.

Speaking at a meeting of West Midland industrialists, he told delegates that the issue of reducing the amount of Government borrowing must not be 'glazed over' and that if the British public wished for public sector provision to remain at a high level then they must be prepared to provide the necessary funds.

Raising taxes on income and expenditure would only further reduce demand and output in the economy as work incentives and consumption plans would be damaged.

Businessmen speculating that double glazed windows may be subject to a higher rate of tax argued that such a move may seriously damage this particular growth area. The Chancellor was, however, quick to reject such fears.

A Green paper looking into the feasibility of the tax should be ready in time for next year's budget which already promises to provide the economy with a major tax shake up.

Divide into groups of three or four. Imagine you have been appointed to research the feasibility of the proposed window tax for the Green Report. You are to write a report assessing the tax on the following grounds:

a   Fairness.

b   The effect on consumption expenditure, output and employment.

c   The cost of collection.

d   The ease with which the tax payable can be calculated.

Your completed reports can form the basis of a class discussion. You may be surprised to know that a window tax did exist in the UK many years ago but has long since been abolished.

Section 7   How the tax system is designed

Progressive, regressive or proportional?

All of the taxes in a country are together called the **tax system**. Governments must decide whether they want a **progressive, regressive** or **proportional** tax system. Each type of system will affect people differently.

A progressive tax system is one where the proportion of income taken in taxation rises as incomes rise. This means better-off people pay a higher proportion of their incomes in taxes than poorer people. Governments use progressive taxation because they feel that people on higher incomes can afford to pay a larger proportion of their incomes in tax.

An example of a progressive tax system

Annual income	% tax paid	£ tax paid
£20 000	20	4 000
£50 000	40	20 000
£80 000	60	48 000

351

A regressive tax system takes a smaller proportion of income in tax as income rises. It may be considered unfair to people on low incomes because a much larger fraction of their income is taken as tax.

An example of a regressive tax system

Annual income	% tax paid	£ tax paid
£20 000	50	10 000
£50 000	40	20 000
£80 000	30	24 000

A proportional tax is one where the proportion of income taken in tax is the same whatever the level of income. For example, a tax of 20% on all incomes of all tax-payers is an example of a proportional tax.

Exercise 5   Tax systems

Look at the following graph.

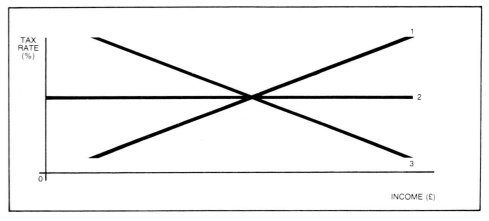

1   Which of the lines, 1, 2, or 3 represents a tax which is:
   a   progressive
   b   regressive
   c   proportional?

Explain your answers.

2   Now look at the three tax systems below. Calculate the percentage of tax paid on each income and state whether the systems are progressive, regressive or proportional?

Tax system 1		Tax system 2		Tax system 3	
Annual income	£ tax paid	Annual income	£ tax paid	Annual income	£ tax paid
£5 000	1 500	£10 000	1 000	£8 000	3 200
£15 000	4 500	£16 000	2 400	£12 000	3 600
£25 000	7 500	£30 000	6 600	£20 000	4 000

Direct and indirect taxation

The main types of taxes, the revenue they raise per £1 of total tax revenue, and what it is spent on, are displayed in the diagram below.

The taxes illustrated in the diagram can be split into two main types: **direct** and **indirect taxes**.

1 Direct taxes collected by the Inland Revenue
Direct taxes are taken directly from incomes and wealth. The main types of direct taxation in the UK are income tax, corporation tax, capital gains tax and inheritance tax.

2 Indirect taxes collected by the Customs and Excise Department
Indirect taxes are taxes on spending. These taxes are only paid when people buy goods and services. For example, when buying a CD for £10, 17½% of the price, or £1.75, is value added tax, or VAT. Customs duties and excise duties are the other main indirect taxes in the UK.

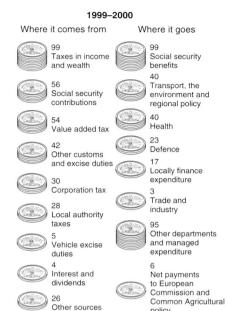

1999–2000

Where it comes from

99 Taxes in income and wealth
56 Social security contributions
54 Value added tax
42 Other customs and excise duties
30 Corporation tax
28 Local authority taxes
5 Vehicle excise duties
4 Interest and dividends
26 Other sources
5 Borrowing

Total Revenue £349 bn

Where it goes

99 Social security benefits
40 Transport, the environment and regional policy
40 Health
23 Defence
17 Locally finance expenditure
3 Trade and industry
95 Other departments and managed expenditure
6 Net payments to European Commission and Common Agricultural policy
26 Debt interest

Total expenditure £349 bn

The proportion of tax revenue raised by each of the main direct and indirect taxes between 1956 and 1999 is given below.

Leading taxes 1956–99 (as a percentage of total taxes)

Year	1956	1964	1982	1991	1999
Income tax	36.1	32.1	27.8	27.9	27.3
Tobacco	11.4	9.7	3.3	2.9	2.2
National insurance	10.7	14.8	20.2	17.5	17.3
Local authority taxes	9.3	11.3	11.2	10.4	8.8
Alcohol	6.9	5.7	3.1	2.4	1.9
Corporation tax	–	–	5.0	8.9	9.3
Customs duties	2.1	2.0	1.8	0.9	0.6
Petrol and diesel	5.5	6.6	4.7	5.3	7.2
Vehicle excise duties	–	–	0.6	1.4	1.4
Capital gains	–	–	4.7	0.6	1.0
Value Added Tax	–	–	17.8	17.1	16.8

Income tax

Every tax-payer is allowed to earn a certain amount of income, known as a personal allowance, before they start to pay tax. For example, in 1987 a single person could earn £2 425 each year and a married man £3 795 before they became liable for tax. The introduction of independent taxation for married people in 1990–91 replaced the married man's allowance with a single married couple's allowance, set initially against the husband's income, but payable in addition to the single person's allowance, set against the wife's income. It was removed in April 2000.

Exactly how much tax is paid depends on how much is earned. Before 1989–90 there were a number of progressively higher tax bands rising from a basic rate of 27% on that slice of a person's taxable income from £0 to £17 900 to 60% for any taxable income over £41 200. In the budget of 1988–89 the basic rate of tax was cut to 25% and the four higher rates replaced by a single rate of 40%. This dual rate tax structure remained in place until joined in 1992–93 by a lower rate of tax of just 20% on taxable income between £0 and £2 000. A 10% starting rate of income tax was introduced in April 2000 on taxable income between £0 and £1 520. A basic

UK Income tax structure

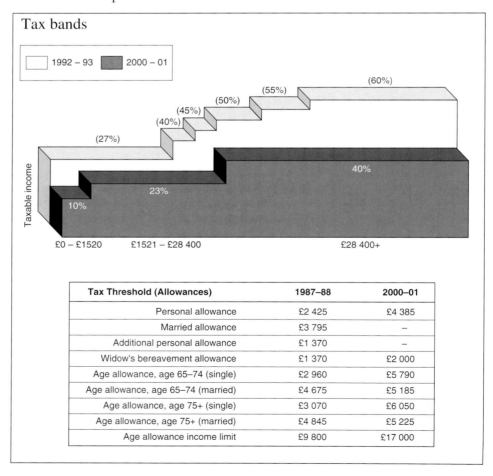

Tax Threshold (Allowances)	1987–88	2000–01
Personal allowance	£2 425	£4 385
Married allowance	£3 795	–
Additional personal allowance	£1 370	–
Widow's bereavement allowance	£1 370	£2 000
Age allowance, age 65–74 (single)	£2 960	£5 790
Age allowance, age 65–74 (married)	£4 675	£5 185
Age allowance, age 75+ (single)	£3 070	£6 050
Age allowance, age 75+ (married)	£4 845	£5 225
Age allowance income limit	£9 800	£17 000

rate of 23% will then apply to taxable income between £1 521 and £28 400, above which the higher rate of 40% will apply.

Income tax is collected from employees' pay by their employers. This is called the Pay As You Earn (PAYE) system. Employers then send the money on to the Inland Revenue. In this way PAYE allows the Government to receive a steady flow of income and prevents the tax-payer from receiving a large tax bill at the end of each year.

Corporation tax Just as individuals are taxed on their incomes, companies are taxed on their profits. The tax on company profits is called **corporation tax**. In 1999 the standard rate of corporation tax was 30% for large companies and 20% for companies with profits of less than £300 000 per year.

From April 2000 small companies earning less than £10 000 in profit each year will pay only a 10% rate of corporation tax.

Petroleum revenue tax Since the UK discovered oil and gas in the North Sea the Government has imposed an additional tax on the profits of companies involved in drilling for oil and gas. Newer fields in the north sea pay significantly lower rates of PRT and so PRT revenues have fallen significantly over time as production from older fields has fallen.

Capital gains tax It is possible to make profits by buying shares, property, etc., at a low price and then selling at a higher price. Profits made in this way are called **capital gains** and are subject to tax by the Government. Profits made on an individual's home, private cars, winnings from gambling and assurance policies are not subject to capital gains tax.

Inheritance tax Inheritance tax is a tax on transfers of wealth made at death. When an individual dies and leaves property or money to somebody else, inheritance tax might be payable on the value inherited. In 1999 inheritances of less than £231 000 were free of the tax, but for inheritances above this minimum a tax of 40% applied. The share of inheritances taken by the Inland Revenue using 1999 tax rates is shown in the picture below.

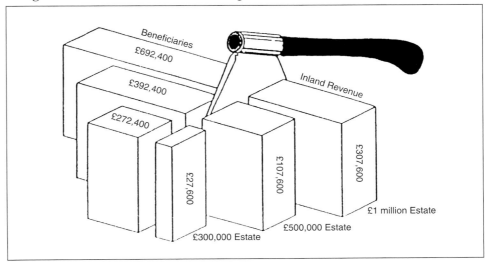

National insurance contributions These contributions are used to pay for the social security benefits of the old, the sick and the unemployed. In this way national insurance contributions are rather like other insurance premiums, insuring against loss of income in the face of unemployment, etc.

| **Section 9** | Types of indirect tax |

Value added tax (VAT) Value added tax is a tax on spending and from 1991 has been charged at 17.5% of the price of the good or service. This VAT money is then passed on by the shopkeeper to the Inland Revenue.

VAT is regressive because it takes a larger proportion of a poorer person's income. For example, if an unemployed man receiving £30 per week from the Jobseekers Allowance buys a hamburger for £1 and pays 17.5 pence VAT, this is 0.58% of his income. If a lawyer earning £500 per week buys a hamburger 17.5 pence in VAT only represents 0.03% of her income, a much smaller figure. Because of this, the prices of certain goods that people on low incomes are likely to consume do not carry VAT. For example, children's clothing, food, books, newspapers and public transport were all free of VAT or **zero rated** in 1999. Some products are also free or exempt of VAT when the consumer pays for them, but producers buying materials to make such goods still pay VAT on these materials. Items exempt of VAT at purchase include medicines, medical services, education and land.

Customs duties Some goods imported into the UK are taxed. These taxes are called customs duties and are used to discourage foreign companies from selling their goods in the UK.

Excise duties Excise duties are taxes placed on certain goods and services. Examples include duties on fuel, tobacco and alcohol, the air passenger duty, insurance premium tax and landfill tax. In 1999–00 excise duties raised over £40 billion.

Other taxes A host of other taxes, such as vehicle excise duty, oil royalties and council tax, are forms of indirect taxes levied in the UK. European Union duties are an indirect tax on goods coming into the UK from countries outside the European Union (EU). This tax money is paid to the EU (see Chapter 18).

Exercise 6 Taxation

1 What is the name of the tax paid on each of the following?
   a A footballer's weekly wages.
   b A gift of £1 million.
   c Imports of machinery from the USA.
   d Profits made on the buying and selling of shares.
   e The purchase of a meal from a restaurant.
   f A company's profits.

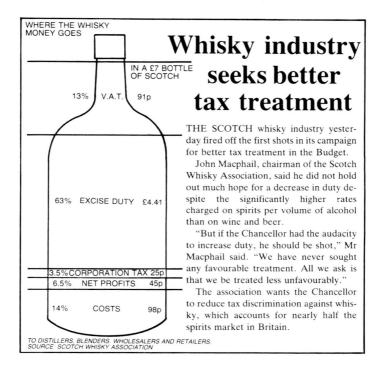

WHERE THE WHISKY MONEY GOES

IN A £7 BOTTLE OF SCOTCH

13% V.A.T. 91p

63% EXCISE DUTY £4.41

3.5% CORPORATION TAX 25p
6.5% NET PROFITS 45p

14% COSTS 98p

TO DISTILLERS, BLENDERS, WHOLESALERS AND RETAILERS.
SOURCE: SCOTCH WHISKY ASSOCIATION

Whisky industry seeks better tax treatment

THE SCOTCH whisky industry yesterday fired off the first shots in its campaign for better tax treatment in the Budget.

John Macphail, chairman of the Scotch Whisky Association, said he did not hold out much hope for a decrease in duty despite the significantly higher rates charged on spirits per volume of alcohol than on wine and beer.

"But if the Chancellor had the audacity to increase duty, he should be shot," Mr Macphail said. "We have never sought any favourable treatment. All we ask is that we be treated less unfavourably."

The association wants the Chancellor to reduce tax discrimination against whisky, which accounts for nearly half the spirits market in Britain.

2 Name:
   a the direct taxes, and
   b the indirect taxes, in the article above.

3 Why do you think the Government taxes whisky so heavily?

4 What problems could arise if the Government taxes alcohol in the UK more heavily than other countries in the EU, such as France and Spain?

5 'VAT is a regressive tax.' Explain the meaning of this statement.

Section 10 | Direct taxes and indirect taxes – advantages and disadvantages

Advantages of direct taxes

1 Revenue

The chief advantages of direct taxes, like income tax and corporation tax, are that they have a high yield of revenue compared with their cost of collection. The total amount of money collected can be estimated with reasonable accuracy in advance, which is of great help to the Chancellor of the Exchequer when planning how much the Government can spend.

2 Redistribution

The progressive nature of many direct taxes means that wealthier members of society are taxed more heavily than poorer groups. Many people think this is fair.

3 Ability to pay

Direct taxes are constructed so that they take account of firms' and people's ability to pay tax. Family commitments, dependents, etc., are taken into consideration and a system of tax allowances are used to reflect these responsibilities.

Disadvantages of direct tax

1 Work incentives

A high rate of tax on income may cause people to work less hard because they know that the more they earn the greater the proportion of their income they will have to pay in tax. UK governments have lowered the starting and basic rates of income tax over time to increase the reward from working.

2 Enterprise

Corporation tax on a firm's profits reduces the incentive for entrepreneurs to start up firms to earn a profit. It also means that a firm will have less profits to re-invest in their business.

3 Tax evasion

High tax rates increase the advantages of evading taxes and finding loopholes in tax laws. As a result, revenues are lower and the trouble of trying to catch up with tax evaders increases costs.

In recent years the British Government has started to rely a little more on indirect taxes to raise revenue because of the disincentive effects high direct taxes have on work efforts. Indirect taxes offer the following advantages.

Advantages of indirect taxes

1 Cost of collection

Indirect taxes are cheap to collect. The burden of collecting taxes in this way lies mainly with the manufacturers, wholesalers and retailers collecting VAT, and importers paying custom and excise duties.

2 Wider tax base

Indirect taxes are paid by young, old, employed and unemployed alike when they buy goods and services, not just by people with earned incomes. As a result, the effects of indirect taxes are spread more widely throughout the community.

3 Selective aims

Indirect taxes can be used to achieve specific aims. Taxes on cigarettes and alcohol can discourage harmful consumption. Taxes on oil can reduce the demand for a valuable resource which will one day run out and help reduce air pollution.

4 Tax alterations

The Chancellor has the power to change the rate of VAT and custom and excise duties up or down by 10% at any time thought necessary. Such taxes are therefore more flexible than direct taxes which take a long time to change and to have an effect on the amount spent by consumers.

Disadvantages of indirect taxes

1 Regressive

Indirect taxes are regressive in nature. That is, they fall more heavily on people with low incomes. This may be thought unfair.

2 Prices

Indirect taxes add to the prices of goods and services and can therefore boost the rate of inflation if the Chancellor increases them.

3 Uncertainty

Because the Chancellor can only guess how much people will spend on goods and services, he or she will be uncertain of how much revenue indirect taxes will raise.

Section 11	The budget

The purpose of a Budget

At the very least, a Budget — as we know it in this country — is necessary to arrange for the raising of tax revenue in the coming year. In the 19th century it was little more. Budget speeches consisted mainly of a very detailed and technical discussion of taxation and borrowing.

Nowadays, the Budget is the most important occasion during the year when the Chancellor reviews the progress of the economy against the world economic background, describes the economic policies of the Government and sets out any new measures for which he seeks Parliament's approval. The reasons for this development are not hard to find. Since the war, governments have accepted a responsibility for determining the financial conditions within which the economy operates. Also, there has been the growing share of national output produced by the public sector or channelled through it in, for example, social security payments or regional development grants. The Budget speech was bound to broaden out.

Fortunately, the speeches have not grown longer. One of the longest was given by Gladstone in 1853, lasting around 4¼ hours. They have recently tended to last about two hours. And they have been broadcast since 1978.

A **budget** is an estimate of government spending and revenue for the coming year. The budget is presented to Parliament by the Chancellor of the Exchequer each year in March.

The two main purposes of the budget are to announce plans for government spending and taxation and through these to influence the economy.

In the budget the Government sometimes announces new taxes, abolishes old taxes and usually changes tax rates. The Government also uses the budget to announce spending plans. For example, programmes of job creation for the unemployed or more spending on defence.

Because Government spending and taxation are so great, changes in them can have important effects on the economy and the Government uses this fact to influence inflation, employment and output. For example, if the Government budgets for a deficit the Government pumps more money into the economy. A **budget deficit** means the Government is spending more than it receives in tax revenue. More money in the economy is likely to cause increased spending on goods and services and so increase employment.

If the Government reduces its deficit by raising taxes and spending less, the amount of money flowing around the economy is reduced. Less money in the economy is likely to cause spending on output to fall and may lead to lower price rises, possibly at the cost of higher unemployment.

If the Government raises more in tax revenue than it spends, it is said to be budgeting for a surplus. If the Government spends as much as it raises in tax revenue exactly, the budget is said to be balanced.

Using public spending and taxation to influence the level of demand or spending in the economy is known as **fiscal policy** (see Chapter 15).

Section 12 | Public sector borrowing

Very often the Government spends more than it earns in revenue. Just as an individual has to borrow if s/he spends more than s/he earns, so does the Government. The amount of public sector borrowing each year from the private sector and overseas is called the **public sector net cash requirement**. Part of the central government net cash requirement is needed to finance lending to local authorities and public corporations (see Chapter 5).

The public sector net cash requirements for 1987–99 are given in the table below. Positive numbers are amounts borrowed. Negative numbers are debt repaid.

Financial year	£ billion	as a percentage of GDP
1987–88	−3.1	−0.7
1988–89	−14.5	−3.1
1989–90	−6.9	−1.4
1990–91	−0.8	−0.1
1991–92	13.8	2.4
1992–93	36.2	6.0
1993–94	46.2	7.2
1994–95	36.7	5.4
1995–96	31.5	4.4
1996–97	22.7	3.0
1997–98	1.1	0.1
1998–99	−5.2	−0.6
1999–2000	4.5	0.5

For example, in 1993–94 the Government had to borrow £46.2 billion to pay for spending over and above revenues. During times of economic recession, as the UK experienced in the early 1990s, tax revenues tend to fall but expenditure on unemployment and social security benefits tend to rise.

However, during periods of surplus revenue, such as in 1988–89, the net cash requirement becomes negative. That is, surplus revenues can be used to reduce the total amount of public sector debt.

The Government can borrow money to finance the PSBR in a number of ways. It can sell IOUs or **debt** to the general public, banks and foreign countries. **Treasury bills** are short-term debt repaid by the Government, with interest, after 91 days. **Gilt edged securities** can last for up to 25 years before the Government repays them. Each year, however, their holder receives interest rather like a dividend on a share. The Government also borrows the savings of people in the National Savings Bank.

Exactly who the Government borrows from is quite important. As we shall see in Chapter 19, borrowing from the banks increases the money supply which many economists believe causes prices to rise.

Section 13   The national debt

Each year the Government must sell enough debt or IOUs to finance the net cash requirement. However, the Government does not always pay the borrowed money back quickly. All the money borrowed by the public sector over the past which has not been repaid is called the **public sector debt** or **national debt**. In 1999 the national debt of the UK public sector totalled £380 billion or 34.6% of GDP. The national debt has usually risen every year because the Government has normally borrowed more each year

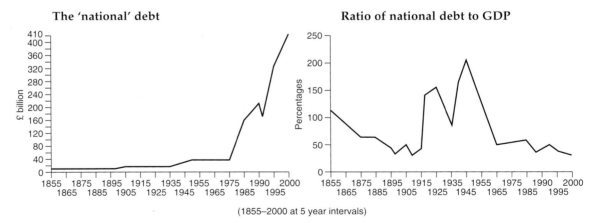

(1855–2000 at 5 year intervals)

than it repays on old loans. Only when the net cash requirement is negative, when public sector revenue exceeds expenditure, can the public sector debt be reduced. For example, in 1998–99 around £5 billion of debt was repaid. Interest must be paid on the public sector debt. As the debt rises so must total debt interest payments. In 1999 a total of £29.5 billion was paid as interest on the public sector debt.

Gross debt interest payments

UK public sector 1987–2000

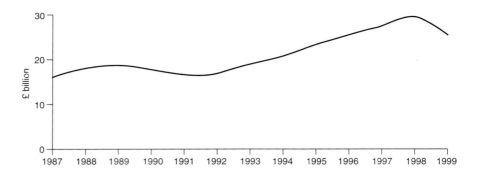

Rising public sector debt and rising interest payments need not be a bad thing. This is because as long as the UK income or GDP rises quicker than the debt, the burden of the debt will fall. For example, if a person gets a larger bank loan, the burden of the loan will not be higher, if at the same time their income or ability to pay back the loan also rises.

This has, in fact, happened in the UK in recent years. Even though public sector debt and interest payments have increased, the UK's ability to pay has increased by more.

Some politicians and members of the public still claim that the public sector debt is a burden on the country. This is because the Government must raise money for the interest payments from tax-payers. Yet this is not true if the interest payments are made to people in the UK who have lent money to the Government. This is because the Government taxes one group of people in the UK and then uses this money to pay another group of people in the UK holding the debt. Interest payments made to holders of national debt in the UK are simply a transfer from one group of people in the UK to another, and so the country as a whole is no worse off.

However, that part of national debt held by foreigners who have lent money to the UK Government is a burden on the UK. This is because interest payments leave the UK, and the country as a whole is worse off. Tax-payers in the UK have to pay some taxes simply to pay interest to foreigners.

A Treasury stock certificate

(The design of the stock certificate is the copyright of the Bank of England and is reproduced at less than its actual size with the permission of the Bank of England.)

362

Local authority expenditure

Local authorities or local councils spend many millions of pounds each year.

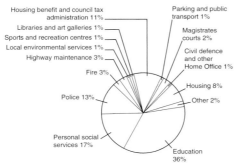

Central Government cannot provide all of the goods and services in the correct amounts needed in each area. Local authorities exist to provide goods and services locally, such as roads, public transport, parks, cemeteries, schools and social services, simply because the Central Government cannot control all of these things for the whole country.

Local Authority Spending, 1998–99
£85 billion

Sources of income for local authorities

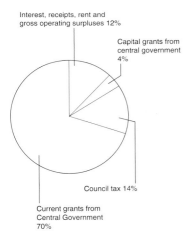

Local Authority Income, 1998–99
£85 billion

Local authorities receive their income from four main sources.

1 Income from the sale of goods and services
Local authorities receive money from council rents on council homes and other property, charges for recreational facilities, such as swimming baths, revenue from public transport and interest on loans they make.

2 Central Government grants
Most of all local authority income comes from central government grants. This is not surprising since much of the work of local authorities is on behalf of the Central Government.

Each local authority receives a grant of money based on a central government calculation of what the local authority needs. In its calculations the Central Government looks at things like the number of children of school age and the number of pensioners as well as many other indicators of need in local council areas.

The Central Government has the power to give local authorities spending targets and to punish them if they spend too much. If an authority spends more than the target, the Central Government can reduce the amount of grant it gives to the authority. The result of this in the early 1980s was that some local authorities received no grant at all.

3 Non-domestic rates
Businesses do not pay council tax. Instead they pay a tax called business rates based on the value of business property. Business rates are collected by local authorities but paid into a national pool. The Central Government then shares out the revenues among councils based on the size of their local populations.

A unified business rate poundage is set nationally every year by the Central Government. The poundage tells a business how many pence it must pay for every pound of the rateable value of its property. It is raised periodically through time. In 1999–00 the poundage was set at 48.9 pence in the pound for businesses in England. So, for example, a business with premises valued at £1 million would pay £489 000 in rates.

363

4 Local taxation

Up until April 1990 local residents also had to pay rates on their homes. Every property had a rateable value. In general, the larger the property the more its rateable value, but properties of the same size could have very different values depending on the area they were in. Each local authority would then decide its own poundage depending on how much money they needed to raise from local taxpayers. If, for example, the poundage was set at 20 pence in the pound, a person with a house valued at £90 000 would pay £180 a year in rates.

In April 1990 rates were replaced with the community charge or **poll tax**. The poll tax was a lump sum tax. The amount of poll tax in each area was set by individual councils and everyone over 18 years of age was required to pay the tax. People on very low incomes could apply for a reduction in the amount of poll tax they had to pay.

Many people objected to the poll tax system because both rich and poor people had to pay the same amount of tax. The tax was considered highly regressive and in some areas people refused to pay. The amount of tax payable also varied greatly by area. For example in 1992–93 the London Borough of Wandsworth set a poll tax of zero while people living in Brent had to pay £550 each.

The poll tax was replaced by the **council tax** in April 1993. The council tax is a local tax based on the values of property in an area. Only one tax bill per household is issued regardless of the number of people living in the property. However, where there is only one adult living in a house, flat, mobile home or houseboat, whether owned or rented, the council tax bill is reduced by 25%.

All properties in England were valued by an Inland Revenue valuer on the 1st April 1991. Values were based on estimated sale prices, and properties were then placed in one of eight council tax valuation bands. The less expensive a particular property is the lower the band it is placed in and the less tax the household will pay. A home in band A will pay two thirds of what someone whose home in band D pays in tax and only a third of what someone in a home in band H pays.

The actual amount of council tax payable in band D is set by each local council. The amount set depends on how much each council and certain other bodies, such as the National Rivers Authority, Police and Fire services, spend and how much revenue they raise from other sources. For example, in 1999–00 the Royal Borough of Kingston upon Thames set a council tax of nearly £800 for households living in band D properties.

Council tax valuation bands in England

Valuation band	Range of values (at 1 April 1991)
A	Up to £40 000
B	Over £40 000 and up to £52 000
C	Over £52 000 and up to £68 000
D	Over £68 000 and up to £88 000
E	Over £88 000 and up to £120 000
F	Over £120 000 and up to £160 000
G	Over £160 000 and up to £320 000
H	Over £320 000

Exercise 7   What local tax?

You are on a government working group. It has been set up to investigate the operation and fairness of the new council tax. The working group consists of a number of economists who are to write a report setting out the arguments for and against the council tax compared to the old systems of the poll tax and rates. They are also to suggest possible future ways of raising local revenue from residents and business owners, local consumers and/or motorists.

The working group starts its investigations by comparing two local authority areas and calculating how much each household would pay under past and present local tax systems.

The Thrifty Town authority
An area of decline. Many firms have closed and there is high unemployment. Many properties are in need of repair. There is a large old age pensioner population in need of care. Average household income is below the national average but local taxes are relatively high to finance high spending on social services.

A typical street in Thrifty Town
(Rateable values of properties and council tax bandings are given in left- and right-hand corners respectively.)

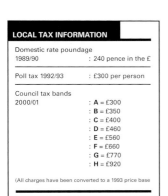

LOCAL TAX INFORMATION

Domestic rate poundage
1989/90   : 240 pence in the £

Poll tax 1992/93   : £300 per person

Council tax bands
2000/01   : **A** = £300
                               : **B** = £350
                               : **C** = £400
                               : **D** = £460
                               : **E** = £560
                               : **F** = £660
                               : **G** = £770
                               : **H** = £920

(All charges have been converted to a 1993 price base)

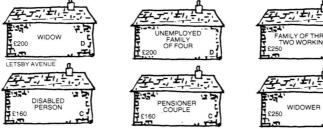

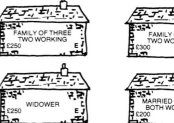

The Green Town authority
A new town with many young working couples. Thriving shopping centre and business district. Household income above national average. Local taxation has historically been low with a large proportion devoted to finance education for the young and the upkeep of parks.

A typical street in Green Town

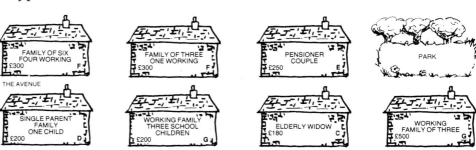

Exercise 8   Learning from the past

'I'm a pensioner on a low income. Why should I have to pay the same as my neighbours, both of whom are at work and earn good salaries?'

'I really don't think it is fair that a family of four should pay the same as a single person in the same type of property'.

'Revenue from the rates is used to pay for local services from which people on low incomes receive the most benefit. Yet many pay little towards their provision because they receive rate rebates. It is in their interest to vote for councils who plan to spend more on these services, but it is people like me earning a good salary that have to foot the bill!'

'Our friends live in exactly the same type of house as we do but because they live in a different council area they pay less than we do in rates. Why can't all councils charge the same?'

'I run a local farm and I would like to know exactly how they estimate how much my business could be rented for. I expect they also find it difficult to estimate the rental value of business premises such as petrol stations and factories.'

Many people were very critical of the rates when they were used to raise revenue by local councils. Examine the statements above. Do you think the poll tax and now the council tax have overcome these problems?

Key words

Key words search

Using the definitions below, find the key terms they refer to in the box of letters.

B	U	D	G	E	T	I	W	I	S	H	T	N	O	F	L	N
U	Y	O	N	C	A	P	I	T	A	L	G	A	I	N	S	A
D	T	H	E	W	I	R	N	G	S	F	O	T	D	V	E	T
G	O	U	P	D	O	A	N	T	P	U	R	I	N	A	R	I
I	N	C	O	M	E	T	A	X	R	E	N	O	M	D	A	O
E	O	U	L	S	E	E	T	X	O	I	L	N	V	E	O	N
V	Y	Z	L	O	R	S	E	F	G	O	R	A	M	F	E	A
A	C	A	T	L	E	S	S	T	R	X	A	L	F	I	O	L
T	A	X	A	E	V	D	I	R	E	C	T	D	R	C	Y	I
P	E	R	X	L	O	V	T	X	S	Z	N	E	O	I	F	N
S	O	N	W	X	Y	B	I	G	S	T	O	B	N	T	O	S
C	C	O	R	P	O	R	A	T	I	O	N	T	A	X	R	U
I	N	D	I	R	E	C	T	Z	V	W	K	L	F	T	N	R
F	I	N	D	B	R	E	G	R	E	S	S	I	V	E	I	A
P	S	B	R	Z	X	K	W	O	Z	E	T	T	A	L	C	N
K	T	Z	I	A	I	N	H	E	R	I	T	A	N	C	E	C
C	U	S	T	O	M	S	A	E	X	I	S	E	T	Z	T	E
L	T	R	A	N	S	F	E	R	P	A	Y	M	E	N	T	S

1 These taxes are levied on incomes and wealth.
2 These taxes can be avoided if you do not buy anything.
3 The total stock of past and present public sector borrowing.
4 Payments made to one group in society from another group. For example, benefits for the unemployed paid from the taxes of the employed.

367

5   This is a tax on wealth held at death.

6   If the Government spends more than its tax revenue the budget is said to be in this state.

7   A tax on company profits.

8   This tax is paid as you earn.

9   A tax levied by local authorities.

10   A tax added on to the price of many goods and services.

11   An estimate of government spending and revenue, and any changes in them over the coming year. It is delivered yearly by the Chancellor of the Exchequer.

12   A tax which takes a greater proportion of a high income than a low income.

13   A tax which falls as a proportion of income as income rises is said to be this.

14   This tax is imposed on profits made by people selling shares, property, etc., for a higher price than they paid for them.

15   Duties imposed on goods imported into the UK from non-EU member countries.

16   Duties on alcohol and cigarettes.

17   Contributions made from incomes as an entitlement to a number of welfare benefits.

Chapter 17 | The Distribution of Income and Wealth

'if we make everyone's size proportionate to their income... we keep on seeing dwarfs...and a few giants.'

J. Pen

Aims

At the end of the chapter, you should be able to:

1 Understand the meaning of and differences between **human** and **non-human wealth**.

2 Understand the relationship between **income** and **wealth**.

3 Describe the **distribution of wealth** in the UK and give reasons for differences in the amounts of wealth held by people.

4 Describe the **distribution of income** in the UK and give reasons for differences in incomes received by people.

5 Understand the importance of **GDP per capita** and be able to calculate it.

6 Be able to describe, in outline, the world distribution of income.

A key objective of the UK Government elected in 1997 was to create 'a fairer society'. That is, it wanted to make sure economic growth and increasing prosperity take place in a way that is fair; by protecting the environment and making sure the benefits of growth are shared out more equally between people by the economic system (see Chapter 3).

The distribution of incomes and wealth in the UK is at present unequal. However, the Government is able to influence this through changes in taxation and public spending.

Section 1 | Wealth

Anything owned by people with a money value is **wealth**. For example, machinery, housing, shares, and bank accounts are wealth.

A nation's wealth is measured as the stock of things with value in that country at a particular moment in time. At the end of 1997 the stock of personal wealth in the UK was estimated to be £3 600 billion. Around £1 900 billion of this wealth was in financial assets, such as pension funds, shares, and bank and building society deposits. Just over £1 000 billion was in housing.

All of the physical goods and financial assets in a country are known as that country's **non-human wealth**.

Nations also possess **human wealth**, that is, the education, training, skills and work experience of their people. It is very difficult to calculate the money value of a person's education, training and skills, and because of this there are no reliable estimates of human wealth in the UK.

Non-Human wealth

Human wealth

Section 2 | Income

Income is a flow

While wealth can be measured at a point in time, income can only be measured over time. For example, the wealth of a particular family could be calculated by adding up the money value of all the physical goods and financial assets held by the family on a particular day. However, if we were to ask what is the income of this family, the answer might be, for example, £25 000 per year or £480 per week. That is, income is measured as a flow of earnings over time.

In 1998 a quarter of all full-time employees in the UK earned less than £256 a week before tax, and a quarter received more than £460 per week.

Where does income come from?

1 Human wealth produces earned income
A highly trained and educated worker, for example, a computer engineer, will earn a relatively high income. This high income is earned because of the large amounts of training and skill, or human wealth, possessed by the worker.

370

Other workers with less human wealth, for example, an unskilled factory worker, will earn far less income. Earned incomes are produced by the stock of human wealth in a country.

2 Non-human wealth produces unearned income

People receive unearned income from their non-human wealth. For example, a person with a stock of non-human wealth, such as a house, shares, bank or building society accounts, may lend their wealth out to others and receive interest, rent and profit. In this way, people receive income without having to go to work. That is, non-human wealth produces unearned income.

Exercise 1 Ms Jones's wealth

Ms Jones is employed as a doctor in a local hospital earning £45 000 per year. Ms Jones has the following investments:

    a   £10 000 in a building society earning £500 per year.

    b   a house worth £140 000 with one room rented out for £85 per week.

    c   £3 000 of shares in a company paying £500 in dividends per year.

1. List the things that might make up Ms Jones's human wealth.
2. List the things that make up Ms Jones's non-human wealth.
3. What is Ms Jones's income for the year?
4. Explain why differences in wealth between people create differences in income.

Everybody knows that there are large differences in incomes between people. In 1997 incomes ranged from an average of £7 060 a year for the lowest earning 20% of UK households up to an average of £45 780 for the highest earning 20%.

We have discovered that earned and unearned incomes arise from the owner-ship of human and non-human wealth. This means that differences in incomes must result from differences in the amount of wealth owned by people.

Section 3	Fair shares? The distribution of wealth in the UK

While there are large differences in income between people, differences in wealth are even greater. The ownership of housing, shares, building society and bank deposits in the UK is very unequal.

Shares in UK wealth

The diagram above shows that the richest 1% of the population owned 19% of all non-human wealth in 1996, the most wealthy 10% of people owned 50% of all wealth, while the most wealthy 50% owned 92% of all wealth. These figures illustrate great inequality in the ownership of wealth. If one-half of the population owns 92% of all wealth, the other half of the population owns a mere 8% of total wealth.

Reasons for differences in wealth

1 Inheritance Studies in the UK suggest that nearly two-thirds of the most wealthy people inherited large amounts of money.

The chances are that if you have wealthy parents, you too will be wealthy. Inheritance is the main reason for the continuing control of 50% of the nation's wealth by just 10% of the people.

2 Savings Savings allow people to increase their wealth, yet savings alone are not enough to allow an individual to match the wealth of the very rich.

3 Self-made wealth Around one-third of the most wealthy people in the UK have made their own money. The main ways in which they have done this are as follows:

　a　The invention or development of a new product. For example, Sir Clive Sinclair became a millionaire by being the first man to produce a home computer.

　b　By being able to forecast future consumer needs. For example, Jack Cohen became a millionaire by opening the first supermarket chain, Tesco.

　c　The ownership or discovery of natural resources, such as oil, has produced many millionaires.

　d　Most important of all is luck. Being in the right place at the right time and being willing to take risks is something most self-made people would claim is important. The National Lottery in the UK had produced over 100 new millionaires by the year 2000.

Trends in the distribution of wealth

Although the distribution of wealth is unequal, it is not as unequal as it has been in the past. There are two main reasons for this:

1 Women in the past owned very little wealth. Today more and more women own property and have high-paying jobs allowing them to increase their holdings of wealth.

2 Home ownership has grown rapidly in recent years so that by 2000 67% of homes were occupied by their owners. As home ownership and the price of housing rise, so does the wealth of the average home owner.

Exercise 2   A wealth of information

Look at the two tables below.

1 Describe what has happened to (a) the distribution of wealth, and (b) the composition of wealth in the UK over time.

2 What factors may explain the changes you have identified in question 1?

3 What measures could a government take to reduce inequalities in wealth?

Distribution of wealth

UK	1986	1991	1994	1996
Percentage of wealth owned by:				
Most wealthy 1%	18	17	19	19
Most wealthy 5%	36	35	38	38
Most wealthy 10%	50	47	51	50
Most wealthy 25%	73	71	73	73
Most wealthy 50%	90	92	93	92
Least wealthy 50%	10	8	7	8

Composition of net wealth in the personal sector

UK	1987	1991	1995	1996	1997
Net wealth (*percentages*)					
Life insurance and pension funds	24	26	35	35	36
Residential buildings net of loans	35	32	23	24	23
Securities and shares	10	11	15	15	17
Notes, coins and deposits	16	17	17	16	15
Non-marketable tenancy rights	9	8	5	5	5
Other fixed assets	6	5	4	4	4
Other financial assets net of liabilities	1	1	1	1	1
Total net wealth, £ billion (100%) in 1997 prices	2 515	2 800	2 979	3 159	3 582

Social Trends 1999

Reducing wealth inequalities The ownership of wealth in the UK, and indeed around the world, is very unequal. This has caused concern and there are a number of methods that are, or could be, used to try and make wealth ownership more equal.

1 Inheritance tax
This is a tax on wealth imposed at death (see Chapter 16). At the time of death a wealthy person's wealth is valued and a percentage taken in tax. However, this allows people to give away their wealth to their family or even friends during their lifetime, so as to reduce wealth ownership and taxes on death.

2 Wealth tax
Some people in the UK have proposed a tax on wealth based on valuing people's holdings of wealth each year, and making them pay a percentage of its value in tax. The problem is that this requires many more tax inspectors to value people's wealth and, of course, people may hide part of their wealth, or if they are rich enough, move it out of the country.

3 Others
Other methods may include:

    a   giving more people a better education so that they could earn more in work and build up more wealth.
    b   encouraging people to buy their own homes.
    c   encouraging more people to own and run their own businesses.

Section 4 | **The distribution of income in the UK**

Income distribution We discovered in section 2 that income is derived from the ownership of human and non-human wealth. We also discovered that wealth is very unequally shared out in the UK. This means that incomes must be unequally distributed in the UK.

Between 1987 and 1997 average household income in the UK rose by 64% from £256 to £420 per week. However, at the same time the gap between those with high incomes and those with low incomes grew. In 1997 fewer than 2.5% of households received a before tax income of more than £50 000, this compared to over 47% with incomes of less than £12 000.

Reasons for the unequal distribution of incomes

1 Differences in salaries
Some workers, such as company directors, have very high incomes. High earnings are a return on human wealth, such as business experience and abilities possessed by workers. For a full discussion of how wages are determined see Chapter 11.

2 Self-employment
Some people have very high incomes because they are self-employed. Self-employment has been growing in the UK. 3.3 million people or 12% of the labour force were self-employed in 1999.

Distribution of incomes in the UK, 1997

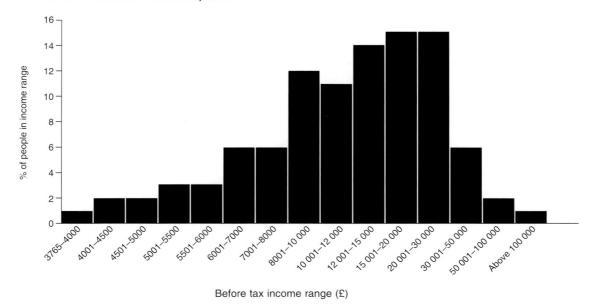

This chart relates only to those individuals who have some tax liability on their incomes
Source: Board of Inland Revenue

3   Family status
Single parents with children are more likely to appear in the lowest income group in the UK than people living alone or couples with children. In 1997 42% of single parent families in the UK were in the bottom fifth of income earners.

4   Old age, unemployment and full-time study
Many pensioners, students and unemployed people in the UK rely on fixed payments given to them by the government. The real value of their incomes has fallen over time as increases in pensions, unemployment benefits, and student grants and loans have not matched price inflation.

The redistribution of income

In Britain, people earning low incomes receive benefits, such as sickness and housing benefits, from the government. The purpose of these benefits is to raise the incomes of the poor so that they can enjoy a reasonable standard of living.

State benefits are paid for by taxing people. The more income people earn, the more income tax they pay.

375

Exercise 3 Redistributing income

Income group 1997	£ Average income before tax and benefits	£ Average income after tax and benefits
Bottom 20% of earners	7 060	8 310
Next 20% of earners	11 250	10 600
Middle 20% of earners	18 070	14 490
Next 20% of earners	26 180	19 040
Top 20% of earners	45 870	31 790

Social Trends, 1999

1 Why are there differences in the average income of earners between the two columns?

2 a Which group of earners benefits the most from taxes and benefits?
   b By what percentage has their average income increased?

3 a Which group of people is least affected by taxes and benefits?
   b Why do you think this is so?

4 a Which group of people loses the most because of taxes and benefits?
   b Why is this?

5 Do you think the present system of taxes and benefits in the UK has a significant effect on the distribution of income? Explain your answer.

The exercise above illustrates how the distribution of income is made more equal by taxes and benefits. The poorest 20% of income earners pay little tax but receive more in state benefits, such as the working families tax credit, jobseekers allowance, old age and disability pensions. In contrast, high income earners pay far more in tax and receive few, if any, state benefits. However, even after tax and benefits are taken into account the average income of the top 20% of earners was still nearly four times as much as the average income of the lowest 20% in 1997.

Exercise 4 Moving income groups

The table opposite splits up the adult population in the UK into groups according to their incomes, from the bottom fifth of adults on the lowest incomes to the top fifth of the highest earners. It does this for 1991 and 1996 and shows how much movement there was between these income groups over this period. For example, 52% of those people in the lowest income group in 1991 were still in that group in 1996. However, 4% of them had made it into the highest income group by then. In contrast, 59% of those in the highest income group in 1991 were among the highest income earners in the UK in 1996, but 41% of them had fallen down the income scale.

1 Describe what is happening in the table opposite. Do you think it shows the distribution of income has become more or less equal, stayed the same or remained about the same over time?

Adults moving within the income distribution between 1991 and 1996

UK						Percentages
	1996 income grouping					
	Bottom fifth	Next fifth	Middle fifth	Next fifth	Top fifth	All adults
1991 income grouping						
Bottom fifth	52	26	12	7	4	100
Next fifth	25	35	22	12	6	100
Middle fifth	11	21	33	23	12	100
Next fifth	7	12	20	37	23	100
Top fifth	4	6	11	21	59	100

2 From the article below, suggest why households with children might on average be poorer than households without children.

3 Why might single parent households be worse off, on average, compared to couples with children.

4 Suggest ways a government could try to reduce inequalities in incomes.

Family finances fail to keep pace

A report by the Institute of Fiscal Studies shows that households with children have become increasingly poor relative to those without children over the past 30 years. The average weekly income, after housing costs, of households with children rose from £152.20 to £235.2 between 1968 and 1996. But that compares with a rise from £200.70 to £338.50 among households without children over the same period.

The study also shows that single parents have lost ground even more dramatically relative to other single adults. Between 1968 and 1996 the average weekly income, after housing costs, of single people with children only rose from £145.70 to £151.80. The average weekly income for single adults with no children rose over the same period from £197.20 to £304.60.

The study also illustrates that poor families with children consistently spend higher than their income. This is not the case for families living above the poverty line. The average income in households with children that were living below the poverty line rose from £65.40 to £91.20 between 1968 and 1996. Expenditure in these households rose from £91.70 to £122.37 over the same period. Among families living above the poverty line the income rose from £151.37 to £283.90 between 1968 and 1996 while expenditure rose from £145.70 to £231.20.

The findings suggest that many poor families see their low income position as temporary and envisage they will at some stage be in a position to meet the shortfall between their income and expenditure.

The Times, 20.7.99

Section 5 The world distribution of income

Just as there are wealthy people and poor people in the world, there are wealthy nations and poor nations. Wealthy nations are known as developed countries, whilst poor nations are called less developed or under-developed countries. (See also Chapter 3 for the characteristics of LDCs.)

In this section, we investigate how to compare living standards between different countries and discover some of the reasons for the vast differences.

How to measure the
standard of living
in a country

Gross Domestic Product (GDP) is a very important measure of how much a country earns. GDP is the total money value of all of the goods and services produced in a country in one year, and is therefore equal to the total national income of the country because someone must be paid for producing these products.

Exercise 5   GDP around the world

Table 1

Annual GDP (billion US $) 1997	
Kuwait	26.65
India	338.79
Nigeria	65.62

1   Using the GDP figures in Table 1 above, state which country has the highest standard of living, and which has the lowest.

Table 2

Population (millions) 1997	
India	960
Nigeria	118
Kuwait	1.8

2   Using the population figures in Table 2 above, can you give different answers to question 1? Explain. (**Hint** How much on average does each person earn in these countries?

Exercise 5 illustrates that it is impossible to judge how well off people are in a country from the size of its GDP alone. For example, India has a very high GDP of $338.8 billion and yet it is a poor country. This is because India has a large population of 960 million people. If India's GDP was shared out amongst its population each person would have only $352 to spend on goods and services. That is, India has a low standard of living because the amount of **GDP per capita** (or average income per head) is low.

If the $65.6 billion of GDP of Nigeria was shared out amongst its population of 118 million people each person would have on average $555 to spend on goods and services each year.

Similarly, in Kuwait, a GDP of $26.7 billion and a population of under 2 million people means that GDP per person is $14 830 per year. Of the three countries discussed, Kuwait has a higher standard of living because the amount of GDP available per person is $14 830. However, even this is misleading because many people remain poor in Kuwait because there are some people who earn very high incomes far in excess of $14 830 per year. That is, the total GDP of Kuwait is concentrated in a few people's hands and not shared evenly amongst the population.

Therefore, it is the amount of income per head, or GDP per capita, which is important, rather than the total size of GDP, when measuring the standard of living in a country. However, as the example of Kuwait illustrates, it is not always an accurate measure.

Other factors are often considered by economists attempting to reach a conclusion about the standard of living in a country. The ownership of many consumer durables, like cars and televisions, by households in developed countries contrasts with the lack of such possessions in less developed nations. Social indicators, like the birth rate, the percentage of the population who can read and write, are also considered while crime rates and suicide rates are often high in developed countries as a result of the pressures of modern-day living.

Availability of households with certain consumer durables, United Kingdom 1998

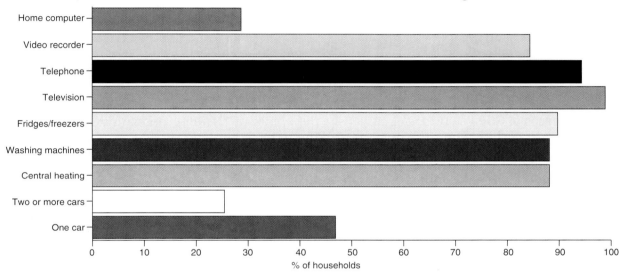

How many homes in less developed countries are likely to own these goods?

How countries compare on GDP per capita

By splitting the world into a Northern half and Southern half it is possible to divide the world up roughly into rich and poor countries.

The rich North includes North America, Europe, Japan, Australia and New Zealand. Countries in the poor South include large parts of Africa, Asia and South America. The figures below illustrate these differences in standards of living between countries.

In the developed countries GDP per capita is high enough for most people to enjoy good health care and education, enough food, clothing and housing and a long life expectancy. Yet in less developed countries, GDP per capita is so low that most people have little or no health care or education, scarcely enough food to survive and a very low life expectancy. For example, in China in 1996 around 270 million people lived on less than one US dollar per day. China accounts for over 70% of East Asia's poor. GDP per capita averaged just $582 in China in 1997.

GDP per capita ($) 1997	
Switzerland	42 416
Denmark	33 191
USA	26 037
Luxembourg	35 109
France	26 444
UK	18 913
Congo	1 008
Bolivia	909
Morocco	1 265
Egypt	973
Pakistan	504
Ethiopia	96
Mozambique	77
China	582

Why are there large differences in GDP per capita?

Developing countries have five times the population of the developed world. Yet to satisfy the wants of all these people developing countries produce only one-quarter of the goods and services produced by the richer developed countries.

High population growth means that as soon as GDP increases there are more mouths to feed. High population growth means people in developed countries very rarely get better off and, in fact, often get worse off. (See Chapter 20 for an in-depth discussion of population changes.)

Exercise 6 Cutting the cake

In the exercise below imagine the GDP of a country to be like a cake waiting to be shared out amongst its population.

1   In the year 1985 the imaginary country of Dimis had a GDP of £100 000. Dimis had a population of 1 000 people. What is the GDP per capita in Dimis in 1985?

2   In 2000 the GDP of Dimis had risen to £150 000, yet the population of Dimis had risen to 2 000 people. What is the GDP per capita in Dimis in 2000?

3   **a**   What has happened to GDP per capita in Dimis between 1985 and 2000 and why?
   b   Are people in Dimis better off? Explain your answer.

4   From the table opposite, calculate for each country the annual average percentage rate of negative growth in GDP per head.

5   Suggest reasons why these countries have experienced negative economic growth, and possible ways their governments could attempt to reverse the decline.

In some countries rapid population growth has outstripped growth in GDP. As a result GDP per person has fallen. In other words, the size of the cake has grown more slowly than the number of people who want a slice. This is true of many African and South American countries. War has also blighted some of these countries and in some cases GDP has been shrinking anyway.

380

Some countries experiencing negative growth in per capita income

Country	GDP per person per year (US $)	
	1990	1996
North Korea	943	271
Kazakhstan	4 122	995
Mexico	2 932	2 700
Ghana	415	397
Senegal	793	572
Angola	1 113	355
Russian Federation	4 308	4 014
Croatia	6 523	2 451

Economic crises and wars have also plagued some Eastern European countries like Croatia, causing GDP to fall despite only modest, or even negative growth in their populations.

GDP per capita can only fall so far before people begin to starve or suffer disease due to poor living conditions. For example, average life expectancy has already fallen by up to 10 years in some African countries due to war, famine and disease.

Key words

Write definitions for the following terms:

Human wealth	**Income and wealth distribution**
Non-human wealth	**GDP**
Inheritance	**GDP per capita**

Now go back through the chapter and check your understanding of these terms.

| Chapter 18 | The European Economy |

Aims

At the end of this chapter you should be able to:

1 Describe the **European Union (EU)** and its objectives

2 Explain **European and Monetary Union (EMU)** and what member countries must do to achieve it

3 Describe the **European Exchange Rate Mechanism (ERM)**

4 Understand the role of the **European Central Bank (ECB)**

5 Assess the arguments for and against a **single European currency**

The UK has been a member of the **European Union (EU)** since 1972. Many of the policies agreed by the member countries of the EU are adopted by the UK Government. The UK economy is, therefore, closely linked to the European economy. In years to come the UK may even share a common currency with the rest of EU members and have interest rates and economic policies set by a European Central Bank.

| Section 1 | The European Union |

What is the European Union?

The European Community (EC) began in 1958 when six countries – West Germany, Italy, France, Belgium, the Netherlands and Luxembourg – committed themselves, in the Treaty of Rome, to the formation of a *common market* in which to trade in goods and services.

By 1993 the UK, Spain, Portugal, Greece, Eire and Denmark had also joined making a total of 12 member states (the 'EU12') and forming a market of over 350 million people. The European Union was formally created on 1 November 1993 by all the member countries. In the EU members agree to work together on legal, political and economic matters.

The number of EU countries increased to 15 on 1 January 1995 as Austria, Finland and Sweden became full members (the 'EU15'). Turkey, Cyprus, Malta, Hungary and Poland have also applied for membership, with many more countries considering joining.

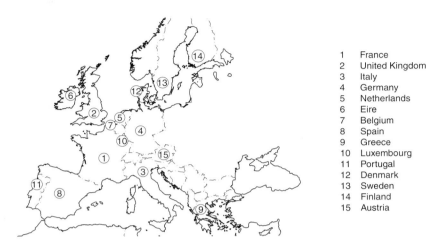

1	France
2	United Kingdom
3	Italy
4	Germany
5	Netherlands
6	Eire
7	Belgium
8	Spain
9	Greece
10	Luxembourg
11	Portugal
12	Denmark
13	Sweden
14	Finland
15	Austria

The European Union 2000

European Union objectives

The EU has a number of broad objectives which will dramatically alter the way in which people live and conduct business in member countries:

1   To form a customs union

Before the EU was set up European countries used to impose tariffs on imports from each other. This meant, for example, that people in France would have to pay much more for goods imported from, say, Germany and the UK. In this way the French Government hoped it would encourage French people to buy goods and services from producers in France even if they could be imported at lower prices from overseas. Because of this protectionism, many firms were unable to sell their goods and services abroad and this raised unemployment among European workers.

The EU has formed a **customs union** and has removed all taxes on trade between EU members. So now, for example, the UK can export freely to all other EU members. However, any imports coming into the EU from non-EU countries are taxed in order to make them more expensive and so discourage EU consumers from buying them. This tax is called the **common external tariff**.

The common external tariff is designed to protect business and jobs in the EU from cheap imports from outside the EU. Tariff rates applied to the price of imported goods and services have to be the same in each EU country otherwise there would be problems. For example, suppose the UK applied a 20% tariff to the price of imports from non-EU countries while France only applied a 10% tariff. A Japanese firm exporting to the UK could first export their products to France and then ship them to the UK without incurring extra tax.

2 To encourage freedom of movement

The EU wants to remove all barriers to the free movement of goods and services, capital and people across EU borders. People in the EU are free to live and work in any member state and be entitled to the same conditions of employment, health care and social security benefits as anyone else in their chosen member country.

3 To operate a Common Agricultural Policy

The European Community felt that it was vital for Europe to produce its own food and not rely on foreign supplies. In order to achieve this aim the EC introduced the **Common Agricultural Policy (CAP)**.

Under the CAP farmers are guaranteed a high price for their produce by the EU Government. However, this has often caused farmers to overproduce every year. Excess supplies are bought up by the EU Government.

The CAP has been criticized because it has often resulted in huge stockpiles of surplus produce and high food prices for EU consumers. The excess output cannot be sold in the EU because it would cause food prices to fall and reduce farmers incomes. The food stockpiles are also very expensive to store and so are sold off cheaply to non-EU countries. Sometimes the surplus food is fed to animals or even destroyed.

4 To provide help to less prosperous regions in the European Union

The EU regional policy provides money to less developed areas in the EU by providing jobs and improving schools, housing, roads, etc.

5 To establish a single European market

The **Single European Market** (or **internal market**) was created on 1 January 1993. EU members have agreed to remove all remaining barriers to movement and free trade such as frontier checks at custom posts, cumbersome importing documents designed to raise importing costs, different national product and safety standards, the application of separate – and sometimes unnecessary – health checks, and major differences in indirect taxation such as rates of value added tax, excise duties and duty free allowances.

6 To create economic and monetary union

On 7 February 1992 the Heads of State or of Governments of the European Community signed the Maastricht Treaty agreement on European Union. The main focus of that agreement is the creation of a framework for European **economic and monetary union (EMU)**, involving the creation of a single currency and common economic policy by 1 January 1999.

For the agreement to come into effect in full, each member state has to approve it. Not all have done so. Denmark voted against the Treaty and the UK opted out of adopting a single European currency. This means the UK Government will have to have a Parliamentary vote before it can join.

Section 2 | Towards Economic and Monetary Union (EMU) in Europe

What is EMU?

Member countries in the European Union have agreed to closer economic and monetary co-operation between their economies and governments. In 1992 the Maastricht Treaty was agreed by EU members to set a timetable for **economic and monetary union (EMU)** between them. EMU involves the creation of single European currency and common economic policies. The single European currency was given the name the 'euro' at a meeting in Madrid in 1995.

A three stage plan for EMU

The Maastricht Treaty set out a three-stage plan for the introduction of economic and monetary union across the European Union.

Stages 2 and 3 have proved controversial. The UK and Denmark have opted out of them for the time being.

---

1 Increased co-ordination of macroeconomic policies between EU members and completion of the internal market

2 A gradual transfer of economic decision making power from national central banks, such as the UK Bank of England and German Bundesbank, to a new single European Central Bank

3 Fixing the value of exchange rates between EU member currencies, a single European monetary policy and the eventual replacement of national currencies by the euro

---

The Maastricht Treaty states that no EU member can join EMU stage 3 unless it 'fulfils the necessary conditions' on:

- **Inflation**: annual average price inflation to be within 1.5% of the rate of price inflation of the three EU members where it is lowest

- **Interest rates**: the average long term interest rate over 1 year to be within 2% of rates in the same 3 members

- **Budget deficit**: a member must not have a deficit between public expenditure and tax revenues that is considered 'excessive' (over 3% of GDP)

- **Exchange rates**: the national currency of the member country must have been within the narrow band of the **European Exchange Rate Mechanism (ERM)** for at least 2 years

Member countries that met with these criteria in 1998 were able to qualify for the third stage of the EMU which began on 1 January 1999. At this time eleven member countries introduced the euro and transferred control over interest rates to the European Central Bank. Between January and June 2002 their national currencies will be withdrawn. Remaining EU members who meet the Maastricht criteria will be allowed to join stages 2 and 3 of EMU at a later date if they wish to do so.

The stability and growth pact	To make sure EU members keep to the Maastricht condition on Budget deficits they all agreed a **stability and growth pact** at a meeting in Dublin in 1996. This agreement is designed to prevent national EU governments spending more than they raise in tax revenue and running up deficits in excess of 3% of their GDP. A country will be penalized if the government budgets for a deficit of more than 3% unless the country is in a deep recession and increased government spending is needed to boost aggregate demand.

Section 3 — The European Exchange Rate Mechanism (ERM)

What is the ERM?	The ERM is thought of as the first step towards economic and monetary union in the EU and the introduction of a single European currency. The ERM requires member states to agree exchange rates between their currencies and then 'fix' them. Interest rates could be used to stabilize currency rates. National central banks in EU member countries would also buy up or sell a particular EU member currency in order to raise or lower its value, if necessary, to keep it at the agreed exchange rate (see Chapter 14).

Exchange rates in the ERM are pegged to the value of the strongest currency in terms of its value against the currencies of non-EU member countries. For many years, the strongest currency in the system was the German mark, being an indication of the strength of the German economy. When the UK joined the ERM in October 1990 the value of sterling was fixed at £1 = 2.95 DM. As the value of DM appreciates or depreciates against non-EU currencies so too will all the other currencies tied to it in the ERM. Thus, if £1 = 2.95 DM = US$1.5, then an appreciation of the DM would take their values to say 2.95 DM = US$1.7 = £1.

Currencies in the ERM are allowed to fluctuate within a narrow band around the strongest currency. When the UK joined the ERM in October 1990 there were two bands set at 2.25% and 6%. The first band allowed currency values to rise above or fall below its fixed rate by up to 2.25%. The wider band allowed the values of weaker currencies to vary by up to plus or minus 6%. Sterling initially joined the wider band which included the currencies of Spain and Italy.

Why did the UK leave the ERM?	During September 1992 increasing pressure on the pound due to a large balance of payments deficit and uncertainty about the UK economy, caused the value of the pound to fall to its lower limit of 2.78 DM, being 6% below its value on entry to the ERM. Speculation that the pound would be devalued caused many financial institutions around the world to sell their holdings of sterling causing the value of the pound to fall further.

Intervention by the Bank of England and other Central Banks in Europe failed to support the pound. Billions of UK pounds worth of foreign currency reserves were used to buy up pounds in an effort to raise the value of the pound. Interest rates were also raised from 10% to 15% briefly in an attempt to attract flows of hot money into the UK (see Chapter 14). However, the value of the pound continued to fall below its ERM floor and so the UK withdrew from the ERM on 16 September 1992.

Because of this experience, many think the ERM is unstable and the UK has not yet rejoined. In 1999 confidence in the good health of the UK economy meant that the pound was strong and its value was high against other currencies. Some economists have argued the pound would need to fall in value before it could rejoin the ERM. However, a fall in the value of the pound would increase the price of imports and boost imported inflation (see Chapter 13).

Exercise 1   Falling through the floor

The articles below describe the events that lead to the withdrawal of sterling from the ERM in September 1992.

Countdown to crisis

■ **AUGUST 20:** Pound hits new low in ERM of DM2.8070 after being dragged down by sharp fall in dollar.

■ **AUGUST 24:** Central bank intervention around world fails to support dollar: investors pile into D-Mark. Pound closes at new low of DM2.7975. Lira slumps.

■ **AUGUST 25:** Pound tumbles as poll shows French could reject Maastricht. Devaluation fears send pound to half pfennig above absolute floor. Major and Lamont meet on growing crisis, pound closes at DM2.7875.

■ **AUGUST 26:** Lamont insists government will not devalue. Markets unimpressed. Massive intervention by Bank of England leaves currency wobbling at DM2.7950.

■ **AUGUST 27:** French rule out realignment of ERM. Pound unmoved at DM2.7950.

■ **AUGUST 28:** EC finance ministers add to no-realignment chorus but D-Mark continues to soar and sterling slumps to DM2.7875.

■ **SEPTEMBER 3:** Lamont unveils plan to borrow £7.25bn of D-Marks to prop up sterling. Pound up to DM2.80, highest for two weeks.

■ **SEPTEMBER 4:** Italy raises rates. Pound holds at around DM2.80.

■ **SEPTEMBER 5:** EC finance ministers reaffirm no plan for realignment or devaluation-strongest statement from EC on crisis.

■ **SEPTEMBER 9:** Pound drops to DM2.7875. Investors continue to buy D-Marks. Sweden hikes rates to 75 per cent Italian government seeks powers for rescue of lira.

■ **SEPTEMBER 10:** Major says realignment will be 'betrayal' for ERM. Pound closes still in critical zone.

■ **SEPTEMBER 13:** Lira devaluation and German interest rate cut. Pound surges to DM2.82 in anticipation of German cut.

■ **SEPTEMBER 14:** German cut of 0.25 per cent smaller than hoped but sterling holds up. Pound closes at DM2.8144.

■ **SEPTEMBER 15:** Pound plunges. Crisis as markets sell sterling. Rumours of 2 per cent interest rise or and devaluation. Pound down to DM2.7780 lowest possible.

■ **SEPTEMBER 16:** Intervention, interest rate rises from 10% to 15%, and then suspension from ERM.

■ **SEPTEMBER 17:** 16% depreciation in value of sterling interest rates lowered back to 10%.

THE GOVERNMENT last night suspended Britain's membership of the Exchange Rate Mechanism after a tidal wave of selling the pound on the foreign exchanges left it defenceless against international currency speculators.

Britain's decision pushed the ERM to the brink of collapse early today, with the EC monetary committee locked in crisis talks aimed at holdings the system together.

The Chancellor, Norman Lamont, announced that the Government could no longer hold the line at the end of a day of desperate and futile attempts at propping up sterling, which included spending what the City estimated as £10 billion from Britain's reserves and a two-stage rise in interest rates to 15 per cent.

Mr Lamont later rescinded the second rise and said interest rates would be pegged at 12 per cent today, two points above the rate on Monday night.

The decision to suspend membership of the ERM represents a humiliating reversal for the chancellor and the Prime Minister, who have staked enormous credibility on being able to resist devaluation. Britain joined the ERM less than two years ago, and until last night's decision membership has been the centrepiece of the government's anti-inflation strategy.

Guardian, 17.9.1992

Gamblers poised to make huge profits

by Tony Maguire

WHILE the pound crumbled, the Government tottered and homeowners tightened their belts another notch, banks were preparing to reap enormous profits on the currency's fall.

Like sugar, gold, rubber and coffee, the pound is just another commodity to be traded by the men and women who run the money markets and ultimately run our lives.

Only a tiny percentage of the estimated $1,000 billion in currency traded every day is "legitimate" — used to pay for imports and exports or to redress the balance when travellers take money across borders. The rest, possibly 95 per cent of the total, is pure speculation, with the big securities houses and banks electronically moving huge amounts of currency around the world, gambling that it will rise or fall.

When interest rates were forced to rise, the banks stood to make enormous short-term gains on their entire operations. If the pound is forced to devalue, the banks will be able to buy back the sterling they are now selling for much less.

Sterling's slide downhill has gathered pace as the banks and speculators gambled on John Major's inability to prevent devaluation. The 0.25 per cent cut in German interest rates temporarily helped the pound on Monday, but by yesterday morning punters were back in betting against sterling's ability to survive.

While the pound sits at the bottom of the European Exchange Rate Mechanism, the prospects of either devaluation or another rise in interest rates remain the most likely options for Mr Major, despite the political ramifications.

Evening Standard, 16.9.1992

1   How does the ERM differ from a floating exchange rate system?

2   Explain how UK interest rates may be used to alter the value of sterling.

3   Explain the term 'devaluation'.

4   Describe the events that eventually caused the UK to withdraw sterling from the ERM.

5   Why did intervention by European central Banks fail to stop the pound from falling in value?

6   What is meant by a '16% depreciation in the value of sterling'?

7   What would be the implications of a depreciation in sterling on
    i.   UK inflation,
    ii. The UK balance of payments?

Section 4 | The euro

What is the euro? The final step towards economic and monetary union in Europe is the introduction of a single currency and transfer of decision making on European interest rates and monetary policy to a **European Central Bank (ECB)**.

The **euro** is the name given to the money, or currency, that will replace the national currencies of the EU member countries. So, for example, by mid-2002 the French Franc, German Deutschmark, Spanish Peseta and other EU currencies will not exist. Instead people in these countries, or travelling to them, will use euros to buy and sell goods and services. Even UK pounds and pence may be replaced with the euro one day.

Eleven EU countries started using the euro on 1 January 1999. Countries using the euro form the **euro area**. Only the UK, Sweden, Denmark and Greece have not joined the euro area, although Greece hopes to meet the Maastricht criteria soon to be able to join.

The euro will be used alongside existing currencies until they are withdrawn from use in 2002. This is so people have time to get used to paying for goods and services in euros. One euro is worth about 6.5 francs in France, 1.95 marks in Germany, and 1936 lire in Italy. These rates are fixed until national currencies are eventually phased out in July 2002.

⊜ The Euro rates

GERMANY	1.95583	marks
FRANCE	6.55957	francs
ITALY	1936.21	lire
HOLLAND	2.20371	guilders
SPAIN	166.386	pesetas
PORTUGAL	200.482	escudos
FINLAND	5.94573	markka
IRELAND	0.787564	punts
AUSTRIA	13.7603	schillings
BELGIUM	40.3399	francs
LUX'BOURG	40.3399	francs

The European Central Bank The creation of a European Central Bank (ECB) accompanied the introduction of the euro. Its main objective is to keep price inflation low and stable across the euro area. To do this it takes decisions on the single monetary policy and interest rate for the euro area. If it thinks price inflation will rise it is likely to raise interest rates, and will cut them if it believes price inflation will fall (see Chapter 15). The ECB also holds and manages the foreign exchange reserves of all the member EU states.

The ECB heads the **European System of Central Banks (ESCB)**, which is made up of the national central banks of all the EU countries, including the Bank of England in the UK (see Chapter 19). The Bank of England is a member of the ESCB with special status because the UK is not in the ERM and has not introduced the euro. This means it is allowed to take decisions on monetary policy and interest rates in the UK but does not take part in decision making concerning the single monetary policy for euro countries.

It is the job of the ESCB central banks in the euro area to apply the interest rate and meet the inflation targets agreed with the ECB in their own countries.

Exercise 2   Why go euro?

Imagine the UK has joined in the single European currency and has replaced pounds and pence with euros. This may actually happen in the future. Read the quotes below and use them to make a list of the advantages and disadvantages of joining the euro. Do you think it is a good or bad idea for the UK to scrap its national currency in favour of the euro? Discuss this in your class group.

1   2   3   4   5   6   7

1 *Female holidaymaker* 'Everytime I went on holiday to say Spain or Portugal I would have to change my pounds into pesetas or escudos. Foreign currency exchanges usually charged a commission to do this of around two or three percent. Then if I had any foreign notes left over after my holiday I would have to change them back into pounds and pay commission again. Now I don't have to do this. Using Euros makes it so much easier and cheaper.'

2 *Businessman*: 'We might have to close down next year if demand for goods overseas doesn't pick up. Exports are way down and I have already laid off 30% of my workforce. I blame the high fixed value of the euro. If we had kept the pound it's value could have fallen against other currencies like the US dollar. This would reduce the price of our exports overseas and help boost demand for them.'

3 *Shopkeeper*: 'Don't talk to me about the bloomin' euro. When we first joined I had to price everything in pounds and euros. All my price lists and catalogues had to be reprinted. Then when the pound was finally replaced I had to reprint them all again!'

4 *Male holidaymaker*: 'Shopping overseas was never easy for me when there were lots of different national currencies. For example, I was in Italy a few years ago. A bottle of wine in a restaurant cost me 8 000 Lire. That's expensive I thought. Then I realized it was only around £3 because there were over 2 600 Lire to every pound. Now everything is in Euros I can easily compare prices in different countries.'

5 *Female Politician with rosette saying 'Anti Euro Party'*: 'The European Central Bank has set interest rates too high for the UK. The UK is in recession and needs to have lower interest rates to stimulate demand for goods and services. However, because inflation is high in the rest of Europe the ECB has raised interest rates. This will just create unemployment in the UK.'

6 *Business man*: 'We import many component parts from suppliers in mainland Europe. Paying for them in Euros has reduced our costs. Trade has increased because we have been able to cut our prices. And as we sell more we need to import even more form Europe. When we had the pound import prices would fluctuate because of changes in exchange rates. For example, we could order £100 000 of components from Germany one morning when the pound was worth 2 Marks, and by the afternoon the cost could have gone up to say £105 000 because the pound had fallen to 1.9 Marks.'

7 *ECB spokesperson*: 'The ECB is committed to bringing down inflation across the European union. Because of this commitment interest rates can be lower than they would have been in some individual countries. This is because some countries have a poor inflation record. If people think there is a risk of higher inflation they will press for higher wages. As a result a country will have to raise interest rates. People will believe the risk of inflation is lower if there is a strong ECB controlling inflation in their countries.'

Arguments for and against the euro

The UK has yet to adopt the euro and commit itself to replacing the pound with the single European currency. The issue is very controversial. There are a number of economic arguments for and against joining the euro.

Potential benefits

1 Reduced transaction costs
If there is just one European currency there will no longer be a need for Britons to exchange pounds for Spanish pesetas, or French francs for Irish punts when travelling to different EU countries or paying for their imports. Changing money into foreign currencies costs money because many banks and foreign exchange agencies charge commission to do so.

2 Increased European competition
Because all prices will be quoted in euros, comparing prices in the different member countries will be easier. There will be no need to convert prices in one currency to another. Because of this people may be more tempted to shop around for the best deal, either during the course of travelling or via the internet. This will increase price competition between suppliers in the different EU countries.

3 Reduced exchange rate uncertainty
International trade between EU members may become less risky and cheaper. This may encourage more trade and help create jobs. This is because businesses will no longer have to pay for imported goods and services in foreign currencies which can rise or fall in value against their own currency. For example, when the French franc fell against the German mark, French businesses had to pay more for imports from Germany. Because they now use the euro this will no longer happen. However, the euro can still change in value against non-member currencies like the US dollar and Japanese yen.

4 Lower interest rates
If the European Central Bank can show it is firmly committed to keeping inflation at a low level across the euro area, it may be able to do so with lower average interest rates. Low interest rates may encourage firms to borrow money to invest, which can raise economic growth in the EU (see Chapter 13). In contrast, individual countries with a poor inflation record may have to keep interest rates higher and for longer to control inflationary surges in aggregate demand (see Chapter 15).

5 Increased inward direct investment
A European Union with a single currency forms a very large market for goods and services. Firms from Japan and other non-EU countries may be tempted to set up factories, shops and offices in the EU in order to sell their goods and services into this large market. This is called **direct inward investment** from overseas. In this way firms from non-EU countries are able to avoid the common external tariff on their goods.

Potential costs

1 There may be economic misalignment resulting in higher unemployment and/or lower real income growth in some countries.
It is possible that European countries' industrial and economic structures, or degree of development, differ to such an extent that over time it will be

391

necessary for their exchange rates to adjust. For example, Greece still relies heavily on agriculture for jobs and incomes compared to many other EU members who have highly developed service sectors.

If one EU country has a high level of unemployment and has a large trade deficit, it might like its exchange rate to fall to boost demand for its exports. A falling exchange rate makes exports cheaper in foreign markets and imports dearer (see Chapter 14). However, a single currency rules this out. If the value of the euro is too high for that country, it will be unable to boost export revenues, and unemployment may remain high.

2   National Governments will no longer be able to use economic policy to control inflation and unemployment in their own countries.
This is because EU countries that have entered stages 2 and 3 of the EMU rely on the European Central Bank to set interest rates across them. They are also committed to a budget deficit of less than 3% of their GDPs. A member country with high inflation relative to the others is likely to want higher interest rates than the ECB would set. A country with relatively high unemployment may want much lower interest rates and to increase public spending. Joining in the euro prevents it from doing this.

3   Changeover costs
Introducing the euro will cost businesses money. These additional costs will be passed on to consumers as higher prices. The costs arise because firms will have to have to change all their price lists, menus, catalogues, wage payments and accounts into euros. The Government will also have to change its public accounting, taxation and social security systems.

Many countries have already committed themselves to stages 2 and 3 of EMU and have introduced the euro believing that the benefits of doing so will outweigh any costs. In 2000 the UK was still unsure and was prepared to wait and see how these other countries get on. What do you think the UK should do? Read newspapers and watch the TV news to keep up to date with the debate over whether the UK should join the euro area or stay out.

Key words

Use the chapter to help you write full explanations in your own words for the following terms:

European Union	Customs union
Common external tariff	CAP
Internal market	EMU
ERM	Euro
Stability and growth pact	Euro area
European Central Bank	ESCB

ILL NEVER GET THAT IN MY WALLET!...

Aims

At the end of this chapter you should be able to:

1   Give reasons for why there is a need for a commodity that everyone will accept in exchange for all other goods and services, that is, a **money**.

2   Support the view that **specialization** and the **division of labour** would be impossible without a money.

3   Critically assess the suitability of various objects being used as money.

4   Trace the historical development of our present form of money.

5   Understand the problems involved in defining what is money.

6   Describe the main forms of money in existence today.

7   Outline the organization of the banking system in the UK and understand the role played by **commercial banks, savings banks, merchant banks, financial houses, building societies, discount houses** and the **Bank of England**.

8   Understand likely future changes in the banking system and be aware of reasons for these developments.

| **Section 1** | Why do we need money? |

Money is something we use to buy that new record or pair of jeans we always wanted, or even just to pay the gas bill. Money is in constant use, but we often take it for granted. Without it, life would become very difficult. Yet in the past, man existed for many thousands of years without the help of money.

Our primitive ancestors relied on the direct swapping of goods and services. For example, if any early farmer had some spare corn and needed an axe he would travel to the local market with his corn. There he would try to find someone who would exchange an axe for the corn. This early form of trade is known as **barter**.

Exercise 1

ye olde swap shop

Imagine there is no money and we have to rely on swapping goods with each other. In groups of three, each member of the group acts out the role of either a ruler-maker, a pencil-maker or an eraser-maker.

1 Firstly, the pencil-maker wishes to exchange some pencils for some rulers. Try to arrange a swap on the best possible terms for yourself. What problems do you encounter?

2 Now the eraser-maker wants to exchange erasers for some pencils. But the pencil-maker is not interested in obtaining erasers. Your only hope is to involve the ruler-maker in the swap.

3 Imagine now that the goods being traded are eggs, milk and cheese. What problems would arise if you could not find any one to swap your goods with? (Remember fridges have not been invented yet!)

You may have discovered that **bartering** is a most inconvenient way to carry out business. In fact three main problems arise:

1 Fixing a rate of exchange
How many pencils are worth one ruler? How many pencils are worth one apple? How many oranges are equivalent in value to one ruler? Indeed, how many rulers could Farmer Giles get for a cow? And so it goes on.

In a barter system the value of each and every good must be expressed in terms of every other good.

This 1lb of
Apples
ONLY ↵
7 pencils
or
2 rulers
or
1 leg of cow
or
½ lb of cheese
or

Special Offer

BUT I'VE ALREADY GOT FOURTEEN.

2 Finding someone to swap with

Miss Swap may want some apples from Mr Trade and in return may be prepared to offer him some cheese. If by chance Mr Trade would like some cheese they can barter. But, if Mr Trade does not like cheese no deal can take place. In this case an economist would say no **double coincidence of wants** exists. In other words, before two people can barter they must both want the goods that the other person has.

3 Trying to save

A final problem is how to save under a barter system. A carpenter could store tables and chairs but would need a large room, but imagine trying to save some meat or cheese for a long period of time.

| Section 2 | The functions of money |

By now you will be familiar with the problems involved in swapping goods and services in a barter system. It would be much easier if there was one commodity that everyone would be willing to accept in exchange for all other goods and services. This commodity would be called **money** and overcomes the problems with barter by performing the following functions.

Money is a medium of exchange

Because money is a commodity that is generally acceptable in exchange for all other goods we do not have to search for a person who is willing to barter. That is, money overcomes the problem of needing a double coincidence of wants. Now, Miss Swap can sell her cheese to anyone who is prepared to buy it with money. In turn Miss Swap can use this money to buy the apples she wants from Mr Trade, or anyone who is willing to sell her some apples. Therefore, trade is brought about by two transactions with money being used in each.

Money is a measure of value

Just as a thermometer measures temperature and a ruler measures length, so money measures value. Using money helps traders to avoid the problems of fixing prices of goods and services in terms of all other goods and services.

Instead of arguing and attempting to remember how many pencils to one ruler, all goods have a price expressed in terms of one single commodity called money.

Money is a store of value

One of the problems with barter is that many commodities are difficult to save either because they use up too much space or they lose their value.

Money generally does not lose its value over time and so acts as a store of value. In other words, it allows people to save in order to make purchases at a later date.

However, today some people save by storing valuable antiques and works of art, things that we do not regard as money but which can be exchanged for money in the future. People often save in this way because as prices of goods rise over time, each £1 will buy less and less. Therefore, the purchasing power of money, or what it will buy, is reduced.

With a continued rise in prices, or **inflation**, money is unable to be such a good store of value (see Chapter 13).

Money is a means of deferred payment

When a person buys goods on credit the consumer has the use of the goods but does not have to pay for them immediately. The consumer can pay some time after he or she receives the goods. In the case of hire purchase, payment is made by instalments spread over a number of months or years.

Credit in a barter system would be very confusing and open to cheating. For example, imagine a person who trades a box of nails for a dozen apples to be paid one month later. Would the apples be fresh? Would they be large or small apples? Using money to pay later overcomes these problems and therefore encourages people to trade, reducing the worry of giving credit.

Exercise 2

RAMPANT INFLATION HITS ISRAELI ECONOMY

One month ago this car cost . . .	One week ago it cost . . .	At 12.29 pm last Wednesday it cost . . .	At 12.31 pm last Wednesday it cost . . .	This week it will soar to over . . .
4,628,726 shekels	5,313,272 shekels	5,594,544 shekels	5,673,370 shekels	6,000,000 shekels

Israel is increasingly moving over to the US dollar as the only stable measure of value in an economy where rampant inflation slowly erodes the value of their currency (the Shekel). Most companies moved over to the dollar age a long time ago. The president of one company said a year ago that there was no point in asking him anything about the company's performance in Shekels.

'I simply can't understand anything in Shekels,' he said with a dismissive wave of his hand.

If you are paying for a babysitter or a cleaner on an hourly wage rate only dollars will do. Disbelievers need only look at any newspaper; the price of a new house or even a second-hand car are all listed in dollars. Many shop windows also only display dollar price tags.

Financial Times, 20.3.1984

1 For what reason did the Israeli economy move over to the US dollar as a measure of value in 1984?

2 Which of the following functions of money was the shekel failing to perform? **a** a medium of exchange, **b** a measure of value, **c** a store of value. Give reasons for your answers.

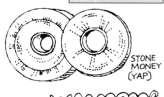

STONE MONEY (YAP)

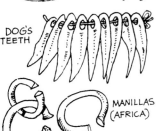

DOG'S TEETH

MANILLAS (AFRICA)

KNIFE MONEY (CHINA)

In different countries around the world, and at different times, a vast range of objects have been used as a medium of exchange. These have ranged from beads used by the American Indians to large stone discs used by the inhabitants of Yap, a small island in the Pacific Ocean.

Money, as we know it today, is the product of a long period of development. Man has slowly discovered, by a process of trial and error, that some objects fulfil the functions of money better than others.

Exercise 3   What is a 'good' money?

In groups discuss which of the following items would make a good money. Appoint a spokesperson for your group to record your views and to present your arguments to the class.

CIGARETTES

MOUNTAINS

CHEESE

GOLD

Your discussion may have led you to the conclusion that characteristics like the following are important for a good money to possess.

1   Acceptability
Anything can be used as money as long as it is generally acceptable. This is why a worthless piece of paper can be used as a £5 note. It is only worth £5 in spending power because everyone accepts it as such. Thus our present money is a **token money** – as a piece of paper it is worth much less than the face value printed upon it.

2   Durability
Any commodity used as money must be hard-wearing. Money would be useless if it just melted away in your pocket. Coins and notes must be strong and durable so that they may act as a store of value.

3 Portability

Money should be easy to carry. A house would clearly be far too heavy to move. A cow would be reluctant to go shopping with you, and even more reluctant if you tried to squeeze it into your wallet or purse. Metal coins and paper notes are lightweight and fit easily into your pocket.

4 Divisibility

If cars were used as money a problem would arise if you tried to buy something priced at half your car. Sawing the vehicle into half would reduce its value. One whole working car is worth much more than two halves. Therefore it must be possible to divide money of a large value into smaller values to make small purchases or to give change, without it losing value.

5 Scarcity

Pebbles on a beach could not be used as money simply because anyone can pick them up. A shopkeeper would not exchange her goods for freely-available pebbles that she could gather at any time, and in any quantity she wished. Only if money is scarce will people value it as a commodity that can be used in exchange.

Exercise 4 The £1 coin

The new £1 coin was issued on 21 April 1984. A coin of this denomination is, of course, nothing new. In 1489 Henry VII minted the first English gold coin with a value of 240d (old pence). It was called the 'pound sovereign' and has been around in many forms since that time.

The decision to introduce the £1 coin was made because the £1 note had become increasingly inconvenient to the public at large. In normal use, experience has shown that, as inflation erodes the value of currency, a point is reached at which the lowest denomination note is treated by many people as though it were a coin – we had that experience with the ten shilling note. People tend to keep the £1 note loose in pockets rather than in a wallet, and it circulates among the public without returning periodically to the banks as higher denomination notes do.

Clearly, when that point is reached, the note deteriorates very rapidly, as we have seen recently with the £1 note. Moreover, its purchasing power is now rather less than that of the ten shilling note. Note when that was replaced by the 50p piece in 1969. The only solution has been to offer a coin in substitution for the note.

The note lasts on average for only about nine months, while a coin has a life of about 40 years.

Economic Progress Report, April 1984

Using the article above try to provide answers for the following questions:

1   Why was the £1 note becoming 'increasingly inconvenient' to people?

2   Give reasons why there was a need to replace the £1 paper note with a £1 coin.

3   If prices continue to rise over the next twenty years what do you think may become of the £5 note, and even the £10 note?

So why is money important?

In Chapter 4 we learnt how people living in a self-sufficient society began to specialize in the jobs they were most able to do. Specialization was the first step towards a wealthier society and a community which practised specialization was for the first time able to produce more than enough food, clothes, pots and other things that they needed. They had some left over – a surplus.

If people specialize they must trade. A man concentrating on making pins could not satisfy his need for food by eating them or his need for clothes by wearing them. Therefore trade is a necessity for the individual to obtain those things they cannot make on their own.

But in a barter system trade is difficult. There is no guarantee that an expert pin-maker will be able to find someone willing to swap their goods for his pins at a fair rate of exchange. The result is the pin-maker and others will be unable to specialize to their full potential. They would have to spend their time and effort producing a range of goods and services in order to increase their chances of trading successfully for the things they needed.

This would mean that much less would be produced by whole economies than if they had specialized in their production.

Money encourages specialization by making trade easier and so enables an economy to increase the level of national income and allow people to enjoy a much higher standard of living. In turn, the more an economy specializes the more money is needed to finance an increasing amount of trade.

Money is needed by consumers, firms and the Government to make payments to buy up the output of the economy. The banking system can provide this money and make it easier to make payments. Therefore, as output grows and more trade takes place, so the banking system must develop and create more money.

the history of money

There have been five main stages in the development of money. Each stage being the result of man's attempt to find objects that display the characteristics of a good money.

Stage 1

The earliest form of money was goods. Knives, beads and shoes among other objects were used as money because many people were willing to accept these in exchange for their produce. However, such **commodity money** was quickly abandoned because many of the goods did not possess the essential characteristics of a good money: divisibility, portability, durability, scarcity.

KISSIE PENNIES (AFRICA)

SPADE MONEY (CHINA)

COWRIE SHELLS

SHOE MONEY (CHINA)

Stage 2

Precious metals, such as gold and silver, have always been scarce enough to make them a possible money. However, trading with metals involved carrying around a weighing scale and tools to cut the metals.

Stage 3

The problem of portability that cursed metals led to the natural development of **coinage**. Precious metals in predetermined weights were often stamped with the face of king or queen, and with another stamp to show their value.

But one problem remained. Throughout history the temptation to 'clip' coins, trimming a fine filing of the precious metal from the edges, has been greater than the fear of being caught.

The invention of the ribbed edge on coins overcame the problem of

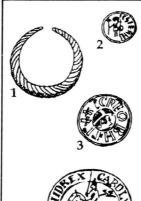

1   Ring money, Gold, 100–50 BC

2   Sceat, Silver, AD 734–766, Anglo-Saxon

3   Silver, AD 802–839, King Ecgberht, Anglo-Saxon

4   Halfcrown, Silver, AD 1644, Charles I

'clipping'. Another problem with the early precious coins was that kings and queens debased them. Coins would be called in for reminting on a special occasion. The monarch would then mix cheap metals with gold or silver, producing perhaps six coins for every four received, cleverly keeping two for themselves. The result of this today is that the metal content of coins is virtually worthless, yet people still accept such coins in exchange for goods because they know they are generally acceptable. It is the duty of the Royal Mint, located in Wales, to issue these coins.

Stage 4

The first **paper money** in the UK was issued by the early goldsmiths who accepted deposits of precious metals for keeping in their safes. In return they issued a paper receipt to the owner. It was quickly realized that these paper claims to gold were far easier to exchange for goods than spending time and effort withdrawing the gold only for it to be given to someone who would then re-deposit it with a goldsmith for safe keeping.

Stage 5   Goldsmiths' receipts for deposits of precious metals were to become the first paper money, and goldsmiths the first banks. Today the government-owned Bank of England has the sole right to issue paper notes, but this money can no longer be converted into gold. Below is an example of an early paper note issued by the Bank of England.

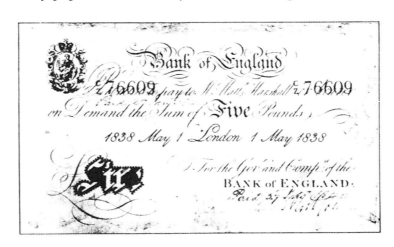

As goldsmiths' receipts became an acceptable medium of exchange, people began to demand the issue of a number of separate claims or receipts for their gold in convenient amounts, for example, £1, £5, £10. These receipts were made payable to the bearer, that is whoever was in possession of the receipts so that they could withdraw the gold from goldsmiths. These early notes were therefore fully convertible into gold.

Goldsmiths soon discovered that on average people would only withdraw a small amount of gold at any one time. For most of the time people were willing to exchange paper receipts and so gold and other precious metals remained in the goldsmiths' vaults for long periods of time. As a result, goldsmiths were able to issue more paper receipts of a value greater than they had in gold knowing full well that those people who owned these receipts were unlikely to convert them back into gold. Therefore, the goldsmiths were creating money, not backed fully by gold.

There came a time, however, when too many receipts not covered by deposits of gold were issued and goldsmiths could not meet demands for withdrawals. Owners of these receipts found themselves holding worthless pieces of paper and the goldsmith bankers collapsed. The Government stepped in to regulate the banking system and the Bank of England now has the sole right to issue paper notes in the UK.

It was possible to convert these notes into gold up until the start of World War 1, but since that time banknotes are no longer convertible into gold.

From the collapse of goldsmith banks grew the large High Street banks of today. Banks, such as Midlands, Barclays, Lloyds, National Westminster and other **commercial banks**, exist today to accept people's and firms' deposits and to make loans. Deposits with these banks may be converted back into cash so bankers must ensure they have enough cash to meet depositors' demands to withdraw. But like the goldsmiths, they realized that withdrawals of deposits would be less than 100% of total deposits. For example, if a bank had deposits of cash totalling £100 000, on average perhaps only one-tenth or £10 000 would be withdrawn in any one month. (Meanwhile, other deposits will be made.) Thus £90 000 cash remains idle. The banks can lend this money to their customers. For example, in the diagram on page 304, rich Mrs Bow has received a £90 000 loan from her local bank. With this money she buys a luxury yacht from Mr Nautical, who promptly deposits the £90 000 he has received into his bank. If this bank keeps one-tenth or £9 000 of this amount then £81 000 can be re-lent. Miss Houseman borrows the £81 000 to buy a house from Mr Builder. On receiving the £81 000 payment Mr Builder deposits it into his bank. If this bank keeps one-tenth, or £8 100 of this amount, then £72 900 can be re-lent. Mr Brown borrows the £72 900 to buy machinery for his new business from Mr Techno, the machine supplier. On receiving payment for his machines, Mr Techno quickly deposits the £72 900 with his bank. And so it goes on. This process is known as **credit creation**. That is, banks are creating money for their customers to borrow and lend. If banks did not lend money,

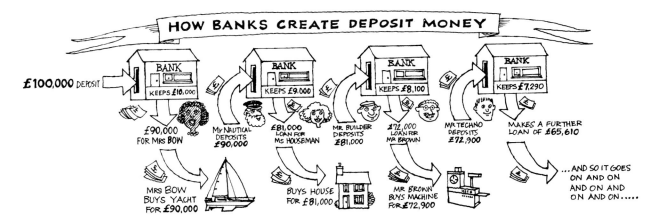

HOW BANKS CREATE DEPOSIT MONEY

£100,000 DEPOSIT

BANK KEEPS £10,000

£90,000 FOR MRS BOW

MRS BOW BUYS YACHT FOR £90,000

MR NAUTICAL DEPOSITS £90,000

BANK KEEPS £9,000

£81,000 LOAN FOR MS HOUSEMAN

BUYS HOUSE FOR £81,000

MR BUILDER DEPOSITS £81,000

BANK KEEPS £8,100

£72,000 LOAN FOR MR BROWN

MR BROWN BUYS MACHINE FOR £72,900

MR TECHNO DEPOSITS £72,900

BANK KEEPS £7,290

MAKES A FURTHER LOAN OF £65,610

...AND SO IT GOES ON AND ON AND ON AND ON AND ON.....

customers who wish to borrow would not have the money to spend and so other customers could not receive money to put back into banks.

Indeed, from an initial £100 000 cash deposit the banking system has created an extra £233 900 (i.e., £90 000 + £81 000 + £72 900) of deposits as each bank lends out money to their customers. If this process continues with each bank keeping one-tenth of any cash returned to them as a deposit (this is known as the **cash ratio**) then from the initial £100 000 a total of £900 000 loans and therefore deposits can be created. The initial £100 000 will still exist in cash but will now be that one-tenth held by banks just in case customers, like Mr Nautical, Mr Techno and many other depositors, wish to make a withdrawal from the total of £1 million of deposits the banking system has on record. Thus the banking system is creating **deposit money**, which are claims to cash held by the banks. Such bank deposits have become the most important form of money in our modern society.

Section 6 — What is money?

Money is a generally acceptable medium of exchange. However, we know that to be money a commodity must also act as store of value. Given this, our savings in bank deposits and other financial institutions, for example, building societies, can be classified as money because one day we may withdraw these deposits so that they may be exchanged for the goods and services we want.

Notes and coins circulating in our economy and deposits with banks and other financial institutions make up the **money supply**.

Exercise 5   Mrs Mint's money

Mrs Mint is tempted by a luxury cruise advertised in the local travel agency. The only problem is the cost of £3 000. At home she tries to figure out just how much money she has.

Emptying the contents of her purse she finds that she has £50 in notes and coins. The jar on her sideboard contains £100 in crisp notes. But not nearly enough for that cruise!

Remembering that she has a current account at the bank which allows her to withdraw any cash immediately, Mrs Mint calculates that another £300 can be added to her list. But still not enough to pay for that cruise!

After waiting seven days Mrs Mint can withdraw her savings from the deposit account she also keeps at the bank. This account contains £400. It appears that she will have to withdraw her long-term savings. In 90 days she can obtain £600 from a Post Office savings scheme. In 120 days £700 can be withdrawn from the building society that she saves with each month. Mrs Mint also has £800 tied up for two years in a building society bond scheme. Finally, she considers selling some of the jewellery she has kept for several years to enable her to sail away on the luxury cruise liner for the holiday of a lifetime.

In the above passage Mrs Mint has a variety of ways by which she can raise the necessary money to pay for the luxury cruise.

1   If money is classed purely as a medium of exchange, list those items included in the passage that you consider would be money and give reasons for your choice.

2   If instead we focus upon money as a store of value, which would you class as money, giving reasons for your choice?

It is not an easy task to decide exactly what is money. For example, a 90-day Post Office savings account is a way of storing value but cannot become a medium of exchange or a measure of value until the end of that 90-day period. Savings tied up for two years will become a medium of exchange after two years has lapsed. So although such methods of savings, or **assets**, can possess all of the functions of money they do not possess them all at the same time or in equal amounts. Cash is a medium of exchange but loses its value due to inflation. Jewellery and other such physical assets may be a good store of value but are not generally acceptable in exchange for other goods.

A deposit account in a bank may become a medium of exchange after seven days when it can be converted into cash. Assets that can be converted relatively quickly into cash are termed **near money** by economists. But jewellery and antiques act as a store of value for many years and may eventually become a medium of exchange given a long enough time to exchange them for notes and coins. However, if on converting such assets into cash the owner can only get less than they originally paid for them, that is, they lose their value, then these assets are **not** near money.

In summary, some assets are nearer money than others, for three main reasons.

a   Some assets fulfil the functions of money better than others. For example, cash is a good medium of exchange, but antiques are not.

b   Some assets can be converted to cash more quickly than others. For example, a bank deposit account can be withdrawn in 7 days, whereas some building society saving schemes cannot be converted into cash for two years or more.

c   Some assets retain their value on conversion to cash better than others. For example, building society accounts hold their value because the society rewards a person who saves with them with periodic payments or **interest**, whereas cars often lose their value.

In our modern economy bank deposits have become the most important form of money as can be seen from the table below. Banks are able to create this **deposit money** by constantly re-lending any cash that returns to them in the form of bank deposits.

The supply of money in the UK, February 1999

	Amount (£ billion)	Percentage share of total
Notes and coins	27.96	3.43
Bank deposits	786.87	96.57
	814.83	100.00

The national income is not the same as the supply of money. This is because notes and coins can be exchanged many times each year. For example, imagine you have just received one pound in return for some work. You use the coin to buy a magazine. The shopkeeper then uses the pound to buy some petrol. Already this one pound coin has been used three times and created £3 of income.

The number of times notes and coins are exchanged, or circulate in an economy, each year is called the **velocity of circulation**. This can vary over time but in the UK has been around 31 each year since 1993. This means, each note and coin in the UK has on average been exchanged 31 times each year. £27.96 billion of notes and coins in 1998 circulated 31 times equals £868 billion – more or less the gross national income in the UK that year.

Two ways of creating money: the Royal Mint and bank loans

405

Economists say that the more swiftly an asset can be converted into a medium of exchange, and the more able it is to retain its value on conversion, the more liquid that asset is. **Liquidity** is therefore the ability to exchange an asset for cash, without a loss of value.

Exercise 6

1   Try to think of all the assets that could be classed as money if they could be converted into cash within:

    a   1 year
    b   5 years
    c   10 years
    d   50 years

In each category arrange all the assets you have managed to think of in order of their liquidity.

2   Compare your thoughts with your class neighbour to see if both your lists can be expanded.

Monetary aggregates

It is possible to imagine a whole 'spectrum of liquidity', that is, a range of assets that could, given long enough, become a medium of exchange.

A simple liquidity spectrum

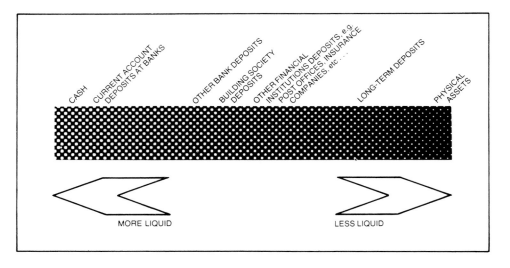

This brings us back to our problem of what exactly is money? If we concentrate on the medium of exchange function then money is simply cash or any asset that can be converted into cash almost immediately. If, however, money is also seen as a store of value, a whole range of assets, that eventually may be converted into cash, can be classed as money.

The Government often wishes to control the amount of money in the economy. But if we cannot pin-point exactly what money is then we cannot know how to control it. To try to overcome this problem the Government has adopted several different definitions of what it thinks money is. These definitions are known as **monetary aggregates**.

The monetary aggregate, known as M0 or base money, concentrates on money being a medium of exchange. It therefore defines money as cash held by the general public, cash held in banks at their various branches and any cash they keep in an account with the central Bank of England.

A wider definition of money is M4. This views money as possessing a store of value function, as well as being a medium of exchange. M4 views notes and coins held by the general public as performing the medium of exchange function, while the savings of people and companies in the UK, held not just in banks, but in all the different financial institutions, are seen to fulfil the role as a store of value.

The growth in the money supply, as measured by M0 and M4 over the 19-year period from 1970 to 1998, is shown on the graph below. Over this period M0 has grown from just over £4 billion to nearly £19 billion. On the wider definition of what money is, M4, the money supply in the UK has grown some £348 billion from just under £27 billion in 1970 to just under £783 billion by the end of 1998.

UK Money Supply 1970–1998

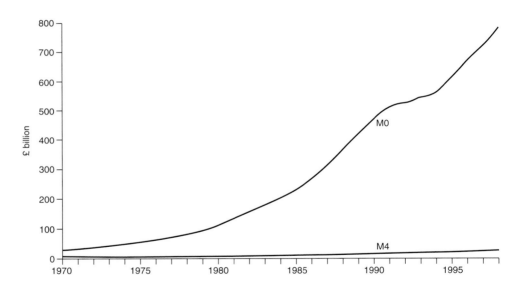

Section 8   The price of money

The market for money

The price of money, like any other commodity in a free market, is determined by the demand for money and the supply of money (see Chapters 8 and 15).

People and firms demand money, or borrow money, to spend on goods and services. People and firms supply money, by saving, to earn a profit. People and firms who lend money to others charge a price for doing so, and this price is known as **interest.** For example, if somebody borrows £1 000 and has to pay back £100, the extra £100 is the price of borrowing this money, or the interest on the loan. Interest is usually expressed as a percentage of the loan. For example, £100 is 10% of a £1 000 loan.

As the interest rate rises, the cost of borrowing goes up and so the demand for money will tend to contract. However, the supply of money is likely to extend as the interest rate rises. The equilibrium interest rate in the **money market** will be determined where the demand for money is equal to the supply of money. When there is an excess demand for money the interest rate will tend to rise. When there is an excess supply of money, the interest rate will tend to fall.

Why charge interest?

People and firms who supply money charge interest for three main reasons:

1 People may lend their money because they do not want to spend it now. However, once a lender has lent her money she may spot a tempting bargain, or need the money for some other reason, but the money has already been lent and she will have to miss out on these opportunities. For this reason, lenders will only lend if they are compensated with interest for not being able to spend their money when they want.

2 Lending money is a risky business. There is always the chance that the borrower may not pay the money back to the lender. In order to encourage people to lend their money and to take this risk they must be paid interest.

3 Because money loses its value over time, people who lend money to others will want some payment to compensate them for this loss of value. If the prices of goods and services rise, an amount of money will buy less and so interest paid should reflect this. Consider a person who lends out £100 at the beginning of the year. That person notices they could buy a compact disc player priced at £100 with this money. However, they have forgone this opportunity. At the end of the year when the loan is due to be repaid, the same compact disc player costs £110. To compensate for this, at least £10 should be paid to the lender as interest on the loan of £100.

Different interest rates

However, you may have noticed that there are many different interest rates offered by organizations lending money. This is because the money market can be split into many different smaller markets for money according to how long a loan of money is for and how risky making that loan is. In general, the longer the loan, and the more risky the loan, the higher the interest rate will be.

There are also many different interest rates on offer to persuade people and firms to save money. People and firms that save money in banks, building societies and other financial institutions, such as pension funds, are in effect lending their money to these organizations. The financial institutions will then use this money to make loans that will earn them a profit from the interest they charge over and above the interest they pay to their savers.

For example, depositing money with a small building society will usually pay more interest than depositing money with a larger building society.

This is because the risk of a smaller building society being unable to repay the money is much greater.

Lending to the Government by saving with the Post Office Girobank pays a lower rate of interest than lending to a local authority. This is because, even though in both cases money is being lent to the Government, the local post office allows money to be withdrawn quickly, while local authorities expect to keep money for longer periods. The longer they keep this money, the more interest they must pay to compensate the lender for going without the use of their money. Thus, in general, the longer the loan and the greater the risk, the higher the rate of interest.

Exercise 7   Why do interest rates differ?

Consider the following cases.

Case 1   As manager of a bank you devise three different saving schemes to suit the differing needs of your customers.

> **Scheme 1**   A deposit scheme (minimum deposit £5) with a withdrawal notice of seven days required.
>
> **Scheme 2**   A Bond share scheme (minimum deposit £500) with a withdrawal notice of 90 days required.
>
> **Scheme 3**   An investment account (minimum deposit £500) with a savings period of two to five years, with 90 days withdrawal notice required.

Your interest rates may vary between 4% and 10%. What rate will you offer to savers on each scheme and why?

Case 2   Which of the following two schemes do you think would offer savers the highest rate of interest? Give reasons for this.

> **Scheme 1**   A building society lends its savers money to house-buyers who repay regular sums.
>
> **Scheme 2**   A Unit Trust uses savers' money to buy and sell shares in companies on the Stock Exchange to hopefully make a profit.

Case 3   Which of the following schemes would offer a lower rate of interest and why?

> **Scheme 1**   This bank scheme involves regular savings and each month the saver receives a statement and interest.
>
> **Scheme 2**   This scheme involves regular savings on which interest is paid yearly, and a statement is sent at the end of each year.

Exercise 8   The supply of money

In 1998 UK households had £583 billion of **disposable income** (i.e. personal income after tax) to spend but only spent £543 billion. The remaining £40 billion was saved. This exercise looks at some of the ways of saving and some of the reasons for doing so. Read the article on the next page and then answer the questions.

Jane Johnson is an accountant. Each month Jane saves £300. Jane does this by paying £50 into a pension scheme, £20 for life assurance, £30 into a bank deposit account and the remaining £200 into a building society.

Jane tries to save for when she retires so that she will have some money to spend. Jane also saves in case of an emergency, for example, her car breaking down or urgent repairs to her house.

Recently Jane has noticed that prices have been rising. Because of this Jane now tries to save £350 per month so that her savings will buy the same number of goods and services as before. Jane is also saving more because interest rates have risen and so savings in the bank/building society earn more interest.

1   Name the main ways of saving

2   List as many reasons for saving as you can

3   Name two things that can influence how much people want to save, and explain why they do

4   Where can people save money? Make a list of as many of the different types of financial institutions you can think of.

Money market or capital market?   You will often read about the **capital market** in newspapers or hear the term used on the business news. The capital market and money market are much the same thing. Just like the money market, the capital market brings together borrowers and lenders of money. However, we often talk about the market for capital when we are considering the supply of large sums of money to big firms to invest in new plant and machinery. Large firms are also able to raise capital through the sale of shares (see Chapter 6). In contrast, we usually refer to the money market when talking about smaller loans of money to private individuals and smaller firms.

Section 9   Money market institutions

The market for money, like any other market, consists of all the people who want money: consumers, firms and government, and all the institutions that supply it, namely the banking system which creates deposit money (see Section 5), and the Government who has the sole right to issue notes and coins in the UK.

Many people nowadays have a bank or building society account of some sort. These and other institutions are known as **financial intermediaries** because they act as go-betweens amongst their customers. They receive deposits of money and then lend out this money to the customers who want to borrow. We will now look at these financial institutions in more detail.

410

Commercial banks

The **commercial** or **high street banks** provide banking services to businesses and consumers through a network of branches. These banks are in business to make a profit for their owners and they are usually public limited companies owned by shareholders.

The table opposite lists the high street banks in Britain in 1999. Together these banks have assets worth around £2 000 billion. Most of this money belongs to firms and to ordinary people. We are willing to place so much of our money with banks because of the functions they perform.

UK Commercial banks in 1999	
Abbey National	Cheltenham and Gloucester
Alliance & Leicester	First Direct
Allied Irish	Halifax
Bank of Ireland	HSBC
Bank of Scotland	Lloyds TSB
Bank of Wales	National Westminster
Barclays	Northern Bank
Beneficial Bank	Northern Rock
Co-operative Bank	Royal Bank of Scotland
Coutts & Co.	Yorkshire Bank
Girobank	Woolwich

The functions of commercial banks

1 Commercial banks keep money safely for their customers
Banks are one of the safest places a person can keep money. It is possible to keep money in a bank by opening a **current account** or a **deposit account** or both.

A current account is used to make payments from. A customer can deposit and withdraw money from this account without giving any notice. To help make payments customers holding a current account are given cheque-books.

Deposit accounts are used for savings and do not offer a cheque-book. Interest is offered to encourage people to save and because notice of withdrawal has to be given.

2 Commercial banks help their customers to make and receive payments

Cheques are the most important method of payment and over six million cheques are paid into banks each and every working day. Indeed, 90% of all payments are made by cheque today. Cheques are not money but transfers of money from one person's current account to another person's account.

Commercial banks can also relieve customers from having to remember when to pay their bills. By filling in a **standing order** or **direct debit** a customer can instruct a bank to make regular payments from his or her bank account to pay gas, electricity, telephone and all other manner of bills. Banks make some of their profits by charging customers for these services.

Credit cards are another important means of making payments. The Visa and Access cards are operated by the commercial banks. People can use a credit card to make payment and receive a bill from the card company for all the payments made within that month. The credit card holder can then pay for all these purchases in total or in monthly instalments by writing a cheque to the credit card company.

3 Commercial banks lend money to customers

As we discovered in Section 5, commercial banks lend money. Individuals, firms and the Government can borrow this money and banks make profits by charging interest on these loans.

4 Commercial banks provide many other services

Banks can exchange UK currency for foreign currencies and issue traveller's cheques for people going abroad. They can arrange insurance for life, houses, cars and other property. They also operate pension funds, help with buying and selling shares, advise on making tax payments or even writing a will. Night safe facilities allow shops to deposit their takings in bank safes after normal banking hours. Many banks will also look after valuable documents like house deeds and property like items of jewellery.

Exercise 9   Do we need banks?

Voce Video Limited is a small but quickly-growing firm manufacturing video equipment.

The company has recently bought its factory building and pays £800 each month to a building society by direct debit.

Voce Video sells much of its equipment by credit card sale and so accepts all main credit cards.

The company keeps most of its sales' receipts in a deposit account where it earns interest. The rest of the sales' money is kept in a current account and the company pays its bills by drawing cheques on this account.

Voce Video has also recently received a £100 000 bank loan in order to build a new factory and has 20 years in which to repay the loan.

1 If there were no commercial bank, how would the way in which Voce Video receives and makes payments change?

2 Where would Voce Video keep its sales' money?

3 Could Voce Video build its new factory?

4 Sum up the main advantages to industry of commercial banks.

National Savings Bank (NSB) The NSB is owned by the Government and money saved in this bank is used or borrowed by the Government. The NSB is run through post offices.

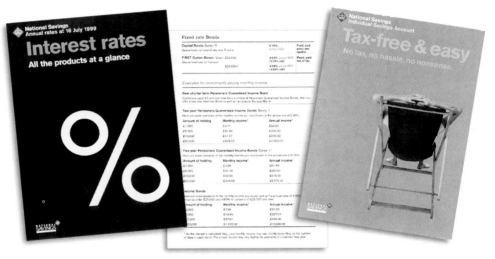

Girobank The Girobank provides a banking service through post office branches.

Merchant banks   The main job of merchant banks is to raise money to lend to industry. They do not lend money themselves but instead help circulate money from those who want to lend to firms who wish to borrow.

Merchant banks may also act as Issuing Houses for companies. (See Chapter 6 on the finance of business.) A merchant bank can help a company to sell its new share issues to the general public.

Foreign banks   There are many foreign banks in the UK, most in London, showing how important the city is in international banking. The USA and Japan have many banks in Britain. These banks set up in the UK to meet the needs of customers from their own countries who have moved to this country, for example, to set up businesses.

The number of foreign banks has also grown because of the increase in the practice of UK public and private sector firms, and the Government, of borrowing from abroad. Foreign banks use their deposits, many in foreign currencies, to make these loans.

Finance houses   Finance houses act in a similar manner to banks by taking deposits from the public and using them to make loans. The type of loan they specialize in is hire purchase (HP) and other types of credit paid by instalment.

Building societies   The main function of a **building society**, as we learnt in Chapter 6, is to provide loans of money to people who wish to buy property. The loans are known as **mortgages**. Building societies, however, also provide other services, such as arranging insurance, cash-dispensing machines, cheque-books and estate agency services to help people find houses.

In recent years building societies have been in increasing competition with commercial banks and it is likely that in the not too distant future there will be little difference between them in the services they provide for the public.

Indeed, many building societies in the UK have turned into commercial banks over time in order to expand their operations and make profits. Building societies are mutual societies owned by their savers. They are non-profit-making organizations so any surplus of revenue over costs is spent on making the business better and/or offering their savers higher rates of interest. Each saver is allowed to vote at annual general meetings to elect directors and determine the business policies and goals of their building society. In contrast, banks are public limited companies owned by share-holders and are in business to make profits. Profits are distributed to share-holders as dividends, and the more shares a person holds in a bank, the more votes that person has at annual general meetings (see Chapter 5).

Exercise 10   From building society to bank

Bradford and Bingley's vote could be the last straw for mutual societies

The defeat of the Board of Directors of the Bradford & Bingley building society – by a far greater majority than anyone forecast – means the end of mutuality. The vote by members took place on the same day the cash and preference share windfall payments from demutualised Birmingham Midshires, which is now part of the Halifax, start to flow to former members. Members of the Bradford and Bingley can expect windfall payouts of estimated at £1,000 each when the society converts to a public limited company some time in 2001.

The B&B vote will now force the remaining building societies to reconsider their mutual status. Supporters of mutuality claim greater commercial freedoms than banks such as being able to borrow larger sums on the money markets as well as bidding for rival or complementary businesses.

Nevertheless, many of the big names in the movement have converted to public limited companies – Abbey National, Alliance & Leicester, Birmingham Midshires, Bristol & West, Cheltenham & Gloucester, Halifax, National & Provincial, Northern Rock and Woolwich.

But whatever the arguments in favour of keeping mutual status, they apply most strongly to borrowers compared to savers. Building societies have priced variable rate home loans around 0.5% cheaper than their public rivals. This is worth about £300 a year to the typical £60,000 borrower, so homebuyers would be better off after around three years than someone voting for a typical £1,000 windfall. However, one in two borrowers has a fixed rate loan, so the benefit is less clear.

On average there are five savers for every one mortgage borrower, and most save relatively small sums so they stand to benefit greatly from a one off £1,000 payout, especially at a time when interest rates are so low. According to figures from the Britannia Building Society, a saver with an average £20,000 is around £200 a year better off because they are offered more attractive rates of interest than banks. As such it would take 5 years before this saver had benefited by an extra £1,000, and it would take much longer for smaller savers to do so.

Remaining building societies claim their presence acts as a brake on 'greedy banks' trying to maximise profits. As if to confirm this, last week Abbey National cut its rates to savers despite prior pledges it had made to help depositors. The Nationwide is giving a mutuality bonus of around £300m a year to its eight million members – but that is less than £40 a head, or a 25-year payback period against a £1,000 payout.

Adapted from 'The Guardian', 27.4.1999

1   What are the key differences between a mutual society and a public limited company?

2   What are the arguments for and against a building society converting to a commercial bank?

3   Suggest what might be the long term results of increasing numbers of commercial banks for **a** savers, **b** borrowers, and **c** the economy. Explain your answers.

4   Takeovers and mergers between banks have increased in the UK. Why do you think this is so?

5   In 1998 UK building societies advanced an additional £24 billion of mortgage loans to around 230 000 people to buy homes. What factors do you think determine **a** the demand for mortgages, and **b** the price of houses and flats?

Many building societies converted to banks in the 1990s

Discount houses   Discount houses are very specialized firms which borrow money, mainly from banks, over a very short period of time, usually for less than a day. They will then re-lend this money to others in the public and private sectors for longer periods of time. They do this by buying a variety of securities, or 'promises to pay', issued by the Government, local authorities, banks and firms. For example, the Government may issue a 'promise to pay' for £1 000. They sell this to the discount house with the promise to repay this loan in, for example, 90 days' time. The discount house will make its profit by buying the security for less than £1 000, say only £950. At the end of 90 days, the Government will repay the loan by repurchasing their security from the discount house for the full £1 000. Local authorities, banks and firms borrow money in the same way from discount houses.

However, because discount houses are using money which can be recalled by banks at short notice, they run the risk of running short of money. Because of this risk, discount houses may have to borrow from the central bank in the economy owned by the Government. The central bank, or **Bank of England**, lends money to help discount houses as a last resort.

The Old Lady of Threadneedle Street – the Bank of England

The Bank of England   The Bank of England, as the nation's central bank, stands at the centre of the banking system in the UK. Founded in 1694 it was taken into public ownership in 1946. The Bank of England has many responsibilities:

1   It is the Government's bank.
The Bank of England is responsible for looking after the money received by the Government, for example, tax revenues, and managing its payments, for example, its spending on hospitals, schools, social security benefits.

2   It stores the nation's gold and foreign currency reserves.
The amount of gold and foreign currency stored at the Bank of England for the Government is known as the **exchange equalization account**. These reserves are used to influence the value of the UK currency Sterling against other countries' currencies (see Chapter 15).

3   It has the sole right of note issue in England and Wales.
The Bank of England is responsible for the printing and issue of banknotes in England and Wales.

4 It manages the national debt.

This involves repaying money the Government has borrowed in the past, and raising new loans for the Government.

5 It is the banker's bank.

The Bank of England acts as a supervisor to the banking system, deciding who can be a bank and how banks should behave.

The Bank of England acts as a bank for the commercial banks. These banks keep deposits of their own money at the central bank so that they can settle debts between themselves following the exchange of cheques and other payments.

6 It is the lender of the last resort.

The Bank of England will lend money to the banking system to try to prevent banks from going bankrupt if they run out of money.

7 It governs the UK Monetary Policy Committee.

The Governor of the Bank of England heads the **Monetary Policy Committee (MPC)**. The MPC was formed in 1997 and is allowed to set the base rate of interest in the UK economy without interference from the Government's Chancellor of the Exchequer (see Chapter 15.)

The MPC consists of a panel of experts who meet each month to make their decision on the interest rate using up-to-date information and forecasts of movements in prices, wages, exchange rates and other economic variables. It will tend to raise the interest rate if it thinks price inflation is likely to rise, and will tend to lower the interest rate if it believes price inflation will fall.

8 It is a member of the European System of Central Banks

The European System of Central Banks (ESCB) brings together the national central banks of all the member countries of the European Union with the European Central Bank (see Chapter 18). Working together the central banks help support the general economic policies of the European Union, conduct foreign currency operations, hold and manage the foreign reserves of member countries, and handle payments between them. The primary objective of the ESCB is to keep price inflation low and stable across the European Union.

Key words

In your own words write down what you understand by the following:

Barter	Current account
Double coincidence of wants	Deposit account
Medium of exchange	Cheques
Measure of value	Clearing
Store of value	Standing order
Commodity money	Credit cards
Paper money	National Savings Bank
Deposit money	National Girobank
Money supply	Merchant banks
Near money	Foreign banks
Liquid assets	Finance houses
Monetary aggregates	Building societies
Interest	Discount houses
Velocity of circulation	Bank of England
Commercial banks	Monetary Policy Committee

Now go back through the chapter to check your understanding.

Chapter 20 | Population

Aims

At the end of this chapter you should be able to:

1 Describe trends in the growth of population in different countries.

2 Examine the concern expressed over rapid population increase.

3 Define what is meant by the **dependency ratio** of a country and calculate it for a number of countries.

4 Analyse **birth rates** and **death rates** and suggest reasons for changes in them.

5 Describe the structure of the present UK population.

6 Analyse how changes in the size and structure of a country's population affect its economy.

Population is the human basis of the whole of economics. People make up the supply of labour able to use capital and land to produce goods and services. They are also the consumers of the goods and services produced.

Section 1 | The world population

The population explosion

Since the eighteenth century the world has experienced a population explosion, and it is still increasing faster than ever before. While there is potential for the production of more goods and services, natural resources are limited, and, as fast as goods and services are produced, so the needs and wants of an ever-increasing world population grow. The population of the world is increasing by over 70 million people each year, or 200 000 a day. Imagine a city the size of London added every month, and the people in that city being on average, only four to five weeks old!

The population explosion started in Europe after the Industrial Revolution in the eighteenth century. Improvements in housing, sanitation and medicine reduced the number of deaths and helped increase the number of births. The population of Europe rose by over 300% in a 160-year period after 1750. Many of these Europeans moved overseas.

In the twentieth century population growth in many western countries has slowed down. The populations of countries like the UK and other western European nations have, over the past few years, hardly changed at all and are currently growing by less than 1% per year.

The new explosion in population is predicted to be in less-developed countries in South America, Asia and Africa. Here, populations are expected to rise by 56% over the period to 2030 compared to an increase of just 6% in more developed countries. Europe is the only continent expected to experience a fall in population.

The world population is expected to reach 8 billion by 2025. About 7 billion of these people will live in less-developed countries.

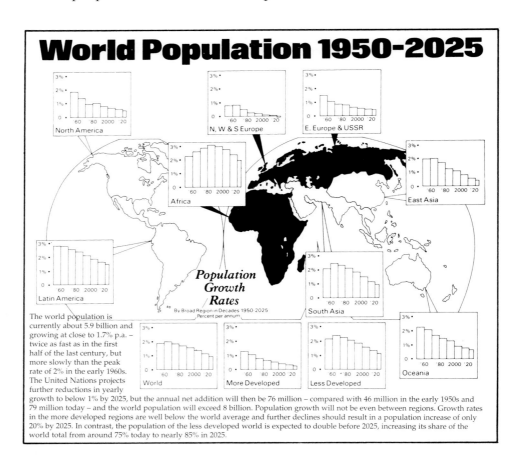

World Population 1950-2025

North America

N, W & S Europe

E. Europe & USSR

Africa

East Asia

Latin America

Population Growth Rates
By Broad Region in Decades 1950-2025
Percent per annum

South Asia

Oceania

The world population is currently about 5.9 billion and growing at close to 1.7% p.a. – twice as fast as in the first half of the last century, but more slowly than the peak rate of 2% in the early 1960s. The United Nations projects further reductions in yearly growth to below 1% by 2025, but the annual net addition will then be 76 million – compared with 46 million in the early 1950s and 79 million today – and the world population will exceed 8 billion. Population growth will not be even between regions. Growth rates in the more developed regions are well below the world average and further declines should result in a population increase of only 20% by 2025. In contrast, the population of the less developed world is expected to double before 2025, increasing its share of the world total from around 75% today to nearly 85% in 2025.

World

More Developed

Less Developed

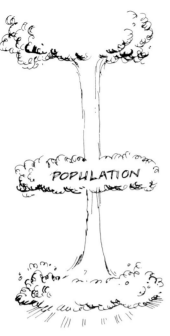

Exercise 1 Explosion

It took until about 1830 for the population of the world to reach its first 1 000 million. The second 1 000 million was added in about 100 years, the third 1 000 million in 30 years, the fourth in just 15 years.

The graph below illustrates this population explosion. By 1998 the population of the world had increased to around 6 000 million and is expected to grow to over 8 000 million by the year 2025.

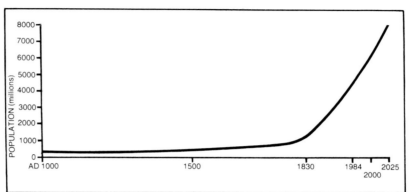

The world population explosion
1   **a**   As the world population increases what will happen to the total number of needs and wants in the world?
     b   If resources are scarce, such as oil, coal, metals, fertile soils, what will happen to the rate at which we use them up?

2   The population of the world rises as less people die and live to old age, and more babies are born. What will happen to the demand for:
     a   Food
     b   Consumer goods
     c   Education
     d   Health care
     e   Housing
     f   Transport?

3   **a**   If one country cannot produce enough goods and services for the needs and wants of its population how will it try to obtain more of these commodities?
     b   What will happen to that country's balance of trade?

Population growth: A cause for concern

Malthus
In 1798 the Reverend Thomas Malthus wrote about population growth in the UK. At the time of writing the UK population was growing fast and this seemed to support his view that increasing numbers of people would only bring misery. There would be too many people and too few resources. That is, there would be **overpopulation**. As a result, people would start to starve and there would be famines and plagues as people lacked the strength to fight off disease. Wars would start as countries tried to take over each others' resources to support their own populations. Population growth would eventually be stopped.

421

However, Malthus was proved wrong in Britain as even though the population increased four times over during the nineteenth century, technology improved to provide for the increased population. Farms' output of food increased and new methods of transport allowed food to be brought to Britain from the vast lands of America. More houses were needed and the building of these provided work and incomes for people. Increasing numbers of people meant more consumers. This increase in demand expanded the markets for goods and services, stimulating investment in new capital equipment to produce them and creating employment for many more people. Economic growth took place, and, despite the costs of increased congestion in growing cities and increasing pollution from factories, living standards rose.

Nevertheless, many people still believe Malthus will be proved right as population growth in less-developed countries outstrips their scarce resources. Wars, famines and disease have plagued countries like Ethiopia and other less-developed nations in Africa, Asia, Central and South America.

Dependency ratios Imagine there are five people living in your home: your mother and father, your sister and a grandparent. Your mother is the only person at work. She earns £150 per week, which is used to provide food, clothing and shelter as well as the other goods and services for five people including herself. That is your father, you and your sister and a grandparent all depend on your mother going to work. Clearly, if there was just your mother and father their standard of living would be much higher. They would have more money to spend on themselves. If, on the other hand, they had more children, all the family would have a lower standard of living as the mother's income and the goods and services it buys would have to be shared out between more people. As the number of dependents rise, everybody will be worse off. The same thing happens in the population as a whole.

People in work produce commodities not only for themselves but also for people not at work. In the UK there are approximately 27 million people in paid employment. The rest of the population of about 33 million people rely on these 27 million to provide the goods and services they need and want. These 33 million people are said to be the **dependent population**. Using these figures we can calculate the **dependency ratio** in the UK. This ratio compares the number of people in work with the total population of the country.

$$\textbf{Dependency ratio} = \frac{\text{Total population}}{\text{Number of people in work}}$$

Using the figures for the UK the dependency ratio is 2.22. That is, every person in work not only supports his or herself but also 1.22 other people. A total of 2.22 UK citizens are supported by one worker.

The dependent population will consist of the very young, schoolchildren, students, housewives, the unemployed and old-age pensioners. Any increase in these groups of people means that the people in work have more people to support and the living standards of most people will fall.

The dependent population includes both young and old

More resources, and expenditure on them, will have to be devoted to education for the young, and medical and welfare services for young and old alike. In a country like the UK, where such services are provided by the Government using tax-payer's money, this means working people may have to pay more tax to support their dependents. In addition, if people in work cannot produce enough goods and services to satisfy the needs and wants of a growing dependent population, the country will have to use some of its income to purchase more and more imported goods from abroad. Its balance of trade may become unfavourable.

The dependency ratio has increased in the UK for a number of reasons; the school leaving age has been increased over time; more young people are encouraged to stay on in full-time education after 16 years of age; people are living longer and the number of elderly people has increased; and an increasing number of people are taking early retirement. To offset this in part, the UK Government is increasing the official retirement age for women from 60 to 65 years of age so that it is the same as males.

Many developed countries are displaying the same pattern. However, it is the less-developed countries which face the biggest problem. Medical help has allowed more people to live to old age and more babies to survive. As a result, their dependent populations are large and increasing, putting more strain on their scarce resources.

Exercise 2   The dependent population

Below is a table of figures showing the total population and the total number of people employed in a number of countries in 1996.

Country	Total population (millions)	Employed population (millions)
USA	271.6	123.0
Switzerland	6.8	3.5
Bolivia	6.4	1.3
Romania	22.8	10.1
Brazil	146.8	62.1
Greece	10.3	3.7

1 For each country calculate:
  a the size of the dependent population
  b the dependency ratio.

2 Which countries have:
  a the highest dependency ratio?
  b the lowest dependency ratio?

3 What effect would the following have on the dependency ratio of a country?:
  a A fall in the number of people in employment.
  b An increase in the number of old people.
  c An increase in the number of births.
  d An increase in employment.
  e A decrease in the number of births.

4 Of the above factors in question 3, which are characteristic of:
  a less developed countries
  b developed countries
  c both types of country.

5 a What is meant by overpopulation?
  b Can the UK be considered overpopulated?

Section 2 | The causes of population change

There are three ways in which a country's population can increase:

1 The number of babies being born can increase.

2 The number of people dying can fall.

3 More people can come to live in a country (**immigration**) than there are people leaving the country to live abroad (**emigration**).

In some countries there are more new babies than others. The average number of children born in a country compared to the rest of the population is known as the birth rate, which is normally expressed as the number of births for every 1 000 people in the country. The birth rate in the UK is 12.3 live births for every 1 000 UK citizens at the present, but it used to be much higher. For most of the nineteenth century the birth rate was about 35 per 1 000.

The reasons behind changes in the birth rate in a country are unclear but here are a number of possible explanations.

1 Living standards

Improvements in the quality and availability of food, housing, clean water, toilet facilities and medical care result in fewer babies dying. Many years ago a high proportion of children would die before they could go to work and earn money for their families. As a result, people had large families in case their children died and they had none to go out to work. As living standards improved in many developed countries, including the UK, fewer

Births

Live births
UK (Annual averages)

	Total live births (thousands)	Crude birth rate[1]
1901–1911	1091	28.5
1911–1921	975	23.2
1921–1931	824	18.7
1931–1941	785	17.1
1941–1951	839	16.7
1951–1961	963	18.2
1961–1971	736	13.2
1971–1981	757	13.4
1981–1991	756	13.1
1991–2001	723	12.3
Projections		
2001–2011	690	11.6
2011–2021	694	11.4

1 Total births per 1,000 of population of all ages

Social Trends 1999

babies died and so people did not have as many children. Indeed, at present, the average UK family has two or three children.

In less-developed countries birth rates remain high because many children still die, and people want large families so that the children can work on their farms to produce food and earn incomes.

2 Contraception
The increased usage of contraception and abortion has dramatically reduced birth rates in developed countries. The pill for women was first introduced in the 1960s and has a 99% success rate in preventing pregnancy. However, because of lack of education on such matters, many people in less-developed countries are unaware of birth control. Perhaps they should learn from Japan's success in reducing her birth rate from 36 births per 1 000 people to 17 per 1 000 people in just 15 years after the introduction of contraception.

3 Custom and religion
Many people, particularly in less-developed countries, hold religious beliefs that will not allow them to use contraception. The Roman Catholic religion is one such belief.

Customs are changing. In developed countries it has become less fashionable to have large families and birth rates have fallen.

4 Female employment
In developed countries, particularly in the UK, more and more women are going out to work. Many women do not wish to break their careers to bring up children. Having children also causes a drain on people's incomes. Not only will the wife have to give up work for a while, but they may also have to pay a baby-sitter to look after the child if they remain at work. This is in addition to the cost of food, clothing and shelter for the child.

5 Marriages
Most people have children when they are married. In many developed countries people are tending to marry later on in life and so birth rates fall. In the UK the average age of a mother at all births increased from 26 years in 1971 to over 28 years of age in 1997.

Births and deaths

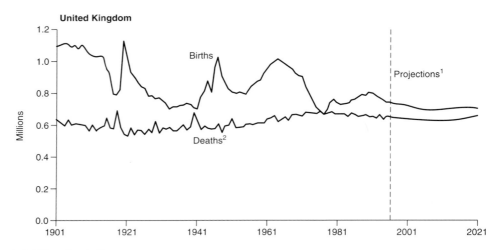

1 1996-based projections
2 Data for 1901 to 1921 exclude the Irish Republic which was constitutionally a part of the UK during this period

Source: Office for National Statistics; Government Actuary's Department; General Register Office for Scotland; Northern Ireland Statistics and Research Agency

Deaths If people start to live longer, this increases the size of the population. The number of people who die each year compared to every 1 000 people in the population is known as the death rate. At present in the UK about 11 people die per year for every 1 000 people in the population. Again, the UK death rate was higher in the past, for example, in the last century it was just over 20 per 1 000. Most countries have experienced a falling death rate, even less-developed countries have had some success in reducing their death rates, but as their birth rates remain high, so their population grows rapidly.

There are a number of factors that affect the death rate in a country.

1   Medical advance and health care

The main killer diseases of nineteenth-century Britain, like smallpox, cholera, tuberculosis, can be prevented or even cured by modern medicine. Advances in medicine and health care have reduced the number of deaths from disease and people in the UK can now expect to live longer. The life expectancy of males and females in the 1990s ranged from 75 to 80 years. However, 100 years ago most people were lucky to live to 50 years of age.

Life expectancy in less-developed countries still remains low, but increasing health care has improved the chance of survival of many of their people.

2   Living standards

Better-quality food, clothing and shelter, and a greater emphasis on cleanliness have helped improve the health and life expectancy of people in developed countries. In the less-developed world a lack of the right types of food to provide vitamins and proteins has meant many people in these areas die from malnutrition. However, in developed nations many people smoke and eat very rich foods, often causing cancer and heart disease. These health problems occur very little in less-developed countries.

The **rate of natural increase** in a country's population is the difference between the birth rate and the death rate in that country. In most countries birth rates exceed death rates and so the rate of natural increase in populations has been positive. The main cause of the increase in the UK population over the past 300 years has been the steady decline in the death rate. The birth rate up to 1900 was quite high but has on the whole been falling since then and so the rate of natural increase in the population in the UK has fallen steadily this century. As a result, the population of the UK grew by only 5.1% between 1971 and 1997.

Migration

A **migrant** is a person who moves from one place to another. An immigrant is a person moving into a country; an emigrant is a person leaving. If the number of immigrants exceeds the number of emigrants the population in a country will rise. That is, if net migration (immigrants minus emigrants) is positive.

Since 1900 the pattern of people entering and leaving the UK has changed. Up until 1930 there was a net loss of 80 000 people each year. In the 1930s there was a net inflow of people to the UK, and during the 1960s and 1970s more people left the UK than entered. However, since then the number of people entering the UK has exceeded the number leaving by around 15 000 each year.

Population changes and projections

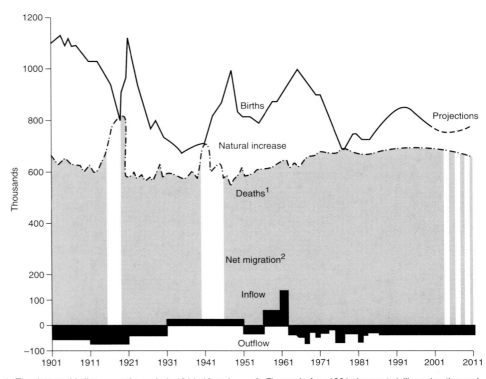

1 The dots on this line cover the periods 1914–18 and 1939–45 which include deaths of non-civilian and merchant seamen who died outside the country.

2 Figures before 1961 show net civilian migration and other changes. Figures from 1961 show net civilian migration only.

427

Exercise 3   Birth and death rates

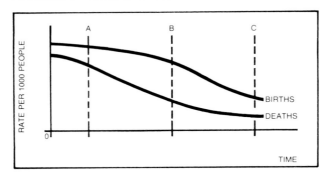

Look at the diagram of birth and death rates over time.

1　**a**　Which of the three position, A, B or C, representing three different countries, is experiencing a rapid growth in population?
　　b　What evidence is there of rapid population increase from the diagram?

2　What do population changes for countries represented by positions A and C have in common?

3　Suggest problems the country represented by position B will face in the immediate future.

4　**a**　Of these positions, which represents a developed country and which a typical less-developed country?
　　b　What evidence is there from the diagram to support your answer?

5　Explain three factors that may have caused a fall in:
　　a　the birth rate
　　b　the death rate shown above.

Section 3	The structure of the UK population

UK population figures have been available for many years. A census has been taken every 10 years since 1801, except in 1941, and provides information on the number of males and females, their age, their work, the number of children in families, the number of marriages, where people live, etc. We shall now consider some of this information in more detail.

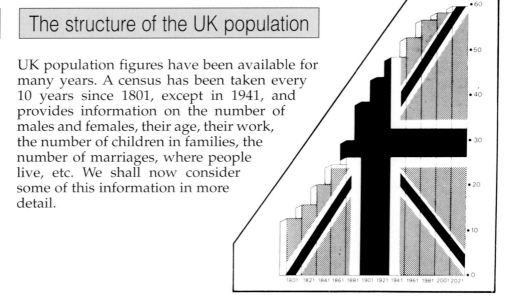

Growth of UK population

Where do the people live? The **regional distribution** of the population refers to where people live. In general, people live near to their place of work. In the nineteenth century, as industries developed, people moved out of farming communities into towns and cities. In fact half the people in the UK now live in seven major conurbations, which consist of a group of towns which have gradually grown together to form one very large city. The largest conurbation in the UK is Greater London, providing a home to nearly 8 million people, a population as great as that of the whole of Sweden and twice as big as New Zealand!

Indeed, London and the South East of England have on average over 660 people living in every square kilometre of its area. The other six conurbations in the UK are Leeds, Liverpool, Manchester, Newcastle, Birmingham and Glasgow.

Today, however, there is a population move out of the large cities into the towns and countryside within commuter distance of the cities.

Improved means of transport and the increasing congestion in cities have prompted this move. Retirement also causes movement. Many older couples move away from their old places of work to retirement homes in areas like the South Coast of England, Lancashire and North Wales.

Population density 1997

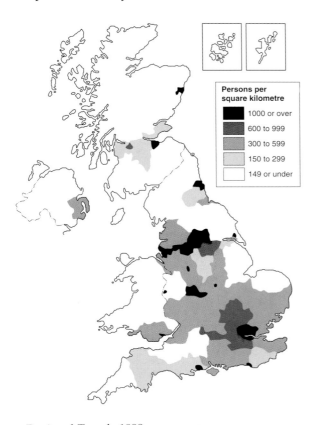

Regional Trends 1999

Projected population growth 1996–2011

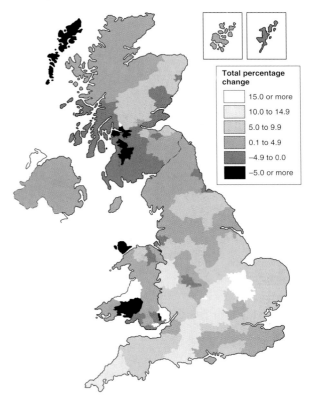

Regional Trends 1999

429

Young or old? The **age distribution** of the population refers to the number of people, or percentage of the population, in each age group. With falling birth and death rates in the UK the average age of the population has increased. That is, on average, each year there are more and more middle to old-aged people. In 1901 only 5% of the population lived to be 65 years old, while around 32% 9.3 million of the population was aged between 0 and 16 years of age. Today around 16% of the population is over 65 years old, and only 20% between the ages of 0 and 16. The UK is experiencing an **ageing population**.

Elderly people as a percentage of the UK Population

Source: Office for National Statistics

As the number of older people grow there will be changes in the economy. For example:

1 A fall in the birth rate will be reflected in a fall in the working population in 16 or more years time. However, the declining working population will have more old people to support as death rates fall.

2 More resources will have to be put into producing goods and services for older people. However, a falling birth rate may mean less resources need to be devoted to maternity clinics, nurseries and schools.

3 An ageing population will also affect the pattern of demand in the economy. Older people will want and need different commodities from younger age groups.

Male or female? The **sex distribution** in a country refers to the number of males compared to the number of females in the population. Although there are more male births than female births in the UK, females tend to live longer than males and so the number of females in the total population exceeds that of males. In 1997, 49.1% of the UK population was male while 60.9% was female. However, due to the longer life expectancy of females, they out-number males by over two to one at 80 years of age and three to one at 89 years of age.

430

The age-sex pyramid for the UK 1997

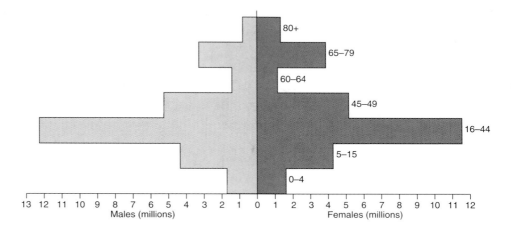

The age and sex distribution of a country's population can be displayed on age-sex pyramids like the one above. Along the bottom axis is the number (or sometimes percentage) of males to the left of the vertical axis, and the number (or percentage) of females to the right. The vertical axis displays age in convenient ranges. The UK age-sex pyramid *bulges* in the middle age groups as the population *ages* due to the fall in its birth and death rates. Many developed countries' age-sex pyramids display the same bulge due to falling birth and death rates.

On the other hand, less-developed nations with high birth rates exceeding falling birth rates display age-sex pyramids with wide bases showing large numbers of teenagers in their populations.

Exercise 4   Population pyramids

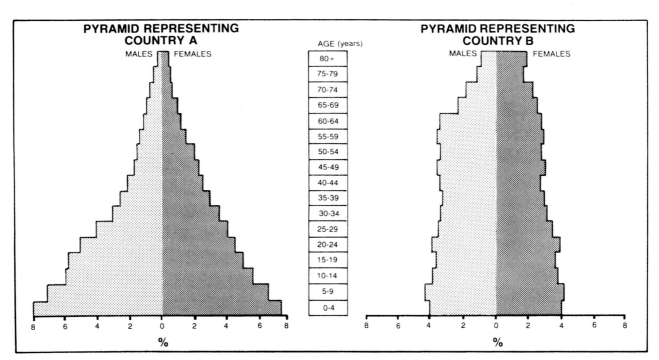

1 Which of these two population pyramids reveals the country with the greatest dependancy ratios for
   a under-15s?
   b over-65s?

2 Is the birth rate for A greater or less than that for B?

3 Which has the highest life expectancy, A or B?

4 Which represents a nation in the less-developed world, A or B?

Where do people work? Of all employees about 36% are employed in manufacturing industries, 4% in primary activities like agriculture and coal mining. Most people are employed in service industries. In contrast, in less-developed countries most people are engaged in primary industries like farming.

Recent changes in employees in employment: all industries (UK)

UK	Thousands	
	1993	1998
All industries	21 613	23 237
Employees in employment		
Agriculture, forestry and fishing	326	272
Mining and quarrying; energy and water supply	91	80
	388	302
Manufacturing	3 906	4 076
Construction	865	1 003
Wholesale and retail trade; repairs	3 562	4 037
Hotels and restaurants	1 185	1 316
Transport and communications	1 317	1 389
Financial services	975	1 064
Public admin. and defence	1 463	1 350
Education	1 829	1 896
Health and social work	2 453	2 582
Other services	3 253	3 870

Annual Abstract of Statistics, ONS

The trend in the **occupational distribution** of the UK is expected to show a continuing increase in employment in service industries.

Female employment is concentrated in industries such as textiles and clothing, food, drink and tobacco, the retailing trade and many office jobs and professions like nursing and teaching. Female employment, although often including much part-time work, has increased dramatically over time. 45% of the UK workforce was female in 1999 compared to 39% in 1979. The same pattern is also true of many other developed countries.

Section 4 | Towards an optimum population

A country is described as overpopulated if there are too few resources for the population. Standards of living are poor as the few available goods and services are shared out among many people.

For example, the UK cannot be considered overpopulated with an average 241 people per square kilometre of the UK land area. Despite the rise in the UK population to its present 59 million or so people, living standards have on average improved as technical progress and economic growth have taken place to provide us all with more goods and services to share.

Neither can Japan be considered to be overpopulated with a population of 117 million living on an area of land much the same size as the UK.

However, countries like Ethiopia, Chad, and Malawi, among other less-developed countries, can be considered overpopulated despite having less than ten people per square kilometre of their land areas in some cases. These countries are overpopulated because they have just too few resources. The few goods and services they produce are shared out among many people. Their standards of living are low.

UNDERPOPULATION *many people but many more resources*   OVERPOPULATION *just as many people but too few resources*

What then is the **optimum population** for a country? This refers to the size of population which, given the existing stock of land, capital and technical knowledge, could produce the maximum amount of output of goods and services per head. As the size of the population in a country grows they are able to produce more and more, but after a point there will be diminishing returns as there are too many people and too few resources. Output per head would fall.

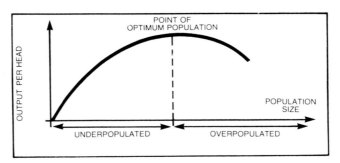

Key words

This word search contains aspects of population studied in economics and geography. Circle or highlight these aspects and then write a few sentences to explain something about each one. Use the chapter to help you.

M	A	X	I	M	I	Z	E	T	R	A	D	E	O	N
X	S	D	E	A	T	H	S	T	O	O	D	E	I	P
L	D	C	O	P	T	F	A	C	Z	C	U	P	M	T
A	G	E	O	I	O	D	G	L	O	C	U	S	M	T
E	C	O	N	O	M	I	E	Z	P	U	P	L	I	A
D	E	P	E	N	D	E	N	T	T	P	G	U	G	E
B	A	L	A	N	C	E	T	R	I	A	D	K	R	O
F	F	S	E	E	M	A	F	U	M	T	K	H	A	E
R	B	I	R	T	H	S	C	O	U	I	T	O	T	N
S	O	C	Z	S	M	A	Y	B	M	O	E	I	I	T
S	B	E	C	E	A	U	S	E	I	N	M	A	O	L
O	N	D	O	X	N	E	R	T	H	A	T	I	N	L
O	E	M	I	G	R	A	T	I	O	N	V	E	L	O
P	W	O	R	K	I	N	G	F	A	M	E	I	N	C
B	O	K	O	R	E	G	I	O	N	A	L	O	M	E

Index